DAVID
King of Israel

Books by F. W. Krummacher

David: King of Israel

Elijah the Tishbite

Elisha: A Prophet for Our Times

The Suffering Saviour

DAVID
King of Israel

F. W. Krummacher

Translated by M. G. Easton

Grand Rapids, MI 49501

David: King of Israel by F. W. Krummacher. Revised edition.

Copyright © 1994 by Kregel Publications.

Published by Kregel Classics, an imprint of Kregel Publications, P. O. Box 2607, Grand Rapids, MI 49501. Kregel Classics provides trusted and time-proven publications for Christian life and ministry. Your comments and suggestions are valued.

This revised edition is based upon the Religious Tract Society's 1838 edition published in London.

Cover and book design: Alan G. Hartman

Library of Congress Cataloging-in-Publication Data

Krummacher, F. W. (Friedrich Wilhelm), 1796-1868.
    [David, der König von Israel. English]
    David: King of Israel / F. W. Krummacher.
        p.   cm.
Originally published: Edinburgh: T&T Clark.
    1. David, King of Israel. 2. Jews—Kings and rulers—Biography. 3. Bible. O.T.—Biography. I. Title.
BS580.D3K713   1994   222'.4092—dc20   93-41453
                    [B]   CIP
ISBN 0-8254-3061-5 (pbk.)

                1 2 3 4 5 printing / year 97 96 95 94

                Printed in the United States of America

Contents

Foreword

The life of David, Israel's shepherd, psalmist, and king, possesses a fascination all its own. A "man after the heart of God," he nevertheless demonstrated the weaknesses of the flesh. The psalms show him to be a man of like passions. He knew fear as well as joy, felt the hurt of injustice and the anguish of ingratitude, as well as the desire to establish an administration of justice as well as relieve the helplessness of the oppressed. All of these facets of David's colorful life and reign are captured by Friedrich Wilhelm Krummacher (1796–1868).

Honored with a Doctor of Divinity degree by the University of Berlin, Dr. Krummacher was widely regarded as one of the most eloquent preachers of his day. In his highly acclaimed David, King of Israel (which originally bore as a subtitle "A Portrait Drawn from Bible History and the Book of Psalms,") David passes before the reader in all the phases of his character. Dr. Krummacher made no pretense at originality of thought and offered no lengthy solutions of difficulties within the text. He also avoided any "controversial sparring" with those whose writings preceded his own. Instead, the narrative flows with the precision and pace of a well-told story. Just emphasis is placed on salient facts or incidents. The reflections of the writer are typical of those of a knowledgeable pastor who is skilled in feeding the "flock of God." And the correlations from the Book of Psalms adequately highlight the earthly trials and triumphs of David as shepherd, outlaw, and king.

We can recommend this volume without reservation to pastors as well as to laypeople. To the former it contains a veritable storehouse of hints for pulpit use, while to the latter it provides the stimulus of a good devotional treatment of the text.

CYRIL J. BARBER
Author, The Minister's Library

Author's Preface

Availing myself of the opportunity afforded me by the respected Translator, I have pleasure in addressing a fraternal salutation to my Christian friends on the other side of the Channel.

If, in the Preface to the German original, where I treat of the "Homiletic use of the Old Testament," I complain of the lamentable neglect and misapprehension which that portion of the Sacred Scriptures has to suffer on the part of many of the faithful in the Church of my Fatherland, I feel myself at liberty, from personal experience, to congratulate the brethren in England and Scotland that they are not open to any such reproach.

It is therefore to me an encouraging thought that the following "Portrait" is in the hands of friends well acquainted with the Scriptures and of one mind with myself in their views of the unity and infallibility of the two Testaments.

I trust it may be favored with a kind reception and that it may in some measure contribute to their joy and edification.

FRIEDRICH WILHELM KRUMMACHER, D.D.

Translator's Preface

The book here presented in an English dress is the most recent that has emanated from the pen of the venerable Author. He needs no introduction to English readers. His name is a household word in religious circles.

The history of David and his times is full of the deepest interest and significance. As we traverse the field here opened up to us, and follow the descriptions of Krummacher, the different scenes and incidents rise up before us with all the vividness of actual events passing before our eyes. The Translator has endeavored to give a faithful rendering of the original and to preserve, as far as the idiom of the English language would permit, the peculiar forms of expression employed by the Author. The reader will sometimes discover in the phraseology and structure of sentences a Teutonic origin; but this, it is believed, will not detract from the interest with which the book will be read.

M. G. EASTON

1

The Call of David

The history of Israel presents to us, within the narrowest limits, a ground-plan of the whole history of the world. The hidden government of the personal God, guiding and training the people, there meets us openly manifesting itself. The veiling curtain of human designs and actions is raised, and we behold, concealed by it, the hand, moving and directing all things, of Him of whom it is written, "He worketh all things after the counsel of His own will."[1] O the adorable condescension of God, who thus would help the weakness of our faith by bringing within the narrow circle of our vision, in the clearest manner, once for all, the secrets of His lofty providence working through all things in behalf of one chosen people! No seeming chaos of the events of time can henceforth astonish or perplex us, when, in the two thousand years' history of that nation, we perceive numberless illustrations of a higher will guiding the most intricate threads which wind themselves through our life, and at length weaving them into a web which, the more it is considered, forces to our lips the words of the apostle, "O the depths, both of the wisdom and knowledge of God!"

How remarkably do we discover, in the life-journey of each one of the saints of Israel, the shining footsteps of him whom Isaiah describes as "wonderful in counsel, and excellent in working," and regarding whom Solomon says, "A man's heart deviseth his way, but the Lord directeth his steps." In the life of none of these Old Testament saints does the exalted Protector of men present, in greater variety of forms, evidences of His guidance and government,

---

1. Ephesians 1:11.

than in that of the man who was deemed worthy to be called "A man after God's own heart." What a fullness, not only of consolation and quickening, but of warning and instruction, is unfolded before us in the experience and the fortunes of this royal Psalmist! To a consideration of his earthly career we now invite attention. This invitation is equivalent to the call of the prophet Amos, "Prepare to meet thy God, O Israel"; for there is no part of David's career in which we shall not meet with that God of whom the royal harper himself sang, "He leadeth me in the paths of righteousness, for His name's sake."

1 Samuel 16:1

> And the Lord said unto Samuel, How long wilt thou mourn for Saul, seeing I have rejected him from reigning over Israel? Fill thine horn with oil, and go, I will send thee to Jesse the Bethlehemite: for I have provided me a king among his sons.

In the books of Samuel we stand on firm historic ground. They form an essential part of the canon of sacred Scriptures, bearing stamped on them the attesting seal, not only of the enlightened in Israel, but also of Christ and His apostles. Grant it, that the Holy Spirit acted, in the composition of the historical books of the Old Testament, more in the way of reminding, watching over, and guiding the writers, while in the production of the prophetic books He put forth an overpowering, creating, inspiring energy; yet in the case of the one, as well as of the other, every suspicion of a mixture of mythic elements is to be utterly rejected, if we would not be guilty of "speaking evil of dignities."

It is well known that the holy apostles, after the example of their Lord and master, so far from showing any scruple at receiving as true the historic narratives, such as those of Noah's ark, Israel's passage through the Red Sea, Balaam's ass, and the miraculous overthrow of Jericho at the blast of Joshua's trumpets, rather added new confirmation to them as undoubted facts. We believe and speak in accordance with these authorities; for who can name any others who are worthy, in the remotest degree, to stand beside them as their peers in holiness and enlightenment? Thus, also, in the representations of David's life, for which we are indebted to divinely instructed prophets, Samuel, Nathan, and Gad, we have to do with pure history, and in no part of it with mere fancies of the poet. With such feelings of confidence in the narrative, let us look more narrowly into this rich life-picture which will unroll itself before us; and first let us turn our attention (1) to the calling and (2) the anointing of the shepherd youth. And may the Spirit of the Lord grant to us guidance, and acknowledge us continually in our contemplations.

From the beginning, the form of government in Israel was theo-cratic. The Lord Jehovah was the only sovereign Lawgiver, Director, and Leader of His people. The human organs through whom His government made itself felt, were, in the earliest times, the patriarchs, Abraham, Isaac, and Jacob: after these, in the sphere of civil life, the heads of the tribes and, in the ecclesiastical domain, the priests, whose sacred office culminated in the mysterious person of the high priest. Yet the Lord reserved to Himself full liberty to raise up others, according to necessity, and to entrust them, as extraordinary plenipotentiaries, with special commissions.

The prophets appeared as watchers and monitors sent and anointed of God as often as there was manifested, in any manner and at any place, among the people, a turning from the path of obedience to the divine laws of the kingdom, as these were delivered through Moses. Neither crown nor breastplate protected transgressors from the stern denunciation they were compelled to hear from the lips of these representatives of the Supreme Judge.

As long as Joshua lived, the condition of the people who were born after the departure out of the infected air of Egypt, during the wandering through the wilderness, was a very joyful one. The last solemn national assembly held by Joshua found them in the heights of enthusiastic resignation to the God of their fathers. After Joshua's death also, they still continued to keep the covenant of the Lord under the direction and fostering care of the elders, with whom their great leader, the worthy successor of Moses, had surrounded himself. But after the watchful eyes of these faithful men also were closed in death, Israel, through the misleading influence of the heathen tribes living around them, entered on that downward course, on which, for a long time, they continued to descend in ever deepening national declension.

They addicted themselves to the dissolute and impure worship of strange gods, and would gradually have been melted into one with the Canaanites, the Hittites, the Amorites, and the Perizzites, had not the

Lord always, at the fitting moment, made use of these heathen hordes as a scourge to check the apostasies of His people. Then, at their cry of distress when the scourge had fallen upon them, even to the shedding of blood, He raised up for them deliverers in the persons of the judges, who rescued them from the very verge of ruin, and led them back to the God of their fathers, from allegiance to whom they had, with accursed ingratitude, departed.

These scenes of apostasy, and of consequent righteous judgment calling to repentance, constantly repeated themselves. At length, under the leadership of the distinguished Samuel, who was at once judge, prophet, and priest, the people seemed willing to be steadfast. Then all at once, with impetuous eagerness, lamentably blinded by passion, they demanded that Samuel should set a king over them, just as the heathen nations had kings.

This demand might not be in itself blameworthy, for it was the purpose of God to let the form of government gradually assume the character of a monarchy; but the motive which lay at the foundation of this demand on the part of Israel was in the highest degree culpable. It was like a renouncing of the theocracy—a godless rejection of the exclusive supremacy of Jehovah. They wished to set themselves free from the condition of absolute dependence on the Lord in heaven. When sorrowful distress filled the land, they were weary of looking to Jehovah's hands, and of being compelled to wait in meek submission to see whether He would help them, and when, and how. It must be with them as it was with heathen nations. They must have in Israel a human ruler, who would have control over an inexhaustible treasure of gold and silver, and over an army of horsemen, prepared at all times for battle, who would become security for the common weal of the land, would relieve his subjects from their cares as well as from the trouble of praying and waiting, and would secure for them, under the shadow of a scepter mildly borne, an undisturbed, cheerful, and agreeable existence.

Samuel, the faithful servant of God, represented to them with holy earnestness the folly of their desire; but he saw his well-meant warnings thrown by them to the winds, while his ears were continually assailed by their boisterous, deafening cry, "Make us a king to judge us, like all the nations." Therefore he brought the matter in prayer before God, and received from the Lord the unambiguous answer, "Hearken unto the voice of the people in all that they say unto thee:

for they have not rejected thee, but they have rejected me, that I should not reign over them." And God "gave them a king in anger," says the historian; while, had they, with childlike trust, allowed Him to do toward them as He pleased, He would one day have given them one in mercy.

The Lord chose for that dignity Saul the Benjamite, the son of Kish, a husbandman and an owner of flocks, a young man, fair, stately, and by a head taller than all the people. The energetic youth, endowed with talents rich in promise, appeared to authorize the best hopes regarding him. His warlike courage and vigor in action corresponded to his knightly form. Besides, witness was borne regarding him that hitherto he had remained unstained by the immoralities of his contemporaries, and that, trained without doubt in the faith of his fathers, there was not lacking in him a lively susceptibility of religious impression, of which we shall find many illustrations in his subsequent history.

The remark we meet with, "God gave him another heart," leads us to think of him as filled with holy emotions, resolutions, and determinations after he had been anointed by Samuel. It was a suspicious circumstance that the humbleness of mind which he gave evidence of while that sacred act was being performed, had its foundation more in the remembrance of his lowly origin than in his consciousness of sin; and that after Samuel had laid his hands on him, we do not see him immediately bow himself before the Lord, nor hear him pray for His gracious help. We will scarcely err if we believe that we recognize in him already, on the day of his call, a man whose heart is yet divided between God and the world, and if we suspect, as lurking behind his promise to govern in the name of Jehovah, the secret reservation that he would do this only in so far as the will of Jehovah would not demand from him any sacrifice of his own will.

So long as Saul bore the scepter, he never laid aside the armor of the warrior. Amid the storms and fury of the battle-field, the days and years of his life fled away. The deliverance of Israel, by the destruction of their enemies dwelling around them, he regarded as the chief business to which he was called. Through the prayers of Samuel and his judicious counsel, Saul gained a victory over the Amorites. This was the first actual seal of confirmation imprinted by the Lord, in the sight of the whole of Israel, on the kingdom of the new ruler. After this victory, Samuel, obedient to an intimation from God, laid down his office of judge, and thereafter stood by the side of the king only as a prophet, counseling and warning him.

A second war, during which Saul was under the necessity of summoning together his whole army, had for its object the subjugation of the hereditary and archenemy of Israel, the Philistines—a war which, though Israel was at that time victorious, broke out ever anew, and continued with varying results till the death of Saul. At its first outbreak the king took a step which opens to us a very sorrowful view into the state of his mind, and which was fraught with sad results to himself. In the name and by the express command of the Lord, Samuel had directed the king to put off the commencement of hostilities against the Philistines till he, the prophet, appeared in the camp in person, and kept a holy sacrificial festival with the army to the praise of God. In the course of some seven days this festival was to have been celebrated.

Saul solemnly promised obedience to this divine injunction. But when, in consequence of the arrival of exaggerated reports of the strength of the enemy's army, the courage of the host of Israel began to be depressed to such a degree, that already bands of deserters sought to conceal themselves in dens and caves, while he waited impatiently for the coming of Samuel who had been hindered by some unforeseen circumstance; and when now the seventh day was already waning toward the evening, and he had not yet made his appearance, then the impatience of the king overcame him, and he determined, though neither priest nor Levite, to present, without any authority, with his own hands red with the blood of men, the holy burnt-offering and thank-offering. He gave orders that the victims for the sacrifice should be brought forward, and then without delay he proceeded to lay them upon the altar.

By this reckless conduct he sinned under the mask of piety, in more than in one respect. His conduct was culpable, as manifesting an altogether unwarrantable distrust in the word of the man of God; culpable, not less as a superstitious degradation of the external act of offering sacrifice into a magical agency, by means of which the covenant fellowship of God might be secured, but especially it was worthy of condemnation as a gross violation of an unequivocal divine prohibition, well known to the king, the slighting of which had on more than one occasion in Israel been visited with the punishment of death.

The smoke of the sacrifice was yet ascending from the quickly erected altar, when Samuel, true to his word, entered the camp. Saul, not a little struck, went forward with feigned composure to meet him. But Samuel, with measured solemnity, beckoned the king aside, and addressed to him the question, "What hast thou done?"

Saul, endeavoring to excuse himself, replied, "I saw that the people were scattered from me, and that thou camest not within the days appointed, and that the Philistines gathered themselves together at Michmash; therefore, said I, the Philistines will come down now upon me to Gilgal, and I"—this he must even confess—"have not made supplication unto the Lord: I forced myself therefore, and offered a burnt-offering."

"Thou hast done foolishly," replied the prophet; and added, yet in a low voice, so that the bystanders did not hear it, the alarming word, "Thy kingdom shall not continue," and then went his way.

To this sin of which the king was guilty at the beginning of the war against the Philistines, there soon was added another yet more grievous, which reveals to us an additional feature in the character of the man. Perhaps he had lulled himself into a state of security by the fact that God not only had not punished him for his offense at Gilgal, but had even crowned him, though certainly not from love to him but to the people, with a brilliant victory over the Philistines. Previous to a battle, during the war against the Amalekites, the express command came to him, through a divine revelation, that after he had subdued this wholly depraved, obdurate, and hopelessly degraded people, he should "slay," that is, completely destroy, "man and woman, infant and suckling, ox and sheep, camel and ass."

But what happened after the long-threatened destruction fell upon this race so sunk in moral debasement, and abandoned as incurable? Not only is Saul reported to have dealt gently with his prisoner, Agag the Amalekite king, but he reserved alive, as lawful spoil, the best and the fattest of the cattle of the enemy. Then the word of the Lord came to Samuel, with whom the Lord was wont, as in former times with Moses, to speak "as a man with his friend," saying, "It repenteth me that I have set up Saul to be king, for he is turned back from following me, and hath not performed my commandments."

This revelation from God agitated the prophet deeply. The whole night, at the commencement of which it came to him, he spent sleepless, weeping, and in prayer on behalf of Israel. Scarcely had the

morning begun to dawn when he arose to meet the king, who—after
he had, with incomprehensible equanimity, erected a monument of
his victory at Carmel, in Judah—was returning with his living trophies
to Gilgal. Here it was that Samuel met him.

Saul saluted him again with the mien of most perfect composure.
It was an unsuccessful endeavor to conceal his troubled conscience.
"Blessed be thou of the Lord," said he; and then, with a bold brow,
though only to betray himself, he added, "I have performed the commandment of the Lord." "Hast thou?" replied Samuel; "what
meaneth then this bleating of the sheep in mine ears, and the lowing
of the oxen which I hear?" Saul, disguising himself, replied, with the
appearance of most pious innocence, "The people spared the best of
the sheep and of the oxen, to sacrifice unto the Lord thy God."

But at that moment the man of God gave free scope to the holy
flame of passion which burned within him, and tearing the mask from
the face of the hypocrite, in the name of the Lord, said, "Thou hast
done evil in that thou didst not obey the voice of the Lord, but didst
fly upon the spoil. And what meanest thou with the seemingly holy
pretext, as if thou didst wish to present an offering to the Lord?
Behold"—(it must be remarked that here even already a man
speaks from the midst of the ancient covenant people and of the
Mosaic economy)—"to obey is better than sacrifice, and to hearken than
the fat of rams; because thou hast rejected the word of the Lord, He
hath also rejected thee from being king."

Thus spoke the seer as the mouth of Jehovah. But how was it with
the king when this storm broke over his head? Truly he felt himself
as if crushed to the ground. He acknowledged the burden that
oppressed him: "I have sinned: for I have transgressed the commandment of the Lord, and thy words." And then he becomes the
supplicant, "Now therefore, I pray thee, pardon my sin"; but adds,
with greater and yet more earnest concern, "Turn again with me, that
I may worship the Lord!"

These words sounded pleasantly and rich with promise; but
what lay at the foundation of this apparently pious request? Nothing
else than a desire to appear in the eyes of his people sheltered under
that high reputation which Samuel enjoyed. So great was his anxiety
to shine before the people in the light of the holiness of this man of
God, and, by means of manifested fellowship with him, to escape the
suspicion of impiety, that when Samuel denied to him his interested

request, and with the repeated declaration, "Because thou hast rejected the word of the Lord, therefore the Lord hath rejected thee,"
turned away from him. Instead of sinking to the ground before the
Almighty with broken heart and crying for mercy, he endeavored violently to hold back the prophet, and seized his mantle so firmly and
with such fury, that he tore it, and a fragment remained in his hand.

But Samuel interpreted this as a prophetic indication of what had
been determined regarding him, and said to him, "The Lord hath
rent the kingdom of Israel from thee this day, and hath given it to a
neighbor of thine, that is better than thou." Then the king repeated his confession, "I have sinned"; but at the same time, in his
anguish, he anew gave open evidence what it was that above all
other things lay on his heart. "Honor me now before the elders of my
people, and before Israel," he entreated, "and turn again with me,
that I may worship the Lord thy God."

Here we see, then, his deepest thoughts disclosed before us.
Instead of being filled with repentance before God, he is only concerned for his honor among men. The prophet pitied the miserable
man, and turned again with him; but with what intention? Was it
that in fellowship with him he might offer sacrifice and prayer, and
thereby strengthen him yet more in his hypocrisy? Far from it! What
then happened? In the presence of Saul, Samuel with his own hands
executed, with the edge of the sword, the sentence of God against
the prisoner Agag, the Amalekite prince, and thereby gave to the
king of Israel a terrible and memorable example, as well of the holy
and inexorable severity of Him who will not be mocked, as of implicit obedience in the eyes of Him who always honors His word and law.

After he had completed this act of blood, he returned again without delay to his city, Ramah, "and he saw King Saul no more" (i.e.,
no more sought after him) "until the day of his death; nevertheless,
Samuel mourned for Saul: and the Lord repented that He had made
Saul king over Israel." Above all things it concerned the Lord that
He should be acknowledged and honored as the "Holy One of Israel."
But a man with a heart so thoroughly unspiritual as Saul's, divided in
his inmost being between God and the world, ready for the service
of God only under the condition that what God laid upon him
should not require him to crucify his personal interests and lusts, and
yet anxiously concerned about the preservation of the external
appearance of unreserved submission to God, which in truth he alto-

gether renounced—an appearance with which he concerned himself only that he might thereby once and again deceive God and man—no such double-hearted man, entangled in the grossest hypocrisy, was fit for being vicegerent upon earth of the thrice holy God. Therefore the "Keeper of Israel," who sets up and casts down kings, chose out for Himself, as was to be expected, another and a worthier, to be shepherd and leader of His people. Where shall we have to seek for such an one?

2. Without some intimation directing us in the right way, we could scarcely conjecture where he will meet us. What was Bethlehem? It was one of the most insignificant towns in the Holy Land. It was indeed pleasantly surrounded by sunny hills and by green pasture lands, yet it was too small and inconsiderable to be even mentioned by name in the numbering of the towns of Judah, as recorded in the fifteenth chapter of Joshua. Who could possibly think that this insignificant little place should ever be raised up to heaven, so as indeed to become distinguished far above all towns on the earth in its relations to the history of the world? And did it not truly so happen? The Lord, whose eyes behold the faithful of the land, knew that little town long ago, and had taken it under His own special protection. In an incomparably noble sense, its name "Bethlehem," that is "the house of bread," must one day correspond with the fact; and is there the name of a single town at which, when sounded, either in prophecy or in song, the heart is so stirred as at that name, "Bethlehem Ephratah"?

In this little shepherd village, the Lord had, with an eye to the accomplishment of redemption in the distant future, some time ago united in a holy marriage, rich with promise, two noble hearts—the hearts of the pious Moabitess, Ruth, and of the excellent husbandman, Boaz. On the nuptial day he put into the mouths of "all the people that were in the gate," and of the "elders" who were witnesses of the celebration, the significant benediction, "The Lord make the woman that is come into thine house like Rachel and like Leah, which two did build the house of Israel; and do thou worthily in Ephratah, and be thou famous in Bethlehem." When, afterward, to the young pair their first little son, called Obed—i.e., "servant"—was born, the inspired words flowed again, not without the influence of the Spirit from above, from the lips of the women wishing joy to the grandmother Naomi, "Blessed be the Lord that hath not left thee this day without a kinsman, that his name may be famous in Israel."

Oh, if these women had foreseen how a remarkably the Lord would, one day, give effect to this their prophetic word, and how He would make the lineage of this son, so joyfully welcomed, an eternal blessing to the whole world! But this was to them, as well as to the whole of Israel, at that time a sealed secret; and it so continued till, 400 years later, the prophet Micah, the Morasthite, opened the last seal with that cry which filled the people with the most joyful surprise: "But thou, Bethlehem Ephratah, though thou be little among the thousands of Judah, yet out of thee shall He come forth unto me that is to be ruler in Israel; whose goings forth have been from of old, from everlasting."

When about half a century had passed after the birth of Obed, Samuel was directed by the Lord to go to Bethlehem. "How long," said the Lord to His servant, in an immediate revelation, "wilt thou mourn (or concernest thou thyself) for Saul, seeing I have rejected him from reigning over Israel? Fill thine horn with oil, and go, I will send thee to Jesse the Bethlehemite" (the son of Obed): "for I have provided me a king among his sons. With not a little surprise Samuel might have heard the terrible word, "rejected." His soul might well have cried in prayer unto the Lord, "Cast him not altogether out of Thy sight!" But that Saul had forfeited the crown of Israel had been long apparent to him, and therefore he bowed to the holy determination of God.

It is possible that, in the first announcement of it, the commission which required him to carry the crown to the unimportant shepherd village of Bethlehem may have seemed to him strange; yet he was acquainted with the ways of Him who ruleth over all, and uttered only this one scruple, "How can I go; if Saul hear it he will kill me." A cowardly fear this, which we would not have expected to find in Samuel.

But the Lord "knoweth our frame," and has sympathy with our weakness. In the most condescending manner the Lord deals with Samuel, His well-approved servant, and directs him to withhold meanwhile from the people the chief design of his mission to Bethlehem, and only to proceed with the offering up of the sacrifice which he was there to celebrate, according to the commandment of the Lord, and to which he was to invite Jesse and his sons. After this festival the Lord will show to him which of the sons of Jesse He has chosen to be prince over Israel. Samuel obeyed, took his staff in his hand, and went forth.

His arrival in Bethlehem created much joy among the inhabitants of the little town; for who was there in Israel who had not at least heard of Samuel, the friend and seer of God? The elders of the place went out reverently, but not without secret fear, to meet the holy man, and saluted him with the question which revealed their misgivings, "Comest thou peaceably?"—i.e., "hast thou a good intention, that thou comest to our poor town?" Samuel quieted the unassuming people, while, in the most friendly manner, he answered, "Peaceably. I am come to sacrifice unto the Lord. Sanctify yourselves"—i.e., prepare yourselves according to the Levitical law, and collect your thoughts for the holy service. Particularly he admonished Jesse and his sons to make such preparation, and gently hinted to them that, in all especial manner, they were the persons to whom, and for whose sake, the Lord had sent him. Those who were invited appeared without delay, in full sympathy with the festive occasion, beside the hastily erected altar; and, after the offering of sacrifice had been completed, amid the heartfelt devotions of all the people, Samuel returned, along with the old man Jesse, to his house, and directed him to bring forward before him his sons, from the eldest to the youngest. And Jesse obeyed the voice of the prophet.

Then came forward before him, first, Eliab, the eldest—a hero in appearance, full of strength and of manly bearing. Ha! thought Samuel, there stands before the Lord His anointed. But the voice of the Lord spoke within him, and said, "Look not on his countenance, or on the height of his stature; because I have refused him: for the Lord seeth not as man seeth; for man looketh on the outward appearance, but the Lord looketh on the heart." Jesse then beckoned to Abinadab to come forward. But again the voice said in Samuel's heart, "Neither hath the Lord chosen this." In like manner it happened when the third son, Shammah, and also the four who were younger, passed by, that Samuel received the same instruction. He said unto Jesse, "Neither hath the Lord chosen these; but are here all thy children?" One of our greatest poets (Goethe) once remembered this question of Samuel's after he had studied and mastered the writings of the most prominent philosophers and wise men of this world, and had found in none of them anything stable and satisfactory. Then with scorn he wrote these lines:

> This case was mine, too, then at leisure,
>   What in the sages wrote I read,
> When with their small wits they would measure
>   The wealth of worlds around us spread;
> I thought of Samuel then, when he
>   Made Jesse's sons in row appear,
> And when the seven were counted, said—
>   Are all thy children here?

O that this prince of poets had not after all omitted to count in One! To Samuel's question Jesse answered, "There remaineth yet the youngest; and, behold, he keepeth the sheep." He said this in a manner which seemed to imply, "this youngest cannot be he whom thou seekest." But "Samuel said unto Jesse, Send and fetch him: for we will not sit down till he come hither." This was accordingly done. After a little the boy came in. "Now he was ruddy, and withal of a beautiful countenance, and goodly to look to." And the Spirit witnessed to the prophet, saying, "Arise, anoint him for this is he." Then, with deep emotion of soul, Samuel took the horn of oil, and anointed with the holy ointment the head of the boy. He accompanied the ceremony with no explanatory words, but contented himself with heartily saluting the youth who had before him such a future. Then, after he had broken bread with the whole family, he took his departure, and returned with a thankful heart to Ramah.

"And the Spirit of the Lord," so the history announces, "came upon David" (i.e., the beloved) "from that day forward." The youth entered upon a new stage in the development of his inner life, which was wholly consecrated to God. The rich talents wherewith he was endowed from his birth received on all sides fresh unfolding. The Law, the holy volume of the books of Moses, in which he had been instructed from his earliest years, opened itself to his enlightened eye more and more. The peaceful stillness of nature amid which, tending his father's flocks, he spent his days, and often also the mild, starry nights, favored his penetration into the secrets of the divine revelation.

His heart, moved and directed from above, already poured itself out in sacred song and poem, which he sang to the accompaniment of his harp, to the praise of that God before whom from his childhood he had learned to bow the knee; and it may well be assumed that even then, amid that rural loneliness, psalms streamed forth from his heart, such as the eighth, which overflows with adoring wonder at the condescension and grace with which the glorious Creator of heaven and earth has concerned Himself with frail man, and has raised him up to be lord over the works of His hands; the nineteenth—"The heavens declare the glory of God"; the twenty-third—"The Lord is my Shepherd, I shall not want"; the hundred and fourth—"Bless the Lord, O my soul. O Lord, my God, Thou art very great; Thou art clothed with honor and majesty"; and others of a similar kind. At all events, a great part of the lovely and thought-ful pictures borrowed from nature, which we meet with in such rich fullness in almost all his psalms, owe their origin to his shepherd life, spent amid the pastures and hills around Bethlehem.

Whether David before his anointing had already met with Samuel, or whether, which is very probable, he had ever associated with the disciples of Samuel at the school of the prophets at Ramah, with whom we find him at a later period enjoying such friendly fel-lowship, cannot with certainty be affirmed. It even remains a question how far he was as yet conscious of the important meaning of his anointing. Probably this knowledge went no further than a faint, dim apprehension, which he regarded it as his duty rather to resist as a bold dream than dare to glory in as a divine promise. The enigma of this, to him, mysterious action, was first solved afterward in the way of manifold experiences. That its meaning was not, indeed, at first fully comprehended by him, is evident from the great frankness of manner with which he, not long after this solemn scene at Bethlehem, obeyed the summons which was sent to him from Saul, which we shall discuss in our next chapter.

We conclude this, in adoring wonder at the providential gov-ernment of our God, to whom, whenever danger threatens His kingdom, it is not difficult "to help by few or by many." We close with the exclamation of the prophet: "O Lord of hosts, Thou art great in counsel, and mighty in work; for Thine eyes are open upon all the ways of the sons of men"; or with the words of the fortieth Psalm: "Blessed is that man that maketh the Lord his trust, and respecteth not the proud, nor such as turn aside to lies. Many, O Lord my God, are Thy wonderful works which Thou hast done, and Thy thoughts which are to usward: if I would declare and speak of them, they are more than can be numbered."

2

The Harper

When we hear Essential Wisdom, whom John in the beginning of his Gospel styles "the Word which was in the beginning with God," by whom, before He became flesh, all things were created, saying, "When God appointed the foundations of the earth, then was I by Him, as one brought up with Him: rejoicing in the habitable paths of the earth; and my delights were with the sons of men"[1]—his words lead us to think of creation as formed by him into a book of pictures, which are full of meaning for all who have eyes to look upon it. From the sun, the king of the heavens, and the moon, which derives from him her light, down to the dewdrop of the morning which fructifies the blade, and to the butterfly which, with glittering wings, springs forth from the death of the larva, the whole of nature is interwoven with symbols which, suggesting lofty thoughts, point upward above this earth to the eternal kingdom. And as it is in nature, so also is it in history, especially in sacred history; in which not seldom an event which in itself may be historically insignificant, contains within it, for those who understand how to solve the enigma, some deep doctrinal or prophetic meaning.

Thus, long ago, Divine Wisdom "rejoiced" over the lowly birthplace of the Savior, which was at first called Ephratah, i.e., "the fruitful," and afterward Bethlehem, i.e., "the house of bread," a name containing in it already a pre-intimation of the "I am the bread which came down from heaven." In like manner, it was an event full of significance that the aged mother in Israel, Rachel, died on the

---

1. Proverbs 8:29, 31: "Then was I the work-master or architect by Him," etc., according to Luther's translation.

27

way to Bethlehem, and thereby unconsciously marked the spot toward which the longing of her children would stretch itself during nearly 2,000 years, even though they also might come to their graves before they reached it. At a later time there was at Bethlehem, as is well known, a marriage celebrated, amid high-sounding benedictions, between an Israelite farmer and a heathen woman from the land of the Moabites: another holy type, which prophesied that from this marriage union would descend One who would be called to break down the middle wall of partition between Jew and Gentile, and would enclose with the band of a holy love all who bear the human countenance.

At last, in a troublous time, we hear joyful melody echoing forth from the hills of Bethlehem. Before its wonderful harmony, not only are the clouds of dark sadness scattered, but even the spirits of the deep are forced to retire, as a presage of that power which the gospel of Christ would one day put forth. We shall find opportunity today to listen to that marvelous song.

1 Samuel 16:23

> And it came to pass, when the evil spirit from God was upon Saul, that David took an harp, and played with his hand: so Saul was refreshed, and was well, and the evil spirit departed from him.

For the first time we now see David emerge from his quiet, peaceful life. Already there begin to appear about him faint traces of that future greatness which in continuous unfolding presented itself to the hopes of the thoughtful in Israel. His first step out of rural obscurity brought him near to the throne of the ruler, to whom, as one of the humblest subjects, he had hitherto looked only with a feeling of reverence. Let us see (1) how he came to King Saul, and (2) what he experienced at the king's court.

1. Rich in power, and in the fame of victory, Saul bore the scepter over Israel. From a distance he appeared to be one of the happiest of men; but seen near at hand, with all his glory, he was a poor, pitiable object. This was not because, as often happens to so many of his rank, ingratitude and misapprehension on the part of his people, or an undeserved destiny, changed the splendid career of the monarch into a life of tears and sadness. The cup of their so-called Godlike felicity is but seldom unmixed, however, to the great ones of the

earth. Yet it avails them much when they are sustained by the consciousness of having been faithful to their people, and of having sought honestly with God, and before God, the welfare of the country. How richly, then, do streams of consolation flow to them in the word of God!

What comfort, moreover, have they in remembering the case of many noble rulers who have gone before them, whose seeds of peace first sprang up over their graves and procured for them in abundant and imperishable fullness that acknowledgment which was scornfully denied to them when living!

But such was not the case with Saul. Look at that dark cloud which shades his brow. What is it that oppresses him and embitters his life? The ground of his deep distress lies not in the conduct of his people, who rather clung to him with new devotion after his victory over the Philistines and the Amalekites, and who willingly, yea, cheerfully, followed him wherever he led them; but it lay in his own inward spiritual relation to God, with whom he stood no more in a condition of favor, and to whom he looked with slavish fear instead of childlike confidence.

This will not appear incredible to anyone after he has seen of the promises of blessing which Samuel once poured over the head of the king. He heard the prophet say to him, "The Spirit of the Lord shall come upon thee, and thou shalt be turned into another man." The history also testifies concerning him, "God gave him another heart"; and once he was found even among the pious sons of the prophets, and heard with animation joining in their songs of praise to the God of Israel.

But God can cause many things fair to look upon and valuable in themselves to happen to a man, without at the same time giving any evidence of delighting in him. He may wish to make use of such an one only as an instrument in His hands, and, in this character only, may, for the welfare of others, crown him with one or another of the intellectual gifts with which he is endowed, without giving him any authority to believe that on this account his name is written in heaven. In this way He bestows on many a ruler the gifts of wisdom, of prowess, or courage; on many a minister of the gospel, those of theological knowledge, of church government, of eloquence, without permitting such as are thus endowed to infer on that account that they are the children of God.

The message of Jehovah, "Fear not: for I have redeemed thee, I have called thee by thy name; thou art mine," appertains only to those who are of broken and contrite heart, who stand in decided hostility against sin, and are with their whole hearts engaged in the service of the Lord. These characteristics are altogether lacking in Saul—at least they are manifestly vanishing toward extinction.

We know that something sorrowful has happened. The king has sinned grievously. When Samuel charged him with his transgression, the whole impurity of his character emerged. His only endeavor was how he might, by all kinds of craftily contrived excuses protect himself from the accusation that had been brought against him; and when these efforts failed, then the only care which lay upon his heart was how he might preserve his character among men. Had he even now, instead of cringingly imploring Samuel for a continuance of his favor, shown a penitent spirit, and, on his knees, cried to the Almighty for pardon, he would have been saved, and would indeed have become "another man," while the Spirit of God which was promised to him would have gained the supreme power within him.

But when did he ever approach the Lord with entire trust, and with open heart? Ought he now, with a guilt-laden conscience to appear before Him? Might he reckon on an audience and on a gracious reception? Without doubt he might, provided he drew near to Him with the tears of a genuine repentance.

To all who are burdened with sorrow, the doors of God's house stand always open. Whatever the guilt that oppresses them, they will find that "with our God is abundant forgiveness." But Saul was not one of these. He was a sharer in the consciousness of guilt which the "spiritually poor" feel, but not in their "repentance not to be repented of." How far was he from entering into that suppliant cry of the malefactor on the cross, "Lord, remember me"; or that earnest, humble spirit of the woman of Canaan, "Truth, Lord: yet the dogs eat of the crumbs which fall from their master's table!"

Was it pride or despondency, self-righteous confidence or secret unbelief which shut Soul's mouth, while an unfeigned confession might have saved him eternally? It was, as it seems, a dark mixture of all these feelings and passions which shut and hardened his heart. Even the awful announcement of punishment in the words of the prophet, "Because thou hast rejected the word of the Lord, He also hath rejected thee from being king," struck him only as a cold hailstorm, making him tremble, but without melting him in penitence.

Instead of being led by this fearful message to resolve, with contrite heart, to seek the face of the Lord, he rather, like Cain, and afterward Judas Iscariot, fled in terror still farther from Him. So it happened to him also at last, as it once did to the unhappy apostle. Through the righteous judgment of God, Satan was permitted to gain dominion over him. The history informs us that "the Spirit of the Lord departed from Saul, and an evil spirit from the Lord troubled him." These words are not to be understood as figurative, nor only as indicating a paroxysm of mental dejection, nor a darkening of his soul under the shadow of a great sadness, but according to the meaning we have indicated, which opens up before us a more dismal sphere than that of a natural melancholy. The power of darkness, which is personal, and in souls in the condition of that in which Saul's now was, finds all open for his operations, wrought in him with prevailing energy to deepen yet more and more that dreadful gulf which separated the king from Jehovah eternally enthroned in the heavens, even, to increase the estrangement of the miserable man from God yet more and more, till it became a demoniacal hatred of God.

What wonder, therefore, that we meet the king today in a state of mind which makes us scarcely able to recognize the man once so cheerful and vigorous in action. His eye appears fixed, his lips are violently compressed, and his whole countenance speaks of a deep, bitter animosity and gloom. How could he have peace after he had put himself into hostility both with God and the world? Condemned he will not be, and yet the voice of the Judge within him says, "Thou art a doomed man." With all his strength, and with all the arts of self-deception, he strives to defend himself against his accusers, both those in his own breast and those that are around him, and to maintain confidence before God and man.

Who would not pity this unhappy man? O that he might yet break through all these inward hindrances and throw himself upon the grace and wrath of the Judge of the living and the dead, with Job's cry of distress, "I am guilty, and repent in dust and in ashes!" To him help would yet come before the door is shut. But for such a hope as this there appears no longer any room. The poison of a reprobate hatred of God has already penetrated into his inmost being. He is lost!

2. The melancholy of the king naturally lay like a dark pall over

the souls of all the courtiers, yea, spread its sorrowful, gloomy shadow even over the surrounding neighborhood. "In the light of a king's countenance," says Solomon, "is life; but the wrath of the king is a messenger of death." The truth of this latter saying was now felt throughout almost the whole land. The royal servants advised this and that, for the purpose of trying to set free from this dismal state of mind their high lord, whose palace was now more like a dull chamber of sorrow than the proud residence of a monarch. The accustomed scenes of revelry, shows, banquets, spectacles, dancing, and such like, are denied to the servants. Then at last there occurred to them, as one would say, a "happy thought." They appeared before their master, and said to him, "Behold now, an evil spirit from God troubleth thee: let our lord now command thy servants, which are before thee, to seek out a man, who is a cunning player on an harp: and it shall come to pass, when the evil spirit from God is upon thee, that he shall play with his hand, and thou shalt be well."

What a saying! Does not the penetration of these people, who, in forming a judgment regarding the melancholy of their master, did not look at the surface, but descended into the depths of the matter, astonish us? The far-reaching enlightenment they here manifest in their knowledge of the existence of a world of fallen spirits, whom God is able to use for putting to trial His own people, as well as for visiting with punishment the wicked impresses us. Must we not conclude that they were indeed already acquainted with the book of Job, and that it was a constituent part of their holy canonical books? An Israelite adhered to his Bible under all circumstances, even when he was destitute of spiritual life, and his conduct was condemned by it. The testimonies of Moses and the prophets were to him in the last resort decisive oracular sayings, and he would have been filled with amazement if anyone had ventured to call in question or to deny anything testified in His sacred book. So deeply rooted in the seed of Abraham was faith in the divine origin and infallible authority of the sacred Scriptures—a faith which it was all the easier for the Israelites to entertain, inasmuch as they were constant ear and eye witnesses of the power and the signs by which God, at one time here, and at another time there—gave testimony to the seers and prophets, who were the instruments of His revelations.

What we further wonder at, in the courtiers of King Saul, is, first, the clearness with which they recognized demoniacal agency in the disconsolate condition of their master; then the frankness, combined, indeed, with the deepest respectfulness, with which they, regardless of the consequences which might arise to them from such a step, announced their opinion of his case, which was by no means flattering to him; and, finally, the suitableness of the counsel which they felt themselves constrained to give to him. They recommend to him the power of music as a means for relieving his mind, but with a wise discriminating judgment regarding its character.

There was, indeed, no lack of musicians at the court at Gibeah; but they appear to have been devoid of the qualifications which were at this time needed. The servants knew well the power of music to produce, according to its kind and quality, not less the most depraved than the holiest impressions. Music can unfetter the most destructive passions; but it can also, at least momentarily, tame and mitigate the wildest storms of the human heart. Whatever noble impulses, unobserved and slumbering, may lie concealed within the breast of man, may be aroused by music and brought forth into the light of day; but, at the same time, it may also stir the vilest passions in the lower regions of human nature, and accelerate their maturity in action.

The music which the servants of the king thought of was not that which pleases the world, and which only opens the door to unclean spirits, but such as, animated by a nobler inspiration, might insensibly elevate the soul by its harmonious melody, as on angels' wings, toward heaven. They thought of the harp, then the most solemn instrument of music, and on the melodies which were wont to sound forth in the sanctuary at the sacred festivals in Israel. And when the king, as if in a waking dream, entered into the proposal of his well-meaning servants, and said to them, "Provide me a man that can play well on the harp, and bring him to me," one of them remarked, "Behold, I have seen a son of Jesse the Bethlehemite, that is cunning in playing, and a mighty valiant man, and a man of war, and prudent in matters, and a comely person, and the Lord is with him."

Welcome information this! He who communicated it proved himself hereby to be a man of understanding, in that he placed in the foreground those qualities of the musician he recommended, which he believed would at once secure the favor of the king. On the contrary, that which was to him the chief matter, and by which he principally expected the deliverance of the king from the demon of dejection, viz., the piety of the harper, and the fact that God was with him, he mentioned last, as if it had been a trivial circumstance. It is, indeed, greatly to be desired that they who are called to the office of seeking to heal diseased souls, and to help into the right path those who have erred from the ways of morality, should not only possess piety, but also have other mental endowments, such as are held in estimation by the world. Oh that it could be said of them, They are people of understanding and intelligence, men of mind and heart, thoroughly educated and of great experience. This would facilitate their relationship with those whom, however much they need counsel and consolation, ignorantly recoil from all serious religion. They are estranged from the gospel. Yet it often happens that even to such persons, after all the world's expedients for obtaining deliverance from deeply rooted sorrow have been found to be only mockery, religion will be recommended as the last remedy, though it may be reluctantly, by their own like-minded associates. They will then, acting on their despairing and reluctant advice, send for a preacher, or some God-fearing man, who is at the same time respected by them because of his pure human virtues. And how frequently has the gospel, in such circumstances, proved itself to be a "power of God," which is a match for every influence which holds the soul in thrall; and substantially, though with more lasting results, there has been frequently repeated what we here today see happen at the court of Gibeah.

How it was that the royal servant became acquainted with the young harper at Bethlehem, then only nineteen years of age, we are not informed. But it is clear, from what he said to the king, that he was himself a God-fearing man; and such men are wont, especially in those times in which, as was then the case, the word of God is precious in the land, to meet with those who are of like mind with them. On the report of this servant, messengers were sent immediately to Jesse, to convey to him, in the name of the king, the command, "Send me thy son David, who is with the sheep."

We may conceive how this would surprise Jesse. David was then in the fields with his father's flocks. The remembrance of his former anointing by Samuel still lingered in his soul as a silent, and to him yet unexplained, secret. In childlike freedom from care, David there, with the sheep and the lambs around him, played on his harp, and sang songs of praise and of homage to the Lord, and left it wholly in His hands to guide and order his future steps. But now, without any intimation of its purpose, he is suddenly summoned home. Obedient to his father's will, he led his sheep away, and when he came to him, learned why he had been summoned. His was the equanimity of one who in simplicity confides in a divine providence guiding all things. Prepared for any service to his king, he declared himself ready to follow the messenger to Gibeah. His father Jesse did not hinder him. Preparations for his journey are immediately made. According to Oriental custom, which forbids anyone to approach a throne without a gift in his hands, Jesse made ready a mule, loaded it with bread and a bottle of wine, and added a young kid of the goats; and with these homage-gifts for his prince, corresponding to the simple habits of the times, he dismissed his beloved David, amid heartfelt and pious benedictions.

At length David reaches Gibeah, carrying his harp hanging on his shoulder-band, and is immediately introduced to the king. Here now they stand opposite each other—the one like the clear shining of the sun in spring, the other like a black thundercloud ominous of evil; the one full of blooming, hopeful life; the other, a dark specter arising from the realm of death.

The king said to him, "Play to me." David bowed his head, and obeyed; and so sweet and grandly solemn was the music which flowed from the strings of his harp, that the clouded brow of the king began visibly to brighten, and his stern features strangely became relaxed and mild. It was a song without words whose soothing melody then fell upon the ear of the king. Words corresponding to the music would have effected the contrary result to that which was aimed at, and might even have increased the ill temper of the king. There are even yet men enough of his sort—persons without faith, yea, at variance both with God and the world—whom solemn music is able most powerfully to delight, and in whom it awakens, at least for the time, dispositions which border on devotion and piety, while yet the words which correspond to the sacred melody would produce in them the very opposite effect.

What is manifest from this, but that in the soul of such persons the last point at which they may be touched by that which is sacred, has not yet wholly decayed away? Let them be on their guard, however, lest by constant striving against the thoughts which, unspoken, echo forth from the harmonies with which they are delighted and refreshed, the last string in their soul on which the heavenly breath gently sounds may at length break asunder, and their aversion to the heavenly message finally terminate in a decided and incurable opposition to all that comes down from above.

The sounds from David's harp had, for the moment at least, wrought a true miracle. To the joy of those about him, the king breathed more calmly, and appeared milder and more serene than they had for a long time beheld him. And often again, when the old melancholy began to gather like a cloud around his soul, the harp-music of the shepherd youth obtained the same happy result. Is it any wonder that Saul loved the young harper? He sent to Jesse, saying, "Let David, I pray thee, stand before me, for he hath found favor in my sight"; yea, so far did the favor of Saul extend, that he received the Bethlehemite into the number of his pages and armor-bearers. The history further informs us that "when the evil spirit from God" (i.e., the spirit that, by the mysterious judicial permission of God, laid hold on him) "was upon Saul, that David took an harp, and played with his hand: so Saul was refreshed, and was well, and the evil spirit departed from him."

These last words surprise us. "Did the music," we ask, "banish the demon?" Not so; but the higher frame of mind into which the king was brought by it sufficed to limit at least the sphere of the operation of the evil spirit within him; while a full, clear, conscious life of faith on the part of Saul would have altogether destroyed the power of the wicked one. Besides, the silent intercessions which David sent up to heaven on the wings of the music of his harp must have contributed to the results with which his melodies were crowned. It appeared to be God's purpose in sending David to the king, to afford to him a new and a last means of grace. He must become conscious of what a man of childlike piety, such as David, is able, by the help of God, to do against all the powers of darkness. In the way of such an experience, he ought himself to have been won to a life of piety. But, alas! all the efforts to deliver the unhappy man were fruitless. His heart hardened itself more and more.

One of our great secular poets has imagined what an elevating, yea, sanctifying power, may dwell in a God-consecrated music. He represents the hero of his poem as saved from an assault of darkest thoughts by harmonies of a sacred choir sounding out from a neighboring cathedral into his chamber. But the poet did not understand the rich harmonious music before which the power of all evil spirits must yield, not for a passing moment only, but forever. This is the music of the holy gospel, for which, however, there must first be created in the heart of him who would listen to it the faculty of hearing, which can only be done by means of repentance and an awakened consciousness of the need of salvation. There cannot be heard in heaven or on earth any music more powerful to pacify and elevate, than that which sounds forth from the spiritual harps of the evangelists and apostles. Here we may listen to melodious notes, which will overpower and make silent every discord within us.

Let us, in conclusion, not overlook the adorable wisdom of God, in the circumstance that He brought David so early near to the throne which he was at an after period to ascend. Then he had an opportunity of obtaining an unprejudiced view of court life in its most diverse aspects, and of learning the numberless dangers to which all are exposed who breathe its atmosphere. The system of lies and deceit, of pretense and hypocrisy, which to surrounds the "gods of the earth," unveiled itself to his view, and instilled into him, for his whole future life, a deep-rooted dislike to courtier-life, with its abounding flattery and eye-service, and a decided love for honorable and faithful counsel and service, even though it might be the less polished. At the same time, the case of Saul strengthened him most powerfully in the conviction that the popular opinion, that a royal crown raises its possessor to the summit of all earthly happiness, is only a delusion, and that, on the contrary, the fear of God, as "the beginning of wisdom," is the only secure foundation of all true happiness, whether in the palace or in the peasant's cottage.

The first of the Psalms of David which we possess may have grown out of the experience he had at that time at Saul's court. With it we conclude our meditation today: "Blessed is the man that walketh not in the counsel of the ungodly, nor standeth in the way of sinners, nor sitteth in the seat of the scornful. But his delight is in the law of the Lord; and in His law doth he meditate day and night. And he shall be like a tree planted by the rivers of water, that bringeth forth his fruit in his season; his leaf also shall not wither; and whatsoever he doeth shall prosper. The ungodly are not so: but are like the chaff which the wind driveth away. Therefore the ungodly shall not stand in the judgment, nor sinners in the congregation of the righteous. For the Lord knoweth the way of the righteous: but the way of the ungodly shall perish."

3

David and Goliath

An occurrence in the life of Joshua, the remembrance of which may have often refreshed the mind of David, may well introduce us to the subject of this day's meditation. It is recorded in Joshua 5:13–15. The leader of the host of Israel, the son of Nun, is just about to enter with his people into the borders of Canaan, which had been promised by God to Abraham as the future inheritance of his descendants. He is fully conscious of all the difficulties of his undertaking. Before him lies the strong, impregnable fortress of the enemy at Jericho. A war, pregnant with important issues, must now be waged. It is night. Joshua's hosts lie encamped around; part are wrapped in slumber; part, in animated conversation, estimate the relative strength of the forces which soon must encounter each other. He himself, the leader, wanders forth alone on the hills which at some distance encompass Jericho.

Did he then survey the ground, and explore the battlefield, and fix on the plan of battle? The history tells us that "Joshua lifted up his eyes"—we know to what place he raised them. He held communion with God. What befell him then? Something wonderful, indeed; but we have no reason to be astonished at it, since God would show, by miracles, to His chosen people, that He was a living God.

Suddenly Joshua saw at a little distance a lofty figure, clothed in warlike armor, standing before him. Is it a human being? Impossible! Is it an angel? Surely it is! May it not be the "angel Jehovah" who afterward became man? At the sight Joshua was well-nigh overwhelmed. He trembles with dread. Then he takes courage and asks, "Art thou for us, or for our adversaries?" The answer is given, "Nay; but as captain of the host of the Lord am I now come." Now Joshua knew at least that he had to do with the representative of the Most High, who alone determines what shall be the issues of battle. He is courageous in being able to stay himself on this Ally. "And Joshua fell on his face to the earth, and did worship, and said unto him, What saith my lord unto his servant?"

We understand him. He renounces all confidence in himself, and desires to be faithful, submissive, and attentive in all things to the will of his Lord. The captain of the Lord's host answers his servant, saying, "Loose thy shoe from off thy foot; for the place whereon thou standest is holy." The language is figurative; but Joshua comprehended what was the spiritual import of the summons thus addressed to him. From that time forward he walked before God in genuine humility; realized God's presence with him wherever he went, confidently expected it; trusted in the Lord; at all times asked first what was His will, and turned away from whatever might be displeasing to Him. And the Lord crowned him with victory after victory, with blessing after blessing. David walked in the footsteps of Joshua, and the word was verified in him, "If ye have faith as a grain of mustard-seed, ye will remove mountains."

1 Samuel 17:45–46

> Then said David to the Philistine, Thou comest to me with a sword, and with a spear, and with a shield but I come to thee in the name of the Lord of hosts, the God of the armies of Israel, whom thou hast defied. This day will the Lord deliver thee into mine hand; and I will smite thee, and take thine head from thee; . . . that all the earth may know that there is a God in Israel.

These words form a portion of the history to which we this day direct your attention. Moreover, they indicate to us what is most essential in the narrative, and, in particular, bring prominently to view the important meaning which the event carries in its bosom

Let us, in contemplating this incident, direct our attention (1) to Israel's danger, and then (2) to the deliverance wrought for them by God by means of David.

1. We hear again in Israel the sound of the war-trumpet. We meet all the men who are capable of bearing arms, already equipped for battle, in the open field. All this was on account of the Philistines, the warlike inhabitants of the seacoast, who unconsciously were

always ready as the Lord's rod of correction against the stiff-necked people of His choice. Anew they had burst into Judea with mighty hosts, with horsemen and chariots of war, and threatened the kingdom in its center and in its strongest fortresses. This nation, always eager for war, and unquiet as the waves of the sea which break in foam upon their shore, had for about a thousand years been in possession of the southern maritime plain of Palestine. They had come partly from Egypt, which was already their second native country since they had left their first and primitive nomad condition in the region of Arabia which borders on the shores of the Persian Gulf, and partly from Crete, whence they retained the name of Cherethites.

Already, during the journey of the Israelites through the wilderness, the Philistines had made themselves sufficiently a terror to them to lead them to prefer a circuitous and difficult route to an uncertain war with these enemies. The chief god of these heathens was Dagon, a sea-deity, represented as in the upper part of his body of human form, and in the lower like a fish. The chief sanctuary of this idol was at Gath. Along with Dagon, the Philistines worshiped Baal, the king of heaven, and Astarte, the queen of heaven. They seem to have been already well skilled in the art of war. At the time of Saul, when their power had reached its highest point, they had no fewer than 30,000 war-chariots, 6,000 horsemen, and their infantry were "as the sand on the seashore" in multitude. The armor of these warriors consisted of an iron coat of mail, a copper helmet, and greaves of brass. Their weapons of offense were the javelin, the spear with heavy iron head, the bow, and the sword. A leathern shield, which covered the whole body, served them for a defense. The Anakims, a race of giants, constituted a part of the host, distinguished for strength and courage. They were the fathers and founders of the whole nation who had come originally from Egypt, and were held in honor as the nobles of the people, crowned with the dignity and fame of ancestral glory.

The history upon which we enter today shows us the Philistines already at Shochoh, three German miles[1] southwest from Jerusalem, encamped on high, level ground. Opposite to them the host of Israel is encamped also on a chain of hills. A valley ("the oak or terebinth valley") separates the two armies from each other. We observe that the army of Israel are by no means confident of victory, in sight of the

---

1. Twelve English miles.

forest of spears and halberts which mark the host of the enemy. And this is not to be wondered at, for they see that the brow of their commander-in-chief is encompassed by dark clouds of care and sorrow, and his eye wanders restlessly. The king now trusts only in the arm of flesh, believing that he has forfeited every claim to help from above. What wonder, then, that the situation in which he is placed should appear to him to be specially critical, and that he should regard it as advisable—unbelief makes men cowards—to limit his warlike operations only to the defense of his position.

The Philistines also delayed the assault, but on a different ground. For the increase of their glory, they sought to show to the world that their warlike strength consisted not only in the multitude of their host, but in the personal warlike dexterity and skill in battle of every separate warrior. They challenged, therefore, the enemy to a duel—a practice common in war among the ancients, as Homer testifies. One of the old race of giants, born at Gath, measuring not less than six cubits and a span in height, Goliath by name, came forward from the enemy's camp, accompanied by his shield-bearer, in full armor, and cried aloud, with a threatening voice, to the army of Israel: "Why are ye come out to set your battle in array? Am I not a Philistine, and ye servants to Saul? Choose you a man for you, and let him come down to me. If he be able to fight with me, and to kill me, then will we be your servants; but if I prevail against him, and kill him, then shall ye be our servants, and serve us." Such is the immeasurable self-confident boasting of the Philistine. On the issue of this combat he places the fortune and the future condition of his whole kingdom. Contempt, such as that expressed in his challenge to the people of Jehovah, could not be more scornful. The boaster is himself fully conscious of this, and cries, confident of victory, with insolent defiance, over to the hostile camp, "I defy the armies of Israel this day; give me a man that we may fight together."

Now it was for Israel, and specially for the king, to recall to remembrance the words spoken by Moses, "The Lord is a man of war; the Lord shall fight for you, and ye shall hold your peace;" and how often in past times the Lord had confirmed this word of His faithful servant, and had sealed it by the events of His providence. And the children of these fathers had so much the greater reason to take heart, inasmuch as the haughty defiance of the Philistine concerned not only them, but also God, who had graciously chosen them as His

people. The cause which gave rise to this war which had newly broken out, was closely connected with the interests of religion, as was,
indeed, the case with most of the wars of ancient times. The heathen
fought for the honor of their god Dagon. They wished him to appear
to all the world as the true god. Jehovah, on the other hand, must
appear to be but a phantom, a shadow without substance, and only
worthy of being despised. In these circumstances the children of
Israel had reason to trust with joyful confidence in the arm of the
Almighty, and, certain of victory, to accept the challenge to battle
made by the heathen. But what happened? Israel is afraid because
their king is fainthearted. They ventured not, with childlike faith, to
appropriate the promises of Jehovah. The wings of faith, which would
have borne them up to the Lord of hosts in confident trust, are broken. What will be the result?

2. They hear in silence the bold challenge of the uncircumcised.
No one in Israel announces himself as ready to take up the gauntlet
thus haughtily thrown down. Then an incident occurred which
seemed at first as if it would interrupt the deeply earnest matter with
an almost enlivening interlude. A tender youth, "ruddy, and of a
beautiful countenance," clothed in plain shepherd's attire, offered
himself to take up the challenge of battle with the giant. This young
Ephrathite is no stranger to us. When the cloud of war darkened
Israel's horizon, his three elder brothers, Eliab, Abinadab, and
Shammah, had to exchange the plow for the spear and the sword,
and the raiment of the herdsman for the war-cloak of the king. But
Jesse had entreated that David, the player on the harp, his youngest
son, might be permitted to return to him at Bethlehem, to assist him
in the care of his flocks—a request which, when his duty now called
the king into the field, was granted to him so much the more readily, because Saul, as it appears, had before this begun to entertain a
dislike to the pious harper, seemingly on account of his religious
earnestness. David, well content with this change of situation, again
went forth to watch his father's flocks amid the peaceful scenes of his
home.

But Jesse remembered also, with a father's solicitude, his sons who
were in the distant camp; and he spoke one day to David, saying,
"Take now an ephah of this parched corn, and these ten loaves, and
run to the camp to thy brethren; and carry these ten cheeses unto the
captain of their thousand, and look how thy brethren fare, and take

their pledge." David, as a faithful, obedient son, accustomed without
hesitation to do as his father commanded, even when the commands
did not correspond with his own inclinations, rose up early in the
morning, and came near to the encampment at the very moment
when the armies stood in battle array over against each other.

Having left the provisions he had brought with him in the hands
of the guards of the baggage of the army, he hastened forward to the
field of battle, and sought out, among the soldiers, his brothers; and
when he had found them, he very heartily saluted them, gave to
them the salutation from home, made them acquainted with the
object of his unexpected visit, and delivered to them the welcome
gift he had been commanded to bring from their father's house. Then
suddenly sounded forth, from the heights along which the camp of
the Philistines extended, the lion-like voice of the gigantic boaster;
for, to the disgrace of the army of Israel, he dared, for several days in
succession, to renew his challenge to battle without anyone venturing to accept it.

Over the whole army was heard the rumor of that dreaded man,
who came forth openly to insult Israel and their God. It was told
how the king had promised a mass of gold to him who would lay the
blasphemer in the dust; yea, that he had even declared himself ready
to give to such an one his daughter to wife, and to free the house of
the conqueror from all subjection to taxation, i.e., to raise them to
the rank of nobles. The flame of warlike courage burnt so feebly in
the breast of Saul that it only influenced him to offer this glittering
prize. How happy would he be were the victory thus purchased,
without blood, to be thrown down at his feet while he reclined in
his royal tent!

With the greatest astonishment David perceives what is now going
on. He doubts whether he may believe his ears when he hears the
insolent call of the uncircumcised warrior again sounding forth, or yet
his eyes when he sees no one of his countrymen in the camp of Israel
burn with holy indignation, and prepare himself to step forward into
the breach, for the glory of God. "How," he asks himself, "is the last
spark of faith extinguished in Israel? or is His arm shortened, who
once buried in the waves of the Red Sea Pharaoh with his horsemen
and their horses; who, at the prayer of Moses, destroyed the power of
Amalek, and guided Gideon so that with his three hundred men he
was able to sweep from the field the thousands of Midian; yea, bent

under the feet of a weak woman the neck of Sisera the Canaanite, who was a terror to the whole land? Has, then, the 'Lord of hosts,' who once was able to do such things, resigned His government to the gods of the Philistines, and must Israel now submit to this change of rulers?"

Thus he reflects with himself, while the flame of a holy zeal as against the slanderer in the camp of the Philistines, so against the despondency of his own people, rises high within him. He inquired among the surrounding warriors regarding the words of the king's proclamation, that he might be sure that the way was open for him to undertake that which his heart with holy impulse prompted him to do for the glory of God. He asked what would be done to the man who would smite the Philistine to the ground, and turn away the reproach from Israel. At the same time, he was not able altogether to conceal from those who stood near him the feelings that were in his mind; and the impetuosity with which he added the question, "Who is this uncircumcised Philistine, that he should defy the armies of the living God?" fully revealed his inmost thoughts. The matter did not escape the notice of David's brothers, but it only filled them with sorrow and anger. "Why camest thou down hither?" said Eliab, the eldest of his brothers. "With whom hast thou left those few sheep in the wilderness? I know thy pride, and the naughtiness of thine heart; for thou art come down that thou mightest see the battle."

Eliab sufficiently knew the brave boy to believe that wherever the honor of God was concerned he would courageously undertake the most perilous enterprise. "But what," thinks Eliab, "will be the result of such an undertaking? Not only the death of the boy, but also, at the same time, the overthrow of Israel; and, worse than even this, the defeat of Israel's God in the eyes of the heathen!" Thus with Eliab also thought his two brothers. We see that even with them faith and courage had disappeared. David replied to the reproachful words of Eliab by quietly asking him, "What have I now done? Has it not been commanded me?" And with these last words he leaves it to his brothers to think on a charge given by their father Jesse, or on some higher and more mysterious command. He is clearly conscious of what it is now his duty to do, according to the will of God. In his continued conversations with the soldiers who stood around him this appears always the more manifest, so that at length they believe it to be their duty to give information to the king of the arrival of this shepherd-boy in the camp, and of his singular declarations.

This was accordingly done. "Bring him to me," said Saul. David appeared, as commanded, and respectfully saluted the king with these words: "Let no man's heart fail because of him; thy servant will go and fight with this Philistine." "What!" replied Saul; "thou art not able to go against this Philistine to fight with him: for thou art but a youth, and he a man of war from his youth." David again addressed the king, and told him of the battles which in his younger years, when a shepherd, he had fought successfully, first with a lion, and then with a raging bear, and added, "And this uncircumcised Philistine shall be as one of them, seeing he hath defied the armies of the living God. The Lord that delivered me out of the paw of the lion, and out of the paw of the bear, He will deliver me out of the hand of this Philistine." Here the heart of the son of Jesse is fully opened up to our view. Jehovah, the God of his fathers, on whose help he relied with perfect confidence, because he was conscious of seeking only His honor, is his support and his strength. Such faith as this called forth wonder and admiration even from the king. Yea, it even communicated to his own timid heart something of that confidence of victory which animated the youth. "Go," said Saul, "and the Lord be with thee."

But the subsequent conduct of the king showed in him a total misapprehension of the position which David occupied when he announced his heroic resolution. He commanded that David should be armed with his armor, his helmet, and his coat of mail, together with his sword. David did not offer any opposition, seeing that such was the will of his master; yet he doubted not but that the king himself would soon be convinced that such an equipment was not suitable for him. And so it happened. "David said unto Saul, I cannot go with these; for I have not proved them"; and Saul therefore did not hinder that David should, to the no little astonishment of all, exchange the heavy war-armor which had been put upon him for his own simple shepherd dress, with his shepherd scrip, his staff, and his sling. Then he went forth out of the camp of Israel; and, after he had taken up five smooth stones out of the dry bed of the brook which ran through the intervening valley, marched on to meet the Philistine, who with his countrymen stood mocking him, while the whole host of Israel, with most earnest, anxious expectation, watched his progress.

History has presented many and diverse examples in the sphere of the spiritual life similar to this heroic march of the youthful David. I now call to your remembrance only a Luther, who, despite the doubts of timid learned men, threw aside the heavy armor of scholastic wisdom, and, stepping forward in freedom, vanquished the giant of Rome with the five heads of his Catechism. And might we not here also make mention of such witnesses and combatants in the region of the Church, as with holy courage have broken through the restraints of homiletic or liturgic forms, and, in the free effusions and creations of their divinely anointed spirits, have given the tone to a new and more animating style of preaching, and thereby have opened the way to a new quickening and elevating of the life of the Church into greater fruitfulness?

When Goliath saw the shepherd youth coming to him, and was convinced that he was really in earnest, unarmed as he was, to venture battle with him, he stepped forward before his shield-bearer to meet the presumptuous boy, and, while yet at a distance, assailed him with words of bitterest scorn and deepest contempt. "Am I a dog," cried he, "that thou comest to meet me with staves? Cursed be thou of my god Dagon! Come on! that I may give thy flesh unto the fowls of the air, and to the beasts of the field." Whom would not this growl of the roaring lion have made to tremble? But David, who knew in his heart for whose honor he now appeared, had no fear, but with noble calmness replied, "Thou comest to me with a sword, and with a spear, and with a shield: but I come to thee in the name of the Lord of hosts, the God of the armies of Israel, whom thou hast defied. This day will the Lord deliver thee into mine hand; and I will smite thee, and take thine head from thee; and I will give the carcasses to the host of the Philistines" (i.e., the carcass of him in whom the host of the Philistines concentrated itself, and came to a point) "this day unto the fowls of the air and to the wild beasts of the earth; that all the earth may know that there is a God in Israel. And all this assembly shall know that the Lord saveth not with sword and spear: for the battle is the Lord's, and He will give you into our hands."

Scarcely had David spoken these words, when the Philistine, with his trusted gigantic spear in his hand, advanced to meet him. But as quickly did his youthful opponent take one of the stones from his shepherd's bag, and nimbly place it in the sling. Then, with vigorous arm, accustomed to use his sling, he swung it round his head, and with the quickness of lightning the stone flew forth, hit its mark, the temples of the Philistine, and with fearful force pierced crashing into the giant's head, scattering the brains. The son of Anak staggered, sank, and fell to the ground with convulsive, quivering limbs, and with a terrible death-moan. The conqueror hastens forward, draws from its scabbard the sword of the fallen giant, and with it separates the head from the body. "And when the Philistines saw that their champion was dead, they fled." By doing this they broke through their compact, according to which they were bound to lay down their weapons before Israel, and submit themselves to the power of the conqueror. Therefore the men of Israel and Judah were justified in pursuing, with loud shouts of triumph, the fugitive Philistines, even to the gates of Ekron—one of the most important of the five great cities of the Philistines—many of whom they slew in their flight, and in taking possession of their forsaken camp and all its contents as spoils of war.

David afterward brought the head of the Philistine to Jerusalem, having previously concealed his armor in his tent which he probably shared with his brothers. A victory, great and glorious and important in the results which flowed from it, was thus gained by Israel. It was Jehovah's, and not man's. A victory of the true, living God, over the whole kingdom of false gods—of faith in the God of Abraham, Isaac, and Jacob, over all the then existing, as well as the future, forms of unbelief and superstition throughout the whole world. Scarcely ever has the Lord so majestically, and with such splendor as here, confirmed that promise spoken to Israel: "I will redeem you with a stretched out arm, and ye shall know that I am the Lord your God"; and that other word, "I will be glorified among the heathen."

But what says Saul now, in this unexpected change of affairs? Naturally he is not a little rejoiced at seeing himself so suddenly and in so surprising a manner set free from that perplexing dilemma in which he had been placed. But there is not the slightest intimation given to us, either that he condemned himself on account of his unbelieving despair, or that, in the dust of humiliation, he presented to the Lord his offering of thanks and praise. Rather, already the poisonous worm of envy seems to have raised itself up within him. He inquired at Abner, "the captain of the host," who the conqueror was, and whose son he was. Abner replied, "As thy soul liveth, O king, I cannot tell." Saul said, "Inquire thou whose son the stripling is." But when, soon afterward, David appeared in person before the king, with the head of the Philistine in his hands, he addressed to him the same question, "Whose son art thou, thou young man?" David simply replied, with the expression of genuine modesty, "I am the son of thy servant Jesse the Bethlehemite," and then stood quietly waiting the further commands of his royal master.

This incident in the narrative, it must be admitted, has in it something strange. Saul did not recognize in David the youthful singer, who had formerly, with the melody of his harp, banished from him the evil spirit, and who on that account had gained his love, and had been received into the number of his pages and armor-bearers. Many interpreters, misled by this surprising circumstance, have been induced to regard the chapter from which our text is taken as a historical supplement to that immediately preceding, and to place the battle with the Philistine before the time of the first appearance of David at the royal court. But this is a mere arbitrary proceeding. How can we explain, then, the enigma of Saul's ignorance of David? In the first place, Saul, to heighten the splendor of his throne, had surrounded himself not only with a bodyguard a thousand strong, and a choir of musicians, but also, as already noticed, with a company of pages and young armor-bearers; and it was not to be expected that amid the continual storms which marked his reign, he could know and remember the names and descent of each one of all these bands. Further, David, by his return to take charge again of his father's flocks at Bethlehem, had, as it seems, for a considerable time been out of the sight of Saul, who had perhaps now only some dim recollections of the comfortless condition in which he was at the time of the first visit of the shepherd boy, but retained no longer any clear remembrance of his person. Lastly, it might possibly be that it was only of the descent and the birthplace of the boy that Saul had now no longer any recollection; for he put the question to Abner merely as to whose son the youth was. Thus we see that one need not by any means despair of being able to explain the difficulty. Besides, as the reverence which he believed to be due to the majesty of his highest lord required, David's answer did not go beyond the question put by the king.

Thus Israel saw themselves honored with another remarkable evidence that the God of their fathers was still truly with them, and that

faith in the promises of their God, when it knows how, with simplicity, to take fast hold of them, can accomplish all things. In the
third Psalm, David sings: "Thou, O Lord, art a shield for me; my
glory, and the lifter up of mine head. I will not be afraid of ten thousands of people that have set themselves against me round about." In
the eighteenth: "Thou hast girded me with strength unto the battle;
by Thee I have run through a troop; and by my God have I leaped
over a wall." In the sixtieth: "Through God we shall do valiantly: for
He it is that shall tread down our enemies." In the sixty-eighth: "He
that is our God is the God of salvation; and unto God the Lord
belong the issues from death." Who perceives not, in these jubilant
notes, the voice of the conqueror of Goliath? These harmonious
strains from his harp, struck by the hand of faith, are they not able
yet, as they have been aforetime, to banish away the demon of faint-
heartedness and despair? May this be the experience of everyone who
needs it! May he learn, as David was not yet enabled to do, to triumph with the Apostle: "I can do all things through Christ, which
strengtheneth me."

4

David in the King's House

Agur, the wise man, specifies[1] three things by which "the earth is disquieted." As the first, he mentions "a servant when he reigneth." He has not here before his mind a person in the station of a servant, but one having a servile disposition as his general habit of mind. A ruler who makes use of the power with which he is entrusted for the purpose of promoting, in low selfishness, his own private human interests instead of the public weal alone, is a calamity to his country. The majesty wherewith God has clothed him is paled in the eyes of his people, who ought rather to see and to honor in him the representative of God upon the earth, ruling over all his subjects with disinterested magnanimity. When the bonds of veneration which bind the people to their king are dissolved, immediately those of obedience become more and more relaxed, till at length, if the kingdom goes not to ruin under a deluge sweeping away all that is called law and order, it is only to be ascribed to the fear of imprisonment and death. With such thoughts as these we begin a meditation, which again brings us near to the throne of Saul, the king of Israel. Let us praise God if it is granted to us to look with feelings of greater satisfaction upon the throne of our own king.

1 Samuel 18:1–2

> And it came to pass, when he had made an end of speaking unto Saul, that the soul of Jonathan was knit with the soul of David, and Jonathan loved him as his own soul. And Saul took him that day, and would let him go no more home to his father's house.

---

1. Proverbs 30:21–22.

We rejoice again to meet with David! Who has not already felt his heart drawn out toward this noble youth? We find him again at the royal court; but now he occupies another and a higher position than that which he formerly held there. Fortune seems to smile upon him; but let us not, however, deceive ourselves by this outward seeming prosperity of his life. He is in the school of the Lord, in which one has to be always ready to exercise, before all others, the grace of humility and self-denial, and learn to know, as an elementary truth, that which is expressed in the well-known verse:

> The path of sorrow, and that path alone,
> Leads to the land where sorrow is unknown;
> No pilgrim ever reach'd that blest abode
> But found the thorns and briars upon the road.[2]

The consequences to David personally of his triumphs over Goliath were these three: His finding (1) a precious treasure, (2) an honor full of danger, and (3) an evil threatening disgrace.

1. The treasure in the possession of which David "was made happy after his victory," was the friendship of Jonathan, Saul's first-born. This princely youth, like the son of Jesse in his disposition and in his noble aims, had perhaps before this time experienced a sympathetic feeling binding him to the amiable young harper of his own age, at the court of his royal father. But afterward, when he was witness not only of his remarkable heroism, but also of his whole behavior, as unassuming and modest as it was manly and free, unrestrained and full of prudence, he felt himself drawn in warm affection toward him; and since this affection was mutual, they framed a covenant of friendship between them which lasted through life, and which has become proverbial because of its truth and genuineness, and is illustrious as furnishing an ideal example of reciprocal affection. It was not a worldly friendship, in which one, in loving another, in reality loves only himself, and in which personal interests, refined it may be ever so far, form the uniting bond. They loved each other truly in God, to whose service they had devoted themselves in the hours of holy consecration; and all their views and aims, their judgments and

---

2. Zu dem Schloss der Ewigkeit,
   Kommt Kein Mensch hin sonder Streit;
   Die in Salems Mauern wohnen,
   Zeigen ihre Dornenkronen." —From a Hymn of the Seventeenth Century

endeavors, were in perfect harmony. They understood the slightest indication of each other's mind; yea, the faintest tone which vibrated on the harp-strings of the soul of the one, echoed full and harmonious in the soul of the other.

When such conditions meet together, there grows the beautiful flower of that love which the apostle calls peculiar, in contradistinction to that which is common. Friendship which thus grows up and blossoms, rooting itself in a similarity of sanctified dispositions, takes a first place among our earthly blessings and possessions. There that communion of heart so unites together that one man becomes to another like a living canal, through which the inner life pours forth to him a stream of enriching and never-failing fullness of refreshing consolations and enjoyments. Happy he to whom it falls to be a sharer in the pearl of such an alliance as this! It will not only be an ornament to him, it will also assist him in life's battles, and, by the power of sympathy, will lighten every burden of half its weight, and in every way will help to brighten his pilgrimage-journey to the eternal home.

Besides this, we call to mind that promise of the Lord, "If two of you shall agree on earth as touching anything that they shall ask, it shall be done for them by my Father which is in heaven"; and not less that in the verse following, "For where two or three are gathered together in my name, there am I in the midst of them." A Cleophas and his companion on the way to Emmaus; a Peter and the disciple who lay on Jesus' bosom; a Paul and his Timothy—how lovely are these double stars of sacred history, pouring forth their rays upon us from heaven! What springs of refreshing gushed forth to those who were united as brethren in such fellowship of heart; and what harvests of happiness and of peace have been gathered home to thousands from the example of such a confiding relationship!

Whoever is the object of such affectionate friendship, let him esteem it as a great treasure of high and precious worth. Whoever, on the contrary, complains that he enjoys no such friendship, let him seek for the cause of this, not in others, but in himself; since to him, without doubt, there are lacking, if not every endeavor after that which is noble, yet at least the heart-attracting virtues of humility, of purity, and of love. For wherever there exists anything of that nobility of mind, it cannot remain without discovering its power of magnetic attraction upon those who are like-minded. While selfishness repels instead of drawing into union with itself, and it assimilates the man to whom it clings to that American tree which is always isolated, within the circle of whose influence nothing grows green or blossoms, and toward which no plant stretches out its tendrils to twine themselves around it. Let no one say that he has no need of his fellowmen, because his Lord and God are enough for him.

That is a proud boast, which seldom has any real truth lying at its foundation, and which, in most cases, seems only as a cloak for coldness of heart and the absence of love, of which such an one must accuse himself. It is true, indeed, that it is only the friendship of the heavenly Prince of Peace which makes us happy; but a part of this happiness belongs to our earthly life, and consists in this, that we are delivered from the dominion of selfishness, and breathe more freely in the element of love, and become partakers of the precious blessings of the "communion of the saints." Christ has not come to separate men from one another, but for the first time to lay the foundation for their being truly united. He desires to see Himself loved by us in our brethren. His Church is so far from existing as a mere multitude of individuals who happen to be thrown together, that it is rather bound together under Him its Head into a living organism, and may be likened to a "spiritual body," whose members, united into one heart and one soul, are active in assisting one another.

Jonathan's love for David must be commended as something altogether peculiarly rare and precious. High, yea, seemingly impassable barriers raised themselves, separating the king's son from the humble shepherd boy; but the affection of the young prince, founded only on a similarity of disposition and of aim, devoted toward that which is holiest and loftiest, not only easily overleaped the barrier of rank and position which separated them, but also stood the test of many heavier trials. Jonathan saw his fame-crowned friend honored by his people with an enthusiasm which might well have had the effect of infusing into him something of that poison which Solomon styles, in his book of Proverbs, "the rottenness of the bones." But Jonathan's love, born of God, was pure and strong enough to tread under foot the offspring of envy and jealousy. Even before this time he may likely have felt within him a foreboding that his father's crown would not descend to him, the natural heir to it, but to his friend David. But even this was not powerful enough to make any breach in his friendship for David. Jonathan's love was truly great; but it was no blossom of nature's growth—it was the fruit of the operation of the Spirit of God, such as one could almost scarcely look for in such perfection in the time of the old covenant.

There were certainly not wanting in David those qualities which could not but tend to promote this sincere and confiding friendship on the part of Jonathan. David's noble self-respect, always associated with unfeigned modesty and humility, as well as his whole general demeanor, as far removed from an unworthy over-estimation of the honor conferred upon him through the favor of the king's son, as his conduct toward that like-minded youth was removed from everything like presumptuous arrogance—how could this fail to gain the whole heart of his friend?

2. "Jonathan," we read, "loved David as his own soul." As an outward pledge of his generous friendship, he sent him, as a present, his mantle and other parts of his own armor, together with his girdle, his sword, and his bow. A very significant present this! Was it the design of the king's son to say anything more by this than "I hold thee as my own brother"? Saul, while he was still under the fresh animation of joy on account of the deliverance gained for him out of the hand of the Philistine, saw without displeasure the friendly relationship of his son with the brave slinger. Yea, he even went so far as to declare to David that it was his purpose to retain him near his own person, and he accordingly entrusted to him the chief command over one of the divisions of his army, probably his bodyguards. David acted in all matters according to the directions of the king, firmly believing that it was the Lord "who, by the hand of Saul His anointed, guided and ruled over him." He behaved himself "wisely," the history informs us. Under all the honors with which he saw himself loaded, he remained master of his spirit, and always like himself. However high they raised him, his heart did not raise itself. In all his actions he conducted himself as became an obedient and submissive servant of his king. Thus he escaped being at any time put to shame, and avoided the jealousy of the other courtiers, if this was indeed in any wise possible. Moreover, he saved himself, by his behavior, from a deeper fall, if at any time (which truly soon enough happened) the favor of his exalted patron should be turned away from him, and he should experience the truth of the well-known lines of the poet:

> The favors of a king are like the sea,
>   Wherein men fish for pearls when all is still
> But when the wind and storms arise, then flee,
>   And haste to guard thyself 'gainst coming ill.[3]

Discretion also counsels to the virtue of modesty, as we see it expressed in these words of our Lord, "When thou art bidden of any man to a wedding, sit not down in the highest room, lest a more honorable man than thou be bidden of him; and he that bade thee and him come and say to thee, Give this man place; and thou begin with shame to take the lowest room. But when thou art bidden, go and sit down in the lowest room that when he that bade thee cometh, he may say unto thee, Friend, go up higher: then shalt thou have worship in the presence of them that sit at meat with thee. For whosoever exalteth himself shall be abased; and he that humbleth himself shall be exalted."[4] It is to be understood, of course, that the conduct which our Lord here commends is such as arises from simplicity of character, and preserves itself unstained by dissimulation and cunning. How often, to one whom we once saw proudly raising his head, and assuming to himself airs, has it been said, "Give this man place," and we now see him sit in the lowest room, while others step forth out of deep concealment, without, perhaps, themselves knowing how highly they are exalted in the esteem and love of their brethren.

David went forward, then, for a while along an even and smooth path; but short enough was this "time of refreshing" granted to him. Already, during the homeward march of the army from the camp to the royal residence, the heart of Saul began to turn against him; and the less easily did the king succeed in concealing the ill humor arising within him, the louder the triumphant applause by which the people celebrated the exploit of the Bethlehemite hero. The women, in particular, vied with one another, from city to city, in demonstrations of joy of every kind. With stringed instruments, tabrets, and trumpets, they went forth to meet the returning conqueror, and, exulting and moving to and fro

---

3. "Wie ein Meer sind Königsgnaden
     Perlen fischt man wo es ruht;
   Aber hüte dich vor Schaden
     Wenn ein Sturm erregt die Fluth."—Friedrich Ruckert
4. Luke 14:8–11.

in rhythmic dances, they cried out ever anew in responsive song, "Saul hath slain his thousands, and David his ten thousands." This threatened to embitter to the king more and more the whole triumph. A cruel jealousy boiled up within his soul. "To me," he murmured angrily to himself, "they have ascribed but thousands, and to that one ten thousands! The kingdom will yet become his!" Now, indeed, a dark foreboding of such an event as this began to take possession of him, and a fire of passion, threatening danger to David, began to burn within his soul. This could not escape the notice of David, for he now read distinctly enough in the countenance of the king, becoming more and more dark toward him, that the honor conferred upon him was one that must be full of peril to him. How willingly would he have heaped upon the head of his king all the wreaths of fame wherewith the people adorned him; but such a thing would inevitably have appeared in the eyes of the people as but an insulting of the king.

A patriotic celebration of the victory in Israel was certainly now in every respect appropriate; but it ought to have been of another altogether different and worthier sort than that now celebrated by the people. The songs of praise ought to have ascended first of all to the Lord, who for this end made use of the humble, unarmed shepherd boy as His instrument, that He might so much the more make it distinctly appear that it was His arm of almighty power which had saved Israel. The people mistook this, and they idolized the instrument. But is not this very error, which lamentably proves a deep estrangement from God, a conspicuous feature of the present generation, which has invented the expression "hero-worship,"[5] and among whom we not seldom see this deification of men rise up even to madness? Well and good. Let men celebrate their heroes, immortalize their memory in monuments, weave laurel crowns for all who have made themselves serviceable to the common weal, or who have extended the empire of elevating and salutary ideas by the power of their creative mental endowments—only let them not forget first to give praise to the Father of Spirits for all that is great and noble and rich in blessing, which the children of men accomplish; for from Him cometh down every good and every perfect gift. And let them render to Him, above all others, in prostrate humility, the

---

5. "Cultus des Genius."

homage which is His due. Let them keep in moderation the rendering of praise to mortal men; and especially let them guard against honoring the unworthy, for thereby they only debase themselves, and set wide open the flood-gates and the channel for all that is ignoble and despicable. Let them be ashamed to lavish their incense on those who, as merrymen, as buffoons, or in such-like ways make themselves a spectacle to others, or carry the greatness that appertains to them to the market, in order to gain the approbation of some tinkling potsherd, or the applause of the rabble.

O what lamentable scenes daily observation in this direction brings before our eyes in our own time! We see the deluded world, having abandoned God and His word, at one time doing homage to the writer of some frivolous romance or novel; at another, to some arrogant denier and opponent of all that is holy; at another, to a pretended reformer, the contemptible ape of those to whom that name truly belongs; at another, to some public orator mirroring himself in his own high-sounding phrases, and calumniating the rulers; if not even to a worthless stage-dancer, or the like; and soon again, after a short intoxication, turning its back on those it adored, to honor others of the same order, with the quickly-expiring straw-fire of its enthusiasm. O that the world of today would mark how already the judgment of God has begun to descend upon them, in that self-degradation which they bring upon themselves by their idolatrous conduct! and how to those who venture to refuse to do homage to the Most High, that happens which is threatened in the fourth verse of the second Psalm, "He that sitteth in the heavens shall laugh: the Lord shall have them in derision!"

But to return to David. We think him fortunate in having been brought by the Lord into friendly fellowship with his Jonathan. For how isolated would he have been when, within a short time after, the sun of the king's favor no longer shone upon him? Where in that circle, whose air he now breathed, could he find a single truly sympathizing heart in whose fellowship he might be able to triumph over all those sorrows he has now from this time forward to endure? To him there was now given the opportunity, and certainly not to his disadvantage, of perceiving what usually happens to persons in circumstances similar to those in which he was at this time placed at the courts of the great ones of the earth. Everything there depends, as it certainly is fitting it should, on the favor of the prince.

Men look to his countenance, however, not only that they may discover from it his commands, but also that they may learn to regulate
their own conduct in conferring favors on anyone by the direction
and measure in which he does so. Woe to him toward whom, in the
highest places, a coldness begins to be manifested! For the most part
he will discover such a change of temperature for the first time in the
changed demeanor toward him of those who were wont to be his
most enthusiastic admirers so long as his course was prosperous. Now
he sees their warm respect suddenly cooled into a formal politeness,
if he does not even make the discovery that these so-called friends
have aimed at hastening his complete overthrow.

    David was bitterly undeceived at this time, when the favor of Saul
was turned away from him. He makes frequent reference to this in his
Psalms. There we hear him complaining, "My lovers and my
friends stand aloof from my sore." At another time he calls upon God
for deliverance from "the deceitful and unjust man." But David had
before this learned to expect his truest happiness not from the good-
will of men, whose fickleness did not long remain concealed from
him, but from the favor of his God alone. Nevertheless he had reason most heartily and always to give thanks to the Lord who had
bound him in the precious fellowship of genuine love with
Jonathan, and thus lightened to him the burden of so many sorrowful
trials, and gave him experience of the truth of the words of Sirach,
"A faithful friend is a strong defense; and he that hath found such an
one hath found a treasure. A faithful friend is the medicine of life."

    3. Saul gradually fell back, in consequence of his burning jealousy
against the conqueror of Goliath, into his former miserable condition. The "Saul has slain his thousands, and David his ten
thousands," still echoed in his ears. He "eyed," as the history expresses it, the young hero through whom Jehovah had wrought so great a
deliverance for Israel, and who thereby had become the man of the
day. Poor Saul, the spirit of Cain moves in his soul! "Why art thou
wroth?" was once said to the first fratricide; "and why is thy countenance fallen? If thou doest well, shalt thou not be accepted? and if
thou doest not well, sin lieth at the door. And unto thee shall be his
desire, and thou shalt rule over him." We sound these words of warning in the ears of the king of Israel; but notwithstanding their
awakening earnestness, they glance from off his heart, which hard-
ens itself more and more. Ever deeper darkness gathers round the

brow of the king, and wilder becomes the threatening glance of his restless eye. The godless thoughts within him grow up speedily into maturity. Again the evil spirit seizes him with all his might. "Saul," says the history, "began to prophesy"; i.e., there appeared in him the dark image of that agitation under which the prophets poured forth their discourses and sayings when overpowered by the might of the Holy Spirit, which for the moment raised them, if not above their own consciousness, at least above their understanding. Saul wandered and raged about his palace like one bereft of reason, and saw in his unbelieving imagination, full of suspicions, visions which at one time made him tremble and shudder, and at another hurried him on to madness and wild outbreaks of passion.

Were it granted us, in our own immediate circles of society, to look everywhere behind the curtain, how often would such-like scenes meet our view—scenes of wild overflowings of a wounded sense of honor, or of unbridled anger because of some loss sustained, or of burning and heart-consuming envy, so that we could not forbear to use the expression "demoniacal" as fittingly designating such paroxysms.

The people about the court found themselves, by this condition of their royal master, placed in circumstances of extreme perplexity. But what was their counsel? The player on the harp must again be brought hither. David is ready. Trusting in his God, and as free from suspicion as he is full of sympathy, he appears before the raging monarch, and begins, as he had formerly done, to strike the cords of his harp. But this time his gentle music did not calm the tiger-like ferocity of the tyrant. Before the harper was aware of it, the king had seized his spear, which he always carried with him instead of the scepter, as kings in ancient times were generally wont to do, and with the whole weight of his vigorous arm hurled it against the savior of his crown, that he might smite him even to the wall with it. The murderous dart, however, missed its aim, and, quivering, remained fixed in the wall over against him whose life had been thus greatly endangered.

Hoping that Saul will now recognize the Invisible Hand which with wonderful power protected him with its shield, the harper again seizes his harp. But when Saul a second time, in his madness, renews his murderous attempt, and sees it once more and in a similar manner frustrated, he begins at last to discover who it is against whom he fights. Fear is now added to his hatred and rancor, which, however, does not restrain him from continuing his persecution of David. He now only meditates on a plan by which it might be possible for him to remove out of the way the object of his jealousy, without exposing himself to the suspicion of personal participation in guilt. He therefore conveys to him the positive command to place himself immediately at the head of a thousand armed men, and to go against the Philistines, who were anew disquieting the land. He reckoned on this result: David will this time be struck down on the field of battle by the hands of the revengeful enemy. That he might the more provoke the enemy, and draw their attention toward him as a mark for their weapons, he hastened to raise the hated conqueror of their great champion Goliath to the dignity of his son-in-law, in accordance with his promise made before all the people, and therefore irrevocable, however reluctant he might be to fulfill it. "In wounding him," perhaps He thought, "they will now imagine that at the same time they wound me."

But the crafty scheme of the king, as we shall immediately hear, went still further. He betrothed to David his eldest daughter Merab, although with true modesty he declared himself unworthy of so high an honor, and said to the king, "Who am I? and what is my life, or my father's family in Israel, that I should be son-in-law to the king?" Some time after this, however, Saul, for unknown reasons, changed his mind, and gave Merab to Adriel the Meholathite to wife, instead of giving her to David, to whom he now betrothed his daughter Michal, because he had heard that she loved the young hero. David was anew reminded of his humble rank and of his poverty. But the king persisted in his purpose, and craftily sent information to the betrothed youth that he expected from him, as a nuptial gift, nothing but a hundred foreskins of the Philistines. Thus he believed he had laid for him a trap which he could not avoid, and that David would surely perish. David, without any remonstrance, at once went forth with his men to meet the faithless hereditary enemies of his people. Not many days passed till, again crowned with honors, he returned with twice the number of the bloody trophies which had been demanded of him. Thus the cunning plot of the king to accomplish his death was again frustrated. In forming his plan, it had not entered into his calculation that Jehovah the Lord stood by the side of His servant David. He could not now, on account of his people, withhold from him Michal any longer. But the history records that "Saul was yet the more afraid of David; and Saul became David's enemy continually."

We can scarcely conceive of a single trying situation in life in which David, at some period of his earthly course, did not find himself placed. Even for His own sake, that he might not be too much elevated by the abundant favors that were heaped upon him, he stood in need of being continually reminded of his dependence on Him who dwells in the high and holy place, and with those who are of broken and contrite spirit. Besides this, however, David was to become, even for thousands of years, a beloved and comforting companion to the oppressed and the miserable of every kind, and therefore from him must no cup of affliction pass untasted. Through what depths of affliction must not his way lead him? But into every darkness which casts its shadow around him the light of the opened heavens penetrated; and after every storm which raged against him there followed the gentle breathings of divine consolation, that all his followers on their pathway of sorrow might thereby be encouraged. Thus is he qualified for being the harper for all afflicted and oppressed souls, just as he once was for the king of Israel; and to this day it is true that wherever the melody of his Psalms sounds and echoes in the heart, there the shadows of sorrow and sadness are scattered, and courage and peace and joy return and take possession of the soul.

Among others, the following may be taken as specimens of those Psalms in which David gave utterance to the feelings he experienced while in the camp of Saul: "Deliver me not over unto the will of mine enemies: for false witnesses are risen up against me, and such as breathe out cruelty. I had fainted, unless I had believed to see the goodness of the Lord in the land of the living. For in the time of trouble He shall hide me in His pavilion: in the secret of His tabernacle shall He hide me; He shall set me up upon a rock. And now shall mine head be lifted up above mine enemies round about me."[6] Again: "Without cause have they hid for me their net in a pit, which without cause they have digged for my soul. But my soul shall be joyful in the Lord: and all may bones shall say, Lord, who is like unto Thee, which deliverest the poor from him that is too strong for him,

6. Psalm 27.

yea, the poor and the needy from him that spoileth him?"[7] "The Lord
is my rock, and my fortress, and my deliverer; my God, my strength,
in whom I will trust; my buckler, and the horn of my salvation, and
my high tower. I will call upon the Lord, who is worthy to be praised:
so shall I be saved from mine enemies."[8] And, finally, "Blessed be the
Lord, who daily loadeth us with benefits, even the God of our salvation. He that is our God is the God of salvation; and unto God
the Lord belong the issues from death."[9]

How often, from such notes as these, have wearied pilgrims, on
their thorny pathway, had new quickening breathed into their spirits! May this precious influence be more abundantly felt in ever
widening circles! May God grant it!

7. Psalm 35.
8. Psalm 18.
9. Psalm 68.

5

A New Storm

Among the peculiarities of all biblical history commanding our respect and strengthening our faith these stand in the foremost rank—that it is unadorned, natural, and simple. The Old Testament history is that of the "chosen people," and it was written by men of that nation; yet we meet in no part of it with the slightest trace of a design to bring this people before us in a manner corresponding to their lofty title. Let one compare it with the pictures of the Romish Church drawn by itself in its Legends and Acts of the Saints: here everywhere he will discover an intentional effort to gloss over what may be blemishes, and to color the brighter side into the supernatural. The biblical narratives, on the contrary, commend themselves on the very first look we take of them, as unadorned pictures of the truth, reflected as in a mirror. The Old Testament history is for the most part the history, not of the virtues, but of the sins of Israel. In it the Lord alone appears holy, worthy to be praised and great. Thus it bears on its brow the stamp of its thorough truthfulness, which makes it easy and natural for us to say, as the Apostle Peter does in his Second Epistle, "We have a more sure word of prophecy."[1] This word, worthy of unlimited confidence, has described to us the course of David's life.

1 Samuel 19:11–12

> Saul also sent messengers unto David's house, to watch him, and to slay him in the morning: and Michal, David's wife, told him, saying, If thou save not thy life tonight, tomorrow thou shalt be slain. So Michal let David down through a window; and he went, and fled, and escaped.

---

1. 2 Peter 1:19.

The Lord in every way takes care that His servant David may not raise his head, adorned with its laurel, too loftily. David richly experienced the truth of the apostle's word, "Whom the Lord loveth He chasteneth, and scourgeth every son whom He receiveth." It was the safety of our young friend that he knew how to interpret to himself the mystery of his "wonderful guidance"; and, amid all the adversities which befell him, to hold fast the faith which he expresses in these words of the eighteenth Psalm, "Thy right hand hath holden me up, and Thy gentleness hath made me great."[2] A new storm bursts over his head. Here let us see (1) what it was that threatened David, and (2) how he escaped from the danger.

1. We meet him this time as the husband of Michal, at Gibeah, in his own house. He is, however, not yet "the sparrow which hath found an house, nor the swallow a nest for herself." When will the time indeed ever come for him, when, according to the words of the prophet, he "will sit under his vine and under his fig-tree, and none shall make him afraid"? In the royal court a new plan is contrived to accomplish his death.

Well might it now have been said to him, as was once said to Judah, "From the prey, my son, thou art gone up!"[3] He was a terror to the enemies of Israel; he was the honored of the people; and, besides, he was the husband of his king's daughter: and what a promise, as yet scarcely half understood by him, rested upon him! But notwithstanding all this, he probably many a time looked back from his lofty elevation with sorrowful homesickness on those days when, as a lowly, unknown lad, he tended the flocks of his father on the pasture-fields and hills of Bethlehem, and, alone in the peaceful temple of creation, sang, accompanied by his harp, his impassioned songs to the Lord of glory. How gently and happily then did his life flow on, like a crystal stream in whose peaceful rippling waves are reflected only the flowers along the banks, and the stars of heaven. No malice had yet spread its nets for him; no tongue of envy had yet poured upon him its poison. God took him into His arms as His own favored child; and now only songs of praise and gladness, such as Psalm 145, rose up, accompanied by the harmonious melody of his harp, to the throne of the Almighty, from his heart overflowing with joy.

---

2. According to Luther's version—"If Thou humblest me, O Lord, so Thou makest me great."

3. Luther's version—"Thou hast become eminent through a great victory."

But now it was far otherwise with him. When today we come to the palace at Gibeah, we find the king, in whose ears the insufferable triumphal song of the women is even yet sounding, engaged in an earnest conversation with his son Jonathan and certain other confidential friends. David is the subject of this animated discussion. "Bring his head to me," we hear the king angrily saying. Jonathan, who had already secretly given information to his friend of the new danger which hovered over his head, and had pointed out to him a place of refuge where he might keep himself concealed, speaks in every way in favor of David, and begs his royal father not to commit sin against the most faithful of his servants, who not only had never plotted any evil against him, but, on the contrary, had been a powerful support to his throne. "He has," said he, among other things, "put his life for thee in his hand, and slain thy hereditary foe the Philistine, and the Lord through him hath wrought a great salvation for all Israel: thou sawest it, and didst rejoice on account of it: wherefore then wilt thou sin against innocent blood, to slay David without a cause?"

How good it is to hear such words as these spoken by Jonathan, which, in their peaceful, gentle tone, their reverential utterance, contradicting in nothing the duty of a child, and in their noble purpose breathe already something of the spirit of New Testament times. And yet, as John at a later period testifies in his Gospel, "the Holy Ghost was not yet given"—a truth which we ought particularly to keep in mind in all the opinions and estimates we form of the morals of the men of Old Testament times. The hereditary nature of man, fallen in Adam, had then allowed to it a much wider scope than in the post-Pentecostal days of the New Covenant. The natural affections and passions shot forth, when once they broke through the barriers of the divine commandments, into monstrous, gigantic manifestations and wild forms, which may be compared to the luxurious growth of the primeval forests. Saul, with his colossal hatred, and his jealousy breathing forth fire and flames, may be regarded as a witness of this fact.

Even the most pious men of those days, as regards the delicacy and keenness of their moral perceptions, and thorough decided heart-holiness, stand far behind the "born again" of the Church of Jesus Christ, and were not so preserved as these are against dangerous backslidings, under the power of their corrupt nature. As they enjoyed the means of grace more sparingly, so they are to be judged by a different standard from that by which we judge of those who "have seen and heard what many kings and prophets before them desired to see and to hear, but did not."

They have substantial claims on our forbearance; and we are guilty of confounding the times, when we would weigh, in the balance of the New Testament sanctuary, the many false steps in which we see the most excellent and God-fearing men in Bible history now and again forgetting themselves. Yet it is undoubtedly true that, even during the Mosaic economy, individual personages appeared like shining meteors, lovely and rich in promise, who present themselves before us as prophetic types of believers of the coming age. To this class belonged Abraham, Moses, Joshua, and certainly now also our Jonathan. The example of disinterested friendship, rooting itself in love to God, which the latter presents to us, remains at least as a fitting model for Christian times, wherein its equal is not often to be found.

Let us remember that in Jonathan the foreboding grew more and more toward a complete certainty that not he, the natural and lawful heir, but his friend David, would at some time succeed his royal father on the throne of Israel. It may be remarked, also, that Jonathan had by no means any ground to conceive of himself as unworthy of succeeding to the throne, for he had performed valiant deeds in arms against the enemies of his fatherland, which scarcely in any respect came behind those of his friend, and which made him not less than he a favorite with the people. Besides, it must be remembered that, together with manly resoluteness and heroic intrepidity, Jonathan showed himself in no way destitute of the other virtues of a ruler.

Notwithstanding all this, however, he not only was prepared to renounce, with the most magnanimous self-denial, his hereditary rights, if the Lord had so determined it, but he also prudently and energetically endeavored, even to his own danger, to frustrate whatever was contrived and undertaken in opposition to the purpose of God; insomuch that, by the hands of his own father, toward whom he was in no respect culpable, either in regard to the duty of filial love or reverence or obedience, and, we might add, of fervent intercession on his behalf, he might have fallen a sacrifice to his submissiveness to the will of God, and his fidelity toward his bosom friend.

Jonathan's friendly and earnest persuasion, to which a report of a new incursion of the enemy lent additional force, pacified for the moment his father's wrath. We read that "Saul hearkened unto the voice of Jonathan: and Saul sware, As the Lord liveth, he shall not be slain." Alas! how this scene fills us with sorrow, especially when we remember the words of the Lord by Malachi, "I will come near to judgment, and I will be a swift avenger against false swearers, for I am the Lord, I change not."

Full of joy and of thankfulness to God for this change of mind in his father, Jonathan forthwith brought David into the palace; and after explaining all that had happened favorable to him, he led him into his father's presence, who came forward with apparently true courtesy and graciousness to meet the hated one. The history records that "David was in his presence as in times past." Just at the moment when this meeting took place, there came the report, most agreeable to David, of the renewed advance of the Philistines. The young hero, always ready for war, rushed forward at the command of the king, and placed himself at the head of the host over which he had been appointed. It was not long till he again returned from the field of battle crowned with victory.

A bloody battle had been fought, and the enemy, after suffering severe losses, had been driven back into their own land. Is it surprising, then, that the Bethlehemite should again be the hero of the day? The people anew immediately proclaimed him as such, with loud and jubilant voice, in all their streets. Then again the brow of the king was overshadowed. All his former wretchedness soon returned to him again. The evil spirit came upon him as before, and all the former scenes were re-enacted, only on a more extensive scale.

David hastened once more to try the power of his harp; but even the dreadful spectacle of which we have already been witnesses was repeated. The royal spear was again hurled at the heart of the faithful harper, and only a sudden spring aside saved the endangered youth from a bloody death. Now he knew that he ought not to continue longer in the neighborhood of the king, and therefore he hastened back home. But who may describe the sorrow of Jonathan at what had happened? He stood as if confounded. The last hope of reconciliation with his father was lost.

Saul continued to storm and rage, and he gave command to a troop of his bodyguards secretly to surround during the night the house of his son-in-law, and to fall upon him and slay him, when, according to his custom, he should go forth from it in the morning. This murderous plan would have succeeded had not the Lord again appeared as his deliverer for his help. Through the providence of the Lord, Michal received information of the plot against the life of her husband, before, however, the assassins had yet, under the cover of darkness, beleaguered the house. Without delay she communicated it to her husband: "If thou save not thy life tonight, tomorrow thou shalt be slain." What tidings this for David, and what a situation that in which he now again saw himself placed!

"A man according to God's own heart," he is called. The most precious promises from God are poured into his bosom. But who that sees him now, hunted like a wild beast, would ever think that he was so highly accounted of by God? There seems no end to the evils which oppress him on every hand. Those who are nearest to him reward his beneficence with ingratitude, his generosity with misapprehension, his love with deadly hatred, and his most willing self-sacrifice and fidelity with base calumny. For the wreath of victory wherewith he had adorned the throne and the altar of his fatherland, he is rewarded with ignominious disgrace; and if at any time a cup of refreshing is reached to him, immediately a drop of wormwood is mingled in it, so bitter, so repulsive, that he would willingly have resigned the joy intended for him because of the bitterness following it.

What a lot was his! "How much softer," he might have thought with himself, "is the bed of the humblest day-laborer, who, unnoticed but also undisturbed, eats his scanty meal, earned by the sweat of his brow, than is mine, against which, on my so-called enviable elevation, every storm beats!" And who, notwithstanding all this, if he looks only a little deeper into his life, would hesitate for a moment to speak of David as a man whose lot was truly blessed, and to be envied, however he was crucified according to the flesh? In the midst of his afflictions, with what gracious visitations was he honored of God! In what manifestations of divine help, amid all the dangers which threatened him, could he always rejoice!

"One may conceive," remarks a pious old author, "that God raised the soul of David, in his deepest distresses, up above all mists and clouds, granted to him the clearest insight into the kingdom of truth, refreshed him by distinct messages from Himself and by friendly consolations, and through Him, as the Psalmist, instructed all the gen-erations of men in true happiness: and it must indeed be confessed that his good fortune outweighed his misfortune, his honor all the disgrace with which they clothed him, his abundance all the want he externally suffered a thousand-fold." "If such," continues this author, "was the happy condition of David, even amid his deep dis-tresses, how immeasurably is the fullness of its felicity heightened when we take into consideration his eternal deliverance out of all dis-tress, and, finally, his glorious condition in a blessed eternity?" From the heart we echo these words. But it becomes all God's children, and such even as possess the ordinary measure of grace, with confidence to say with the apostle, "The sufferings of this present time are not worthy to be compared with the glory which shall be revealed in us."

Yet David seems to be not a little surprised by the tidings con-veyed to him. Did he fear death? He had already proved that he could boldly look in the face of the king of terrors. But it is not grant-ed, even to the children of the New Covenant, to do this at all times; and how could we expect such a preparation to face death without fear, in those to whom, as the Scripture says, "the way into the holi-est of all was not yet made manifest"? It is enough that God should then, for the first time, give to His own all that is necessary for their last journey, when He gives them the signal to arise and depart. It is certain that at that time there did not prevail in the soul of David the desire to depart from the earthly field of battle; and much less could he reconcile himself to the thought that he should end his life by the hands of assassins, to the triumph of his own enemy, and of the enemy of God. Much rather did it give him joyful satisfaction to find that a way of deliverance was opened for him; and the prudent resoluteness of his wife Michal pointed out to him this way, as we shall immediately see.

2. How David felt during that night, so full of important issues, under the roof of his dwelling, beset by assassins, he has himself informed us in the fifty-ninth Psalm. From that Psalm it appears evi-dent that it was not the fear of death which was uppermost in his mind, but, as we have already indicated, a noble, holy solicitude for the honor of his God, which would have been greatly obscured by the success of the fiendish plot of his enemies. In his own deliverance he saw illustrated the consoling truth that God not only preserves from disgrace, but that He also covers with His sheltering wings all

who trust in Him and fear His name. Therefore he willingly gave ear to the counsel of the prudent Michal, which was, that he should let himself down by a rope through a window at the back part of the house, which was unguarded, and flee to a distance under cover of the night, nothing doubting but that the Lord Himself, who does not at all times help by means of miracle, gave into his hand this means of escape. David seized the rope, slid down—as at a later period, in similar circumstances, the Apostle Paul once did at Damascus—gently and unnoticed over the wall, and then hastened away for a long time through the darkness.

If we may be allowed to give to this event a typical meaning, we would indicate the following as reflections it suggests: When, in a spiritual sense, we do not any longer dwell in safety, when not bands of assassins indeed surround us, but murderers of our peace—be it sorrows, or apprehensions, or cares about our food or clothing, or anything else that threatens our souls—then is it not our duty to seek for ropes which might be able to deliver us out of the dilemma and set us free? Indeed, such are at hand, and are ready for our use among the treasures of the divine word. These are the sure testimonies and promises of our God. Did we but understand how to lay hold of these with childlike faith, we would thereby glide gently out of every difficulty and danger, and be delivered from every strait, and again breathe with freedom, in patience and in hope.

But now, while our fugitive is pursuing his lonely way in the midst of darkness, yet in this sad condition conscious that he is under the special guidance of his God, and confidently looking for further intimations from the Almighty, Michal spins out the thread of her stratagem. She perceived that when her husband did not go out of the door of his house at the dawn of day, his enemies would immediately suspect that he had escaped, and that as soon as they received certain information of the fact, they would forthwith seek for him in all directions. To guard against such a result, she resolved to announce that her husband was sick; but at the same time, lest it might happen that they would personally search into the truth of the report, and so discover her deception, she contrived the following plan:

She brought out from a corner of her house a carved image of wood, some house-idol which David had probably brought back with him as a trophy from the war with the Philistines, as a memorial of

the triumphs won by the help of God over the heathen. This figure
Michal laid on David's camp-bed, covered it carefully up to the head,
and spread over its face a net of goats' hair, such as was in use in the
East during the night as a prevention against the assaults of gnats.
When it was announced to King Saul that David was sick, and that
he had not left his house, he sent new messengers, with the command that they should force their way into the house, and bring to
him, well or ill, the object of his hatred. Michal did not hinder these
hirelings of her father from entering her dwelling. On the contrary,
she led them to the pretended sick-room, and showed them,
though only from a distance, through the opened door of the apartment, the figure lying motionless on the bed, and whispered to them,
"Ye see that it is impossible for him to follow you to the king." The
messengers being convinced of this, hastened to give their report to
their master.

But the king, who could have no rest so long as he knew that the
man who was to him as a thorn in his eye was not removed out of
the way, sent them again with express orders to bring his son-in-law
to him, on his sickbed if indeed he was sick, and to give him information, as soon as possible, that he had given up the ghost in some
apartment of his palace. They therefore again visited David's
house; and now the fraud Michal had practiced was completely
uncovered. Instead of finding David, when they came near to the
bed, they found only a wooden image. Strictly in accordance with
the letter of the king's command, they took up the same, along with
the bed whereon it lay, and carried it to the palace.

Saul was transported with rage at this trick which had been played
upon him, and sternly ordered that his daughter Michal should be
brought before him. She appeared; and to her father's question,
whether she was the contriver of the artifice, gave no denial. Saul
spoke angrily to her, and said, "Why hast thou deceived me so, and
sent away mine enemy, that he is escaped?" Michal, adhering to the
dubious course on which she had entered, replied, "David said unto
me, Let me go; why should I kill thee?" Therefore, to save her own
life, she said that she had aided the flight of her husband. This was
a manifest falsehood, having nothing to excuse it—not even the
necessity of defense against her father's wrath, which threatened her.
We shall see, at a later period of her history, that the reward for this
conduct did not escape her.

According to the example of the Apostle Paul, who in his Epistle to the Galatians makes reference to a certain event in the history of the family of father Abraham, and says of it, "which things are an allegory,"[4] we may venture also to say the same thing, though not with the same authority as the apostle, of the scenes which we have just witnessed under David's roof, and in the royal palace. In a spiritual sense, these scenes frequently repeat themselves, and in diverse ways, in the life of believers.

For example, we find on the part of the enemies of the cross of Christ, assaults made with all the weapons of bitterest scorn and most malicious condemnation, against any brother who, alas! like Simon Peter of old, has fallen under great temptation, and thereby made the cause of the gospel to be evil spoken of. "This man," they say, "gave himself out as a saint. He stands now uncovered before all eyes. But such are all the so-called pious men—hypocrites, Pharisees, are they all." In this way they assail the poor fallen one. But whom do they hit? Is it the man himself? Not so; but only his "not I,"[5] while the true man escapes. They saw not the tears of contrition which streamed from the eyes of the fallen penitent. They heard not the sighs in which his soul poured itself forth before the throne of God.

They know not that the true Simon Peter has escaped into freedom through a window, by the rope of grace, and now stands before God as one against whom "there is no more any condemnation," and is entitled to appropriate the words with confidence and joy of heart, "Bless the Lord, O my soul: who forgiveth all thine iniquities, who healeth all thy diseases." So it is only an unsubstantial image of the sinner that they load with ignominy, while the sinner himself has long ago escaped, pardoned and saved.

Again condemnation is pronounced by the adversaries against someone who is dead, who indeed departed from the scenes of earth laden with heavy guilt; but, what his judges understood not, he went from hence crowned with the pardon of the malefactor. They freely pronounce against him the judgment of condemnation, and quite give him up as eternally lost, if to them the judgment on that other side has not become an idle tale. But what these misguided persons pronounce condemnation against is only an image, a figure, which lies on the bed of their short-sighted contemplation, but as a

4. Galatians 4:24.
5. See Romans 7:17, etc.

true person is no longer there; while the man about whom they converse has shaken from off his feet the dust of the pilgrim's journey,
and now, adorned with the white robe of the heavenly marriage
guests, mingles his voice in the great hallelujah which they there
above sing to the praise of the Lamb who has borne the sins of the
world.

It must be admitted that the psalm—it is the fifty-ninth—which,
like a mountain stream, poured forth from the deeply-riven soul of
David on the occasion we have now been contemplating, has in its
stern contents something strange to our ears. But let us never omit
to distinguish from each other the times and the diverse economies,
and to place ourselves, as far as is possible, in sympathy with the
experience of a heart which burned for nothing more than for the
glorifying of God in this world. Everything that tended to obscure the
theocratic relation of God to His people, called up in the soul of
David the most vehement passion. The scornful oppression with
which Saul and his venal satellites visited him, the man of God,
could not but have, upon the eyes of all, the appearance as if Jehovah
were no longer Lord in his own land, who inexorably adhered to His
laws and rights. Treason, falsehood, and every kind of evil then prevailed unchecked. What wonder that, as formerly Moses in the
wilderness was provoked against the stiff-necked people, so also
David, whom the awful holiness of God had already made to tremble, should feel his spirit stirred against the ungodly who surrounded
him, and should say with Job, "My bowels boiled within me." If what
he says in the fifteenth Psalm—"Who shall dwell in Thy holy hill?
Only he that walketh uprightly, and worketh righteousness," and so
on to the end of that psalm—formed the basis of his character, we
need not be surprised that his prayer for deliverance from the "bloody
men" who laid wait for his soul without a cause should be accompanied with the petition that the arm of divine justice should be
stretched out in vengeance against them. It may well sound fearful
when we hear him say, "Be not merciful to the transgressors. Slay
them not, lest my people forget: scatter them by Thy power; and
bring them down; and let them make a noise like a dog, and go
round about the city. Let them wander up and down for meat, and
grudge if they be not satisfied."

But for what end does he call down such judgments against the
workers of iniquity? Let us hear him further as he continues, "And

let them know that God ruleth in Jacob unto the ends of the earth." It is Jehovah's honor, and nothing else, which arrays the prayer of this psalm with its dreadful armor of thunder and lightning.[6] But did not the singer in this psalm, breathing forth curses and vengeance, find also room for a sigh for the conversion and regeneration of those over whom he had imprecated such a storm of wrath? Had he not at least for the king, the anointed of God, whom he had already called by the name of father, room for the prayer, "O Lord, enlighten, redeem, and sanctify him?" We perceive nothing of this kind. The psalmist closes this storm-song with the words, "But I will sing of Thy power; yea, I will sing aloud of Thy mercy in the morning: for Thou hast been my defense and refuge in the day of my trouble. Unto Thee, O my strength, will I sing: for God is my defense, and the God of my mercy." But without doubt there were not awanting, in the inmost depths of his soul, the sighs of compassion which we miss in his psalm. Yea, among those whom he wished to see brought, by means of the punishments he had imprecated, in penitence to bend again under the yoke of Jehovah which they had cast off, they certainly would take the first place from whose hands he had personally been made to suffer; and the terrible words, "Be not merciful to them," we have not to interpret as if they meant more than simply "spare them not." But certainly it was the vindication of the honor and glory of God which, in that hour when this psalm was composed, formed the ruling desire and interest in David's soul; while concern for the salvation of the souls of his despisers for the moment fell more into the background.

The spirit which animates believers under the New Covenant scarcely permits them to pray as we hear David do in the fifty-ninth Psalm—not because the same zeal does not become them, of which David in another place says, "The zeal of Thine house hath eaten me up," but because the consciousness of a participation in the divine mercy which is in Christ, which rests on the foundation of a deep knowledge of themselves and of their sins, outweighs every other feeling, and therefore on the altar of their souls the holy fire of compassion toward their fellow-sinners is made to burn more clearly. Once, indeed, we hear from the mouth of Paul the startling

---

6. Psalm 59.

words, "Alexander the coppersmith did me much evil: the Lord reward him according to his works."[7] Yet we surely must interpret that hard utterance in the sense of that other, in which the same apostle says regarding two transgressors, that he had "delivered them unto Satan, that they might learn not to blaspheme."[8]

But even though we keep out of view the significance of this latter saying, we must remember that Paul was an apostle, a man who was honored by immediate divine revelation, and to whom the final judgment of God against the hopelessly lost might be made known. It might indeed happen that, against obdurate sinners, such, namely, as dare to insult the Holiest, and to calumniate both the Majesty in heaven and the rulers on earth, such "words may force themselves to our lips as those of David in the fifth Psalm—"Destroy Thou them, O God: let them fall by their own counsels; cast them out in the multitude of their transgressions; for they have rebelled against Thee." But if in such a case there remains not in us room for genuine, hearty, intercessory prayer on their behalf, then we lay ourselves open to the stern reproof which the two "sons of thunder" once received, "Ye know not what manner of spirit ye are of. For the Son of man is not come to destroy men's lives, but to save them." Let this saying of our Prince of Peace hover always before our eyes, especially in these days of general rebellion against God and His anointed, in which there are not lacking to believers provocations to wrath and maledictions against the ungodly. Perhaps it even sometimes happens to us as it once did to Job, when he broke out in the words, "Behold, my belly is as wine which hath no vent; it is ready to burst like new bottles. I will speak, that I may be refreshed."

But that we may take care not to sin against the commandment of love, but to preserve always in our hearts freedom and room for genuine intercession for others, we are to keep constantly upon our minds how much more of meekness and placability are expected, and ought to be expected, from us the children of the New Covenant.

---

7. 2 Timothy 4:14.
8. 1 Timothy 1:20.

6

David at Ramah

"Whom have I in heaven but Thee? and there is none upon earth that I desire besides Thee. My flesh and my heart faileth: but God is the strength of my heart, and my portion forever." Thus prayed Asaph, in the seventy-third Psalm, a man of kindred spirit with David, and, according to the statement of the book of Chronicles, even "a seer and a prophet," and afterward David's chief musician in the sanctuary. By the overpowering force of his psalms, David awoke the slumbering spirit of poetry in many in Israel. And without overlooking the direct influence of the Holy Spirit, we may speak of a Davidic "school of poets." That is an enviable position to which the sacred poet in the psalm above quoted comes. He does not reach it, however, by a smooth pathway, but only after a deep inward struggle.

In the first part of this psalm he thinks on the folly into which he had fallen when he envied the godless in their wantonness, when he saw how it went with them so well, and how they were not plagued like other men. They stand fast, he had thought, even like a palace, and therefore are they proud and bear themselves loftily. They set their mouths against the heavens. Therefore the people join with them, and blasphemously say, "How doth God know, and is there knowledge in the Most High? Behold, there are the ungodly, who prosper in the world, while they who have washed their hands in innocency are never free from plagues." Asaph confesses that he had almost given room in his heart to such thoughts, yea, he had already uttered them, and thereby had committed treason against all the children of God.

For a long time he had not known how to solve the dark enigma of these facts, which were apparently irreconcilable with a divine providence of the world, till at length he went to the sanctuary of God, and then he saw what was the end of the ungodly; then he saw how God set on slippery places those who turned their backs upon Him, that they might come to a terrible end. But before he discovered this, his heart was grieved, and he was pricked in his conscience. He was foolish and ignorant, and as a beast before God. "Nevertheless," he concludes, "I am continually with Thee; Thou hast holden me by my right hand, while Thou wouldst have done righteously hadst Thou hung over me the punishment of a total rejection from Thy presence."

This experience of the faithfulness of Jehovah had moved the psalmist's heart with deepest emotion, and broken it in genuine repentance. How humbled stood he now before God, who so faithfully had held him up when he was sinking! but how exalted, also, through the tender mercy of God, and how full of holy confidence that the Lord would now henceforth guide him with His counsel, yea, would bring him at last to honor! The singer now gained a firm standing place in life. After this what could make him to err? "If I have only Thee," he cries out with a deeply moved soul, "I ask nothing more. They who depart from Thee shall perish; but it is my joy that I keep close to God, place my confidence in the Lord, and, praising Thee, declare all Thy doings."

Happy Asaph! Happy he who participates in that heart-experience! There is one who did so. Long before him, and with yet more decision of mind, had David uttered this as his watchword, "If I have only Thee, O Lord, what need I more?" We shall today see him finding new occasion to remain always true to this the watchword of his life.

1 Samuel 19:18

> So David fled, and escaped, and came to Samuel to Ramah, and told him all that Saul had done to him. And he and Samuel went and dwelt in Naioth.

We wish our fugitive happiness! After the storm at Gibeah, a calm soft breath of peace refreshes him again. (1) He comes to Ramah, (2) enjoys the fellowship of the saints at Naioth, and (3) sees a new plan contrived to accomplish his death wonderfully frustrated. These are the historical events which today claim our attention.

1. We seek out the son of Jesse where we last left him, in that stormy night when he fled under the open heaven of God. There he wanders over mountain and valley a banished man, who could nowhere feel himself safe. If there was a rustling among the bushes, he thought of an ambuscade. If he saw the glimmering of a light in the darkness, it was perhaps the torches of the hired murderers who pursued him. How easily might it happen that he might miss the direction, and, in the darkness of the night, stumble into a marsh or into a deep chasm. A critical situation this; and we find in it one who was peculiarly the object of Jehovah's love, and was destined by God to great things. Let no one reckon on prosperity according to the flesh who has renounced the prince of this world and devoted himself to the service of God the Lord. Whoever lusts after earthly prosperity, let him remain among the bands of those whom Asaph describes to us. What the "children of the kingdom" have to expect as regards their life on earth, the author of the Epistle to the Hebrews has, in the eleventh chapter of that book, presented to our view. Of temporal goods scarcely anything further is promised with certainty than food and clothing, and even for these necessaries they have not seldom first to knock in prayer at the gates of heaven. The whole of their training tends to the crucifying of their flesh with its affections and lusts; and Paul rightly says, in the name of all God's children, "If in this life only we have hope in Christ, we are of all men most miserable."

But if to no one who has entered through the narrow gate into the kingdom of Christ the experience is spared that the way to life is strait and thorny, yet all such have the advantage over the children of this world, even while they are yet on earth, in realizing that they are no longer their own but God's, that all things must work together for their good, that the God who "brings them into the depths" is He who will also "bring them up again," and that at last all things will result in their being raised to excellency and glory. If one knew but how to penetrate through the veil of the form of a servant in which the chosen of God live in this world, and on account of which they are regarded as only worthy of pity, they would be spoken of as only truly blessed.

Consider David. There he prosecutes his way through the dark night as an exile whom many dangers threaten; but the shield of God is over his head. He goes forward under divine guidance, accompanied by unseen companions who have been sent to defend and to help him, and high above him in the firmament he is greeted by the stars shining like lamps from a blessed home, where the place is already prepared for him, and where his Sabbath rest awaits him, which will scarcely permit him any more to think of the anxieties and disquietudes of his short earthly journey. What could be wished more, and what could hinder him from making the confession of the apostle his own, "I have all things, and abound"?

Protected most faithfully by his unseen guardians, David at length reached the gates of the little town, to which he probably looked forward when he set out from Gibeah as the wished-for termination of his night-wanderings. It is Ramah, which was situated among the mountains of Ephraim, surrounded by groves of the ever-green tamarisk trees, the birth-place, as well as now the dwelling-place, of Samuel. His heart longed after this man. Amid his perplexities and difficulties he reckoned on hearing from him encouraging explanations, and counsel, and instruction. And he was not disappointed.

It is impossible that a man baptized with the spirit of God can wholly disown the new nature of which he had become a partaker. It may indeed happen that, by providences unexpected and apparently contradicting all the promises of his God, his faith may be deeply shaken, yea, altogether broken and disjointed. Yet he will always be recognized by the "image and superscription" wherewith his heavenly King has marked him out: it may be only a longing look upward, or the anxious question forced to his lips, "Lord, why this, and how long?" or the sigh, "Have mercy on me," or a desire after fellowship with those like-minded in the Lord. Particularly will this last feature make itself manifest in the hours of trial and of affliction. How he is hindered and restrained when he sees himself surrounded only by the children of the world, who understand him not, and with their consolations only increase the anguish of his soul! On the contrary, how much is his soul refreshed when he meets with an experienced and tried fellow-pilgrim to the Jerusalem which is above, and is able to disclose to him his heart, and to hear from his mouth consolations such as these: "Be not dismayed, my brother, as if some strange thing happened to thee. Many a time a like thing has happened to me; but how does the remembrance of my complainings then, now bow me down to the very dust! The Lord dealt in faithfulness with me, and when His hour came, how gloriously He helped me out of all my straits! Wait and know—when the gold is in the crucible, the refiner is near!"

Such and such-like brotherly words as these, spoken from his own experience, and therefore with the tone of perfect truthfulness and hearty sympathy, how they echo in the soul of the suffering one, and how he begins again to breathe more freely, and to see more distinctly the path in which God is leading him! What a fullness of encouragement and quickening the God of all grace has laid up in the communion of the saints, words cannot sufficiently express. If anywhere here below the atmosphere of his future heavenly home is to be breathed, it is in such fellowship. David will joyfully confirm to us the truth of this. How heartily we wish him joy of that consolation which is prepared for him.

Having reached the little town of Ramah, he knocks at Samuel's door; and how his heart leaps with joy when the venerable servant of God receives him with the hearty salutation of peace! It is probable that this was the first time after his heroic exploit that Samuel had seen the fame-crowned conqueror. Yet we do not read that, in their conversation, any mention was made of the victory over Goliath. Both of them well knew to whom the honor of that victory alone was due. The history only informs us that David poured into the bosom of his fatherly friend all the evil that Saul had done to him; and I seem to hear how Samuel comforted him; how he exhorted him, under all circumstances, to hold fast by the promises of his God, who could not lie; and how he then, for David's refreshing, laid open to him the rich fullness of his own life-experience of many years in the way of the Lord, and pointed out to him that the counsel of the Lord of Sabaoth was indeed wonderful, but that he always knew how gloriously to carry it into effect. And I see in spirit how the brow of the lonely fugitive became more and more freed from clouds, and his eye began to brighten with the beam of gladness. It was as if a new divine power had streamed through him, and as if henceforth nothing could again shake the courage of his faith.

Happy Church, which numbers amongst its members God's pilgrims, who, grown gray in the service of the Lord, and approved as faithful servants of their God, have, like a Samuel, the power, on account of the riches of their experience of salvation, to initiate such as are only novices in the life of faith into a knowledge of the snares laid for them by the powers of darkness which they may expect to meet with in the narrow way, and to point out to them, at the same time, the well-tried spiritual armor by which they may certainly obtain a victory over the wicked one, and at the same time to give to them beforehand the key to the mysteries of divine providence, and when they know nothing more, to go to them with the counsel of the wisdom of old age! Veterans in the kingdom of God of this kind, whose old age, by the wonderful operation of the holy God, is "as their youth," cannot be sufficiently held in honor. O that we met oftener than we do in the Church, such as those whom the ninety-second Psalm thus describes: "The righteous shall flourish like the palm-tree: . . . they shall still bring forth fruit in old age; they shall be fat and flourishing." Of Moses, when 120 years old, it is said, "His eye was not dim, nor his natural force abated." This could be truly said also, and perhaps in a higher sense, of the aged Samuel. I am inclined to believe, indeed, that it was he who sat for that beautiful portrait which David has drawn for us in the words of the first Psalm.

2. After these two had spent some time there, under the hospitable roof at Ramah, in confidential soul-sharing, Samuel asked his beloved guest to accompany him to Naioth. This was one of those blessed settlements which owed their origin to the wisdom of Samuel, and which are known to us under the not altogether appropriate name of "the schools of the prophets." Naioth, situated amid rural quietness, not far from the little town of Ramah, was the first of those colonies, and was the mother of all the rest that were afterward established.

We must conceive of these noble institutions as free unions of pious and earnest-minded Israelitish youths, who, under the guidance of one or more of the prophets, devoted themselves to the deepening of their knowledge of the word of God; but besides this, they devoted themselves to the study of many other sciences, such as history, only raised into a higher spiritual sphere, and sacred music, more especially choral song. Although they (to whom it was even then known that "godliness with contentment is great gain") had to labor with their hands in garden and field, or in the workshop, to procure their daily bread, yet they understood also how to redeem time, in the most excellent manner, for their sacred studies. Thus at one time we find them sitting, with open ears, listening at the feet of enlightened and anointed teachers; at another, deeply engaged in the study of the mysteries of revelation; at another time, united together in social prayer and singing of psalms, or employed in other efforts and activities tending always toward their mutual strengthening in the divine life.

These were blessed associations, to which most of the cloister-brotherhoods that have been formed in later times are related only as caricatures to the original likeness; blooming gardens of God in the desert-waste which Israel then presented; sources of spiritual salt and fruitfulness for the whole people; yea, seed-plots and nurseries of the kingdom of God, where the very letters of the word of God appeared quickened into life, and where the actual and indubitable proofs present themselves to one, that if the spirit which animated these young men prevailed everywhere, the whole world in a short time would change its appearance and its very being, and would become glorious as an outer court of paradise, where righteousness and peace kissed each other. Undoubtedly there were such peaceful asylums, which bloomed like spiritual oases in the wilderness of the Israelitish people, from which many sacred writings mentioned here and there in the Holy Scriptures were sent forth, though none of them have descended to us. Such, for example, were the "Book of Gad the Seer," the "Visions of Iddo," and the "Book of Iddo the Seer," and others. The Lord may have called many of those who attended these schools of the prophets to be His most eminent instruments in carrying on His work, and have clothed them with the office of teacher and judge in Israel; while in the choice of His prophets he was always free, as, for example, when He chose the Prophet Amos to be His seer immediately from the fields and from among the herdsmen.

How refreshing it must have been to David's mind, when, at Samuel's side, he entered this peaceful brotherhood, and found himself most heartily and most respectfully welcomed by all, who greatly rejoiced that they had the opportunity of looking upon the conqueror of Goliath and the deliverer of the fatherland! How pleasant and how quickening to his spirit would the days and hours be that he spent there in intimate converse about the highest and holiest events of his life, and in singing songs of thanksgiving and of praise to the honor of Jehovah! In the words of the twenty-third Psalm, "Thou preparest a table before me in the presence of mine enemies: Thou anointest my head with oil: my cup runneth over." Perhaps the recollection of his sojourn at Naioth hovered before the eye of his memory. To him, only just escaped from the lion's den, it could not but be a source of inward gladness and thankfulness, thus suddenly to find himself again in fellowship with men sincere and like-minded with himself, and to breathe again the refreshing air of holy love and heavenly peace which he had so long been deprived of. In many other effusions of the Davidic Psalter we perceive undoubted traces of his experiences at Naioth, and believe that we are especially justified in the conclusion that, for the strengthening of his inner life and the aiding of his spiritual efforts, he owed much to his interviews with the schools of the prophets.

But to him, Naioth, as he perhaps himself then anticipated, was only a place in which he might be equipped for new warfare. Before he was aware of it, he again received intimation that he must leave this lovely Elim, and a command to set forth again in his wanderings through the wilderness.

3. The sound of arms broke in upon the holy, peaceful stillness of the rural brotherhood. The horsemen of the king penetrated to this corner of the land—an unwonted spectacle. Saul, from whose eyes sleep departs till he has overtaken his prey, had sent them out as spies, and had ordered them to bring back the hated fugitive living or dead. The command of their master the king was to them as the very command of God. They obeyed it in silence; and how happy they were to discover so soon the object of their miserable pursuit, and in a situation to allow them to seize him without shedding blood, and to bring him as prisoner to the king!

But suddenly, and in a very wonderful manner, their whole enterprise was frustrated. At the very moment that they reached Naioth, which had been made known to them as David's hiding-place, the children of the prophets were all engaged in the presence of their two highly honored guests, who joined with them in the exercise, in "prophesying." By these "prophesyings" we are not to understand, as we are already aware, a foretelling of future things but a pouring forth of the heart, under the impulse of the Holy Spirit, in lively songs of praise of God, and of His wonderful works. With anointed lips, and with an animated oratory, they praised the mighty deeds through which Jehovah had from of old made Himself glorious to His people.

In responsive chorus they sang, with the harmonious accompaniment of harps, flutes, cymbals, and trumpets, sacred songs to the honor of God, and called down in earnest prayers upon themselves and all the people the blessings of the Almighty, and the fire-streams of His Spirit. From time to time it pleased God, in the days of the Old Covenant, to bring into prominence the exalted life of His own children in contrast with the children of this world, abandoned by the Spirit, and unable to rise above the earth, in so unmistakable and overpowering a manner, that in view of it even the most blinded among the people might gain some apprehension of the depth to which they had fallen from the elevated height of their former calling. At the same time, from these inspired ones there went forth among the people a light to show in what sense the Lord, by the coming of the Messiah, for whom they were then waiting, would create a "new thing in the earth," and what was meant by the regeneration and purifying of the world, which would be brought about by the coming of the Messiah.

Under the New Testament, such operations of the Holy Spirit, in these clear and distinct forms of manifestations, come rarely now to view. Operations approaching them, and of kindred character, meet us only on the first days of Pentecost, as also in the assembly for prayer, of which we read in the Acts of the Apostles,[1] and in the "speaking with tongues" at Corinth, of which the apostle makes mention in his First Epistle to the Corinthians.[2] Perhaps, also, in our own day, many of those religious movements, often degenerating, indeed, into fanaticism, of which we see examples in the well-known field and camp meetings on the other side of the ocean, and which are by no means to be always ascribed to a morbid action of the nervous system, may well be compared to what was experienced at this time at Naioth. But the Holy Spirit now generally operates in a manner more secret and peaceful, but also, at the same time, more fundamental and lasting. The seat of the Spirit's work is the chamber of the heart, and the aim of His creative energy the gradual transfiguration of the inner man into the lovely image of Him who is "fairer than the children of men," brightly shining in the mild splendor of gentleness, of humility, and of love.

The armed servants of the king came to Naioth at the very time when the stream of divine inspiration was flowing in lofty waves over the assembly. Whether they were pious people, who unwillingly had undertaken the ungodly commission of their vengeful master, or

---

1. Acts 4:32.
2. 1 Corinthians 14.

belonged to the thousands of their people, who, in their estrangement from God, yet knew something of a union of heaven with
earth, though it were only by tradition from their fathers—enough;
before they were aware of it, they were overcome with the holy
thoughts and feelings of those who were "prophesying," and, powerfully moved, they also mingled involuntarily their voices in the
inspired songs of praise.

When the king learned the surprising reason of his messengers not
returning, he quickly sent thither in the storm of his impatience, a
second and then a third company of soldiers. But to all of them a like
thing happened, in a very wonderful manner, as to the first; and it
need not astonish us greatly. Even among the roughest and wildest
spirits in Israel, the religious feeling was in only a few instances so
completely dead that it could not be kindled up out of its ashes,
although only temporarily, when touched by the right spark. There
are even at the present day, in our own fatherland, districts of the
Church where almost a similar thing may be said of those who
belong to it. In times of great spiritual awakening, or even of solemn
Church festivals, one sees persons who, on account of their spiritual dullness and their thorough worldliness of character, were
believed to be incapable of being lifted up into the kingdom of God,
suddenly glow with devotion and with zeal for the service of God
when brought into fellowship with believers.

This sudden religious elevation to which they are thus drawn along
with them, shows itself, as a rule, to be by no means steadfast and
enduring. But they also "prophesy" a while with the congregation of
the saints, and perhaps even rise higher than many of them, in the heat
and enthusiasm of their religious profession. It often happens even that
they who are only passing travelers, when they breathe the air of such
a district, feel themselves, before they are aware of it, deeply interested
in religious and ecclesiastical matters. Moreover, the religious elevation of mind on the part of the royal messengers at Naioth may be
attributed partly to the appearance of the aged Samuel, the man of
God, known and highly venerated throughout the whole land. It is
enough that at that time they could not venture on any account to
rush with violence into the midst of the solemn scenes to which they
had come. How could they by any possibility lay hands on him whom
Saul hated in so unrighteous a manner, and who was so visibly under
the protecting care of God—the young hero by the side of Samuel?

Saul, however, by whom these proceedings were rigorously directed, strove obstinately against the discovery that he was persecuting one who was protected by the Almighty. He even now resolved to execute personally his bloody decree against his hated son-in-law, and set out for that end, with an armed retinue, on the way to Ramah. Arrived at the outskirts of the little town, by the great well of Zophim, so named in commemoration of the founder of Ramah, Zuph the Ephrathite, he asked the water-carriers whom he there met concerning the residence of Samuel and David. The neighboring town of Naioth was named, and therefore he hurried there. But what a wonderful thing happened! While he was yet on the way, there fell upon him a solemn awe. He found himself here amid the well-remembered scenes of his early home. The recollection of the days of his youth overcame him, so that he could say with Job, that when "the Almighty was yet with him in the way, His candle shined upon his head, and by His light he walked through darkness."

It was here, beside Naioth, that Samuel once made known to him the secret of his high calling, and with words of holy encouragement, and with precious promises, anointed him, and honored him with the kiss of homage. Oh, how joyous and full of hope his heart was then! How his soul then melted within him with pious emotion, and with childlike thankfulness! How blessed, and full of confidence, he then lay at the feet of God!

The memory of all this, in vivid pictures, rose up all at once before him. It was the Spirit of God that again breathed upon him, and called back into life, whatever of good was yet remaining in the man. This inward emotion of his soul became every moment more intense, and when he approached the houses of Naioth, and heard the solemn music come forth from the circle of the children of the prophets, and float in waves of melody over him, the recollection also was revived within him of the exalted delight which he experienced at that time, when in like manner, as now, he was greeted on "the hill of God, at Kirjath-jearim." It was not long till the whole mysterious scene of that time rose up anew, and with vivid impressiveness, before him.

Having dismounted from his horse, he concealed his royal armor under a light mantle, such as the children of the prophets were wont to wear, and went forward into the circle of the worshipers with animated movements of his hands, and holy gestures, pouring forth, with loud oratory, the language of praise to God. Disturbed, rather than gladdened and edified, they received their king with becoming reverence. But he, as if shaken by convulsions, fell into a condition which was more like madness than pious excitement; and at one time singing with a loud voice, at another declaiming, at another falling to the ground in the attitude of prayer, presented to the assembly a spectacle not less painful than fitted to awaken compassion. Of him it was again said, and that cry of surprise afterward became a proverb, "Is Saul also among the prophets?"

But it did not escape the notice of Samuel, that too soon a new outbreak of his old anger would follow this apparently pious animation of the king. Therefore he thought it necessary to give the advice to David to tarry no longer in Naioth, but without delay to betake himself anew to flight. The history makes no mention whether, during his stay at Ramah, Samuel had opened up to him more particularly the meaning of the anointing at Bethlehem; but it may well be presumed that he did so. It is certain, however, that Samuel did not dismiss Saul without solemnly reproaching him, face to face, in the name of the Lord, with his godless conduct, and admonishing him, in the most earnest manner, to repentance and conversion.

David had again, meantime, to hold himself ready for some time longer to encounter new sufferings and conflicts. But it is certain that he did not depart from the school of the prophets without having obtained an essential increase of confidence in God, and of strength of faith; and often afterward, with heart moved to gratitude, would he look back on those blissful days he spent at Naioth and at Ramah in fellowship with Samuel. It is indeed very possible that it was the refreshing remembrance of that most precious and never-to-be-forgotten experience that suggested to him the peace, joy, and love which breathe through Psalm 133: "Behold, how good and how pleasant it is for brethren to dwell together in unity!" It is like the precious ointment upon the head that ran down upon the beard, even Aaron's beard; that went down to the skirts of his garments; as the dew of Hermon, and as the dew that descended upon the mountains of Zion: for there the Lord commanded the blessing, even life forevermore.

7

Hallowed Friendship

It is important to bear in mind that the world in which the life of David was spent was not the same as that whose air we now breathe. It is true that it also was already illuminated by the light of revealed truth, and that the living God walked through it in mighty deeds and wonders, making Himself glorious sometimes by displays of beneficent love, and sometimes by a holy righteous indignation. But "the Word" was not yet made "flesh," and the Holy Spirit looked not upon this earth, estranged from God, as a place for His continuous operation; and the throne of grace appeared to sinners then only as an object of hope in the dim light of a distant future.

The twelfth chapter of the Epistle to the Hebrews discovers to us the wide chasm which separated the dispensations of the Old and of the New Covenant. "Ye are not come," it is said to believers under the Christian economy, "unto the mount that might be touched, and that burned with fire, nor unto blackness, and darkness, and tempest, and the sound of a trumpet, and the voice of words; which voice they that heard entreated that the word should not be spoken to them any more (for they could not endure that which was commanded. And so terrible was the sight, that Moses said, I exceedingly fear and quake): but ye are come unto Mount Zion, and unto the city of the living God, the heavenly Jerusalem, and to an innumerable company of angels, to the general assembly and church of the first-born, which are written in heaven, and to God the Judge of all, and to the spirits of just men made perfect, and to Jesus the mediator of the new covenant, and to the blood of sprinkling, that speaketh better things than that of Abel."

Hence we ought not to lay the same measuring rod to the life and actions of the members of the ancient kingdom of God existing before the coming of Christ, as we apply to the life and actions of such as, redeemed by Christ, have been raised to the enjoyment of peculiar privileges and honors. But the less we are entitled to do this, so much the more ought it to put us to shame to find among the children of the old covenant so many praiseworthy examples of moral greatness. Among others that we meet with, such is the altogether remarkable pattern of friendship which today we are to look upon, and which is presented to us for this end, that we, among whom the complaint is so frequently to be heard that no longer any fidelity is to be found in the land, and that "friends in need" belong to the rarer pearls, may be humbled in deepest sorrow. David and Jonathan present to us this picture. In the same measure in which it calls forth our lively admiration, it may also condemn us; but not without at the same time raising us to a purer life and animating us with the desire to imitate it.

1 Samuel 20:16–17

> So Jonathan made a covenant with the house of David, saying, Let the Lord even require it at the hand of David's enemies. And Jonathan caused David to swear again, because he loved him: for he loved him as he loved his own soul.

The love of Jonathan to David was put to a severe test by a threefold discovery which he made. There opened up before his mind a view (1) of the true intentions which his royal father cherished toward the young hero; (2) of the lofty destiny determined by God for his beloved friend; and (3) of the danger which threatened him by reason of his fellowship with David. It will nobly stand the test. Let us revel in the contemplation of this heart-elevating spectacle.

1. David first returned from Naioth to Gibeah. A sense of duty and a longing after his bosom friend may have principally moved him to this. It became him also to let Michal his wife see that, whatever storms might burst upon him, he was not forsaken by God. We meet him again by his own hearth, and at the very moment when he is opening up to Jonathan his overflowing heart, moved with the deepest feeling. After relating to him what had befallen him at Ramah and at Naioth, we hear him say, with the tone of painful sadness, "What have I done? what is mine iniquity? and what is my sin before thy father, that he seeketh my life?" Jonathan endeavored to

represent this fear of his as excessive. He said unto him, "God forbid; thou shalt not die: behold, my father will do nothing, either great or small, but that he will show it me; and why should my father hide this thing from me? it is not so." David assured his friend with an oath that Saul intended nothing less than his death. "Thy father certainly knoweth," said he, "that I have found grace in thine eyes; and he saith, Let not Jonathan know this, lest he be grieved: but truly, as the Lord liveth, and as thy soul liveth, there is but a step between me and death."

We are astonished. Has David's courage suddenly given way? Far from it. But how could it be a matter of indifference to him whether he lost his life by the hands of assassins, or hazarded it in the service of God for some important object pleasing to God? That he was always prepared to venture all in the service of God, we cannot for a moment doubt, after all we have already seen of him. But what a curse would King Saul bring down upon his own head, and what an evil upon the people whom he represented, if he should succeed in his wicked design! Would he not thereby make Israel a scorn to all nations? The thought of this could not but make David tremble at the purpose of his royal master. Besides, it must not be forgotten that to believers, under the Old Covenant especially, death was not yet the angel with the palm-branch of peace, as we, to whom "life and immortality are brought to light by the gospel," know it, or at least ought to know it. If, notwithstanding, the thought that there is "but a step between us and death" fills us also with horror, as too frequently happens, how shall we venture to blame the man living under the Old Testament economy, if we hear him, in his trying situation, express the wish that he might escape at least that form of death which was intended for him?

Jonathan will not further contradict the solemn asseveration of his friend that his father thirsted for his blood, though he could not altogether escape from doubts as to the foundation of the dark supposition entertained by David. "I will do for thee," said he, "whatever thy heart desires." Only too soon, however, did he find an occasion to convince himself that the concern of David was something more than a mere imagination. The time of the feast of the new moon came. It was the custom in Israel that at this feast, for two days in succession, they ate at a solemn banquet the flesh of thank-offerings that had been sacrificed. It was observed after this manner

also in the royal palace; for Saul, with all the disloyalty and obstinacy
of his heart, yet failed not, for the sake of his people, to attend to the
Levitical ordinances of worship as accurately as possible. At all times
there are princes who take part thus in the public worship of God,
which in the narrow circle of their like-minded associates they perhaps make sport of; because they well know that with the religious
faith of the people the authority of an oath also perishes, and with
that at last their thrones and all social order would fall to ruin.

At the feast table at Gibeah the royal son-in-law would naturally
be expected, after his return from his flight had been made
known. After all that had happened, however, how could the king
reckon on David's being present at the feast? Without doubt Saul
flattered himself that David would have concluded, from the king's
behavior at Naioth, that he had undergone a change of mind, and
would dream of the possibility of a reconciliation. But David had by
no means seen any reason to entertain such ideas. Rather he now
knew full well how the king's heart was affected toward him. He
therefore informed Jonathan of his resolution not to appear at this
time at the king's table, and indicated to him a place in the neighborhood of the city—perhaps some country cottage, or some
rocky cavern—in which he would hide himself and to which
Jonathan would bring him information, after the second day's festival, whether the king had said anything regarding him, and what
he might expect from him.

In the event of his royal father asking after him, he was to say that
David had gone for a short time to Bethlehem, his father's city, to be
present at a sacrificial feast. Was this a subterfuge only? Certainly not.
Bethlehem lay near to Gibeah, and was to be the next resort after the
hiding place where Jonathan would meet his friend, and communi-
cate to him tidings. David further said to Jonathan: "If, when thy
father hears of my journey to Bethlehem, he says then, It is well; thy
servant shall have peace: but if he be very wroth, then be sure that
evil is determined by him. Therefore thou shalt deal kindly with thy
servant; for thou hast brought thy servant into a covenant of the
Lord with thee: notwithstanding, if there be in me iniquity, slay me
thyself; for why shouldest thou bring me to thy father?" To these
words, as affecting as they were noble-hearted, Jonathan replied, "Far
be it from thee: for if I knew certainly that evil were determined by
my father to come upon thee, then would I not tell it thee?"

After this conversation, the two friends walked together into the field, and agreed as to the manner in which David was to learn the result of Jonathan's observations. If it could be done unperceived, Jonathan was personally to bring word to him but if otherwise, he was, on the evening of the third day, to shoot as if practicing archery, at the stone Ezel lying near to David's hiding-place; and if he called with a loud voice to the boy whom he sent to bring back the arrows he had shot, "Behold the arrows are on this side of thee, take them," this was to be a sign to him that it was peace, and that there was no danger. But if, on the contrary, he said to the young man, "Behold, the arrows are beyond thee," then this would serve as a sign to his friend that it was dangerous for him to appear before the king, and that it was the purpose of the Lord rather that he should flee. But why should he not personally bring the tidings to him, if for David no danger was to be feared? All this was for David's sake, that he might avoid the appearance as if he needed to be persuaded to show himself to the king. Besides, Jonathan intended to avoid giving any room to the suspicion that David's journey to Bethlehem was only a deceitful pretense. It was therefore only a delicate consideration for David which led Jonathan to make choice of the signs that have been named; and the prudence which he displayed in this matter, in no respect leaves him open to reproach.

At this time Jonathan found himself in very difficult circumstances. Not only was he under the necessity of mediating between his father, who was at the same time his king and master, and his friend, who was persecuted by his father, but of taking part with the one against the other. But he knew how, on all sides, to discharge the very difficult duty with a truly holy tact. He could not be led to give up his friend, notwithstanding the hatred which his father cherished against him. The covenant with David was, as we have seen, truly entered into in the Lord.

Jonathan loved David, the beloved and chosen of God, and his companion in the kingdom of God. He would have regarded a renunciation of his friend as the tearing asunder, with a wicked hand, of a bond which Jehovah Himself had formed, and a denial in the person of David, who was to the Lord as the apple of His eye, of the Most High Himself. Yet in all this Jonathan offended not in a single instance against the reverence and love and sincerity of affection which were due from him to his father and king.

By means of the plan which he formed for the protection of David, he intended only to cut off occasion of sin from his father, on account of which the anger of God would have descended on his anointed head. Jonathan had not for a moment been unmindful of the divine command, which enjoins that honor should be rendered to father and mother; and on that account, also, the promise which accompanies this command was in him richly fulfilled. Jonathan "lived long in the land which the Lord his God had given him." In the ninth chapter of the first Book of Chronicles we find mention made of his descendants to the twelfth generation, and perceive that this race were distinguished for their knightly virtues hundreds of years after their noble ancestor.

One of our great poets has made the confession that, when misfortune falls upon any one, even of his best friends, he finds something that he does not wholly dislike. Another maintains, from his own experience, that the first impression which the intelligence of disaster having overtaken any one makes in the human heart, is that of secret joy that he himself was not the subject of it. We see such selfishness condemned by this example of Jonathan. Moreover, pure, self-denying love, such as that of Jonathan, has not yet, God be praised, died wholly out from the earth.

2. While they were on the way through the fields to David's hiding-place, a moving and heart-quickening scene presents itself to us in the conversation carried on between the two friends. After Jonathan had repeated to David the assurance, solemnly swearing by the God of Israel that he would immediately bring to him information of whatever might be planned and determined concerning him in his father's house, he says, greatly agitated, and with an elevated voice, "The Lord be with thee, as He hath been with my father." A deeply significant "as"; for the Lord had been with Saul in this, that He had raised him to the throne of Israel, and had crowned him with victory after victory over his enemies. Jonathan continued: "And thou shalt not only, while yet I live, show me the kindness of the Lord, that I die not: but also thou shalt not cut off thy kindness from my house forever; no, not when the Lord hath cut off the enemies of David every one from the face of the earth."

We understand the king's noble-hearted son. The secret of David's future greatness had already begun to unseal itself to him. Whether he had arrived at this conclusion from marking the course of his friend's life hitherto, or whether he received it as a divine revelation—enough; it is no longer a hidden mystery to him what has been concluded regarding David in the counsel of his invisible Protector. What other heir to a throne would not have been in extreme agitation by such a discovery as this which Jonathan made, and have flamed up into inextinguishable hatred against his unrighteous rival? Jonathan, on the contrary, with manly self-denial and joyful resoluteness, laid down the crown and scepter, his future inheritance, at the feet of David, because it was to him, beyond all question, that he made this offering to the Most High Lord in heaven, who had reserved to Himself the undivided sovereignty over Israel. He presented to his friend, as if he now already saw him clothed with royal purple, the request that, when the just judgment of God would descend upon all his enemies, he would deal gently and kindly with him and his house.

Where in the wide world do we meet with such an example of self-sacrificing submission to the divine determination, and of hallowed friendship, so full of self-denial, as this which now lays claim to our admiration? One must have spent the life of a hermit, and passed his days far from the courts of the "gods of this earth," to be able to deceive himself with the imagination that, even in the midst of the light of Christianity, souls like Jonathan's are not as pearls which are very rare.

What most lamentable scenes present themselves to us there only too abundantly! It needs not that so great a thing as a crown should be the object sought for—no; let them only be ambitious of gaining some title, some elevation of rank, some mark of honor, or any kind of human favor, and then what eager emulation, what despicable envy, what jealous pressing forward of one before another, even among friends, do we too frequently observe! And would that these so-called "friends"—these candidates for honor anticipating one another in burning envy—were only the children of this world, who make no claim upon the Christian name! But, to the injury of the gospel, there are not wanting in this crowd some who make a public profession of the faith, and perhaps even who strut about in priestly attire.

It is a thing even not altogether unheard of, that the rivals in such a racecourse prepare pitfalls for each other, and, under the mask of friendship, yea, even with the appearance of commending and justifying their fellow-competitors, both cunningly and clandestinely disparage, and give rise to suspicions against one another, in the eyes of the dispensers of fortune and of favor. Oh, how this example of Jonathan condemns such a spirit! May these false brethren, especially if they know and name the name of Christ, take heed to themselves that they do not come under the condemnation of the apostle, which he utters against those who, in works, deny Him whom they know, and are an abomination in the sight of God, and "unto every good work reprobate!"

David heard the significant words of his friend in silence. How they must have taken hold upon him, and moved him in the deepest manner! They opened up for him a new seal of that secret which had lain concealed in his bosom since the anointing at Bethlehem. His present situation, indeed, appeared to be in entire contradiction to that lofty destiny to which the anointing, and also now the remarkable words of Jonathan, pointed. But he thought on that which is expressed in Psalm 135, "Whatsoever the Lord pleased, that did He in heaven, and in earth, in the seas, and all deep places," and with such reflections calmed the storms of emotion in his heart. His soul was prostrate in the dust, bowed down in humility before God.

But without taking into account the view which was thus opened to him into the future of his own life, how could he find words sufficient to express the feelings which overpowered him at the sight of that love and self-denial and resignation which, like a reflection of heaven itself, he here discovered in the conduct of Jonathan toward him? His whole soul was melted within him in thankfulness to the Most High for the treasure with which He had blessed him in his friend Jonathan. Jonathan knew how to interpret David's silence, and, not less moved, reached to him his hand on departing, in the hope of soon meeting him again. Thus David was left alone in his hiding-place, which was perhaps enclosed on all sides by a thick forest. That it was to him as a quiet little chamber for prayer cannot be doubted. For a while we must separate ourselves from our friend, in order to be witnesses of a scene which presents a striking contrast to that we have been contemplating.

3. The feast of the new moon came round. The solemn act of offering up the sacrifice is over. Saul's guests already fill the courts of the palace. The king comes in amongst them. Jonathan respectfully salutes him, and sits down at his left hand at the table. At his right

hand sits Abner, his uncle, the captain of his host, a man skilled in war. David's place remains empty. The king is silent; his eye looks sullen. He misses his son-in-law from his place, but thinks that some unavoidable hindrance may have prevented his presence. But when David did not appear on the second day, then Saul directed to Jonathan the inquiry, "Wherefore cometh not the son of Jesse"—thus he coldly, and as if he were a stranger, speaks of him—"to meat, neither yesterday nor today?" Jonathan excuses his friend, without alleging any untruth, by saying that he had gone to Bethlehem to be present at the yearly sacrifice offered there for all his family. The old anger of the king suddenly blazed up again, and he poured out against his first-born a storm of insulting and opprobrious words: "Thou son of the perverse rebellious woman," he cried, "do not I know that thou hast chosen the son of Jesse to thine own confusion, and unto the confusion of thy mother's nakedness" (as if he were not his son, and therefore not the rightful heir to the throne)? "For as long as the son of Jesse liveth upon the ground, thou shalt not be established, nor thy kingdom: wherefore now send and fetch him unto me; for he shall surely die."

One can imagine in what perplexity this outbreak of passion on the part of his father would place Jonathan. Leaving out of view the painful impression which it must have made on the heart of the son to hear himself maligned by his own father as the son of a perverse rebellious woman, he saw with horror that his father, who without doubt had also received some light as to David's future destiny, had, with determined purpose, sworn that he should be put to death. He endeavored to appease his raging father. "Wherefore shall he be slain?" said he "What hath he done that thou art so angry against him?" But his words are interrupted in a dreadful manner. The king seized his spear to pierce him through. Jonathan avoided the murderous aim, and hastened—since he must, for the present at least, abandon all hope of pacifying and reconciling his father—away from the table in extreme excitement, and with the deepest sorrow.

On the following day he neither ate nor drank for grief of mind. Who will be surprised at this? Let any one place himself in his situation. That word of God, "The father's blessing buildeth up the children's house, but the mother's curse pulleth them down again," he had not yet heard; but he well knew with what earnestness and emphasis the divine commandment impressed upon children the duty of reverence, submission, and obedience to their father and mother. And now he had kindled against himself his father's anger and hatred, and must take care that the curse of his mother do not also accompany it, if he remain true to his friend, yea, even help to open up to him the way to his father's throne. Ought he to sacrifice the love and the blessing of his parents, and, besides this, the fortune and the perpetuation of his father's royal house, to his friendship for David? What perplexing thoughts this question would awaken within him, especially since, after the terrible scene at the royal table, he could no longer conceal from himself that through further relationship with his friend he would provoke his father to the uttermost, and only place his own life in danger.

Notwithstanding all this, he did not hesitate in his resolution. Without detriment to his filial faithfulness, he is prepared, although his heart bleeds at the thought of all the sorrow that would grow out of it, to make this great sacrifice without hesitation, and principally on this account, because he is clearly and fully conscious that he makes it not so much to his love for David, as rather to the Most High, whose unambiguous resolution regarding the son of Jesse was to him no longer an enigma. One could almost believe that these words of the Son of God had been revealed to Jonathan: "He that loveth father or mother more than me is not worthy of me." He loves God his Lord more than all things; and therefore there already burns within his soul a spark of that flame of love which afterward the Lord had in view when He said, "Greater love hath no man than this, that a man lay down his life for his friends."

On the morning of the third day Jonathan hastens out into the field, accompanied by a young armor-bearer, and gives to his friend, in his hiding place, the appointed signal. Thrice the arrow from his bowstring flew to the stone Ezel, and as often did the lad, and with him also the friend in the hiding place, hear the words from the mouth of the archer, "Is not the arrow beyond thee? make speed, haste, stay not." Then David knew how matters stood. But when Jonathan perceived no one near at hand by whom he thought he could be noticed, he sent back the lad with his bow and quiver to the city, perhaps under the pretense that he wished to wander forth alone and undisturbed for a little time in freedom, and then he went forward to the place where his friend was concealed.

Before he reached it, David hastened to meet him and how excit-

ing is the scene which we now witness! David, overcome by the tide
of feeling that arose within him, testified to his friend his thanks, his
high esteem, and his love, while, after the Eastern custom, he "fell on
his face to the ground, and bowed himself three times." Jonathan
restrained him, raised him up, pressed him to his bosom, and the two
hung weeping in each other's arms, sealing their bond of friendship
with the warm brotherly embrace. And how expressive of his deep
inward emotion were the silent tears which streamed copiously from
David's eyes! Along with his sorrow at separation from Jonathan,
what a deep grief he felt because of the misery that had come upon
the king's house; what a sorrow, also, to find himself forced into a
relation to that house which was so little in harmony with the divine
order; and what a crowd of alarming apprehensions and fears filled
his mind for the immediate future, not so much of himself as of Saul,
whom they both called their father, and for the future of the whole
people! Inexpressibly sad are their hearts.

They found relief only in God. Jonathan is the first to compose
himself. "Go in peace," he says, and reaches to his friend, whose
flight seemed now for the second time to be commanded by God, his
hand of farewell; "forasmuch as we have sworn both of us," he added,
"in the name of the Lord, saying, The Lord be between me and thee,
and between my seed and thy seed forever." David, silent from inward
emotion, signifies his "Amen," and then the two friends separated
from one another.

Feelings in harmony with those which then rose up in the soul of
David, when he was informed by Jonathan that a heavy thundercloud hung over his head, threatening his life, and that only a speedy
flight could save him, are frequently expressed in his psalms.
Among others, they are found expressed in the eighty-sixth Psalm.
Is it not the sadness, penetrating even to the heart of God, of a lonely fugitive cast upon the Lord alone, which finds utterance in the
following sentences of that psalm? "Bow down Thine ear, O Lord,
hear me; for I am poor and needy. Preserve my soul, for I am holy"
(i.e., separated by Thee, and for Thee, from the multitudes of the
godless): "O Thou my God, save Thy servant that trusteth in Thee.
Be merciful unto me, O Lord: for I cry unto Thee daily. Rejoice the
soul of Thy servant: for unto Thee, O Lord, do I lift up my soul. In
the day of my trouble I will call upon Thee: for Thou wilt answer me.
I will praise Thee, O Lord my God, with all my heart: for great is Thy

mercy toward me; and Thou hast delivered my soul from the lowest hell. O God, the proud are risen against me, and the assemblies of violent men have sought after my soul, and have not set Thee before them. But Thou, O Lord, art a God full of compassion, and gracious, long-suffering, and plenteous in mercy and truth. O turn unto me, and have mercy upon me: give Thy strength unto Thy servant, and save the son of Thine handmaid. Show me a token for good, that they which hate me may see it, and be ashamed; because Thou, Lord, hast holpen me, and comforted me."

How many, under similar circumstances, have already imitated the holy singer in giving expression to these suppliant words! And let no one doubt that, wherever this is done in the same spirit with which David prayed, the tokens of favor which are sought will not need to be long waited for. With the author of another psalm, we say, "Truly God is good to Israel, even to such as are of a clean heart!"

8

False Steps

"I have set the Lord always before me: because He is at my right hand, I shall not be moved." Thus with a joyful spirit David sings in the eighth verse of the sixteenth Psalm. It might appear as if in using these words he overstepped the bounds of humility. But he speaks, as he intimates in the tenth verse, not so much in his own name as in the name of the "Holy One," with whom he supposes there was a constant walking before God, such as he himself, agonizing in prayer, sought for. He speaks, therefore, the truth.

"To have God always before the eyes," says Luther, "makes a lively spirit and an undismayed heart, which is joyful and willing to bear patiently wherever misfortune, the cross, and suffering need to be borne: such a faith is unconquerable." It was David's deepest and purest desire not to let God and His holy commandment out of his sight for a single moment; but however willing his spirit, his flesh was weak. With his naturally excitable disposition, it could not fail that storms of temptation gave him much to do, if they did not throw him out of his right path, though only temporarily.

Thus we find that at different times he quite wavered. But he was like the magnetic needle, which, indeed, yields to mechanical pressure forcing it out of its direction, but as soon as this pressure is withdrawn, returns by its own inherent force into its previous position which is natural to it. If David, in an unguarded hour, makes a false step, the note of triumph in the camp of the enemy is always premature. Before one is aware, the fallen man again stands up, whole and uninjured, with the tears of repentance on his cheeks, and is again "the man after God's own heart."

100

2 Samuel 21:1, 10

> Then came David to Nob to Ahimelech the priest. And David arose, and fled that day for fear of Saul, and went to Achish the king of Gath.

These words show to us the scenes which we will this day visit in spirit. David's experiences (1) at the one place, and (2) at the other, claim our most lively interest.

1. On his second flight from Gibeah, David came first to *Nob*, a little town lying in the neighborhood of Jerusalem. Probably this town was that which bears the modern name of El Isawijeh, i.e., "Esau's" or "Edom's village," so named from the horrible deed committed there by Doeg the Edomite, of whom we shall hear further. The tabernacle was then at Nob, that mysterious symbol of Jehovah's dwelling-place, which only wanted its holy furniture, the ark of the covenant, which was at that time at Kirjath-jearim (i.e., "the city of the wood"), in the house of Abinadab the Levite whither they had fled with it twenty years before, after it had been rescued from the hands of the Philistines. For so long a time in Israel had the order of divine worship been broken through, and ecclesiastical anarchy had prevailed. The priests erected altars and offered sacrifices wherever it pleased them, and Saul was not the man to put an end to this lawless state of things. Yet the holy tabernacle remained the central point of the worship of God for those among the people who aimed at walking steadfastly in the ways of the law of Moses.

To this number David belonged, who had not forgotten the word of Jehovah, spoken long ago: "In all places where I record my name, I will come unto thee, and I will bless thee!" At Nob also the high priest waited upon his holy office; and the people believed that they testified becoming reverence to the holy ark, by turning their faces in prayer toward the place where it was at that time preserved. Besides this, the high priest was in possession of the mysterious breastplate, the "Urim and Thummim" (i.e., illuminations and perfections), by which Jehovah was wont, in a manner no longer understood, to reveal Himself regarding weighty events and undertakings in Israel.

What now moved David to make his way to Nob was perhaps the double hope of finding protection from his persecutors beside the altars there, and of obtaining, through the intervention of the priest, divine direction as to his future course. That he reckoned on this latter result is manifest from the tenth verse of the following chapter, where it is expressly said that the high priest had "inquired of the Lord" for him. We do not, it is true, observe that an answer was given to his inquiry. If the Lord was silent, David had to attribute this to himself, inasmuch as his conduct at Nob was by no means pleasing to God. When Ahimelech the high priest discovered that the wanderer who had come to him was David, the first impression which this unexpected meeting created within him was that of great surprise to see the king's son-in-law come thither unarmed, and also without any retinue; and the second, a secret concern lest he might be the bearer to him of some unwished for command from the king. With deepest reverence he approached his distinguished guest with the question, "Why art thou alone, and no man with thee?" And how did David answer? Perhaps many a time afterward the remembrance of the lamentable weakness which revealed itself in him there may have brought the blush of shame to his face.

But we make allowance for him. David, greatly wearied with his long journey, stood much in need, first of all, of bodily refreshment If he found no harbor at Nob, where could he turn? And perhaps, also, it was necessary for him to be careful lest he should be denied shelter if he made known to the high priest that an outlaw, pursued by the king, stood before him. He therefore resorted to a subterfuge, and gave out that the king had entrusted him with a commission which, for the attaining of his object, he had under all circumstances to keep secret. He said that he had left his attendants at a distance behind, and had directed them to remain there till, after a short interval, he should return to them again. He asked that Ahimelech might give him a loaf, or, in order that these his servants might also be refreshed, five loaves of bread.

It is sad to see David sink thus suddenly down from the heights of his faith into such cowardice. This is the first moral blemish which we find in him. It is indeed true that we often see Old Testament saints, under like circumstances, fall into the same sin; yet no one of them escaped divine chastisement on account of it. David's great ancestor, the patriarch Abraham, once stained himself with a lie, when, from fear of the king of Gerar, he said that Sarah his wife was his sister; but we know also with what anguish of mind and confusion he was visited on account of this cowardly stratagem. And this penitential sorrow was also not wanting in David's case, as we shall afterward see.

The fugitive gained at once his object by means of his scheme. The priest, who had not at that time ready in his house any "common bread," did not delay to set before the husband of the king's daughter consecrated loaves from the table of shew-bread in the tabernacle of the covenant. He did this so much the more unhesitatingly, because David assured him that he with his followers were pure, according to the Levitical law; and he justified his willingness in this matter by considering that the Bethlehemite stood before him not only as the representative of Saul, the anointed of Jehovah, but also, as a lively presentiment would suggest to him, as one destined by God to great things. On the holy table of shew-bread stood at all times, according to the directions of the divine law, on golden trays, twelve loaves of unleavened bread. These were removed every Sabbath and replaced by new ones.

They symbolized to the twelve tribes of Israel the covenant relationship into which God had entered with them, when He, like the father of a household, spread for them a table and cared for all their necessities. They reminded the people also of their departure out of Egypt, as well as of their duty to consecrate to Him again all that the Almighty Preserver of their life made, according to His loving-kindness, to grow in their fields and gardens, and to use all to His glory and in His service. Finally, they pointed prophetically forward to the days of the New Covenant, and typified the spiritual Bread which would then come down from heaven to earth as the Bread of eternal life. The bread which was removed from the holy table every Sabbath belonged to the priests, who, according to certain prescribed regulations, might give it also, in cases of necessity, to others who did not belong to the tribe of Levi. David was in this case, and he thankfully took the bread that was offered to him.

It is well known that Christ once made reference to this incident, ratifying its historical veracity, when He replied to the Pharisees, who made it a reproach to His disciples that they had plucked off the ears of corn on the Sabbath-day to appease their hunger.[1] He said unto them, "Have ye not read what David did, when he was an hungered, and they that were with him? how he entered into the house of God, and did eat the shew bread, which was not lawful for him to eat, neither for them which were" (according to David's statement) "with

1. Matthew 12.

him, but only for the priests?" By this the Lord showed to the
Pharisees that already, under the economy of the law, the Sabbath
commandment was put in abeyance by a danger threatening life, and
that wherever the saving of a human being was concerned, departure
from a Levitical arrangement was not at all taken into account before
God. But in that occurrence even something more important
than this must be observed, for in the New Covenant the Levitical
constitution has to be regarded as only a shadow of that substance
which had now appeared, and that the children of the heavenly
kingdom now made free would no more be bound by it.

"I say unto you," said Christ, in concluding His address, "that in
this place is one greater than the temple. But if ye had known what
this meaneth, I will have mercy, and not sacrifice, ye would not have
condemned the guiltless. For the Son of man is Lord even of the
Sabbath-day." A sublime and highly important statement this,
which, like a ray shining down from above, reflects a light over the
whole plan of the kingdom of God! The meaning of it is this: The
Old Testament economy is revoked and abolished, because it is realized and fulfilled, spiritualized and transfigured, in the New.

After David had refreshed himself with the consecrated bread, he
asked, still, alas! carrying out his deception, whether the priest could
supply him with a spear or a sword, because that, on account of the
haste with which the king had given his command, he had been
forced to leave without his armor. Ahimelech replied, "The sword of
Goliath the Philistine, whom thou slewest in the valley of Elah,
behold, it is here, wrapped in a cloth behind the ephod: if thou wilt
take that, take it; for there is no other save that here." And David
said, "There is none like that; give it me." The priest then gave it to
him. Once the shepherd's sling alone was necessary for our hero; now
he asks for that sword which had not even availed him for whose
giant hand it had been fabricated; and, besides, he says of it, "There
is none like it," as if the victory were connected with a weapon, and
did not depend on the arm of the Lord alone. Poor David! But
patience! the Lord will yet know how to lead him back again into the
right path.

At the very time that all this happened at Nob, there sat, concealed in the holy tabernacle, a man named Doeg, an Edomite, one
of the servants of the king. Saul had committed to him the oversight
of the royal flocks and herdsmen. This guest was a silent witness of

all that had taken place between the fugitive from Gibeah and the high priest. For what reason he was in the holy tabernacle, whether as a proselyte or on account of some vow, is not mentioned. Enough: his presence betokened no good either to the high priest or to the distinguished fugitive under his protection. He was the chief occasion of a great evil which fell upon both of them.

2. Over David's head the sound of the approaching storms was already heard. On all sides armed spies were lurking around him. When he received information of this, he fled into the enemy's land, because he believed himself no longer safe anywhere in Israel. He committed himself, however great might be the hazard, to the protection of Achish, king of the Philistines, who also, as did all the kings of the Philistines, bore the name Abimelech (i.e., "father-king," signifying the same thing as "head of the royal house"), and held his court at Gath, the birthplace of Goliath. Probably he thought that what he had once done to the Philistines, since a considerable time had now passed by, would by this time be forgotten by them, or at least would be overlooked; but principally he founded his hope of protection on the rights of hospitality, which are everywhere in the East held in high estimation, and are observed even toward an enemy. But he deceived himself in the one respect as well as in the other. He had not tarried there long when he heard the servants of Achish whispering to one another, and saying, "Is not this David, the king of the land? did they not sing one to another of him in dances, saying, Saul hath slain his thousands, and David his ten thousands?" and he saw the attention of those around always directed toward him in a manner threatening danger, and he heard his name mentioned, and his former heroic exploit calumniated with ever-increasing bitterness of tone. Even the brow of the king began visibly to darken toward him.

Unhappy fugitive! what plan did you now fall upon? It was a new labyrinth in which you did lose yourself. Did the Keeper of Israel sink into slumber, that you did see yourself under the necessity of seeking, near the altars of Dagon and of Ashtaroth, an asylum which you thought could no longer be found in the land which the God of your fathers had chosen for the place of His glory? Lo! the Almighty, who will not give the glory due to His name to any other, and of whom Moses testifies, saying, "The Lord is a jealous God," has for a moment, to your humiliation, in the anger of His love, given the reins to your cowardly conduct and the anguish which has come upon you in the region where you now sojourn. That its very atmosphere is heavy with storms against you, you may well regard as a part of the punishment which you have exposed yourself unto by your faint-hearted and unhallowed proceeding at Nob! We may well, therefore, call upon the erring one to awaken out of his lamentable infatuation. But perhaps his own conscience already says the same thing to him. He does not, however, as yet regain his lost position.

What now takes place? When he saw his situation become the longer the more dismal, and thought that he must every moment expect the lightning to flash forth from out of the clouds which gathered over his head, which would utterly destroy him, he takes refuge in a new artifice, and, alas! in one yet more doubtful and more inexcusable than the former one. Perhaps that he might awaken compassion toward him and thereby obtain deliverance out of the painful situation in which he finds himself, he pretends to be mad, distorts his countenance, begins, when the king's servants would seize him, to roll about and prance like one frantic under their hands, and, letting his "spittle fall down upon his beard," to "scrabble" unintelligible writings "on the doors of the gate." Everyone stands amazed but he gains his object. "Lo, ye see," cried Achish, "the man is mad! wherefore then have ye brought him to me? Have I need," he continued, with a scornful glance toward him, "of madmen, that ye have brought this fellow to play the madman in my presence? Shall this fellow come into my house?" Thus he speaks, and gives orders that without delay they should convey into his own country the miserable man, who would now no longer be dangerous to the Philistines.

Many interpreters think they see in that convulsive paroxysm of David not a pretext, but a real attack of insanity, or of falling sickness, which, partly through the fear that he must here die a dishonored death, partly through bitter repentance over his error, which boiled up within his soul, overpowered him, though only for a time. And certainly the supposition appears to find support in the circumstance, that it is scarcely conceivable how anyone would willingly place himself in a situation such as that in which he is here described to us.

However, our interpretation, following an old Jewish tradition, is favored by this, that we do not find in the vigorous healthful life of David anything whatever indicating in the remotest degree nervous weakness, or a tendency to nervous fits. That mighty inward tempest then raged in his soul is certainly manifest, from the fact that he could so far forget himself as to make choice of so repulsive and so sinful a means of obtaining deliverance as that dissimulation was.

It might possibly, indeed, be true that God the Lord, for the punishment of His erring servant, may have permitted that, for the time, to become a dreadful reality, which David intended only to feign. If this opinion were granted, both views of that terrible occurrence would then be united. Besides, the Lord dealt gently with David in permitting him to succeed in his scheme, which can in no way be justified, for thereby his deliverance was brought about. But for this, also, the son of Jesse had to praise the free grace of his God alone, as he afterward did not fail to recognize.

It is always a dangerous course when believers look to the children of this world for protection and help. Without taking into account that too easily in the circle of such benefactors and deliverers do they lose their balance, and, making court to them for their favor, yield to the temptation to disown their faith, and in word and conduct to place themselves on an equality with the world. Such a step gives to the latter occasion secretly to triumph, that they who are so willing to be called "the chosen," when distress comes upon them know not how to be contented with their God and His help alone, but gladly permit themselves to seek aid from those to whom they do not otherwise concede the name of brethren. Never will they succeed in truly reconciling the enemies of their faith by means of affected accommodation to them and their forms of life for, according to the well-known testimony of God, the enmity between those who are "after the flesh," and those who are "after the spirit," is a fixed principle, and though covered with many a fair garland of courtesy and politeness, yet, even when universal love bears the scepter in the heart of God's children, that enmity cannot be abolished till regenerating grace has made of the "twain one."

Among the psalms of David we find two in which the holy singer looks back upon his sorrowful experience at Nob and at Gath. Of the first tears of repentance which without doubt streamed from his eyes over the errors of which he was guilty at these places, the walls of some secret little chamber, if a tongue were granted to them, could give us information. When David sang the two psalms referred to, divine grace had already dried his tears. Their keynote is thanks for the grace and deliverance he had experienced. But whoever has an eye to observe it, will also perceive that they are even yet bedewed with tears, and will not fail to discover in the heart-gushings of the singer the most sorrowful recollections of his former guilt and error.

David begins the thirty-fourth Psalm with praise to God, who had graciously delivered him from his sorrows and anguish. "They who look to Him," says he, "and run to Him" (instead of laying hold of an arm of flesh), "will not be put to shame. This poor man cried" (the poor man is himself), "and the Lord heard him, and saved him out of all his troubles. The angel of the Lord encampeth round about them that fear Him"—(ah, how deeply the singer had darkened for himself this truth!)—"and delivereth them." Hereupon he conjures all his fellow-pilgrims to fear the Lord, because to such no good thing will be wanting. Affectionately, as well as urgently, he calls unto them in these words: "Come, ye children hearken unto me, I will teach you the fear of the Lord," and the first thing he impresses on them is this, that they should keep their tongue from evil, and guard their lips that they speak no deceit. He warns them against dissimulation, of which he himself had once to his own injury been guilty in so gross a manner before Abimelech and before Achish.

"The eyes of the Lord," he continues, "are upon the righteous, and His ears are open to their cry." Is it not as if in these words there mingled the sigh, "Ah, would that what I say had been present before me at that time!" "The face of the Lord," we further read, "is against them that do evil." He speaks thus from his own bitter experience. Although that which he adds, "that He may cut off the remembrance of them from the earth," did not happen to him, yet his conscience testifies to him that in justice it might have done so. And wherefore did it not? He himself gives the answer: "The Lord is nigh unto them that are of a broken heart; and saveth such as be of a contrite spirit. Many are the afflictions of the righteous, but the Lord delivereth him out of them all. The Lord redeemeth the soul of His servants; and none of them that trust in Him shall be desolate."

Thus precious fruits to the son of Jesse were made to grow, under the blessing of the divine compassion, "Out of those sorrowful events at Nob and at Gath came a more thorough knowledge of himself, a deeper humility of heart before the Lord of lords, and a strengthened confidence in His grace and faithfulness.

The fifty-sixth Psalm seems to lie, in point of time nearer to the

events to which it refers than the thirty-fourth does. The keynote in
the latter is praise and thanks, while in the former the sigh for help
and deliverance predominates. This psalm undoubtedly arose out of
David's flight to Gath and to the land of the Philistines. David had
with deep sorrow recognized his errors, and had solemnly passed sentence against himself; and now he cries unto the Lord for
preservation from the snares of his many enemies.

"Be merciful unto me," he begins: "for mine enemies would daily
swallow me up." Yet he will no more despond. "What time I am
afraid, I will trust in Thee. In God I will praise His word" (i.e., I will
trust in His promises): "I will not fear what flesh can do unto me."
Hereupon there follows a description of the obduracy and the plots
of his enemies, and then the prayer, "In Thine anger cast down the
people, O God. Thou tellest" (i.e., observest) "my wanderings: put
Thou my tears into Thy bottle." Then, with increasing confidence,
he exclaims, "Are they not in Thy book?" His assurance that God
will hear him becomes stronger. "When I cry unto Thee, then shall
mine enemies turn back: this I know; for God is for me. In God will
I praise His word: in the Lord will I praise His word. In God have I
put my trust: I will not be afraid what man can do unto me." The
singer concludes with the vow that he would pay to the Lord the
thanksgiving which was due. "For," says he, "Thou hast delivered my
soul from death: wilt not Thou deliver my feet from falling, that I
may walk before God in the light of the living?"

Oh, the splendid gain which accrued to the son of Jesse through
the grace of God, not only from his sufferings, but also from his most
grievous errors! May it be granted to each one of us in like manner
to gather grapes from thorns, and figs from thistles!

9

David in the Wilderness

Moses gives us in his dying song a beautiful description of the protection and defense with which their covenant God had hitherto made glad the people of Israel. "The Lord found him," says he, "in a desert land, and in the waste howling wilderness; He led him about, He instructed him, He kept him as the apple of His eye. As an eagle stirreth up her nest, fluttereth over her young (so cherished He the seed of Abraham), spreadeth abroad her wings, taketh them, beareth them on her wings; so the Lord alone did lead him, and there was no strange god with him."[1] Happy people who are the objects of such care! And it happened to them for an example of the manner in which God deals with all His people, yea, with every individual member of His kingdom. For if we are among those who are with their whole hearts "on the Lord's side," we shall not fail to experience the same protection. No doubt even then the journey through the wilderness may still be appointed to us, but only in order that there the Lord may find a place and an opportunity for helping us in a wonderful manner.

We are threatened by many and dangerous enemies, who lie in wait for us; but without these, what experience could we have of the protection which the Almighty extends toward us? Without all wavering, we shall scarcely reach the goal; but as the eagle bears up, on the soft feathers of her wings, her young when unable to fly, so the Lord winds around us all the closer the arms of His grace, and the band of love which unites us to Himself. If anyone will seal with his "yea and amen" what we now say, it is David. Oh, how had the Lord

---

1. Deuteromy 32:10–12.

protected him, even as the apple of His eye! Today we shall meet with new proofs of this.

1 Samuel 22:1–2

> David therefore departed thence, and escaped to the cave Adullam: and when his brethren and all his father's house heard it, they went down thither to him. And every one that was in distress, and every one that was in debt, and every one that was discontented, gathered themselves unto him; and he became a captain over them,: and there were with him about four hundred men.

Such is the commencement of a chapter which leads us forward to three new scenes in the life of David. None of them is without instruction for us. Let us direct our attention more closely to them, and see what befell the fugitive (1) in the cave Adullam, (2) in the land of Moab, and (3) in the wilderness of Hareth.

1. It was a great folly, only to be accounted for from the violent agitation by which he was then overpowered, for David to seek safety and protection against the plots of Saul among Israel's hereditary and most bitter foes. Perhaps he imagined that the circumstance of his now seeking refuge among the Philistines from the persecution of Saul, whom they so much hated, would awaken their sympathy, and that they would be disposed to act in a more indulgent and amiable spirit toward him. But how could he who had slain their hero, the pride and joy of their country, hope for such a thing? Yet in his extremity he did venture into their land.

But did he go only into a remote province of their country? No; he went direct to the residence of the king of the Philistines, which was, moreover, the birthplace of the giant whom he had slain. It might be that prudence advised him before this to ungird from his side the sword of Goliath, and to entrust it to the care of some confidential friend. Yet how imprudent to seek an asylum in the very jaws of the raging lion. Though he had bitterly to repent of this unwise step, yet, under the protection of the wings of the free grace of God, he comes forth again safe, at least with his life.

The history does not inform us how he made his way from Gath farther through the land of the Philistines. Enough: we see him today cross again the borders of the tribe of Judah, and make a halt not far from Bethlehem, the place of his birth. What must have been his feelings when he trod once more this peaceful region of the land of his youth, where he once was so happy, while yet an unknown shepherd boy, conscious of no other enemy than the bear and the lion, which he felt himself able to vanquish with his spear, as he peacefully watched his flocks! Now he came hither like a sheep driven from the fold—ah, even like a hunted deer—pursued by him whom he called his king and lord, yea, his father, and for whom he would so willingly have shed his last drop of blood.

The southern mountain ranges of his beloved land, among which David now tarried, abound in large and capacious caverns, some of which are dry in their interior, and therefore are habitable, and they even still, as in former times, serve as folds for the shepherds and their flocks. One of these is so extensive that it could even afford a secure encampment for a large army. In later times, Christian hermits and ascetics were often wont to take up their abode within its extensive recesses; and during the Crusades, on one occasion, the whole population of the neighboring Tekoa, with their sheep and cattle, fled to it for safety against the attacks of the destroying invaders.

This was the cave of Adullam. In it our fugitive now sought shelter and protection. That this lonely grotto served him at first as a peaceful oratory there can be no doubt. At all events the hundred and forty-second Psalm sounds forth to us from amid its darkness. Let us hear him! "I cried unto the Lord with my voice; with my voice unto the Lord did I make my supplication. I poured out my complaint before Him; I showed before Him my trouble. When my spirit was overwhelmed within me, then Thou knewest my path. In the way wherein I walked have they privily laid a snare for me. I looked on my right hand, and beheld, but there was no man that would know me: refuge failed me; no man cared for my soul. I cried unto Thee, O Lord: I said, Thou art my refuge and my portion in the land of the living. Attend unto my cry; for I am brought very low: deliver me from my persecutors; for they are stronger than I. Bring my soul out of prison" (my distresses), "that I may praise Thy name: the righteous shall compass me about; for Thou shalt deal bountifully with me."

This heart-cry from the lonely cave had found its way to the heart of the Almighty. It is gladdening to behold how the Lord hastens to crown the concluding utterances of that prayer with the blessing. Before even David is aware of it, "the righteous" assemble themselves together unto him. In the circles of the pious at Bethlehem and its surrounding districts, it was soon known that David was again in the land of Judah, and that he hid in the cave of Adullam.

In order that we may be able to estimate the joy with which they received tidings of David's arrival in their midst, we must know to what a degree at that time the mournful state of the government, under which the land groaned, bowed down in sorrow the faithful and God-fearing in Israel, and how deeply the general falling away from the faith, the want of reverence for God, and the abandonment of the customs and manners of the fathers throughout the land, went to their hearts. At the same time consider how the thought within them became always the stronger and stronger, that the son of Jesse was destined by Jehovah to great things, and particularly to be the instrument in effecting a restoration and a revival of the old sacred ordinances of God. Though they did not yet venture to speak it out, they saw in him their future king and the deliverer of the dissolving theocracy. What wonder that they who, by the necessity of the times, were pressed to a kind of self-defense and self-preservation, felt themselves now drawn in the most powerful manner to the man of their hopes!

They came from all sides as pilgrims to his hiding-place, the cave of Adullam. His relatives—father, mother, brothers, and cousins—came to him from Bethlehem. Oh, what delight for him to breathe again the air of love in the fellowship of those dear ones from whom he had been so long separated! After these his relatives, there came to him people of all classes, particularly the poor and lowly, but God-fearing, whose hearts were specially affected by the spiritual hurt of Joseph, but who not less also sighed under worldly oppression, because they were burdened by exorbitant taxation, and were under a load of debt, seeing that there were men in Israel who regarded not, yea, who without fear trampled under their feet that commandment of God against usury, which was so benevolent in its object, and so favorable to the poor.

Of these men there were about 400, and among them were some whom we shall afterward meet with as David's bravest heroes and generals. They belonged to the best among their people, and were firmly resolved no more to depart from David's side. And David consented to their congregating about him, and "he became captain over them."

Whom do we find here? Is this a rebellious band risen up against their king? By no means. These men believed that they were assembling under the banner of their king against his enemy the Philistines, and in this they were not mistaken. They formed a band of volunteers, devoted only to the service of the fatherland, and, if God gave them grace, as a remnant of the children of Abraham according to the spirit, the founders of a better generation that was to arise.

Who can fail to recognize in David, as he here appears, a remarkable type of the divine Prince of Peace, who at a future age could go forth from his house. As David then stood, so Christ, his illustrious descendant "according to the flesh," now stands almost everywhere, misapprehended by the world, if not hated and persecuted, and only surrounded by a little band of devoted followers, comparatively small and insignificant, and for the most part contemptible in the eyes of the world, and, moreover, reviled by bitter enemies. "Not many wise men after the flesh, not many mighty, not many noble are called; but God hath chosen the foolish things of the world to confound the wise; and God hath chosen the weak things of the world to confound the things which are mighty; and base things of the world, and things which are despised, hath God chosen, yea, and things which are not, to bring to nought things that are, that no flesh should glory in His presence."

The true and living Church of the heavenly David corresponds in general, at the present day, to this apostolic description. Those who gather themselves together unto Him in truth are only such as are spiritually "in distress and discontented," and therefore are filled with joy that "He came not to call the righteous, but sinners to repentance." They are helpless bankrupts, who know themselves to be debtors to the whole law, and to whom free grace remains as their sole confidence, their only hope. To them He addresses His invitation, "Come unto me all ye that labor and are heavy laden"; and He is not ashamed to be called their "Captain" and Leader, yea, their Mediator, High Priest, and eternal Savior. Let them flee then to Him to whom their soul is precious!

The dwelling-place of the exalted Son of David upon earth is meanwhile as unlike to a royal palace as was David's cave of Adullam to a lordly mansion. The true Church is as yet concealed under a dark covering, as with a widow's veil. Her Lord is not yet present to the sight. Her people walk by faith and not by sight, and know that they are surrounded by the powers of darkness, against whom their weapons of war are to be laid aside neither by day nor by night. A world stands in arms against the decided followers of the crucified King of glory, and they are dealt with as very outlaws, on whom any one may lay his hands. But even to them also the time comes when, as our fugitive must exchange the cave of Adullam for the gorgeous palace on Mount Zion, even so for those who are not offended at the "form of a servant" assumed by the divine Son of David, and at the lowly aspect of His kingdom upon earth, the simple dwelling in which the Church now gather together shall become transformed into a glorious building, irradiated with heavenly splendor, whose dome shall tower upward into the ever-opened heavens, whose pillars shall encompass the whole earth, and whose inhabitants, after they have waited patiently with their Head here below, shall reign with Him forever.

2. Precious hours of edification, of enjoyment, and of mutual encouragement must these have been which were spent in the cave by these companions in the faith, who were congregated around David as the center of their hopes. In times of distress, when danger and persecution assailed the Church, often has one seen the faithful gathering together, from their separations and disunions, as these did at the rocky cave. We need only refer to those unions, blessed of God, of the first Christians amid the darkness of the catacombs, when they were assailed by the bitter persecution of the emperor of Rome; or those solemn assemblies of the Protestants in France, in the deserts and amid the forests, when threatened by fire and sword, where a hill encompassed by woods served them as a pulpit, and a moss-covered rock as an altar and a communion table. But never has the life of Christian faith and love blossomed in greater beauty than at these very times.

Days like these might return; and who knows how soon, if the anti-Christian power continues to make progress with the same gigantic steps with which it has been seen to advance during the past ten years? As yet there are only, as it were, rhetorical firebrands for the most part, and the sword of a word full of poison and gall, with which the enemy shows his rage against God's Israel. But let there be a new volcanic outbreak of the revolutionary elements which ferment and boil in the depths of the predominant spirit of our days of apostasy, and, before we are aware of it, the spiritual weapons of assault may be changed into the material.

Then, indeed, would a speedy end be put to the unholy quarrels among brethren which at present rend the Church, the body of the Lord. Then would become again one what God had joined together; and it would become manifest that faith, love, and fidelity to the death had not yet altogether disappeared from the earth. May not one, therefore, sometimes even entertain the wish to see the storm arise which shall kindle into a new flame the smoking torch of spiritual life in the "remnant" of the people of God, and drive the sheep of the Good Shepherd, now separated from each other, into one fold, united together in love?

But perhaps other ways are known to the wisdom of the Lord, by which this desired end may be attained before it must come to that extremity. Oh, may He only help, in whatever way it may seem good to Him, that this scandal, occasioned by His own people, may become less and less, and that no longer the word, and with it the way of truth, may be evil spoken of through the fault of those who boast themselves here on earth that they are His, and that they are under the guidance of His grace.

Soon after these days of rest and refreshment in the cave of Adullam, we again meet with David in his wanderings in the midst of his faithful followers, who will no more depart from him. It did not escape him that new dangers and new wars were just before him, and therefore it became him, like a dutiful son, to place his aged father, above all others, in a place of safety from the approaching storms. But where could he go with him? He was separated by only a few hours' journey in a southerly direction from Moab, lying along the eastern coast of the Dead Sea, on the other side of Jordan—a land traversed by high mountain ranges and steep precipices, but also blessed with green valleys and fruitful plains. The Moabites were indeed a heathen nation, who worshiped the god Kamos or Baal-peor, and stood for the most part in an attitude of bitter hostility toward God's people. Yet they were related to the Israelites in their origin, inasmuch as they boasted of Lot, the nephew of Abraham, as their ancestor, on whose account they were spared at the time of the conquest of Canaan.

At a later period—indeed for a long time—this relation to Israel was of so friendly a character, that, during a famine which fell as a scourge from God upon the Holy Land, several families of the latter people had no hesitation in going to the Moabites for help. Among those who did so were Elimelech the Bethlehemite, and his wife Naomi—pious people, who, without doubt, like others of their kind, carried with them into that dark land, on the east of Jordan, the seeds of the divine word, and helped many of the inhabitants there to a knowledge of the true God. The two sons of Elimelech and Naomi had married daughters of the land, after they had renounced the service of idols and acknowledged the faith of Jehovah. One of these was the God-fearing, faithful Ruth, who afterward incorporated herself as, in spirit, a true daughter of Abraham, with the chosen race, and indeed with one of its most distinguished tribes; and at Bethlehem, whither she had accompanied her widowed mother-in-law when she returned to her native land, became the wife of Boaz, and the great-grandmother of our David.

Perhaps it was the case that David had still in Moab remote family relationships, and that yet here and there some of that spiritual seed was still growing green which the Israelite emigrants had left behind them. This will serve to explain the circumstance that, at a later time, we find a believing Moabite among the heroes and captains of David. There was, at the time when David set out for Moab, peace between the two nations, and therefore he believed that he might reckon most safely on a hospitable reception among that neighboring heathen people.

He was not deceived. As soon as he reached the land of Moab, he directed his steps straight to Mizpeh, the royal residence; and having been brought before the king, he respectfully presented to him the request, saying, "Let my father and my mother, I pray thee, come forth and be with you" (i.e., grant to them a hospitable residence in thy kingdom) "till I know what God will do for me." Far from concealing his faith in the presence of the heathen prince, he freely acknowledged himself to be a true servant of the God of Israel, to the intimations of whose mind he had at all times respect, and without whose will he entered on no undertaking. The king granted him his request, and promised him, both for his parents and for himself, protection and shelter. We see anew how sacred the rights of hospitality were regarded in the East. After he had provided for his parents in the meantime, David pitched his camp on a neighboring mountain height. It was a place fortified by nature, whence he was able to look far and wide upon the surrounding region; and here, conscious of the purity of his cause and of his intentions, he waited in trustful composure for the further directions of his God.

It happened that on a certain day he was surprised by the arrival of a highly welcome visitor. God had sent to him the prophet Gad. David, perhaps, at the first did not imagine all that he would afterward become to him. After this we shall frequently meet with him in his company under the title of "David's Seer." From first to last we will find him faithfully attached to him. Nothing more wished for could have happened to our fugitive than that this friend should have been associated with him, who, more experienced in the ways of the Lord than he, and perhaps also at the same time more intimately acquainted with the word of God, was always at hand to aid him both by word and deed.

Moreover, the Lord will never permit any prince who is heartily disposed to conduct the affairs of his government in His name, to be at any time altogether without some such Gad among his soldiers or officers around him—some man who, because he seeks not his own, unites the most incorruptible fidelity with his allegiance, and by whose mouth the Lord, as often as the foot of the prince is like to slip, will by his warnings and his counsel show to him the right and safe way. Woe to the land on the steps of whose throne there is not found, in the circle of dignified officers surrounding the ruler, at least one man who bears not only in his profession, but at the same time also in his entire consecrated personality, the stamp of a man of God, and who knows at the right time to throw the weight of the divine word and commandment into the balance-scales of the government!

The first message which was communicated to the prophet Gad for David was that he should, without delay, leave his place of refuge in Moab and return again to the land of Judah, into which the Philistines had anew made an incursion, and where they, even at that time, had encamped against the city of Keilah. Thus, again, David must go forth to war. David bowed to the divine command, and prepared without delay for the march. He secured for his beloved parents their place of refuge in that strange land; bade them farewell—ah, perhaps for the last time in this world!—thanked the king, as was his due, for the hospitable reception he had met with, and then departed thence, in the name of God, with his followers. His soul is not without anxious forebodings of the new troubles which awaited him, for Saul had not yet laid aside his hatred against hint, and he will be the less disposed to do this, should it please the Lord to grant new victories to him who was the object of his envy and his hatred.

It was probably at this time that Psalm 27 arose from David's heart. He expresses in it first his confidence in the Lord: "The Lord is my light and my salvation; whom shall I fear? the Lord is the strength of my life; of whom shall I be afraid?" Then he goes on to say, "Though an host should encamp against me, my heart shall not fear; though war should rise against me, in this will I be confident." After this declaration of his confidence, the singer gives expression to the wish that he might always enjoy the most intimate fellowship with God, and the blessing of the nearness of His grace. He is animated by the hope that the Lord would "hide him in His pavilion" (i.e., grant him protection); "in the time of trouble, and in the secret of His tabernacle hide him" (guard him faithfully); "and set him upon a rock."

Then the psalm proceeds in the language of fervent prayer: "Hear, O Lord, when I cry with my voice: have mercy also upon me, and answer me. When Thou saidst, Seek ye my face; my heart said unto Thee, Thy face, Lord, will I seek. Hide not Thy face far from me; put not Thy servant away in anger: Thou hast been my help; leave me not, neither forsake me, O God of my salvation. When my father and my mother forsake me then the Lord will take me up. Teach me Thy way, O Lord, and lead me in a plain path, because of mine enemies."

Then he concludes with the sigh: "Deliver me not over unto the will of mine enemies: for false witnesses are risen up against me, and such as breathe out cruelty," but at the same time, with the renewed expression of his confidence: "I had fainted, unless I had believed to see the goodness of the Lord in the land of the living. Wait on the Lord: be of good courage, and He shall strengthen thine heart: wait, I say, on the Lord!"

3. As soon as he had arrived in his own land, David first, according to the direction of Gad, pitched his camp in the forest of Hareth. But he had scarcely rested in this place with his followers, when the exciting news was brought to him that Saul was at Gibeah, sitting enthroned on a high place under a tamarisk tree; and that with the great men of his kingdom, and particularly those who were of his own

tribe, gathered around him, and having his spear, the symbol of his power, in his right hand, he had addressed to them the following words: "Hear now, ye Benjamites; will the son of Jesse" (i.e., if he becomes my successor, for the king had already an apprehension that such a thing might happen) "give every one of you fields and vineyards, and make you all captains of thousands, and captains of hundreds; that all of you have conspired against me, and there is none that showeth me that my son hath made a league with the son of Jesse; and there is none of you that is sorry for me, or showeth unto me that my son hath stirred up my servant against me, to lie in wait, as at this day?"

It was further told to David, how that, after Saul had given utterance to these words of sorrowful complaint, Doeg the Edomite stood up and reported to him what he had seen at Nob, when the son of Jesse came to Ahimelech the priest, for the purpose of asking him to inquire at the Lord for him, and how the priest had thereupon presented before him bread, and had given him the sword of Goliath. That, in consequence of this report, the king had immediately sent armed messengers that they might lay hold of Ahimelech and all his father's house, the priests that were in Nob, and bring them to him. The messenger also said that Saul then asked Ahimelech, the son of Ahitub, why he had entered into a conspiracy against him with the son of Jesse, in that he had given him bread and a sword, and had inquired of God for him—all this to incite the traitor to lie in wait against his king, as at this day.

Then Ahimelech had stood forth in behalf of David, and had said to the king, "Who is so faithful among all thy servants as David, which is the king's son-in-law, and goeth at thy bidding, and is honorable in thine house? Did I then begin to inquire of God of him? Be it far from me. Let not the king impute anything unto his servant, nor to all the house of my father: for thy servant knew nothing of all this" (viz. of rebellion and treason), "less or more." But that this apology by the priest had only the effect of pouring oil on the flame of the king's wrath, who replied to him with a voice of thunder, "Thou shalt surely die, Ahimelech, thou, and all thy father's house"; and that then he commanded his footmen that stood about him, saying, "Turn and slay the priests of the Lord; because their hand also is with David, and because they knew when he fled, and did not show it to me."

The messenger further told David that the footmen did not venture to lay their hands on the Lord's anointed, and that Saul then said to Doeg the Edomite, "Turn thou, and fall upon the priests." And that this venal stranger had showed himself willing, and had on that day slain with the sword "fourscore and five persons that did wear a linen ephod." And not only this: he had visited with the same fearful vengeance, Nob, the city of the priests, which was regarded and dealt with as a city doomed to destruction, together with every living thing within it, "both men and women, children and sucklings, and oxen, and asses, and sheep."

Such was the report that was brought to David. These heinous cruelties were indeed perpetrated. Let anyone think what Israel would have become under such tyranny, had not the Almighty in His mercy looked upon it, and at the right time terminated the terrible rule of the arbitrary, God-forsaken monarch. What wonder that the pious in Israel gathered about David, the longer the more numerously, and placed in him their whole hopes for the future of the kingdom! But to the honor of the people it must be said, that it never, even in a remote degree, came into the mind of anyone of them to raise the hand of rebellion against the furious despot. He was, and continued to be, "the anointed of God," so long as it pleased Him who sets up and dethrones kings. Surely there cannot be a greater misfortune for a people than to see themselves subjected to the iron scepter of a ruler who has thrown from him the restraints of the fear of the Lord, and, instead of obeying the divine word and command, prefers his own whim as the rule of his government. But where such a misfortune exists, a people in whom all faith is not yet dead see in it only a merited judgment from God, bow themselves under the mighty hand of God, and, praying and waiting, hope for the rising again of the sun of God's favor after the storm, and will never find themselves deceived in such a hope.

The priest Abiathar, Ahimelech's son, had escaped unhurt from the slaughter at Gibeah and Nob. It was he who had sought out David, and brought to him, in the forest of Hareth, the fearful tidings. One may conceive how this report would agitate the mind of David. "I knew it that day," we hear him say, "when Doeg the Edomite was there, that he would surely tell Saul," and with a deeply contrite heart adding, "I have occasioned the death of all the persons of thy father's house!" At the same time he entreated Abiathar that he would remain with him, because his presence would be comforting to him, and that there was no room for fear, for "he that seeketh," said he, "my life seeketh thy life"; that is, "only over my dead body will the hand of the enemy be able to touch thee; therefore remain."

And Abiathar remained. Oh, how faithful God is, who, after He had given Gad the prophet as a counselor to His servant, who had passed through great yet salutary trials, turned to him now also the heart of the priest, who was a confidential companion to him during his whole life, rendering to him the most essential service! Solomon says, "When a man's ways please the Lord He maketh even his enemies to be at peace with him." With equal truth he might also have said, "He will never want for faithful and trustworthy friends."

The state of mind into which David was brought by the tidings concerning the traitor Doeg, and Saul's murderous command, has found its expression in Psalm 52. An excellent expositor of this psalm has truly remarked, that "the tidings of such villainy could not but fill the mind of David with anxious and sorrowful thoughts. Against an enemy armed with the weapons of such wickedness as Saul, he believed that he was able to do nothing more. When he remembered the slaughter of the 85 priests, who were put to death as a warning to him of what might at some time happen to himself, he could not but despair of his own life." But David restrained himself, and in spirit addressing the king, he begins the psalm with the words, "Why boastest thou thyself in mischief, O mighty man? the goodness of God endureth continually. Thy tongue deviseth mischiefs; like a sharp razor, working deceitfully. Thou lovest evil more than good, and lying rather than to speak righteousness. God shall likewise destroy thee forever: He shall take thee away, and pluck thee out of thy dwelling-place, and root thee out of the land of the living. The righteous also shall see, and fear, and shall laugh at him: Lo, this is the man that made not God his strength; but trusted in the abundance of his riches, and strengthened himself in his wickedness." Not only does God glorify Himself in the destruction of His enemies, but also in the deliverance and protection which He graciously extends to His friends. Full of joyful confidence, the singer therefore continues, "But I am like a green olive-tree in the house of God: I trust in the mercy of God forever and ever." He closes his psalm with the utterance of praise: "I will praise Thee forever, because Thou hast done it: and I will wait on Thy name; for it is good before Thy saints." David sang this song for us for every similar situation in life in which we may be placed.

10

New Divine Interpositions

Thou'rt often in need of thy God,
  And askest each day for His care;
His blessings He richly bestows,
  He helps thee in answer to prayer;
He comes to thy house with His gifts,
  But, alas, He finds thee not there!—Tersteegen

How true are these words of the pious poet! Who that is given to prayer does not feel himself impressed by them? And who is there that does not at least sometimes pray? Even with the most unbelieving, when the waters of tribulation press in unto his soul, not seldom an involuntary "Lord God, have compassion on me, I pray Thee," forces itself to his lips. But as to such persons, so also it often enough happens even to the pious that, when the help they prayed for comes, they are so completely carried away by the natural joy on account of it, that they do not any longer remember their prayer, and in the help they receive they altogether overlook and mistake the gracious aid of the divine Hearer of prayer. Even a Job, of whom the honorable witness is borne that he was "a perfect and an upright man, and one that feared God and eschewed evil," finds himself forced to confess that he was not free from such an evil. "If I had called," says he, "and He had answered me; yet would I not believe that He had hearkened unto my voice."[1]

It was indeed true that that of which Job here complains was not so much a thoughtless disregard of the answer granted to him, as rather a false humility, in which he looked upon himself as too mean

---

1. Job 9:16.

for the God of gods to listen to his voice. When the Lord came at his
cry for help, he was "not at home" to receive Him with reverence, and
on bended knees to render to Him the thanks which were His due.
When the singer of Psalm 119 says, "Open mine eyes that I may
behold wondrous things out of Thy law," we may have occasion to
add to it for ourselves, "and that I may know the wonders of Thy
guidance and government." Our life is full of such wonders, even as
we now ourselves conceive of it. We do well, therefore, to take to
heart the counsel given to the Church in Laodicea, "Anoint thine
eyes with eye-salve, that thou mayest see."

With these words we come now again to consider the life of
David.

1 Samuel 23:14

And Saul sought him [i.e., David] every day; but God delivered him not
into his hand.

1 Samuel 24:4

Then David arose and cut off the skirt of Saul's robe privily.

We see our fugitive today threatened by new dangers: (1) at Keilah,
(2) in the wilderness of Ziph, and (3) in the wilderness of En-gedi. May
the contemplation of the scenes which we shall witness there contribute to the strengthening of our faith!

1. We left the son of Jesse with his band of men in the forest of
Hareth. There we again seek for him. But as we approach the wood
we hear the watchword: "On to Keilah!" The Philistines had fallen
upon this city of the tribe of Judah, lying on the borders of their land,
and plundered the granaries and barns, only lately filled with the
fruits of the harvest-field. Saul delayed to adopt measures of
defense against those hordes of robbers; and the loyal city seemed to
be about to fall an easy prey to them. What was therefore to be done?

This question pressed heavily on David's heart. He was one of the
king's field-generals. If he attacked the enemy, it would be under the
banner of the king, and for his king and fatherland. The king, however, had given him no command to do this. Dare he then cherish
the belief that he might now draw the sword notwithstanding, with
the approbation of God? That was not a matter to him altogether
clear. He longed, therefore, to obtain an infallible judgment as to the

path of duty. But how could he obtain it? Fortunately he had with him not only the prophet Gad, but also the high priest Abiathar— men faithful to the Lord, and enjoying fellowship with Him, and, next to the king, the most distinguished representatives of the theocracy. Since, then, the matter was one which in the highest degree concerned the kingdom of God, it seemed good to him to cause inquiry to be made of the Lord by means of the "Urim and Thummim" (the "Licht und Recht," i.e., Light and Right, according to Luther's interpretation).

Investigation has been made with great care and industry into the peculiar nature of the mysterious means by which revelations were thus communicated, and of the form and manner in which they were made, but as yet without any very satisfactory results. The Urim and Thummim was not, as many suppose, the breastplate itself of the priest, with its twelve precious stones, but a something which was concealed in a pouch formed by the folds of the breastplate. But what that was, whether the name Jehovah, or a sacred emblem giving assurance of God's presence, as the ark of the covenant and the two cherubim above it did in the temple, or something else—who can decide? But Israel, who was not yet able to pray, as we can, in the name of Jesus, needed for the strengthening of their faith the outward proof that God, the exalted One, regards the voice of poor sinners and such a purpose was served by the divinely appointed mediation of the priesthood, and, in particular, by that mysterious treasure laid up by God Himself in the Urim and Thummim, as a visible pledge to the high priest of the gracious nearness of God.

When the high priest arrayed himself in his robes of office, and along with these put on the Urim and Thummim, by virtue of such an act he silently confessed himself anew to the God of Abraham, Isaac, and Jacob, as the representative of all the people, and thereby testified at the same time his confidence in His gracious condescension toward sinners. And God confirmed this his confidence when He revealed Himself to him by an inward message of His Spirit, as a proof to the whole congregation that He was near at hand, and would grant an audience whenever the honor which was His due was with uprightness rendered to Him.

But the divine communications were not given only by means of the Urim and Thummim. How frequently did the Lord reveal Himself to David in answer to prayer, and without any priestly intervention? But, at the same time, the presence of the divine promise, embodying itself, as it were, in that sacred emblem, conduced always to the essential strengthening of the faith of those who sought for counsel from on high and this end it accomplished at that time, when, in the matter of Keilah, a decision of weighty consequence for David needed to be made. It was not a little to his comfort, therefore, to know that he had with him in his camp, and among his followers, the anointed of the Lord, together with that holy thing, giving assurance of the willingness of Jehovah to grant the wished-for counsel.

To David's inquiry, made through the priest, at the Lord of hosts, "Shall I go and smite these Philistines?" the divine answer was returned, "Go and smite the Philistines, and save Keilah." Thus he was certain of his cause, and felt himself perfectly at rest regarding the path of duty. He had now received the word of command from the mouth of Him who is infinitely higher than the human vicegerent on an earthly throne. But will the men also, his friends, be now willing to follow him? For a moment we see they hesitate. "Behold," said they, "we be afraid here in Judah: how much more then if we come to Keilah against the armies of the Philistines?" But David again inquired at the Lord in the presence of them all, and the answer, decided and unambiguous, was given anew by the mouth of Abiathar, "Arise, go down to Keilah; for I will deliver the Philistines into thine hand." All fears among his companions are now put to flight.

The march is begun. Without meeting with opposition, they at length reach the suburbs of Keilah. But here suddenly the enemy present themselves in full array against them. A fierce and bloody battle is fought. The Philistines, who without doubt overestimated the number of their assailants, were slain in flight, were stripped of their herds of cattle and other stores, and all that remained were driven across the neighboring boundary of their territory. Thus Keilah was saved and set free. After the Lord had thus given to His servant David, in this triumph, a new pledge of His divine kindness and grace, David's little host appeared highly encouraged, and within a short time was increased to a band of 200 valiant men of Israel.

David intended to remain now for some time in the town he had just recovered from the enemy, because he thought he might regard himself as so much the safer, the greater the claims which he had earned for himself on the gratitude of the inhabitants. Now once more there was an interval of peace in his storm-tossed life. He felt himself happy in Keilah, especially after Abiathar, the high priest, had followed him there with the ephod, the holy garment. But that rest was only of a short duration. Soon new dangers threatened him. But let us not be too much astonished that the Lord hung over "the man according to His own heart" so heavy a calamity, and allowed him to pass from one danger into another. This was the school for the future king; the Lord thereby gained room to mark him out, by means of continually renewed helps of a wonderful kind, always more distinctly as the man of His choice, and already to incline the hearts of the people to their future ruler.

But what new danger was it that threatened David? Saul received information of the glorious victory which the young hero had once more gained over the old enemy of Israel at Keilah. But these tidings were so little fitted to render the king more gentle toward the conqueror, that they rather gave new nourishment to the demoniacal flame of anger in the heart of the jealous and passionate monarch. "God the Lord has now delivered the traitor," cried he, "unto mine hands. He is shut in, by entering into a town that hath gates and bars." Thus he spoke, and without delay gave the command to his host: "Up now, let us go to fight against Keilah! Besiege and burn the town, and spare not mine enemy nor his companions!"

David heard what was in progress against him. But what could he do? Here it was well for him again to ask the Lord. Abithar must come to him once more in priestly attire with the Urim and Thummim. He appears, and David is the first to speak. "O Lord God of Israel," he cried out, "Thy servant hath certainly heard that Saul seeketh to come to Keilah, to destroy the city for my sake. Will the men of Keilah deliver me up into his hand? will Saul come down, as Thy servant hath heard? O Lord God of Israel, I beseech Thee, tell Thy servant!" Thus David. And what was the answer of the Lord? It was given by the mouth of Abiathar: "He will come down!" David asked a second time: "Will the men of Keilah deliver me and my men into the hand of Saul?" The answer of God was returned: "They will deliver thee up." Such an evil is in their hearts. Therefore David knew that it was time for flight.

"Again to flight?" Yet what else could he do? Must David place himself with armed force against his king and lord? No! His whole soul rose up against bringing dishonor on his cause by such an act.

But how came it about that even the citizens of Keilah, whom he had saved from destruction, offered him no protection? Perhaps they, unthankful, saw in him now only the rebel against Saul, their liege-lord, of whose vengeance they stood in fear; or their conduct toward their deliverer arose from a mistaken patriotism.

So David with his 600 men departed. "They went," says the history, "whithersoever they could go"; that is, hither and thither, unconscious of any definite object. They went first to an extensive lonely desert, intersected by deep ravines and rugged precipices. The origin of Psalm 31 is to be traced to this period of wandering, although there is nothing contained in the title of it which authorizes this supposition. We meet, however, with many passages in the psalm which quite correspond with the circumstances in which David was then placed.

The singer begins with the humble but confiding prayer that God would never let him be put to shame (he was so at that time, when the citizens of Keilah would no longer allow him to dwell amongst them), but that He would deliver him (the guiltless outlaw) in His righteousness. He prays that the Lord would bow down His ear to him, and deliver him speedily, and be a strong rock to him, and a protecting fortress. The imagery here is plainly suggested by the wild scenes of nature which surround the singer. He prays that, for His name's sake, the Lord would lead him and graciously be near him in the pathless and inhospitable wilderness, and that He would guard his feet from the net which they had laid on all sides to catch him.

"Into Thine hand," he continues, "I commit my spirit: Thou hast redeemed me, O Lord God of truth," namely, from the violence to which they would surrender me. Moreover, David speaks of himself as one who was forsaken by all the world, and was covered with unmerited reproaches and slanders. He was even guilty of high treason, and had placed himself in opposition to the greatest part of the people, because he was the object of the king's displeasure. Yet he is far from speaking of himself as free from all guilt. He feels himself as a poor sinner before God, and, with a sigh, gives utterance to the prayer, "Have mercy upon me, O Lord." Nevertheless he trusts in His mercy whom he confidently calls His God; and, after giving praise to the Lord for all the wonderful goodness and the help which He had hitherto vouchsafed to him "in his flight," he concludes with this call to his brethren in the faith: "O love the Lord, all ye His saints: for the Lord preserveth the faithful, and plentifully rewardeth the proud doer. Be of good courage, and He shall strengthen your heart, all ye that hope in the Lord."

The singer was not always clearly conscious, as he was in this instance, that he composed his songs not only for the relief of his own heart, but also at the same time for the use of his companions in the faith in the worship of their God. In his songs he often gave expression, following an inner impulse, only to his own personal experiences, and had no one but God and himself in view. But in the process of composing these psalms, the Spirit of God was also putting forth creative energy, in so far as He gave, unobserved, to these spontaneous effusions of the singer's heart, a shape and direction, as to their form and their contents, which marked them out as at the same time Church-songs for the congregations of the faithful for all ages. On this view rest the apostolic injunctions, such as that of St. James, "Is any one merry? let him sing psalms"; and that of St. Paul, "Teach and admonish one another with psalms and hymns."[2]

2. At the news of David's flight, Saul naturally abandoned his undertaking against Keilah, but by no means did he desist from following after the hated fugitive, who was now tarrying in the mountainous wilderness of Ziph, in the tribe of Judah, not far from a town of the same name, and eight miles southeast from Hebron. Without any plan, and apparently by accident, he was directed thither; but he knew at a later time that it was God the Lord who here, as always, guided him, and directed his going even without the pillar of cloud and of fire.

In the desert of Ziph, after all the heart-sorrow which had hitherto fallen upon him, a refreshing surprise awaits him. Before he was aware of it—scarcely dare he trust his eyes—his beloved friend Jonathan stood before him. He had secretly stolen away from the king's host and who may describe the emotion and the pleasure with which both of them praised the Lord, who had so unexpectedly brought them together again! This trusted companion appeared to David almost like a comforting angel, at a moment when, after the occurrence at Keilah, he felt himself forsaken and rejected by all the world. "Jonathan," we are told, "strengthened his hands in God" (i.e.,

---

2. Colossions 3:16.

quickened and animated his faith, undoubtedly by a reference to the
gracious guidance of the Lord with which he had hitherto been
favored). He said to him, moreover, in a prophetic spirit, with great
precision, "Fear not: for the hand of Saul my father shall not find
thee; and thou shalt be king over Israel, and I shall be next unto
thee; and that also Saul my father knoweth." Thus it was now spoken out without reserve: "Thou art the heir to the throne of Israel."

Jonathan bowed himself to the determination of God—gave God
the honor—and was submissive. Where in the history of the world do
we meet with such an example of purest self-denial, and of most
cheerful subjection to the divine will? David now sees the last seal
unloosed from the secret of his anointing by Samuel. "Let it happen
to me according to the will of God," he says in genuine modesty, and
places his cause wholly in the hands of Him to whose guidance he
had hitherto unreservedly committed himself. The two renew
their heart-covenant "before the Lord," and then, deeply moved,
reach to each other the hand of farewell—ah, from this world forever!
But the image of this friendly pair sends out its inextinguishable rays
as a faithful ideal of hallowed, manly friendship in God, flaming forth
to the quickening of the Church.

Scarcely had Jonathan, who had departed from the side of his
royal father without his knowledge, entered upon his journey back
again, when David, yet deeply moved by the surprising meeting with
his dear friend, and the significant conversation which he had
enjoyed with him, received the sorrowful information that he was
betrayed by the Ziphites also. Probably from fear lest, if they
granted a hospitable refuge to the fugitive, a similar fate might await
them to that which had fallen upon the inhabitants of Nob, they had
sent messengers to Saul at Gibeah to say to him, "Knowest thou not
that David is concealed with us in strongholds in the hill Hachilah,
which lies on the south of Jeshimon? Now therefore, O king, come
down, according to all the desire of thy soul to come down; and our
part shall be to deliver him into the king's hand." And Saul replied
to the wretched men with a show of piety, "Blessed be ye of the Lord;
for ye have compassion on me"; and then sent them away with the
charge that they should inquire yet more particularly in what direction the traitor had set out, and bring him word again; and that then
he would follow them immediately, and on his part would "search
him out throughout all the thousands" (i.e., among all those divisions

of the tribe, each of which counted a thousand heads). It was at once done as he said.

As soon as David heard of the march of the royal forces toward his hiding-place, he fled with his men to the wilderness of Maon. Saul followed after him. Danger increased upon the fugitives from moment to moment, and seemed to be unavoidable. A chain of hills divided the two camps from each other. Saul purposed thereupon with his mighty host to surround the little band of his son-in-law, and to seize it unexpectedly in the rear. David appeared to be indeed lost. Suddenly a swift messenger comes running up to Saul and brings the news, "Haste thee and come; for the Philistines have invaded the land." A fear of God fell upon the king's host. Saul instantly abandoned further pursuit of David, and went with his cavalry to meet the Philistines. David was saved indeed at the last hour. But ever does the Lord give proof even in such an hour to those who put their trust in Him, that His word, "I will never leave thee nor forsake thee," is yea and amen! The place where this fortunate turn in David's situation happened has since been called "Sela-hammahlekoth" (i.e., the rock of escape). Where shall we find a friend of God in whose life-course there is not more than one place worthy of this name?

At the time when David received tidings that the Ziphites had betrayed him, his soul poured itself forth in Psalm 54. Here he first directs his eye from the earth, where faithlessness and wickedness surrounded him, upward to heaven, and prays to God that He would save and judge him (i.e., justify him), since the people of his own tribe had risen up against him as enemies, yea, like the heathen. But not less does he give utterance to his confidence that the Lord would be his helper and would uphold his soul, and that the wickedness of his enemies would recoil upon themselves. "Cut them off in Thy truth," he cries out; adding, "I will freely sacrifice unto Thee; I will praise Thy name, O Lord, for it is good"; and concludes with the words of joyful confidence, "For He hath delivered me out of all trouble; and mine eye hath seen His desire upon mine enemies." We have already been witnesses how this confidence did not deceive him, and it shall yet be further seen.

3. The repose which was granted to David after the departure of Saul did not continue long. For scarcely had Saul victoriously driven the Philistines over the frontiers, when he again put his army in motion against the poor hunted one. He had meanwhile withdrawn

into the extreme south of the tribe, into the wilderness of En-gedi, bordering on the Dead Sea, which also afforded in its rocky cliffs and spacious caverns excellent hiding-places for whole hosts. Once more Saul received, by means of his spies, tidings regarding David's place of refuge, and marched after him with a host of 3,000 men, gathered from all Israel. In every lurking-place he sought the fugitive, and directed men to climb the loftiest crags, the abodes of the chamois and the wild-goat, to see whether his anguish had driven him thither. But all this trouble was in vain.

When now the day began to decline, the king, who was wearied with the marchings, was glad to lay himself down for a short rest in the valley, at the "sheep-cotes by the way." At the entrance of a cave, covered with his mantle, he stretched himself out and fell asleep. And lo! it was this very labyrinthine cavern in the inner recesses of which David also and his men had found refuge. What a situation that in which he then saw himself suddenly placed! Some of his men soon recognized the sleeping one on the threshold of their hiding place, and with gentle steps approaching their leader, whispered to him, "In the entrance lies the king fast asleep. Behold, the day of which the Lord said unto thee, Behold, I will deliver thine enemy into thine hand, that thou mayest do to him as it shall seem good unto thee." And certainly it had the appearance as if they spoke the truth.

The temptation for David was great. A stroke of the sword, and he would have delivered himself from his deadly foe. But all that was within him shuddered at this thought. "The Lord forbid," replied he to his unasked advisers, "that I should do this thing unto my master, the Lord's anointed, to stretch forth mine hand against him, seeing he is the anointed of the Lord"; and, while he said this, he ordered with earnest words the men to withdraw from the neighborhood of the slumbering one, back into the darkness of their hiding-place, and threatened them with the heaviest punishments if they ventured to lay hands on the king. But one thing he did not refrain from. Saul must at length, once for all, in an unmistakable way, be convinced that his servant David bore no evil against him in his heart. Therefore with gentle step he approached him and cut off a corner from his royal mantle. But very probably he did this with beating heart and trembling hand. He might, perhaps, already repent of it the moment after it was done. He probably deemed it like an act of high treason—so deeply rooted in the hearts of the Israelites was the idea of their king and lord as the representative of God upon earth! In addition to that, Saul was David's father-in-law—father of his wife.

The king awoke. Without being aware of what had happened, he rose up to return to his soldiers. Then David, notwithstanding the danger which might threaten him, hastened after the king, and cried out, "My lord the king!" Saul turned round, and how great was his astonishment to see the object of his hatred before him! But David stooped with his face to the earth, and bowed himself (i.e., did homage to his sovereign), and said, "Wherefore hearest thou men's words, saying, Behold, David seeketh thy hurt? Behold, this day thine eyes have seen how that the Lord had delivered thee into mine hand in the cave: and some bade me kill thee; but mine eye spared thee: and I said, I will not put forth mine hand against my lord for he is the Lord's anointed. Moreover, my father"—thus he continued in a tone of greatest tenderness—"see; yea, see the skirt of thy robe in my hand: for in that I cut off the skirt of thy robe, and killed thee not, know thou and see that there is neither evil nor transgression in mine hand, and I have not sinned against thee; yet thou huntest my soul to take it. The Lord judge between me and thee, and the Lord avenge me of thee; but mine hand shall not be upon thee. As saith the proverb of the ancients, Wickedness proceedeth from the wicked" (meaning the same thing as the New Testament proverb, "A tree is known by its fruits"); so (this is the meaning of his language) mayest thou certainly discover, in that I have not laid hands upon thee, who I am and how I stand affected toward thee. "After whom art thou come out," thus he concludes, "O king of Israel? after whom dost thou pursue? after a dead dog, after a flea? The Lord therefore be Judge, and judge between me and thee, and see, and plead my cause and deliver me out of thine hand."

Thus David spoke with perfect candor, and with deepest, unfeigned humility of heart. It was not with fawning self-degradation that he called himself a "dead dog," yea, "a flea." He meant thereby only to say that he, the outlaw, was nothing higher in the presence of all the world, and that his power, when compared with that of the king, was nothing at all.

After David had thus spoken, Saul replied, not without visible mental emotion: "Is this thy voice, my son David?" With so tender a name he had not for a long time named him. Then he continued, and indeed—we are astonished—moved to tears: "Thou art more righteous than I: for thou hast rewarded me good, whereas I have rewarded thee evil. And thou hast showed this day how that thou hast dealt well with me: forasmuch as when the Lord had delivered me into thine hand, thou killest me not. For if a man find an enemy, will he let him go well away? Wherefore the Lord reward thee good for that thou hast done unto me this day."

We interrupt the king for a moment, and give expression to our surprise to meet the sullen, wrathful man all at once in such a mood. Perhaps the selfish joy that he had been safely delivered from the danger of death which hovered over his head, had not a little share in his emotion. Perhaps, also, if all human feeling was not dead within him, he may have been deeply impressed at a display of forbearance so magnanimous as that which David had extended to him. But that we hear him confessing, "Thou art more righteous than I: for thou hast rewarded me good, whereas I have rewarded thee evil"; and that we see the hard and heartless tyrant become gentle, even to tears—this surprises us, and permits us to hope that there might yet come about a moral revolution within him. Without doubt he experienced, in the better feelings which at that moment prevailed within him again, once more a powerful visitation of divine grace.

But did he recognize it as such? And does the history inform us that he was now conscious of his godless life; that, in the presence of God, he pronounced sentence of death against himself; that he sought grace and pardon from the Lord; and that he called upon Him for strength to sanctification? We read nothing of all this. He might think that, by his open confession, he had already given satisfaction to God and men, and had furnished sufficient evidence of humility and condescension. But did we not see him arrested and deeply moved?

Truly he was not by any means destitute of every better feeling. We have already several times been witnesses of that. But it always became easier for him quickly again to smother nobler impressions. Even among persons of the most objectionable character, there is not seldom found an easily excited susceptibility of feeling, as often as anything evidently good and noble anywhere in life presents itself to their view. Even poetical effusions in praise of virtue, which they listen to as spoken from the stage, perhaps make them melt in tears; while at the same time, on returning home, they act like tyrants toward their wives and children, and show themselves capable of every wicked action.

We are able, therefore, to attribute scarcely any moral worth to the gentleness which we observe in King Saul at this scene at En-gedi. Soon enough he will be thoroughly ashamed of his humiliation before David, into which he allowed himself for the moment to be betrayed, as also of all the evils of which he owned himself guilty toward him. He had betrayed a weakness in his presence, and how will poor David be made to atone for that!

Let us hear him, however, further: "Behold, I know well that thou shalt surely be king, and that the kingdom of Israel shall be established in thine hand" (i.e., shall remain with thee and thy house). Evidently he spoke this in remembrance of the judicial announcement which Samuel once communicated to him, in accordance with the revelation he had received from God, in these words: "Thou hast done foolishly, thou hast not kept the commandment of the Lord thy God which He commanded thee. Now thy kingdom shall not continue: the Lord hath sought a man after His own heart. And the Lord hath commanded him to be captain over His people!" The self-control with which the king here in his own person opens up to his hated rival the dark secret of his soul, fills us with greater amazement than all which preceded it. The certainty of his fate, and care for his future, may have for a moment overpowered him. "Swear now therefore unto me by the Lord," he continued, "that thou wilt not cut off my seed after me, and that thou wilt not destroy my name out of my father's house!" It is difficult for us to restrain our feelings at this sorrowful request of the king of Israel. This would indeed be more difficult for David himself. With perfect rectitude he gave the oath asked for by Saul, and after this was done the two separate silently from each other.

Saul returned with his army to the land of Benjamin; David, on the other hand, went forward with his men to camp for a while in the mountain region of En-gedi. The king permitted him to do this so much the more readily, because he knew that with his band he stood as an advanced post against the hostile border tribes. David, however, wavered not for a moment in his judgment of the value of the renewed friendship of his royal master, but regarded it as advisable to wait for evidences of its genuineness in one of the rocky strongholds of the wilderness, rather than in the neighborhood of the royal throne.

Psalm 57 unveils to us the exercises of David's heart during his sojourn in the cave of the wilderness of En-gedi, before the scene with Saul. To that psalm, with several others belonging to the time of Saul, he has affixed as a motto the words borrowed from the fifth book of Moses: "Destroy not" (namely, Thy people and Thine inheritance).[3] While Saul raged about and was furious, David prayed in his dark asylum, "Be merciful unto me, O God, be merciful unto me: for my soul trusteth in Thee: yea, in the shadow of Thy wings will I make my refuge, until these calamities be overpast. I will cry unto God Most High; unto God that performeth all things for me. He shall send from heaven, and save me from the reproach of him that would swallow me up. God shall send forth His mercy and His truth."

The singer is fully conscious of the critical situation in which he now finds himself. This is manifest from the words which follow: "My soul is among lions; and I lie even among them that are set on fire, even the sons of men, whose teeth are spears and arrows, and their tongue a sharp sword." In these words he thought not so much on Saul and his horsemen, as rather on the courtiers and flatterers who surrounded the king, who, by their calumnious suspicions, continually stirred up the fire in the breast of Saul against him. But David confidently waited upon his God; and receiving anew, by the communication of the Spirit in his soul, the assurance of a gracious answer, he exclaims: "Be Thou exalted, O God, above the heavens; let Thy glory be above all the earth!"

He triumphs as if he had already experienced complete deliverance: "They have prepared a net for my steps; my soul is bowed down: they have digged a pit before me, into the midst whereof they are fallen themselves." And his soul becomes continually clearer within him: "My heart is fixed, O God, my heart is fixed; I will sing and give praise. Awake up, my glory; awake, psaltery and harp: I myself will awake early!" And wider and clearer becomes his vision into the distant future: "I will praise Thee, O Lord, among the people; I will sing unto Thee among the nations: for Thy mercy is great unto the heavens, and Thy truth unto the clouds!" After this he closes, as he had begun, his triumphal song of salvation: "Be Thou exalted, O God, above the heavens: let Thy glory be above all the earth."

---

3. Deuteronomy 9:26.

11

Abigail

In the life of David we shall today meet with a dark image, over against which we are able to place for our comfort an image of light. This is Christian marriage, as the apostle describes it to us in his Epistle to the Ephesians 5:23–26. "The husband," says he, "is the head of the wife, even as Christ is the head of the Church; and He is the savior of the body. Therefore, as the Church is subject unto Christ, so let the wives be to their own husbands in everything. Husbands, love your wives, even as Christ also loved the Church, and gave Himself for it; that He might sanctify and cleanse it with the washing of water by the word."

On earth there is no bond closer than the marriage bond which unites husband and wife. Here, as the Scripture says, "two are one"; and of all the reciprocal influences of the spirits of men on each other, none can, for strength and endurance, be compared to that which arises out of the marriage union. As the married are able, if the marriage is a Christian one (i.e., rooted in the love of Christ), to contribute to the improvement and sanctification of each other, so, in the opposite case, they can accelerate the pace of each other's ruin.

As the indispensable condition of a truly Christian marriage, there is a threefold living consciousness which must animate those who are bound together. They must feel, first of all, that in the mutual sympathy and love which they cherish toward each other, a higher will has directed them, so that to them the words of the Lord are applicable, "What God hath joined together, let not man put asunder"; secondly, that they are called of God, supporting, helping, and bearing with each other, to journey as pilgrims, hand in hand, to the heavenly home; thirdly, that it is incumbent on them, before all

137

other things, in order that they may not miss their aim, to give themselves from the heart, with the well-known watchword of Joshua, to the service of the Lord, and to regulate their own wills at all times in subjection to His holy will.

The language of the apostle shows to us the true marriage in its highest aspect, when he likens it to a relation which, in depth and intimacy, comes short only of that which exists between the Eternal Son and the heavenly Father: "The husband is the head of the wife, even as Christ is the head of the Church." This shows the dignity of the husband, but at the same time also the weight of his responsibility. Made happy in the possession of one confided to him by the hand of God, and thankful for the blessing which, through her, is bestowed upon him, he is the faithful leader, the loving helper, the stay and the protection of the wife; while she, although looking up to him as her lord, yet also, as the weaker vessel, cleaves to him as her support, and finds her joy in walking by his side as his helper. With tender tact she advises him, smoothes lovingly the furrows of care upon his brow, strives to sweeten to him the burden of his calling; in days of sickness, with that thorough self-sacrificing willingness, which is more frequently to be found among Christian women than among men, gives herself up to her duty and everywhere, as an active, careful stewardess, knows how to brighten his home till it becomes to him the loveliest spot on earth.

Both, devout and contented with the lot in which God has placed them, exercising patience and forbearance toward each other, because they themselves stand daily in need of, and rejoice in, the same from above; yet when the duty of reciprocal furtherance in holiness demands it, departing not from the severity of truth—for Christian love is no less severe than it is tender—both, I say, discharge in their respective callings and circles, freely and joyfully as unto the Lord, their daily duties. As regards the good things of this life, they are conversant both with want and resignation, yet they feel themselves more than abundantly indemnified for all their temporal wants by the happy consciousness of their heavenly riches.

Thus their house stands, without any ostentatious display of religion, a place of peace in the midst of this valley of tears, like a "tabernacle of God among the children of men"; for in it that love dwells and rules which, because melted into one with love to God, never decays nor grows old. Whoever crosses the hospitable threshold of such a house will never depart without silently blessing it, and yet this house makes no pretensions to present anything special. It is like the dwelling of Daniel in Babylon, which had a secret little window that looked out toward Canaan and the holy city, and through which also there streamed in a ray of light from the everlasting hills. It is true that paradise has disappeared from this earth; but if one may speak of its outer court as anywhere to be found here below, then it must be there, where, as Paul Gerhard sings:

> Husband and wife walk hand in hand,
> Or steadfastly together stand
> In bonds of pure fidelity.

Perhaps the married life never, on this side of eternity, wholly corresponds to its holy prototype. When two frail creatures, daily needing pardoning grace, dwell with each other, the holy relation will not be altogether secured against every darkening cloud. But whatever evil may threaten, it will soon pass away in answer to prayer, and that word of the Song of Solomon be there verified, "Love is strong as death. Many waters cannot quench love, neither can the floods drown it."

In the glory to which Christ was the first to elevate it, marriage was not known even to the most pious under the Old Covenant. We find today opportunity to bear witness to this, as we accompany the son of Jesse further on his life-course.

1 Samuel 25:28, 39

> (Abigail said unto David) The Lord will certainly make my lord a sure house; because my lord fighteth the battles of the Lord, and evil hath not been found in thee all thy days. . . . And David sent and communed with Abigail, to take her to him to wife.

David (1) falls into a new and severe temptation; yet (2) through the grace of God he is once more gloriously helped out of it. These are the two facts in his history which now claim our attention. Let us examine them particularly.

1. We have arrived at the year 1026 before the birth of Christ. A great man in Israel has just disappeared—a man of the highest influence among all the people, and equally beloved and esteemed and venerated. Samuel has closed his eyes upon this world. After he had,

by the change of Israel into a kingdom, been released from the responsibilities of a judge, he still maintained the cause and honor of Jehovah in his fatherland as a prophet and priest. A year ago or more, the Lord had permitted him to withdraw from the sphere of public life, and to enjoy the evening of his days amid the peaceful quietness of the colony of beloved brethren which he had established at Ramah. Elsewhere he was but seldom seen. Nevertheless it was a consolation to thousands that he still at least remained among the living. It was as if a mild beneficent light streamed forth from that noble star over the whole of Israel, so long as he yet, even though behind a veil of clouds, shone in the sky of the Holy Land. That star in Israel was now quenched. In the seventieth year of his age, he calmly departed amid the circle of his beloved disciples, "the sons of the prophets" pouring forth their hearts in thank-offerings and in prayers to God. Weeping sore for their loss, his young friends at Ramah laid him in his grave. Very many felt themselves, in the then disordered condition of the kingdom, as if made orphans by his death, and among these David was not the last.

As our Lord once, after the tidings of the departure of His fore-runner and friend John had been brought to Him, withdrew in silence into a lonely desert, so David also, when the sorrowful news from Ramah reached him, withdrew with his followers into the quiet uninhabited desert of Paran, which at the present day is called El-Tyh. There, according to the report of a recent traveler, the view stretches out on all sides over a mournful wilderness, in which not a single tree nor bush nor green blade of grass refreshes the eye, and where only here and there a streak of white chalk-cliffs shimmers through the monotonous gray of the steppes and the barren hills. Here he found leisure to mourn over the death of that most excellent man of his time, and thankfully to recall to mind the greatness of the blessings which he had brought upon Israel. The time granted him for this purpose was, however, short. He soon saw himself summoned back again to the scene of war, and this time against an enemy for whose overthrow he needed other weapons than those of steel and iron. David fell into a sore temptation. It was the prince of this world who dug for him a new ditch.

On the extreme limits of the wilderness of Paran, in a south-easterly direction from Hebron, lay, in a hilly pastoral region, a little hamlet named Carmel. It is now called Kurmul, where, in the waterpools hewn out of the rock, and in the moss-covered heap of rubbish, we have evidences of a civilization of ancient times. Here at that time lived a wealthy husbandman and prince of flocks, named Nabal, a descendant of the old distinguished family of Caleb. Three thousand sheep fed on his pastures, and he had a thousand goats on the surrounding mountains. His servants were a great number, and he himself was as a king in his dealings. Often did David meet on his excursions with the shepherds of this man, and he had maintained good friendship with them. As he now needed in the barren desert all manner of provisions for his men, and as he could no longer reckon on its being available from friendly circles, he considered whether Nabal might not be inclined to share his abundance with his kinsmen. To this end he sent ten young men to him with a friendly salutation, and directed them to say to him in his name, "Peace be both to thee, and peace be to thine house, and peace be unto all that thou hast. And now I have heard that thou hast shearers: now, thy shepherds which were with us, we hurt them not, neither was there ought missing unto them, all the while they were in Carmel. Ask thy young men, and they will show thee. Wherefore let the young men find favor in thine eyes: (for we come in a good day)," (it was the day of sheep-shearing, which was in Israel wont to be kept as a day of joy with a feast and a banquet): "give, I pray thee, whatsoever cometh to thine hand unto thy servants, and to thy son David."

The messengers depart without delay, and at length reach Carmel, and address to Nabal the words that had been given to them. But how bitterly were they disappointed in their expectations! Nabal, "a man churlish, and evil in his doings," as the narrative describes him, did not comply even so much as to return thanks for the friendly salutation which had been brought to him, but angrily and with a stern countenance said to the messengers, "Who is David? and who is the son of Jesse? There be many servants now-a-days that break away every man from his master. Shall I then take my bread, and my water, and my flesh that I have killed for my shearers, and give it unto men whom I know not whence they be?"

This example of rudely violated hospitality stands almost alone in Israel. In the haughtiness with which Nabal treated David's messengers, may not, however, some spark of attachment to the king have had its influence? Possibly so. But David ought not to have condescended to the flattery in which he calls himself "Nabal's son," and his armed followers "Nabal's servants"; and as little did it become him to reckon it as a particular virtue in himself and his men, that they had not insulted nor robbed nor injured his peaceful shepherds. The scornful reply of Nabal was not therefore unmerited. Enough: the young men returned ashamed, with empty hands, to their leader, and announced to him how unsuccessful they had been.

How did David now receive their report? Did he humble himself and commend his cause to God the Lord? On the contrary, we meet him now, for the first time, not master of his own spirit, but hurried along by his natural passion. With a flaming anger, in which, perhaps, as in that under the influence of which Moses once slew the Egyptian, a feeling prophetic of his future dignity may have formed a part, he gave his men the order of the day, "Gird ye on every man his sword!" And when this was done, and he also had girded on his, namely, the sword of Goliath, which the Lord had given into his hand as the spoil of victory, and which, therefore, had become worthy of a more honorable campaign, glowing with a spirit of revenge, he led his band of 400 armed men to the little town of Carmel, while he left 200 behind "by the stuff."

Thus he stands before us, about to break the peace of the land, to seize on the possessions of strangers, and to stain himself with the blood of peaceful citizens, yea, of his own kinsmen. Surely he had not this time either prayed or inquired at the Lord by the "Urim and Thummim." If he had carried out what his anger suggested to him— and it was not his fault if the intention was never executed—he would have given the deathblow to his own honor and to his cause. Then he would have appeared before God and all the world as an outlaw—a man over whom not only his enemies would have triumphed, but who must also be given up by his friends as unworthy of the crown of Israel, and to whom nothing else would have remained but, as a fugitive, with the mark of Cain on his brow, to beg for protection within the limits of some heathen land.

What a precipice this to which we here see him rushing forward! We tremble for him whose whole future is now at stake. But He will indeed graciously interpose, who always means it infinitely better to His people than they do to themselves, and who has promised His beloved not only deliverance from the dangers which men prepare for them, but also from such as might arise to them out of the temptations of the powers of darkness and the allurements of their own

sinful nature. If David formed his resolution, so also the Lord formed
His concerning him. We perceive, to our joy and comfort, what a surprising turn the affair now takes.

2. Nabal's wife was Abigail. The history calls her "a woman of a
good understanding, and of a beautiful countenance." That the first
of these qualities belonged to her, she has given evidence. She was
also a woman who feared God. When David had already begun his
march toward Carmel, one of her servants came to Abigail and told
her what had happened, namely, that the son of Jesse had sent messengers out of the wilderness to convey friendly salutations to Nabal
her husband; but that he had answered these men, who had
entreated him for food, as if they had been enemies, although they
had been good friends to his shepherds in the remote regions of the
wilderness, and had even served them as a wall of defense against the
threatening bands of robbers from the countries of the heathen.
"Now therefore know," continued this servant, "and consider what
thou wilt do; for evil is determined against our master and against all
his household: for he is such a son of Belial that a man cannot speak
to him." Thus the young man spoke. Who recognizes not in his mission the hand of that God who directs all things?

After Abigail had listened calmly to the communications of her
servant, she—the quiet and considerate housewife—very speedily discovered the course that must now be adopted. Solomon says, "Every
wise woman buildeth her house: but the foolish plucketh it down
with her hands." Who will deny that there never have been wanting
seals confirming this proverb? Seldom will a man be able to pull
down so much as a pious intelligent wife does not build up again with
ready hand. As a rule, it is the wife who puts her stamp upon the
house, and not the man; and where there are children, in most cases
they imitate their fathers less than their mothers.

Abigail hastened immediately to her storerooms, and gave direction to her servants without delay to load several beasts of burden
with 200 loaves, two measures or skins of wine, five sheep ready
dressed, and as many measures of meal, together with an abundant
supply of raisins and figs, and then to drive them forward in the direction which she more particularly pointed out to them. She would
herself follow them immediately, and then she would make them better acquainted with the object of their expedition.

Of course all this was done without the knowledge of Nabal who remained at a distance beside his flocks. The servants departed as their mistress commanded them, and Abigail had her mule quickly bridled, and soon overtook them. The caravan, however, had not proceeded far, when the armed troop, bent on revenge, came upon them as they went along a path under covert of the hill. David, its leader, was not yet calmed from the storm of angry passion with which we saw him set out on his march. He had just addressed his companions in these words: "Surely in vain have I kept all that this fellow hath in the wilderness, so that nothing was missed of all that pertained unto him and he hath requited me evil for good." It does not seem to us as if with these words David intended only to ease his conscience, which without doubt rose up with sternest threatenings against him; for, in the storm of his wild passion, he thus continued, protesting with an oath: "So and more also do God unto the enemies of David, if I slay not all the men that pertain to Nabal, by the morning light!"

Scarcely had these inconsiderate words passed from his lips, when Abigail appeared before him, dismounted quickly from her mule, and, bowing herself with her face to the ground before him, according to oriental custom, addressed him thus, with agitated heart: "Upon me, my lord, upon me let this iniquity be: and let thine handmaid, I pray thee, speak in thine audience, and hear the words of thine handmaid. Let not my lord, I pray thee, regard this man of Belial, even Nabal: for as his name is, so is he; Nabal is his name" (i.e., fool, a word which in the Hebrew has a moral signification, and denotes a perversity not only of the understanding, but also of the heart), "and folly" (estrangement from God) "is with him: but I, thine handmaid, saw not the young men of my lord, whom thou didst send. Now therefore, my lord, as the Lord liveth, and as thy soul liveth, seeing the Lord hath withholden thee from coming to shed blood, and from avenging thyself with thine own hand, now let thine enemies, and they that seek evil to my lord, be as Nabal. And now this blessing, which thine handmaid hath brought unto my lord, let it even be given unto the young men that follow my lord. I pray thee, forgive the trespass of thine handmaid" (of which my husband hath made himself guilty, and which, therefore, I impute to myself also): "for the Lord will certainly make my lord a sure house; because my lord fighteth the battles of the Lord, and evil hath not been found in thee all thy days. Yet a man is risen to pursue thee, and to seek thy soul: but the soul of my lord shall be bound in the bundle of life with the Lord thy God; and the souls of thine enemies, them shall He sling out, as out of the middle of a sling.

"And it shall come to pass, when the Lord shall have done to my lord according to all the good that He hath spoken concerning thee, and shall have appointed thee ruler over Israel, that this shall be no grief unto thee, nor offense of heart unto my lord" (but much more shall make thee glad), "either that thou hast shed blood causeless, or that my lord hath avenged himself: but when the Lord shall have dealt well with my lord, then remember thine handmaid."

How affecting, and how rich in enlightened wisdom, and in tender, holy tact was this heart-cry! Where in the whole heathen world do we find a woman comparable to Abigail, this daughter of the wilderness of Paran? May she not be regarded as of almost equal rank with the Marys of the New Testament? It is true that she is unhappy. Ah, her house, however blessed with earthly goods, is no house of Bethany! She is constrained, with deep sorrow, to call her rude husband, hardened in the service of Mammon, "a fool." But she bears with him with patient and hopeful love and fidelity, and perhaps oftentimes raises holy hands to God for him. She appears before David on his behalf while she takes upon herself, as a sacrificial lamb, the trespass of her husband. But she also holds out to David the grave offense of which he would have been guilty if he had carried out his purpose against her husband.

In how tender a manner, at the same time, did she signify to him that he had reason from the heart to praise the Lord his God that He had at the right moment, and, indeed, by means of her, arrested him when rushing to his own destruction; and with how much tact does she also remind him that he was not yet either ruler or king, and consequently neither judge nor avenger of transgressors in Israel, when she says to him in these and in the words following, "When the Lord shall have appointed thee ruler over Israel!"

And how could David resist her petition for the forgiveness of her husband, after she had in so prudent a manner presented before his eyes the highest blessedness to which anyone on earth could attain, namely this, "to be bound in the bundle of life with the Lord" (i.e., with those who were ordained by the Lord to eternal life); and when she then, with the silent supposition that this dignity was his, and that he would not forfeit it through wickedness, promised to him all blessings for his future course, and then, with the well-considered expression, "Thine enemies shall He sling out as out of the middle of a sling," called back to his recollection the great honor which the grace of God had already conferred upon him especially in his victory over Goliath? Indeed, the truth and sincerity, as well as the dove-like simplicity, united with hallowed prudence, revealed in that childlike, pious address of the excellent wife, merit our liveliest admiration.

Who can fail to perceive that here already the Spirit from above works mightily? Is it not almost as if in her we listened to an advanced disciple of the gospel? The words, "Thou shalt be bound in the bundle of life with the Lord," uttered long ago by the mouth of Abigail, as a favorite expression, and as indicating the most precious thing on earth which anyone could desire, have become naturalized in the language of the whole Christian world.

There was no need that Abigail should add to her words the prayer, "Remember thine handmaid." The impression which her address produced in the soul of David was powerful and decisive. Melted in thankful emotion at the faithfulness of his God, who in so tender a manner had restrained him, storming with passion, from a bloody crime, but not less also penetrated with shame and repentance, he stands at first dumb before the simple woman, and then, with great feeling. breaks out in these words: "Blessed be the Lord God of Israel, which sent thee this day to meet me: and blessed be thy advice, and blessed be thou which hast kept me this day from coming to shed blood, and from avenging myself with mine own hand. For in very deed, as the Lord God of Israel liveth, which hath kept me back from hurting thee" (i.e., thine house), "except thou hadst hasted and come to meet me, surely there had not been left unto Nabal by the morning light any living man in his house." Thus David.

Like one walking in a dream, who wakens up at the sound of his name, and suddenly, with horror, sees himself on the brink of a giddy precipice, and overflowing with thanks toward his deliverer, retraces his steps—such was now the state of David's mind. Besides, he had learned, to his humiliation, as well as also to his safety, to know one side of his temperament, which till now he had not recognized. As long as life lasts, he will not forget his march toward Carmel. And we, perhaps, do not err if we suppose that what he once experienced

at Carmel hovered before his soul as often as in his psalms, particularly in the seventeenth, the eighteenth, the thirty-seventh, and the
sixty-sixth, he raised his cry to the Lord as a God who "holdeth our
soul in life, and suffereth not our feet to be moved."

Thankfully David received the presents which Abigail had
brought for his men, and departed from her whom the Lord had sent
to him like a guardian angel, with the words, "Go up in peace to
thine house; see, I have hearkened to thy voice, and have accepted
thy person."

But when Abigail, the faithful wife, returned home, the whole
unhappiness of her condition came again before her in the clearest
light. Her husband sat at a luxurious banquet, rioting with his companions. His heart, the narrative says, "was very merry within him,"
for he then, as always, only lived for himself, "and he was very drunk-
en." Poor wife! Yet even in the present day, and in the midst of
Christianity, many of her sisters in sorrow may be found. Thus there
appears before me many a sorrowful wife, who might have a happy
home, because her husband is vigorous, and fails not in laboriousness
and industry. But what happens? "At the close of the week"—we
relate here, in the words of another, what came under his observation,
although we ourselves have frequently been witnesses of a similar
misery—"after he has been paid his wages, he returns to his house in
the evening. The children are glad that this time their father will be
longer beside them, because the Sabbath is at the door. With out-
stretched arms the little ones run forth to meet him. But quickly they
return, ashamed and sad, to their mother. The father staggers. 'Alas!'
sighs the poor wife, 'will then all have no effect?' And how great
cause had she for these sighs! During the week she has been provi-
dently careful to put in order the clothes of her husband for the
Sabbath, to repair the dress of the children, to clean the rooms, and
attend to whatever else needed to be put in order or made; and now
again this sad fate! The children hide themselves, trembling with
fear, in a corner! The mother fights against her despair, and silently helps the unhappy man into his bed. Then sings she the lullaby to
her infant child; but God only knows what a secret woe behind that
song gnaws at her heart!"

Oh, the peaceful martyr, with such a cross on her weak shoulders,
and yet bearing it in self-denial, and forgiving seventy times seven,
but yet always anew overwhelmed by the same domestic misery! If

only, once for all, something of that "I and my house, we will serve the Lord!" sounded again in the heart of the husband sold under sin, an end would be put in repentance to all that distress and all that misery. "Yet continue constantly," we say to the sorely tried wife, "to pray for the pitiable man. God knows thee, and he preserves thy secret tears in His bottle. Hope in Him, and remember the words, 'They that sow in tears shall reap in joy.'"

Abigail, however, experienced no such longed-for change. When, on her return, she found her husband in that lamentable condition, she wisely said nothing to him, "less or more, until the morning light." But so much the more, on the other hand, did she pray to God the Lord. But when the day broke, and Nabal had become sober, she honestly and without reserve told him all that had happened. She hoped that this communication would produce a blessed influence on his heart, since he must indeed perceive that there had been only one step between him and death, and that through the protecting hand of God, and the faithfulness of his wife, the evil had been averted. But her hope deceived her. The obstinate Nabal thought himself wounded in his honor by the obliging condescension of his wife toward his enemy, and instead of a feeling of thankfulness, such a spirit of ill-humor and anger overpowered him, that suddenly "his heart died within him, and he became as a stone."

For ten days he lay without consciousness; then the Lord smote him a second time, and his soul departed hence, without doubt accompanied by the unremitting intercession of his faithful wife, under the mighty hand of the Judge of the living and the dead. When David received information of Nabal's death, the remembrance of the wicked deed to which his blind, unbridled anger was hurrying him forward came back upon him with all its strength. At the same time, with adoring thankfulness, he thought on the divine protection of which he had been so wonderfully the object, and broke out in these words: "Blessed be the Lord that hath pleaded the cause of my reproach from the hand of Nabal, and hath kept His servant from evil: for the Lord hath returned the wickedness of Nabal upon his own head." Certainly—and scarcely anything else was to be expected—it is the stern spirit of the Old Covenant, of the economy of the law, and not the milder spirit of the gospel, which breathes out of this expression of thankfulness.

A lovely contrast to this conduct of David is presented in that of the honored veteran of science at Halle, who, while sitting one evening in his study, was suddenly assailed by a murderer. Although sorely wounded, he wrestled, in close struggle with him, the knife from the assassin, and at length had the murderer's life in his hands; but suddenly he remembered God's Word, "Vengeance is mine; I will repay"; and so, instead of making use of the weapon he had snatched, he contented himself with raising a loud cry for help. The murderer, who in that moment thought he heard the noise of the steps of men hastening thither, took flight, and when the neighbors made their appearance and searched for him, they found him hanged in the garret. He had in his despair condemned himself.

What then happened to the man who was thus saved? His soul was indeed full of thanks to God; but his first word was not a word of triumph, as when David said, "The Lord hath returned the wickedness of Nabal upon his own head," but of sorrow over the soul of the unhappy man, which had passed away immediately from amid his transgressions, without repentance and without faith. That is the Christian's revenge!

A considerable time had passed away after this occurrence at Carmel, when David sent messengers to Abigail, his prudent and pious deliverer, who were to speak unto her, saying, "David sent us unto thee, to take thee to him to wife." Abigail, recognizing in this new incident of her life the guidance of a higher Hand, arose from her seat and bowed herself on her face to the earth before the messengers, as the representatives of David, and said, "Behold, let thine handmaid be a servant to wash the feet of the servants of my lord"— an expression of deep humility, but arising from a true feeling of her unworthiness to be chosen as the spouse of him who would one day, as there was now no longer any room to doubt, be ruler over Israel. After she had refreshed the messengers with food and drink, and had entrusted her farm to the management of a steward, who was perhaps one of her own relations, she ordered her mule to be saddled, and by no means concealing from herself the fact that she would encounter many hardships and trials, she "went with five damsels of hers," along with the messengers of David, to the wilderness of Paran, and "she became David's wife."

She became David's third wife. His first marriage with Michal, Saul with wicked hands had disannulled, and, in his anger against David, had given this daughter to Phalti of Gallim, in the tribe of

Benjamin. A second marriage David, before his union with Abigail, had probably contracted, with Ahinoam of Jezreel; so that we thus find, even in the life of the "man after God's own heart," compliance with an immoral custom, which had long ago spread deeply in Israel, and which was directly opposed to the ordinance of God.

According to the divine statute, one man should be bound to one woman in conjugal fidelity till death; but long ago Lamech had violated this command, and had brought upon himself sore chastisement on account of this transgression. But gradually this opposition to the law of God became so general among the people, that the consciousness of their culpability had almost disappeared from among them.

Marriages, such as that between Isaac and Rebekah, had at an early period come to be rare pearls in Israel. Now, as a natural consequence, a hallowed family life, resting on the consciousness that husband and wife had been brought together by God for their mutual furtherance in the divine life, and that they were called upon to exhibit again, under the help from above, the lovely image of the first human pair, and to transform their house into a peaceful temple of God, this also was seldom encountered. The right conception of marriage as the union of a single pair, which indeed it was at the beginning, made itself, at a later period—particularly under the influence of the warnings and personal example of the prophets—the longer the more influential, though it was only for the first time apprehended in its full distinctness and perfectly realized in the time of the New Covenant. Till then that violation of the divine order was dealt with in the same manner as divorce "under the forbearance of God."

Thus David was perhaps scarcely conscious that in his marriage with Abigail, however noble the treasure might be which he had in her, he had made himself, by transgression, guilty before God. He did not, however, escape the merited chastisement of his offense.

It is not certain whether David was the author of Psalm 128; but obviously there is mirrored in this song something of a married and family life consecrated to God, and lifted up into a higher sphere, of which there were some anticipations among the pious in Israel in David's times; yea, here and there they had even already a foretaste of it.

12

The Last Meeting of
Saul and David

L o, all these things worketh God oftentimes with man, to bring
back his soul from the pit, to be enlightened with the light of
the living."[1] Thus spoke Elihu to Job, after he had set him right
regarding those afflictions which fell upon him, showing him that
they were not an evidence of anger or an undeserved visitation of
punishment from God, but rather a wholesome discipline of eternal
love, and appointed only for promoting his humility, purity, and holiness. Elihu praises the unwearied long-suffering with which the Lord
pursues after the sinner, to see whether he will not at last bow himself before Him, and, broken in heart, take hold of His gracious hand.

And truly never will a single sinner go to destruction who will not
be constrained to confess that, on numberless occasions in his life, he
has wantonly torn asunder and cast from him the divine rope of salvation that had been thrown out to him. But that will one day be the
never-dying "worm" in his soul, that he shall have to confess that he
had, even while he was sinning, a conscious knowledge of what God
commanded and prohibited; but that this consciousness exerted its
legitimate influence so little, that, as often as the veil of lying excuses, behind which he sought to conceal himself with his guilt from his
own conscience, began to raise itself up, so much the more violently
did he hold it fast together.

All this is fully applicable to the case of King Saul. We shall today
see him once more experience a visitation of divine grace; but we

---

1. Job 33:29–30.

shall see it again wholly frustrated as to its influence by his skill in the art of self-deception.

1 Samuel 26:6

> Then answered David, and said to Ahimelech the Hittite, and to Abishai the son of Zeruiah, brother to Joab, saying, Who will go down with me to Saul to the camp? And Abishai said, I will go down with thee.

For the last time during their lives Saul and David now meet together, and the scene which presents itself will fill us with the deepest sorrow. Let us see (1) under what circumstances they met; and (2) what resulted from their meeting.

1. We meet the fugitive David again in the wilderness of Ziph. What induced him to return to this region, whose inhabitants had once so faithlessly betrayed him to his persecutor, is not announced. Whether he thought that the Ziphites would now be more placable toward him than formerly, or whether some slight hope that his friend Jonathan would once more seek for him there, enticed him, who can with certainty say? The wilderness of Ziph was certainly more hospitable than the dark wilderness and moorland of Paran. Enough: he went thither again with his men, and pitched his tent not far from the little town of Ziph.

If he had indeed reckoned on a revolution in the disposition of the inhabitants there toward him, he was most bitterly deceived. Influenced more perhaps by the fear of the king's wrath than by patriotic attachment to him, they betrayed David a second time. On an intimation conveyed to him from thence, Saul marched without delay, with a band of 3,000 young warriors, to surprise his hated son-in-law at the hill of Hachilah, which had been pointed out to him as the place of David's encampment. The impression of the affecting scene at the cave in the wilderness of En-gedi, which furnished him with so indubitable a proof of the innocence and fidelity of David, had wholly faded away from his mind, and the old hatred burned within him, if possible, more fiercely than ever. At the hill we have named, however, much to his vexation, he did not meet with David, who had meanwhile retired further into the wilderness, and therefore he pitched his own camp there for a short rest.

When David received information of what was in progress against him, he next sent out spies to inquire after the position of his persecutor; and when they brought back to him the report that Saul lay encamped with his men at the foot of the hill Hachilah, he rose up, with a few of his trusty followers, and crept stealthily through the rocky defiles and thick underwood, till he came so near to the royal camp, that, from the elevation on which he stood, he could distinctly overlook it. It was a hazardous enterprise which he had undertaken; but he trusted in his God, from whom, as he did not doubt, the impulse to undertake this journey had originated.

Yet once more he thought to make an attack upon the heart of the king, to see whether he might not at last be moved to repentance. In a similar but yet in a more indubitable manner than formerly at Engedi, he hoped to be able to make it appear evident to him that he was a faithful subject and a heartily devoted servant, and that he did not harbor in his breast, in the remotest degree, any evil intention toward him.

Already night had spread its veil over the land, and only the moon gave light with her pale beams to the daring band but they revealed to them as much as was necessary. Deep silence reigned in the royal camp and they were soon convinced that, wearied with the fatiguing day's march, they had already sunk in deep slumber. In the foreground, on the threshold of the encampment, lay the king, stretched out on his camp-bed. By his side was Abner the son of Ner, Saul's uncle, and captain of his host, of whom we shall again hear. David soon recognized both of them, regarding this as a token, which he believed was here given to him; and with a quick understanding of the import of the divine intimation, he whispered to his companions, to Ahimelech the Hittite, a descendant of one of the Canaanitish tribes, who had been converted to the faith of Israel, and to Abishai, the son of his step-sister Zeruiah, and brother to Joab, "Who will go down with me to Saul, to the camp?" A bold thought! The Hittite is startled, and hesitates. Abishai, on the contrary, who was related by blood to David, quickly resolved, and said, entering fully into David's intentions, "I will go down with you."

So then the two went down with soft steps from the rocky height into the valley, and without being challenged or hindered, at length reached the royal encampment. There lay before them their royal master, overpowered by sleep. His spear, the emblem of his sovereignty, was stuck into the ground at his bolster. By his side lay the man who ought to have kept watch over him, but who had also resigned himself to slumber—the captain of his host, Abner; and round about were the wearied soldiers, overpowered by sleep.

A lamentable spectacle! Dishonor rests upon such an army as this, and especially upon its general! We hear, meanwhile, the words, "A deep sleep from the Lord is fallen upon them," and therefore it becomes us to lay our hand on our mouth, and at least to moderate our condemnation. What happened? The zealous Abishai quickly came to a resolution. "God hath delivered," he whispered to David, "thine enemy into thine hand this day: now, therefore, let me smite him, I pray thee, with the spear even to the earth at once, and I will not smite him the second time."

Abishai rightly perceived that it was the Lord who had delivered the king into their hands but in his judgment, influenced by a heart estranged from God, he mistook the design for which this was done. The spirit which animated David knew how to interpret better the divine intimation. "Destroy him not," he replied: "for who can stretch forth his hand against the Lord's anointed, and be guiltless? As the Lord liveth, the Lord shall smite him; or his day shall come to die; or he shall descend into battle, and perish. The Lord forbid that I should stretch forth mine hand against the Lord's anointed: but, I pray thee, take thou now the spear that is at his bolster, and the cruse of water, and let us go"; and so it was done. With these things "they gat them away, and no man saw it, nor knew it, neither awaked; for they were all asleep because," the history expressly adds, as we have already perceived, "a deep sleep from the Lord had fallen upon them"; from which may be understood that the Lord had bound them fast for a while in the sleep by which they had allowed themselves, with unaccountable indiscretion, to be overpowered.

Behold now, once more, our David, as he goes away with Saul's spear, the emblem of his sovereign power. At that moment he presents a symbolically significant appearance. Unconsciously he prophesied of his own future, while he stands before us as the projected shadow of that form in which we must one day behold him. In the counsel of the invisible Watcher, it was indeed irrevocably concluded that the Bethlehemite should inherit Saul's scepter, and here we see before us a dim forecast of that fact.

2. After the two had succeeded in their attempt, they again took up their position on the top of the hill, which rose up immediately

behind the royal camp. From this place David made his voice sound forth among the watchmen slumbering in the camp, and thundered out to the son of Ner, who was placed as the life-guardsman nearest to the king, these words: "Abner, this thing is not good that thou hast done. As the Lord liveth, ye are the sons of death" (i.e., ye are guilty of death), "because ye have not kept your master, the Lord's anointed. And now see where the king's spear is, and the cruse of water that was at His bolster."

But while he thus reproached the watchmen who had been negligent and forgetful of their duty, the king also awoke out of his sleep, and, not a little amazed, said, "Is this thy voice which sounds in mine ear, my son David?" "Yea," replied he, with deepest reverence, "it is my voice, my lord, O king." Then in a most sorrowful tone he continued: "Wherefore doth my lord thus pursue after his servant? for what have I done? or what evil is in mine hand? Now therefore, I pray thee, let my lord the king hear the words of his servant. If the Lord have stirred thee up against me" (i.e., in His righteous indignation permits you to fall from one sin into another, so that you rage even against those who are most faithfully devoted to you), "let Him accept an offering" (which may reconcile Him and incline Him to forbearance): "but if they be the children of men" (perhaps the courtiers surrounding thee) "who stir thee up against me, cursed be they before the Lord; for they have driven me out this day from abiding in the inheritance of the Lord" (the people who are Jehovah's heritage and His sanctuary), "saying, Go, serve other gods. Now therefore, let not my blood fall to the earth before the face of the Lord" (since they have banished me into the country of the heathen); "for the king of Israel is come out to seek a flea, as when one doth hunt a partridge in the mountains."

Saul listened to these heart-breaking words, and whatever feelings of goodness or of rectitude yet remained within him began once more to awaken. "I have sinned," he says (this time, however, without tears) "return, my son David; for I will no more do thee harm, because my soul was precious in thine eyes this day: behold, I have played the fool, and have erred exceedingly." So far an honest confession this, but without the slightest trace of a true repentance and sincere humiliation before Almighty God. Even the most abandoned will be able to use these words, "I have committed folly; I have sinned," when he sees himself convicted of a crime against a man

whom he suddenly discovers to be his benefactor, or, as in the case
of Saul with David, the savior of his life.

The king's confession of sin sounds coldly, much more coldly even
than the similar confession which we heard from his lips at En-gedi.
And what a suspicious sign this is, that he meant not a single word
of that contemptible outburst of solemn promise made at En-gedi!
His hardening seemed to be brought by a considerable step nearer to
full maturity.

This would be more apparent to David than it is to us. His falsely tender words, "Return, my son David," awoke no echo in his heart.
David called to him from the top of the hill, "Behold the king's spear!
and let one of the young men come over and fetch it"; and then
added, with significant earnestness, betraying thereby the impression
which the words spoken by the king, so well-meaning according to
their appearance, produced within him: "The Lord render to every
man his righteousness and his faithfulness: for the Lord delivered thee
into my hand today; but I would not stretch forth mine hand against
the Lord's anointed. And, behold, as thy life was much set by this day
in mine eyes, so let my life be much set by in the eyes of the Lord,
and let Him deliver me out of all tribulation."

How precious are these words of David! What an important view
they open up to us into his inmost being! The king seems impressed
by them to a certain degree. "Blessed be thou, my son David," he
says; and continues, almost prophesying: "Thou shalt both do great
things, and also shalt still prevail" (i.e., be always great and prosperous). And after he had thus spoken, David went his way, and Saul
also his. It was a separation forever. In life they saw each other no
more!

What sorrow fills us as we contemplate this scene! From the side
of King Saul had now departed all spiritual counselors, guardians, and
supporters, even to his son Jonathan, who was, however, only as a
thorn in his flesh. The aged Samuel, who, after Saul had tacitly dismissed him, notwithstanding, as long as he remained on the earth,
rose up like an apparition before the memory of the king, and, warning and prophesying from afar, had restrained him from many an
improper step. He was no longer among the living. The pious priest
Abiathar and the stern prophet Gad had long ago separated from
Saul, and had joined themselves to David; and now also Saul saw his
faithful son-in-law no more, who, through the power of his noble dis-

position and conduct, had sometimes rendered to him the service of awakening his blunted conscience. On every ground, therefore, there was reason to fear that he would rush on with redoubled steps to his own destruction. And so it indeed happened.

It was not long till Saul was again, through a new incursion of the Philistines, placed in great difficulty. He was no longer the hero he had formerly been. With his faith, his courage also had gradually disappeared. In vain he sought counsel. Dreams did not impart it to him; the "Urim and Thummim" could no longer be resorted to after the high priest had departed from him; and all the prophets he had thoroughly alienated. And therefore now, as his last resort, he went to a witch at Endor, instead of God, from whom a Cain-like fear had estranged him more and more. He demanded of her, under oaths, that, notwithstanding the express prohibition of God, the act would not be reckoned to her as a crime, that she should raise up Samuel from the kingdom of the dead, that he might once more receive his counsel and instruction. And when, as is well known, God the Lord, by means of His wonder-working almighty power, that He might put an end forever to the Saul's flummery, permitted it on this occasion to change into fearful earnestness, and granted truly to the king the wished-for appearance of Samuel, that he might hear out of his mouth his sentence of death. Then the crowned transgressor, together with the terribly-surprised impostor, overcome with fear and trembling in every limb, fell to the ground; but of repentance, of contrition because of his crime, and of crying for mercy, there is not a single trace to be found in the king. Woe to the unhappy man! He was weighed in the balance and found wanting. He was rejected, because he had forsaken his God, and had willfully departed from His way. Unhappy man! The angels of peace weep over you, and hell triumphs!

The seventh Psalm is unmistakably related to the last persecutions which David had to endure in the wildernesses of En-gedi and Ziph. Its inscription, according to the original text, is briefly this: "A song: Erring" (or Folly, namely, Saul's), "which David sang concerning the words" (i.e., the calumnies) "of the Ethiopian" (Heb. Cush) "from Benjamin": a distinct allusion to the name of Saul's father, Kish, under which, however, Saul himself is meant. But the Ethiopian often serves as an image of the sinner. The psalmist begins his song with the expression of his confidence in God: "O Lord my God, in

Thee do I put my trust: save me from all them that persecute me, and deliver me!" He then directs his look from the multitude of his persecutors to the one who was their head, saying, "Lest he tear my soul like a lion, rending it in pieces, while there is none to deliver." He appeals to his own good conscience: "O Lord my God, if I have done this" (namely, of which my calumniators have accused me); "if there be iniquity in my hands" (the same expression he made use of in his self-justification before Saul); "if I have rewarded evil unto him that was at peace with me; (yea, I have delivered him that without cause is mine enemy): let the enemy persecute my soul, and take it; yea, let him tread down my life upon the earth, and lay mine honor in the dust. Selah." Hereupon he calls unto the Lord for protection and help: "Arise, O Lord, in Thine anger, lift up Thyself, because of the rage of mine enemies; and awake for me to the judgment that Thou hast commanded. So shall the congregation of the people compass Thee about" (i.e., show Thyself to them as the Judge of the universe): "for their sakes therefore return Thou on high" (to Thy lofty throne). "The Lord shall judge the people: judge me, O Lord, according to my righteousness, and according to mine integrity that is in me" (so far as I have these to boast of in respect to my dealings with the king, who hates me). "O let the wickedness of the wicked come to an end; but establish the just: for the righteous God trieth the hearts and reins."

Instead of prayer he now gives utterance to hope: "My defense is of God, which saveth the upright in heart. God judgeth the righteous, and God is angry with the wicked every day. If he turn not, He will whet His sword; He hath bent His bow, and made it ready. He hath also prepared for Him the instruments of death; He ordaineth His arrows against the persecutors." David foresees the terrible end of his persecutor. "Behold," he continues, "he travaileth with iniquity, and hath conceived mischief, and brought forth falsehood. He made a pit, and digged it, and is fallen into the ditch which he made. His mischief shall return upon His own head, and his violent dealing shall come down upon his own pate." He concludes his psalm, praising the righteousness of God: "I will praise the Lord according to His righteousness; and will sing praise to the name of the Lord Most High."

It will be said that this psalm belongs to the Old Testament times, and breathes the spirit of the law. It is so. David the prophet spoke not from himself, but as the organ and representative of God, who from Mount Ebal proclaimed to the world, "Cursed be he that confirmeth not all the words of this law to do them," and whom it became at that period, in the development of His kingdom, especially to make Himself known as "the Holy One of Israel." But if anyone means by this that he recognizes a different God in the Old Testament from that of the New, let him only listen to the latter; and what words of thunder strike upon his ear! Let him hear! "Be not deceived; God is not mocked. He that soweth to his flesh, shall of the flesh reap corruption. Our God is a consuming fire. Depart from me, ye cursed, into everlasting fire, prepared for the devil and his angels. It is a fearful thing to fall into the hands of the living God. If thy foot offend thee, cut it off: it is better for thee to enter halt into life, than having two feet to be cast into hell, into the fire that never shall be quenched: where their worm dieth not, and the fire is not quenched."

Let anyone read these and many similar passages, and he will be convinced that here, as there, the same God meets us, terrible to hardened sinners, but, on the contrary, a God of patience and grace toward the penitent. Therefore the impressive apostolic admonition ought to be specially pondered: "Work out your own salvation with fear and trembling; for it is God which worketh in you both to will and to do of His good pleasure." That this word may pierce us to the heart, and that the Lord may also grant to us both—this is the prayer with which we conclude our meditation for the present.

13

David Among the Philistines

I will hedge up thy way with thorns."[1] Thus spoke the Lord to His people. In form a threat, this word was nevertheless in reality, for the friends of God, a gracious promise. Even the pious, so long as they are in the body, are not unconditionally secured against the deception of sins, however thoroughly they have abandoned them. The old man within them may be wounded to death, but he is not therefore yet dead. Besides, the prince of this world is everywhere busy to mislead them by deceptions of every kind, and to entice them into false ways. As little have the watchmen of Zion under the New Covenant, as had those who were under the Old, to regard themselves as freed from the duty of warning the faithful without intermission against errors. How often do we see, however, the best-meant calls of the watchmen thrown to the winds as "superfluous," and those who are warned heedlessly forsaking the right path. And does the Keeper of Israel, who has promised to His own that He will guard them as the apple of His eye, yet suffer it to happen that they wander from the straight path and go astray?

Indeed He seldom leaves them, even for a wide space, altogether to themselves, that they might afterward find ground and occasion to adopt, to the praise of His name, these words of Psalm 119: "Before I was afflicted I went astray; but now have I kept Thy word. Thou art good, and doest good. Teach me Thy statutes." At some point in the by-path of error, along which they walk as in a waking dream, they suddenly encounter a thorny enclosure hemming them in. Not by words of warning, but by opposing Providence and misfortunes, are

---

1. Hosea 2:6.

160

they brought to a halt. A deep dejection of spirit seizes upon them, but only soon to resolve itself into sorrow and humility. They discover where a further prosecution of their self-chosen path would lead them, and who it is that has in mercy, at a fitting time, barred their way. Many, though perhaps not here, yet on that further side of the grave, shall perceive with astonishment that all the troubles and afflictions they suffered on earth were only such a gracious hedging up of their way by the hand of their heavenly Guide; and for this they will praise the faithfulness of God, that He did not spare the thorns, in order that He might make true to them the promise given to His people by Hosea. Among such as thus praise the Lord, we meet with David in the foremost rank.

1 Samuel 27:1

> And David said in his heart, I shall now perish one day by the hand of Saul: there is nothing better for me than that I should speedily escape into the land of the Philistines.

1 Samuel 29:6–7

> Then Achish called David, and said unto him, . . . Now return, and go in peace, that thou displease not the lords of the Philistines.

1 Samuel 30:1–2

> And it came to pass, when David and his men were come to Ziklag, that the Amalekites had invaded the south, and Ziklag, and smitten Ziklag, and burned it with fire.

The spiritual lessons which are brought before us by the history today are those of warning and of consolation. David (1) goes astray, and (2) is on that account graciously visited with chastisement. These are the two historical elements upon which we more particularly fix our attention.

1. While David, after his last meeting with Saul, tarried again in the lonely wilderness of Judah, there gradually rose up within him an eager longing after some place of concealment, that might be at least less inhospitable. Saul had, it is true, solemnly protested anew that he no more had thoughts of doing him harm. But on nothing could David reckon more certainly than on this, that he would in a short time violate this word also, and would, with his accomplices, not

desist from laying snares for him till he had removed him out of the way. With the unsettled life of a fugitive, David was now at length, however, heartily wearied; and especially it occasioned him pain to be compelled to lead about with him his wives, Ahinoam and Abigail, so long in his wandering life, and to require them to share with him all the hardships and privations of the rough experience of the soldier. He had been, as perhaps was now evident to himself, at all events too precipitate with his marriages. We do not at least read anywhere that, with reference to these domestic events, he sought counsel from the Lord. If he indeed omitted to do this, the grievous condition in which he now found himself must be regarded as a well-deserved chastisement on that account. He had no cause, however, to permit this discipline to have a weakening influence on his faith, though he seems not to have guarded himself against this result.

We meet him today by no means, as we met him a short time ago, on the heights of confidence in God. Instead of appealing to the Lord, he takes counsel with flesh and blood. Tender care for his wives did not justify that which he planned to do. If he was willing no longer to require that they should dwell with him in caves and amid rocky defiles, he could easily have obtained shelter for them at Nabal's farm at Carmel, or in some friendly house in Judah, while he himself waited, amid the privations and the dangers of the wilderness, to see what the Lord might further determine regarding him. Instead of doing that, however, he adopted the foolish resolution of seeking among the Philistines, the hereditary and chief enemies of his people, a place of safety for himself and his followers. We perceive how by such a course he was brought into danger.

It is uncertain whether Achish, who was at that time king of the Philistines at Gath, was the same person with whom he formerly took refuge from Saul, not without having afterward bitterly to repent of that step. Possibly he was the same, since David had come to know him personally as a man well disposed toward him, and first stirred up against him by his courtiers; but it is more probable that we must regard this Achish as the successor of that former monarch of the same name. David reckoned on the hospitality of the man, and found with him indeed the wished-for asylum, but he did so at the high price of his veracity and his fidelity to his religious profession. In order to recommend himself to the goodwill of his protector, he led him to believe that, as he had renounced allegiance to King Saul, so he had also laid aside the national hatred of his people against the heathen; and by doing this David already made himself guilty of a culpable abandonment of the truth.

Some such stratagem, however, is almost always practiced when believers become suitors for the favor and help of the children of this world. That they should, when distress comes, make "flesh their arm" at all, will give their enemies cause to triumph. And too frequently, indeed, do the malevolent find occasion for rejoicing over such conduct. Quickly do they discern that, in order to gain their favor, the "pious" change their language in their presence, that they carefully abstain from the mode of speech in common use among the "brotherhood," and that they even accommodate themselves to many of the views of their opponents, which directly contradict the word of God, and take refuge in ambiguous phraseology and so-called mental reservation, that they may avoid making an open and complete rejection of the faith.

Oh, the contemptible treachery which Christians, by such conduct, are guilty of toward the gospel! The case may indeed perhaps arise when, pressed by necessity, they must seek help even among the despisers of God and of His word; but then let it be done, in however mild and friendly a manner, always with an unmasked countenance, so that, in case they should be spurned, they at all events may save their own souls, and extort from the enemy at least this testimony, honoring to God, that the children of God always remain faithful, and, in whatever situation they may be placed, always know how to stand their ground.

Alas! David does not this time stand the trial to which he is subjected. The simple fact that he threw himself especially into the hands of the Philistines, brought on him the greatest reproach. He led them thereby to suppose that he now earnestly repented of the victory he had once gained over them by the help of his God. As a punishment for his error, he, who had hitherto been an object of fear and hatred to King Saul, must now be the object only of his contempt. Briefly but significantly the history records, "And it was told Saul that David was fled to Gath; and he sought no more again for him." It is plainly indicated by these words that Saul believed he had henceforth to regard the coward as in no way an object of fear to him.

Moreover, David appeared now as a friend of the Philistines, and consequently as a traitor to his country; and without doubt Saul flattered himself with the hope that he would be acknowledged as such by the whole of Israel, and would be forced to renounce forever the prospect of the throne of Israel. "Saul sought no more again for him," but yet he thought about him with scornful contempt. Hitherto his satellites had seen him spouting fire and flame against David; now they heard from his lips perhaps only such mocking words as these: "The deserter assigned to himself the right name when he designated himself a flea, and a timid partridge on the mountains."

Oh, the disgrace which fastened itself to the heels of our friend in this course now pursued by him! Perhaps he was many a time ashamed of himself when it came into his consciousness how he, when he was only the terrified prey in the wilderness, against which horse and horsemen were sent out, was yet an altogether different man from what he was now in his supposed hiding-place among the Philistines.

David was soon convinced of the equivocal nature of his situation in the heathen city. At every step he saw himself watched by evil eyes, assailed by insidious questions, and beset by snares of many kinds. Therefore he appeared one day before Achish, and submissively and with humility said to him, "If I have now found grace in thine eyes, let them give me a place in some town in the country, that I may dwell there: for why should thy servant dwell in the royal city with thee?" By this he meant to say that he was not worthy of such an honor. On whom could this language, however, produce the impression of truthfulness and honesty? It was not, indeed, altogether a manifest falsehood, though it quite bordered on it. Achish granted him his request, and offered the little town of Ziklag as a place of residence for him and his people. The hospitable reception with which the Philistine prince favored the stranger surprises us. But Achish hoped that the Hebrews might be useful to him, if not as scourges, yet as spies and betrayers of their own people; for that the alienation between Saul and David was irreparable, was now to him a matter beyond all doubt.

Ziklag lay close upon the borders of the tribe of Judah, to whom it had originally belonged. At a later period it had been allotted to the tribe of Simeon. At the time of David it was in the hands of the Philistines, from whom it was afterward taken, when it fell to the kings of Judah as a private possession. Here David lived, as much as possible separated from the heathen inhabitants, for a whole year and four months, along with his followers, supported partly at the cost of his princely host, partly from private contributions sent from his native country, lying not far off. But how could a man like him keep his hands so long idle in his bosom? Soon the blood which flowed in his veins began again to boil and prompt him to valiant deeds. He became again the warrior thirsting for heroic achievements. At the same time, he perceived how necessary it was that he should give his men active employment, and thus guard them against sloth and licentiousness.

But where could he go with them? He did not remain long in doubt about that. Not far from the place where he then was, toward the wilderness of Egypt, there dwelt a powerful remnant of the heathen aborigines who had never been driven out by Joshua. These were the Geshurites, the Gergesites, and the Amalekites. Upon them there lay, from ancient times, the divine sentence of rejection. This, together with the fact that in assailing these wild tribes he would only be fighting against hordes of robbers who continually disquieted the borders of his fatherland, appeared fully to justify his plan of action, and tended to the quieting of his conscience, if it should assume the attitude of accusing him on account of his taking the sword against those barbarians without any commission from Saul his royal master.

Confident of victory, he went forth against these hordes, and returned from every engagement in triumph, and rich with booty. The work was a very bloody one. He proceeded strictly in accordance with the divine command of extermination, as it was given to Moses and Joshua. Men and women were given up to the sword; sheep, cattle, asses, camels, together with materials of clothing of every kind, were carried away as booty. Then, after such exploits in arms, David appeared again before King Achish, to give him this and that of the spoil, and to counteract certain accusations which might perhaps be raised against him on account of these expeditions; and if he was asked by Achish who they were against whom his warlike excursions, of which he heard, were directed, he replied, "Against the south of Judah, and against the south of the Jerahmeelites, and against the south of the Kenites." This answer was ambiguous, and went round about the kernel of the king's question. David indicated only the directions which he had taken, and the regions he had entered upon.

His answer might be interpreted, and he wished it to be so, as if he had made war only against his own countrymen, inasmuch as the Jerahmeelites and the Kenites dwelling in the south of the land of Judah were partly descendants of a Jerahmeel who had sprung out of Judah, and partly of the great-grandson of Hobab, the father-in-law of Moses, and therefore they were related by kindred to the Israelites and not to the Philistines, either by descent or by religion. That David, according to his pretense, should rage against his own flesh and blood, could not but be pleasing to Achish the king of the Philistines. But was it not, again, a manifest falsehood, and at the same time a renunciation of his own people, of which David made himself guilty? In the sight of God it undoubtedly was so.

David might perhaps seek in some way to justify himself, by the thought that, in his ambiguous manner of speech, he made use only of an allowable stratagem, and that he was a heathen to whom he veiled the truth—an idea which then commonly prevailed in Israel. But he will yet be made to experience that God will weigh those who would be His, not in the false balance of a self-pleasing public morality, but in the balances of the sanctuary, in which, among others, that inviolable word is found as one of the weights, "Thou shalt not bear false witness." He will fully understand that in his conduct, so deliberately planned, he only prepared for himself the rod of correction, under the painful stroke of which he would learn how the lie, even where it makes its appearance in the most delusive coloring of truth, when measured according to the divine standard, remains still a lie and every lie is an abomination in the sight of God.

We are here once more reminded of the history of Abraham. It happened on one occasion, even to this father of all believers, that he turned aside from the truth in like manner as David now did in the land of the Philistines. On the occasion of a famine he sought refuge in Egypt, where, from cowardly fear lest the heathen should put him to death and then take possession of Sarah his wife, who was fair to look upon, he gave out that she was his sister, she also joining with him in the deception. He could, indeed, with an appearance of truth, conceal the true relation in which he stood to her, since Sarah was in reality his step-sister.

But how bitterly was he led, notwithstanding, to repent of that artifice, exhibiting lamentable lack of confidence in his God! His wife was only just so much the sooner taken from him, and brought to Pharaoh. But he, being visited by God with a severe plague on account of his robbery, gave her back forthwith to her husband uninjured; and Abraham had, in addition to the great anxieties which he endured, to bear also this disgrace, most humbling to him, to hear himself censured sternly on account of his lie by the heathen king. With a calmness and a demeanor which for the time made him appear nobler than that distinguished father of the faithful, he addressed to him the question, why he had done this to him, and had not said to him that she was his wife. "Why," said the heathen king, "saidest thou she is my sister? so I might have taken her to me to wife: now, therefore, behold thy wife, take her, and go thy way." And after he had so spoken, he even gave charge to his men to convey the stranger and his wife, and all that he had, in safety to the borders of their own land. And Abraham departed from thence, ashamed; the thanks which with trembling lips he rendered in the dust to his God, because of His faithfulness toward him, being accompanied probably by a stream of burning, penitential tears.

David had in the meantime, by his cunningly contrived evasion, gained his object with Achish. "Achish," we are informed, "believed David," saying, "He hath made his people Israel utterly to abhor him; therefore he shall be my servant forever." David himself was, however, in the long run, not at all contented with the proceeding, because he was continually tormented with the fear that some fugitive from among those tribes against which he made war might come to Gath and make known to the Philistines the true state of the case, saying, "So did David, and so will be his manner all the while he dwelleth in the country of the Philistines." Therefore it was necessary for him anxiously to take care that the borders of that region should be closely guarded; and for this purpose he issued the command that whoever should be found on this side of it on the way to Gath should be forcibly sent back; or, if they offered resistance, should be slain with the edge of the sword. Thus the evil deed, once begotten, propagates itself without end, and the divine punishment which lays in arrest upon it, how sharp soever it may be, is a blessing.

2. The unpleasant situation in which David had willfully placed himself, was itself a punishment for him. But we shall see the painfulness of it rise still higher, even to the anguish of death, and then we shall see the Lord stretch His hand of deliverance over His servant, and heaps coals of fire upon his head. What happened? The

Philistines break forth anew against Israel, and even with larger and more powerful armies than ever before. Then Achish sends for David from Ziklag, and with true-hearted simplicity and freedom from suspicion says to him, "Know thou assuredly that thou shalt go with me to battle, thou and thy men." One may imagine what were the feelings in David's mind when he heard these words. He must take the sword against his king and his people, and that, too, under the banner of their ancient enemy the Philistines. He shrunk back from the thought of such a thing; but how can he escape from this atrocious act? He must follow, for he will not reveal to the heathen his true position, and thereby place his freedom and his life at stake.

Unhappy man! How his inmost soul was agitated by a storm of conflicting thoughts! Yet he composes himself, and replies to Achish, "Surely thou shalt know what thy servant can do." By this he meant, "The Lord will provide, and make a way of escape for me even here, as He has many a time done before." It is doubtful whether he cherished this thought without at the same time having to bear the accusation of his guilt-laden conscience. Achish interpreted, moreover, the indefinite answer of his guest in his own favor. "Therefore," said he, "will I make thee keeper of my head forever" (i.e., make thee captain of my lifeguards), "and commit my life to thy protection."

The hosts of the Philistines gathered together in the plain of Jezreel, the battlefield of nations from ancient times, at Aphek, not far from Endor, the place where resided the witch by means of whom Saul heard from the mouth of Samuel the sentence of rejection pronounced against him. Here Achish joined his army with his people and the Hebrew forces, at the head of which stood David, trembling with agitation. What now took place? When the lords of the Philistines, at the mustering of the hosts, passed on with their hundreds and thousands before the king their liege-lord, and perceived the foreigners in the retinue of Achish, they said to him, "What do these Hebrews here?" And certainly it was not without a cause that they regarded them with distrust, for it once before this happened at Gibeah of Benjamin that an Israelite division, which had joined the army of the Philistines, suddenly, during the battle, deserted their standard, and went over to the side of the Israelites, their countrymen.

Achish tried to pacify the suspicious nobles, by assuring them that David, the servant of the king of Israel, had been with him as his guest for a long time, and that he had perceived nothing in him to awaken suspicion since he had deserted from his own people. But the princes insisted on the dismissal of the strangers, and with anger replied: "Make this fellow return, that he may go again to his place which thou hast appointed him, and let him not go down with us to battle, lest in the battle he be an adversary to us: for wherewith should he reconcile himself unto his master? Should it not be with the heads of these men? Is not this David, of whom they sang one to another in dances, saying, Saul slew his thousands, and David his ten thousands?" Thus the princes.

Then Achish called David, and said to him, "Surely, as the Lord liveth" (one may notice how the heathen here accommodates himself perhaps not altogether without inner truthfulness, to the faith of David), "thou hast been upright, and thy going out and thy coming in with me in the host is good in my sight: for I have not found evil in thee since the day of thy coming unto me unto this day: nevertheless the lords favor thee not. Wherefore now return and go in peace, that thou displease not the lords of the Philistines" (i.e., that thou continue not with me against their will). How could David hear these words of innocence and simplicity without feeling himself condemned by his own conscience? The blush of shame must have covered his face. He did not, however, in the anguish of his heart, turn again into the path of truth and sincerity. He made Achish believe that if he had not been sent back he would have drawn the sword in his behalf even against his own people Israel, a thing which, under no circumstances, he ought to have consented to do.

"What have I done?" said he, with all the appearance of true-heartedness, "and what hast thou found in thy servant, so long as I have been with thee unto this day, that I may not go to fight against the enemies of my lord the king?" Certainly he did not mean by this the "enemy" then before him. Against all his heathen enemies the king would assuredly have found in him a faithful ally and champion. But naturally by the mention of his "enemies" Achish meant first and exclusively Israel; and David sinned again most grievously against the truth in this, that he acquiesced in his false supposition without attempting to undeceive him. "I know," answered Achish, "that thou art good in my sight, as an angel of God: notwithstanding, the princes of the Philistines have said, He shall not go up with us to the battle. Wherefore now rise up early in the morning with thy master's

servants that are come with thee; and as soon as ye be up early in the
morning, and have light, depart." Thus he spoke, and David did
accordingly.

In how unexpected and wonderful a manner did David again here
see himself set free by the hand of the Lord from the fatal dilemma
into which, in an unhappy hour, through the lamentable weakness
of his faith, he had brought himself! He needed now neither to break
the promise he had, with unpardonable thoughtlessness, made to
Achish, nor to draw the sword against his own covenant people,
which would not only have deprived him of the crown and scepter,
but with the honor of his name would also forever have robbed him
of peace of conscience. As little had he now also on that account to
accuse himself of a violation of faith, in that he turned his back again
against the Philistines, and appeared openly as their enemy. He was
by their princes, even as it were officially, sent back and released from
his service. Oh, what a fullness of new reasons now poured upon him
for his kissing the feet of the Lord his God, and, prostrate in the dust,
praising His free grace! And surely there was nothing wanting for
this, when, after the tumult of sin and hypocrisy in which he had
been bewildered, there returned to him the full, clear consciousness
as well of his great transgression as of the help of God, as unexpected
as it was unmerited, which had been extended to him, in spite of all
these errors into which he had fallen.

Without doubt there hovered before him remembrances of
what he experienced during his sojourn among the Philistines, when
in Psalm 103 he raised his voice in accents of praise for the
unchangeableness of the divine mercy, in opposition to the frailty
and changeableness of the poor sinful sons of Adam, and poured
forth from his deeply moved heart these words: "Bless the Lord, O my
soul: and all that is within me, bless His holy name. Bless the Lord,
O my soul, and forget not all His benefits: who forgiveth all thine
iniquities; who healeth all thy diseases; who redeemeth thy life from
destruction; who crowneth thee with loving-kindness and tender
mercies." And surely he remembered the experience of those days
when he thus further praised the Lord: "He will not always chide:
neither will He keep His anger forever. He hath not dealt with us
after our sins; nor rewarded us according to our iniquities. For as the
heaven is high above the earth, so great is His mercy toward them
that fear Him. . . . For He knoweth our frame; He remembereth that

we are dust." Many effusions assuredly, both of repentance and of
thanks in his psalms, owe their origin to his looking back upon these
transgressions of which he then was guilty, as well as the divine deliverances which he experienced. He had allowed himself to become
deeply entangled in the deceitfulness of sin; but that which might
have led to his eternal death became to him, through the grace of
God, a healing power of wonderful energy for his inner man.

"The lords favor thee not," said Achish to David. A word this which
many of the like-minded associates of the son of Jesse, who have had
communication with the great ones of the earth, could apply to
themselves. It is, alas, a rare case for persons of decided and outspoken adherence to the gospel, to find favor in the eyes of the
so-called gods of the earth! It is true we knew at least one of these, of
whom the friends of God and His kingdom might say with far greater
reason than the Israelites once had for saying of the centurion at
Capernaum, "He loveth our nation." It may not be said that he was
the only one of his kind; yet we cannot but utter the sigh, "Oh, that
all were of his spirit!" The holy Scriptures name in the first rank among
the glories of the jubilee-time of God's kingdom which it places
before the view of the faithful, this, that kings walking in the splendor of the light of divine revelation would become guardians of the
city of God on earth, and that princesses would become nursing-
mothers to the Church. Till the dawning of these longed-for days, it
brings to us not a little consolation, if among the faithful counselors
of a sovereign we know at least one Daniel; but yet it is an incomparably greater comfort when it can be said of the ruler himself as it
was once said to Ananias concerning the man of Tarsus, "Behold, he
prayeth!"

A venerable author of former times accompanies the consideration of David's treatment at the hands of Achish and the princes of
the Philistines with this practical application: "Let us here learn that
the too great favor of rulers, in so far as they are not richer in the fear
of God than Achish, toward a man who desires to walk in the footsteps of the faith of Abraham, is especially dangerous. They exact
altogether too great a tax for the favor which they bestow. If they are
kind, one must be in all things accommodating to them, let the tender conscience say what it will. In the bonds of their favor one walks
as a prisoner.

The mistrust of the Philistine princes helped David out of the dif-

ficulty into which he had hurried himself through the favor of
Achish. So the favor of godless nobles, when it is blended with somewhat of fear, is more advantageous than their favor alone. The
godless nobleman, who is an enemy of God, must know that he has
as servant a friend of God, a servant of Jesus Christ, an upright and
believing son of Abraham, to whom he dare impute no folly and
wickedness. Consequently this servant must not dissemble as
David did with Achish, but profess his faith, trusting in God at all
times.

Achish, who was formerly a worshiper of idols, solemnly assured
David by Jehovah that he pleased him, and said to him that he
regarded him as upright, even, that he was pleasing in his sight as an
angel of God. But he held him as an enemy of Israel, and this David
indeed was not. But the supposition was the result of his own culpable hypocrisy. Let the whole truth be confessed where occasion is
given for it; and if one indeed finds it advisable to hold back a part
of it, let him at least say nothing contrary to it; otherwise, sooner or
later, he brings himself into great danger.

Thus David returned with his band safely from the land of the
Philistines to Ziklag; but what terrible news reached him on the way!
The Amalekites, another of the godless and reprobate tribes, had fall-
en upon the town with fire and sword, converted it into a heap of
ashes, and having driven away the men, who but barely escaped with
their lives, had taken captive the women, and among these David's
wives, together with his sons and daughters. This also was a divine
chastisement on account of David and his hypocrisy. David, indeed,
with deep distress of soul, soon recognized it as such. For when he
heard the evil tidings, he and the people that were with him lifted up
the voice and "wept until they had no more power to weep," says the
history.

These were the tears of sorrow and of anger but with David's tears
there mingled also the more bitter tears of repentance on account of
his conduct hitherto. The consternation into which the dreadful tidings had brought him was completed when he heard that his own
people, whose wives, sons, and daughters had been carried away captive, not only began to murmur against him, but even to threaten to
stone him. Perhaps already the whole expedition with the Philistine
host against Israel had greatly vexed them; but now their indignation
threatened to overstep all bounds.

It will not be difficult for us to credit the history when it tells us that "David was greatly distressed" Where will he go now in this momentous crisis? In his distress, deeply crushed and bowed down, but not hopeless, he lifted his heart and his eyes to heaven, and "encouraged himself in the Lord his God." He sent for Abiathar, with the breastplate, and inquired through him at the Lord (he ought to have always and everywhere inquired at Him at the right time): "Shall I pursue after this band of warriors that have smitten Ziklag, and shall I overtake them?"

The answer from God was, "Pursue, for thou shalt surely overtake them, and without fail recover all!" With revived courage he therefore gives his command, "Forward!" and his band of men, pacified by the prospect of bloody revenge, and of delivering their captives from the enemy, suppressed their animosity against their leader, submitted to the command of David, and by hasty marches went forward to the scene of battle. David left those of his 600 men who were wearied (about a third part of the army) at the borders of the wilderness, not far from Gaza, beside the brook Besor, and with the rest went over into the land of the Amalekites.

While on the way, they came upon a man lying in the fields exhausted, and near to death. David gave him drink and food and after that the spirit of the man had come to him again, they heard from his mouth that he was a young man of Egypt, and servant to an Amalekite, who, because he had fallen sick on the march, had been left behind in a helpless condition by his master. For three days he had lain there, and had eaten no bread nor drank any water. The stranger also informed them that they had made an invasion upon the south of the Cherethites (a tribe of the Philistines who had in former times come from the island of Crete) and afterward that they had invaded Judah and the south of the region not far from Hebron, where the descendants of Caleb lived, and had then advanced against Ziklag for the purpose of burning it with fire, and turning it into a heap of ashes.

"Canst thou bring me down to this company?" David asked. The man was ready to do so, after he had caused David to swear to him by the Almighty God that he would neither kill him nor deliver him into the hands of his master. Under his guidance, they reached the borders of the Amalekites, and came upon the wild hordes at the moment when they were spread abroad, eating and drinking and dancing, because of the spoil. Like a storm after clear sunshine, David's band of heroes rushed in amongst them in their fancied security, smote, in a battle which raged from morning until the evening, the whole of them, with the exception of 400 young men who rode upon camels and fled, and recovered from them all that remained of their spoil—sheep, cattle, and whatever else they had carried away in their incursion.

They recovered from them also all their captives, and among these their wives, and then, under David's leadership, returned to Ziklag crowned with honor while a band marched before, exulting as they went, and apparently to compensate for the offense given to David while on the way thither, repeatedly broke out with the triumphal cry, "This is David's spoil!"

When they came again to the 200 men whom they had left at the brook Besor, David hastened forward to them, and presented to them his friendly salutation. This displeased some of the baser men among his band. "The wives and children," they murmured, "may indeed be given back to them but to them who have not shared with us the toils and dangers of the battle belongs nothing else of the spoil that has been recovered from the enemy." Then answered David, who had recovered all his former self-possession, "Ye shall not do so, my brethren, with that which the Lord hath given us, who hath preserved us, and delivered the company that came against us into our hand." Thus he gave God alone the glory. Then he continued: "For who will hearken unto you in this matter? but as his part is that goeth down to the battle, so shall his part be that tarrieth by the stuff: they shall part alike."[2] Thus it was decided according to the express law of God. This law, however, had not always been observed. But from this time forward, as the history announces, it remained again a custom and a law in Israel. According to our own practices in war, also, those who guard the baggage share with the combatants both the fame and the spoil of victory and so it ought to be.

After his return to Ziklag, David thought also on his friends in the tribes of Judah and Simeon, who, during his excursions in the wildernesses and deserts, had rendered him important service, by conveying to him provisions, and by other acts of kindness. It was pleasing to him to be able to give them a practical proof of his gratitude; and he sent

---

2. Numbers 31:27.

to their elders an appropriate present from the booty which had been taken from the Amalekites. To those who had at one time and another been plundered by these hordes, he sent the gifts, with the words, "Behold a present for you of the spoil of the enemies of the Lord." This was indeed a royal act, performed in lively anticipation of his soon being called on to occupy the throne. Unmistakably already the crown of Israel was dimly seen over his head, while the number of his followers was augmented daily by new bands of valiant men.

Among the psalms of David there is none which, in its superscription or contents, contains an undoubted reference to these last occurrences during his sojourn in the land of the Philistines. But we do not err in the supposition that the remembrance of what he experienced there interweaves itself in many of his songs of thanks for the help from God which he had experienced. Certainly this is the case with Psalm 124, "A Song of Pilgrimages," where David represents the whole of Israel as saying with him: "If it had not been the Lord who was on our side when men rose up against us: then they had swallowed us up quick, when their wrath was kindled against us: then the waters had overwhelmed us, the stream had gone over our soul: then the proud waters had gone over our soul. Blessed be the Lord, who hath not given us as a prey to their teeth. Our soul is escaped as a bird out of the snare of the fowlers: the snare is broken and we are escaped. Our help is in the name of the Lord, who made heaven and earth." In this name, we add, let our help also always be!

14

Mourning for the Dead

A dark cloud overshadowed the life of ancient Israel, notwithstanding all the glory wherewith a whole firmament of stars—divinely revealed truths and promises—irradiated it. That cloud was the fear of death which "the day-spring from on high," by which expression Zacharias announces the appearing of Christ, first fully dissipated.[1] Till that time the power of death was not taken away. This power was not indeed regarded in Israel as able to annihilate. Israel's faith in a personal living God included in it also a belief in the continuance of the personal existence after death of men created in the image of God.

This doctrine found also strong support in the divine commandments, fortified as they were with promises and threatenings as well as in the preparations which the Almighty was carrying forward for the founding of a kingdom which must necessarily extend beyond all the limits of time and the boundaries of this world, into eternity. But the faithful possessed what they knew of a life of happiness beyond the grave, rather as the inference of a reflective mind, than as an express divine revelation shining clear as the sun; and the consolation of a dim anticipation, which was far from sufficient to raise them wholly above the fear and dread of the last enemy, supplied the place for them of the blessed hope.

They knew in general only the Sheol or Hades, a kingdom of the dead, in which self-consciousness was not entirely extinguished, which was proved to them by the appearance at Endor of Samuel, who had come over from that other world into this world again in the whole energy of his personality. Yet the conceptions which they

1. Luke 1:7–8.

associated with this kingdom sufficed not to elicit from them any expression like that of Paul's, "I have a desire to depart." Enoch's translation to heaven showed them distinctly enough the way thither; yet without taking into account that this wonderful meteor shone too dimly from a distant past for them to be able to lean their hopes upon it, that man who was carried up to heaven was one who "walked with God" as no one else ever did, while they knew themselves only as poor sinners who had not yet heard of the blood of the Lamb "which cleanseth from all sin."

To some chosen ones among them—particularly the later prophets—it was indeed granted by the Spirit of the Lord to see the veil of clouds farther withdrawn and to direct their eyes with clearer vision into the life beyond death. Thus it was announced to the prophet Isaiah: "He will swallow up death in victory; and the Lord God will wipe away tears from off all faces"[2]; and in another place: "Thy dead men shall live, together with my dead body shall they arise. For thy dew is as the dew of herbs, and the earth shall cast out the dead."[3] So also it was granted to Ezekiel. In the thirty-seventh chapter of his prophecies, the supposition of a resurrection of the dead to a new and blessed life plainly lies at the foundation of his description. Daniel in like manner announces: "Many of them that sleep in the dust of the earth shall awake, some to everlasting life, and some to shame and everlasting contempt. And they that be wise shall shine as the brightness of the firmament; and they that turn many to righteousness as the stars forever and ever."[4]

So also such glimpses into the future were granted to David, of which we shall afterward have the opportunity of convincing ourselves. And did not the path by which Elijah ascended up to heaven shine over Israel like a waymark to a world of glory? Yet for all that it remains true that, during the economy of the Old Covenant, that which then already existed of a clear revelation of a happy future only with great difficulty found a place in the faith of minds which had been filled with anguish by the law. However, the less "the way into the holiest was made manifest" (the expression used in the Epistle to the Hebrews), so much the more worthy of our admiration must the strength of that faith appear which we see operating in so

---

2. Isaiah 25:8.
3. Isaiah 26:19.
4. Daniel 12:2–3.

many in the near prospect of death, in spite of the dimness of those rays of hope which but feebly glimmered among them.

What we have now said may serve as an introduction to the impressive scenes which we are this day to look upon.

2 Samuel 1:17

> And David lamented with this lamentation over Saul, and over Jonathan his son.

It is a mourning for the dead of which we shall this day be witnesses, one of the most affecting scenes which ever moved the hearts of men in this vale of tears. Let us see (1) on whose account is this lamentation; and (2) how they mourned for them.

1. Was the mourning for "a great one in Israel" and those who were near to him? With deep sorrow we shall hear of it. Saul has passed away from this earthly scene. When a monarch dies, it is usually felt by his people as if the very ground trembled beneath their feet. At the death of Saul, in spite of all that has preceded, feelings of this kind even today come over us. The people's lament for the dead echoes distinctly in our hearts, and in spirit we also lay a cypress wreath on the grave of the departed king.

The Philistines whom we again saw in the plain of Jezreel, in the land of Judah, pressed victoriously with their whole force against the host of Israel, driving them in flight before them to the mountains of Gilboa, the northern barrier of the mountain range of Ephraim. Here, where Saul, after he had already been wounded on the head in a fierce fight at the fountain of Ain, had taken up a supposed place of safety in a natural fortress, a new battle was fought, which was, however, as disastrous in its results for him as the previous one. Why need we wonder at this? We hear nothing of humiliation and prayer having been proclaimed in his camp; nothing of his bowing down in holy penitence before the Lord of Sabaoth before the battle was fought; nothing of the offering up of sacrifices or any act of that kind.

The unhappy king had forsaken God, and therefore, also, God the Lord had forsaken him. With terrible impetuosity the heathen burst over entrenchments and bulwarks into the midst of the legions which Saul, faithful to his warlike character, commanded in his own person. His valiant men fell in thousands at his right hand and his left. But from the moment the enemy discovered Saul himself in the tumult of battle, their whole attention is directed toward seizing him as a prisoner. Indeed, very soon a troop of the enemy's archers succeeded in driving him, already retreating, up a steep hill, and there surrounding him. His cause is lost! The bravest of those who were around him have already fallen, and, alas! among them are also three of his sons—Abinadab, Melchi-shua, and the beloved Jonathan.

The king sees no way of escape. Despair seizes him on his lonely rocky eminence, which will immediately be stormed by the enemy. "Draw thy sword," cried he to his armor-bearer, "and thrust me through therewith lest these uncircumcised come and thrust me through, and abuse me." Thus care for his poor honor before the world is the only thing which, in the last moments of his life, lies on his heart. The armor-bearer trembled and shrunk back with horror at the thought of laying his hands on the sacred person of his royal master. Then the king resolutely drew his own sword, placed its hilt on the ground, and threw himself upon it. When the armor-bearer saw him fall down covered with blood, he also followed his example. He might not survive his master. Alas! Beside these dead bodies watches no angel of God. But he who is called "a murderer from the beginning" celebrates a triumph. A rare prey has here fallen to him! But was it so also with his shield-bearer? It rather becomes us to weep over that faithful man than to condemn him. And we leave him in God's gracious hands.

Ah! that a human being, from his youth upward so highly endowed as Saul, and so richly blessed with promise, should come to such an end! All that was in him—his clear understanding, his active, courageous spirit, his knightly disposition, and, added to that, his high imposing stature—pointed him out as if he was altogether born to rule. Besides, he united by nature to his manly resoluteness and vigor of action a tender disposition, easily moved, and also not unsusceptible of the highest and holiest emotions. But the world, with its pomp and its honors, overpowered within him all his early better impressions, which without doubt he had received in the home of his parents, and particularly in his relationship with that man of God, Samuel. That he had not, with his whole soul and without reserve, given himself to the Lord his God, this was his unhappy case.

He descended deeper and deeper along the path of declension on which he had entered, his soul being divided between God and the

world, and his obedience to the Most High being partial and mer-
cenary, until at last he fell into the gulf of complete estrangement
from God and obduracy of heart. The longer he strove against the
discipline of the Spirit of God, so much the more did his sense of
honor degenerate into a fanatical, immoderate ambition, his natural
irritability into an unrestrained anger, his sternness as a ruler into
tyrannical injustice and cruelty, and, in the degree in which he
departed from the Lord, all pious people were to him as his own conscience—the longer the more disagreeable and repulsive. More and
more he withdrew himself from them, and gradually burned with
demoniacal hatred against them. Thus he had already separated himself from the only man who might have had power to lead him back
into the right path—the venerable Samuel—who, as a pure living
mirror, brought to his consciousness only his own degeneracy, and
who therefore must necessarily be to him a troublesome apparition.

That the example of the king exercised a most lamentable influence on the life of the people was not to be wondered at. Faith
disappeared from among them, the worship of God was abandoned,
and public morality degenerated. "In the days of Saul," as the Book
of Chronicles announces, "no one inquired at the ark of God." Thus,
then, King Saul stands in history as a warning illustration of those
spoken of in the words of Solomon, "who leave the paths of uprightness to walk in the ways of darkness; . . . whose house inclineth unto
death, and their paths unto the dead."

When the alarming tidings of the lost battle at Gilboa and of the
death of the king and his sons spread itself over Israel, all the people
who inhabited the hill-country, reaching even to the Jordan,
betook themselves to flight, and the Philistines took possession of the
forsaken towns and hamlets. But to the fallen king that disgrace was
not even spared against which it was the last care of his life to secure
himself. When, on the day after the battle, plundering bands of
Philistines appeared again on the field to take possession of the clothing and other personal effects of the slain, they found on the
mountain, not far from the bodies of his three sons, the corpse of
their royal father, swimming in his own blood. Hearts of stone must
have been softened at this sight.

It provoked the barbarians, however, only to raise a rude cry of triumph. To celebrate their victory, they separated the head of the king
from the trunk, and stripped off his armor and his weapons. The lat-

ter they sent into the land of the Philistines round about as trophies, that therewith they might publish among the people, in the houses of their idols and in the streets, the triumph they had won. The armor of the king they placed as a spectacle in the temple of the goddess Ashtaroth. His body they hung up on the wall of Beth-shan, while they fastened his head in the temple of Dagon, their chief idol.

And did He who dwells in heaven see such wickedness without whetting His glittering sword, and stretching forth His arm for the destruction of those guilty of such inhuman conduct? Indeed, He permitted this to be done; for He meant, in the sight of all the world, to present an evidence that what was formerly spoken by His servant Moses, and afterward also by the prophet Jeremiah, was truth: "O Lord, the hope of Israel, all that forsake Thee shall be ashamed, and they that depart from me shall be written in the earth, because they have forsaken the Lord, the fountain of living waters." One may read the sorrowful epitaph over the grave of King Saul in these words of the sacred history: "So Saul died for his transgression which he committed against the Lord, even against the word of the Lord, which he kept not, and also for asking counsel of one that had a familiar spirit, to inquire of it; and inquired not of the Lord: therefore He slew him, and turned the kingdom unto David the son of Jesse."[5]

God also gave free scope to the crimes of the Philistines for this purpose, that, in opposition to the better spirit which even in those days of general religious declension among the people had not yet wholly disappeared, the cruelty of the heathen might be made manifest to every one. For immediately after this dreadful scene there unveils itself to us the solemn scene of a mourning for the dead in Israel, by which our minds may be again in some degree relieved after their depression.

2. We first meet with a beautiful illustration of genuine gratitude. It is now a long time since Saul freed the inhabitants of the city of Jabesh-Gilead, on the east of Jordan, from the sore oppression under which they sighed, in consequence of the plundering incursions of bands of warlike Amorites. The Jabeshites had not forgotten this act of kindness. When they heard of the terrible blow that had fallen upon their people and upon their deliverer Saul in the mountains of Gilboa, "they arose, all the valiant men," set out for the distant town

---

5. 1 Chronicles 10:13–14.

of Beth-shan, and journeyed during the whole night. Having
reached it, they took down, with reverential silence, from the walls
where they had been fastened by the Philistines, the bodies of Saul
and his three sons, and brought them away, that they might give
them honorable burial among themselves at Jabesh. Here they
burned them (this is the first instance of burning dead bodies in
Israel), then gathered together the bones reduced to ashes, buried
them solemnly under an oak, and fasted in honor of the dead for
seven days. How it refreshes the heart to witness this act of piety! Yet
we shall behold something even more animating.

Where is David now? After the slaughter of the Amalekites, we
saw him return to Ziklag. Here we find him also after the dreadful
disaster had fallen upon his people at Gilboa. He did not yet know
the things which had happened in his fatherland. But, lo! a man
comes running to him in great haste, with the marks of the deepest
sorrow—with his clothes rent, and earth upon his head. As soon as
he came in sight of David, he fell to the earth, and did obeisance,
such as is wont to be offered to princes. "From whence contest thou?"
David asked. He replied, "Out of the camp of Israel am I escaped."
David further inquired, "How went the matter? I pray thee, tell me."
The stranger answered, "The people are fled from the battle, and
many of the people also are fallen and dead; and Saul and Jonathan
his son are dead also!" David, in extreme excitement, cried, "How
knowest thou that Saul and Jonathan his son be dead? And the
young man that told him said, As I happened by chance upon mount
Gilboa, behold, Saul leaned upon his spear; and, lo, the chariots and
horsemen followed hard after him. And when he looked behind him,
he saw me, and called unto me: and I answered, Here am I. And he
said unto me, Who art thou? And I answered him, I am an
Amalekite. He said unto me again, Stand, I pray thee, upon me, and
slay me: for anguish is come upon me, because my life is yet whole in
me. So I stood upon him, and slew him because I was sure that he
could not live after that he was fallen and I took the crown that was
upon his head, and the bracelet that was on his arm, and have
brought them hither unto my lord." Thus spoke the deserter.

How was David affected by these tidings? Filled with extreme sorrow, and at the same time burning with passion and anger, he seizes
his clothes and rends them asunder; and those who were around him
do the same thing, mourning with their leader, weeping and fasting

until nightfall, for Saul, and for Jonathan, Saul's son, and for the people of the Lord, and for the house of Israel, because they were fallen by the sword. In the evening, David sent again for the man who had brought to him the sorrowful tidings, and said to him, "Whence art thou?" He answered, "I am the son of a stranger, an Amalekite." "How wast thou not afraid," continued David, with most violent emotion, "to stretch forth thine hand to destroy the Lord's anointed?" Then, turning to one of his warriors, he commanded him: "Up, smite this man!" The stroke follows, and the stranger falls dead to the ground. As he fell, David gave utterance to these words: "Thy blood be upon thy head: for thy mouth hath testified against thee, saying, I have slain the Lord's anointed."

Did the man truly slay the king? Possibly it was the case that he found him still living after his suicidal act, and at his request had given him the last death-stroke. But probably his whole story was only a tissue of falsehoods, and all the truth that was in it was confined to this one thing merely, that as he passed across the field of battle for the purpose of plundering the dead, after the manner of the Amalekites, he drew near to that part of the mountain to which Saul and his armor-bearer had fled, at the moment when that scene of despair occurred between the two. Then, when he saw the unhappy men dead, swimming in their blood, he hastened forward to take possession of Saul's royal insignia. His bringing these latter to David was done, without doubt, for the purpose of ingratiating himself for the whole future of his life into the favor of David, whose succession to the throne was now to all the world, as well as to him, a matter beyond doubt.

For a like reason, he made use of the hypocritical mode of expression in his report that Saul "could no longer live," on account of his falling away from Jehovah, and that it was the God of Israel who had condemned him. Enough: whether he spoke the truth or no, the sentence of David against him, especially since there was now no more a king in the land, and he, as captain of his host, exercised the office of judge in it, was an altogether righteous one, and places before us in the best light the character of the son of Jesse. This action of his was also a solemnity in honor of the king of Israel; and the bloody sacrifice was glorifying to the Lord, who by His Holy Spirit had said, "Touch not mine anointed!"

This stormy scene was soon followed by a more peaceful and more noble one. David gave vent to the feelings of his heart in a lamentation for Saul and Jonathan, which, after all the darkness with which we have seen him encompassed for a long time, brings back again to us, in undimmed brightness, "the man after God's own heart." One would have thought that no more welcome news could have been brought to David than this, that his implacable deadly foe had at length been called away from the scene. But we rather hear the tones of genuine, deeply felt sorrow with which he laments his departure. Oh, how it puts us again to shame to meet, in the days of the Old Testament, love to an enemy such as that which David here manifests; a love so pure, true, and honest as this, among us who know the revelation of the love of God in Christ to sinners, belongs, alas, to the rarer pearls!

But let us listen to David's lamentation, as in genuine and unfeigned simplicity it flows warmly from the depths of his heart. It is one of the most pathetic and most beautiful odes that ever flowed from a human breast. The eye of David rests first on the bloody battlefield, and, deeply moved, he makes mention of the triumph which the uncircumcised had there gained over the people of the Lord:

> The beauty of Israel is slain upon thy high places, O Gilboa!
> How are the mighty fallen!
> Tell it not in Gath, publish it not in the streets of Askelon;[6]
> Lest the daughters of the Philistines rejoice,
> Lest the daughters of the uncircumcised triumph!

Then, abandoning himself wholly to his sorrow, he seems to look upon the dead bodies of the two chiefs of the people, and then with opened mouth and heart proclaims their praise:

> Ye mountains of Gilboa, let there be no dew,
> Neither let there be rain upon you, nor fields of offerings:[7]

All nature is summoned to join with him in his lamentation:

> For there the shield of the mighty is vilely cast away,
> The shield of Saul, as though he had not been anointed with oil.
> From the blood of the slain, from the fat of the mighty,
> The bow of Jonathan turned not back,
> And the sword of Saul returned not empty.

---

6. In the towns of the Philistines.
7. Consecrated gifts for the temple from abundant harvests.

Saul and Jonathan were lovely and pleasant in their lives,[8]
And in their death they were not divided:
They were swifter than eagles, they were stronger than lions.
Ye daughters of Israel, weep over Saul,
Who clothed you in scarlet, with other delights;
Who put on ornaments of gold upon your apparel.[9]
How are the mighty fallen in the midst of the battle!
O Jonathan, thou wast slain in thine high places!

David then raises a special memorial of his tender love to his friend, in these words—

I am distressed for thee, my brother Jonathan:
Very pleasant hast thou been unto me:
Thy love to me was wonderful, passing the love of women!

And, as a conclusion, he breathes out at once all his deep sorrow in the sigh—

How are the mighty fallen,
And the weapons of war perished!

David gave to this elegy the title of "The Bow," and thereby designated it as a song of mourning for the battlefield. As such, he bade them teach it to the children of Judah, and especially to those who were able to go forth to war; and commanded that it should be inserted in the collection of songs in the "Book of Jasher," in which also the miracle of the standing still of the sun at the command of Joshua is recorded.[10] But this collection has not come down to us.

One might perhaps consider as exaggerated the expressions which David made use of in praise of Saul, and be inclined to doubt the inward truthfulness of that song of praise. But let it be remembered that at the graves of the departed whom we have associated with in life, almost always the bright sides of their character come prominently out to view, and rise up before the teary eye of memory. Whatever, at some time or other, may have been said to the reproach of the departed then disappears, through knowledge, now without hindrance, making the best of it. One also is led to take

8. Literally, were reciprocally loving and beloved.
9. Of the spoils of war.
10. Joshua 10:13.

guilt to himself regarding those actions, however numerous or what-ever be the importance attached to them, by which they have caused us sorrow.

Such a thing happened to David, who without doubt could not but say to himself that he was not always and everywhere so master of his youthful spirit as he ought to have been, in his bearing toward his king and the father of his wife. And how natural was it for him to conceive that oftentimes the thought that his crown would descend to a stranger, the shepherd of Bethlehem, instead of being inherited by his own house, would call up dark spirits in the heart of the king. And indeed David did not, in his lamentation, speak too highly in praise of the king. Was not Saul truly a warlike hero? Did not also that which was gentle and tender oftentimes find an echo in his soul? And did there not exist between him and his sons, not even excluding Jonathan, a cordial relationship, in spite of all the stormy scenes which sometimes occurred? Did they not show themselves toward him true and faithful children even unto death? All this at that time hovered before the mind of David. With such recollections as these there was associated a deep, sorrowful com-passion for the sad fate of the king. And thus it was David's gentle feeling and sentiment to which he gave full outspoken expression in his lamentation for the dead.

These words of the song—

Tell it not in Gath, publish it not in the streets of Askelon—

have since that time, in the circles of the faithful, become a proverb. It is frequently heard when one of their community has failed to take heed to his ways, and so has given rise to a scandal. Would that that call were more faithfully observed than is for the most part the case! Would that the honor of the spiritual Zion lay always as near to the heart of the children of the kingdom as did that of the earthly to the heart of David! But how often does it hap-pen that they even strive to disclose before the world the weaknesses of their brethren, and thus, by a repetition of the wickedness of Ham, become traitors to the Church which Christ has purchased with His own blood. Thus they make themselves guilty of bringing dishonor upon the gospel, while they open the gates to such dishonor through their perhaps altogether malicious tale-bearing, and to their own great prejudice disown the charity which "believeth all things, and hopeth all things," and also "covereth a multitude of sins."

David's address to the mountains of Gilboa, "Let there be no dew, neither let there be rain upon you, nor fields of offerings," has remained at least without wide-reaching consequences. The region referred to forms, at the present day, one of the most fruitful and blessed districts in all the Holy Land. "The curse causeless," says Solomon, "shall not come." But the words of David are not a curse; they are only a bold figurative expression employed to denote his deep sorrow. At all events this is manifest from his impassioned mode of address, that at least at that time even in him the hope of an eternal blessed life was not strong enough to overcome the terror and dread of death and the grave.

In his song there is no trace of his being able to look beyond the grave to paradise on the farther side. We meet with no word in it of a comforting hope that those separated by death would ever meet again. Even before his eyes there hung a thick veil hiding heaven from his view. It is true indeed that, in the after period of his life, we see that dark veil raising itself more and more from before him; but how infinitely more blessed is our lot than was that of those ancient saints, even in the moments of their greatest enlightenment! Let us also hold, in spirit, a quiet celebration on the mountains of Gilboa. Let us look upon the bloody corpse of the king, not without a shudder it may be, yet still with the hope that, in the last moments of his life, God may have broken his heart with repentance, and that he may have become partaker of the malefactor's pardon. But to Jonathan we may address the words of the poet:

> 'Tis well! All hail to thee now!
> Gone to that blissful land;
> The victor's crown on thy brow,
> Amid a glorious band.
> —Gerhardt

On the graves of both of them we plant in spirit the cross of Golgotha; and let us rejoice in the truth that for all in this world who bend themselves in genuine humility before God the blood is shed which "speaketh better things than that of Abel," and takes away all sin!

15

David, King in Judah

Almost 500 years before Israel became a kingdom, the divine law which was to guide and rule the domestic conduct of its future king was already laid up among the archives of the nation. We find it recorded in the fifth book of Moses. God the Lord, it is there said, would, in the exercise of His sovereign power, always choose out and set up over them the man who should be their king. Israel must not set a stranger on their throne; but their king must always be one from among their brethren. The king was never, through a vain desire after a multitude of beautiful and stately horses, to allow himself to be misled into forming an alliance with Egypt, which would only bring ruin and be a snare to him and his people. Also, he was not to multiply to himself wives, lest his heart might thereby be turned away. He was to guard also against covetousness and an unseemly accumulation of state treasures. He was rather to put his gold and silver into circulation for the welfare of the land.

But, above all, when he sat upon the throne of his kingdom, he was always to remember the law of his God. He was enjoined to cause a transcript of it, by the hand of the priest, to be delivered to him to have this holy record always before his eyes, and to read therein all the days of his life, "that he may learn to fear the Lord his God, to keep all the words of this law, and these statutes, to do them: that his heart be not lifted up above his brethren, and that he turn not aside from the commandment, to the right hand or to the left: to the end that he may prolong his days in his kingdom, he, and his children in the midst of Israel" (i.e., may transmit the scepter to his descendants, and preserve it forever in his house).[1]

---

1. Deuteronomy 17:19–20.

Could there have been given to the kings a more excellent rule of direction for their government in so few words? And is not this rule essentially one of unchanging value for all the great ones of the earth, and may we not claim for it an application also to kings of the present day? Wherever the path here marked out is closely followed with an unfaltering step, there the blessings of heaven will flow down in copious streams over the land. But are we able to trace in history the shining footsteps of many who have followed this rule of conduct? Among those rulers who have at least approximately presented, as realized in their own persons, the example of a prince such as is here described by the hand of God, without contradiction one of the first places belongs to the man whom we today see mount the throne in the name of God.

2 Samuel 2:4

> And the men of Judah came, and there they anointed David king over the house of Judah.

That which has been long anticipated in Israel is now accomplished. David, purified in the furnace of severe persecutions and sorrowful humiliations, and strong in faith through the joyful experience of wonderful deliverances and merciful exaltations, is prepared and ready for the lofty dignity which the Lord has destined for him. He is now called to the throne by the grace of Him who has reserved to Himself the right of absolute sovereignty and supreme power over His covenant people. Three noble features of character distinguishing David, and rich in promise, come before our view today: the first in what occurred between him and the Jabeshites immediately after he had ascended the throne; the second in his treatment of Abner; and the third in his relation to Ish-bosheth.

1. We may well conceive that after the death of Saul, David recalled not only the significant act of anointing which Samuel once performed on him at Bethlehem, but also the many prophetic intimations which here and there he had heard uttered regarding the future of his life. Very far, however, from putting forth any claim on account of them, he turned to the Lord, not indeed without great agitation of mind, and inquired of Him by the high Priest, through the "Urim and Thummim," "Shall I go up into any of the cities of Judah?" The answer from God was, "Go up." David asked for further

instruction. It was then said to him, "Go to Hebron in Judah." But why should he go to Judah? Judah was the place of his birth, and where the most of his friends resided. At the same time, Judah was then free from the Philistines, while they had possession of a large part of the other districts of the land. But where was now the army of Saul? After the battle of Gilboa, it had been disbanded; and only small companies of the soldiers had been assembled again by Abner, the chief captain, on the borders of Gad and Manasseh, on the other side of Jordan, that he might by their help raise Ish-bosheth, Saul's fourth son, to his father's throne.

At the command of God, David, with his two wives, Ahinoam and Abigail, and his men of war, who had recently been considerably increased in number by the addition of a strong reinforcement from Manasseh, went to ancient Hebron. Scarcely had he reached it, when from all sides the people, who had long since recognized in him their future king, gathered around him, being specially strengthened in this presentiment by the circumstance that the high priest, and with him also the prophet Gad, had gone over to the side of David. By means of the former, the son of Jesse now for the first time received confirmation of Samuel's anointing; and, amid universal shouting for joy, he was saluted as the ruler of the nation, chosen and unequivocally pointed out by God for that dignity.

David's first thoughts, after he had received the homage of the people, were of King Saul, his unhappy predecessor on the throne. Where rested the mortal remains of the anointed of God? Had they received an honorable burial, worthy of a king? David heard what the men of Jabesh in Gilead had done. Without delay he sent messengers to them, who were to say, "Blessed be ye of the Lord, that ye have showed this kindness unto your lord, even unto Saul, and have buried him. And now the Lord show kindness and truth unto you: and I also will requite you this kindness, because ye have done this thing. Therefore now let your hands be strengthened, and be valiant; for your master Saul is dead, and also the house of Judah have anointed me king over them." This mark of true piety toward the departed king, this honorable acknowledgment publicly paid to him, in spite of all the harshness of his treatment of David, could not but fill all who heard of it with a deep respect for the truly royal disposition of the new ruler.

The hearty words of thanks which he sent to the men of Jabesh could not fail also to affect them and to gain their hearts. They were persuaded by it that this man, uninfluenced by the low spirit of revenge and malice, knew how to forgive and to forget, and that all the wrongs and injuries which he had experienced had not the power to obscure to him the dignity and sacredness of his predecessor, as the anointed of the Lord. Moreover, by that conduct of David, the decided impression was produced among the people that they might expect from him a humane government, while he would also honor the lowliest and most insignificant praiseworthy actions, which might be anywhere done in the land, with a thankful recognition of their worth.

2. The hopeful frame of mind with which the people already regarded David was soon to experience a yet further strengthening. Abner, Saul's uncle, and captain of the host, a man of an intrepid, active, heroic nature, but also a man of unbounded ambition, had, with the bands which he had again gathered around him after the breaking-up of the army, gradually rescued from the Philistines a considerable part of those provinces which they had seized. He had, under the pretext of fighting for the rightful and legitimate heir to the throne, raised the standard, not in favor of David, but rather of the rival king, Ish-bosheth the son of Saul, and at Mahanaim, in Gilead, had formally proclaimed the man of his choice as king over the whole of Israel, although there were only a few tribes of the land which had as yet acknowledged him and submitted to his authority.

He now proceeded to devise plans against the tribe of Judah, and threw into it first the torch of civil war. He succeeded, in fact, in alienating from David considerable numbers, and in assembling them under the banner of rebellion which he had unfurled. But David also prepared for war, and sent against him Joab, his chief captain, the son of Zeruiah. They met together by the pool of Gibeon, not far from Jerusalem. Abner proposed that the war should be decided by twelve men from each side engaging in single combat. The plan was adopted. But since those who were chosen for this combat destroyed each other in the fierce engagement ("wherefore that place was called Helkath-hazzurim," i.e., "field of swords," or "of the sharp knives"), and consequently neither of the parties could claim the victory, a very sore battle was fought, in which the rebels were completely defeated. Abner was personally involved in the crowd of fugitives.

Asahel, the brother of Joab, a man "as light of foot as a wild roe," pursued after him with naked sword, and turned not to the right hand nor to the left. Abner, the hero experienced in war, for a long time warded off the stroke of the sword of his pursuer, and entreated him to cool his courage against some other one of the host; for he hesitated to slay Joab's brother, because this might have involved a failure of some of his secret calculations. But when Asahel did not listen to his voice, Abner turned himself and smote him through with his spear, so that he sank dead to the ground. "And it came to pass," the history relates, "that as many as came to the place where Asahel fell down and died, stood still." A deep, painful sorrow, that such a hero should fall, arrested the steps of everyone that drew near.

In the host of David, anger against Abner burned most fiercely. Joab and Abishai were both brothers of Asahel, and, bent on revenge, they pursued the murderer with all their might till the sun went down. When they reached to the hill of Ammah, Abner saw himself suddenly strengthened by the addition of a company of Benjamites, and he ventured, under their protection, to offer peace to Joab. Joab replied, "Unless thou hadst spoken, surely then in the morning the people had gone up every one from following his brother." Joab then caused the trumpet to be blown, as a signal to the people to cease from the pursuit, and they obeyed. But Abner with his men during that same night crossed over the Jordan, and came back to Mahanaim. Joab, on the other hand, after he had solemnly laid his brother Asahel in his father's sepulcher at Bethlehem, came with his men to Hebron. The victory was wholly on his side. Of his men he had lost only nineteen, besides Asahel. But of those who followed Abner there were left 360 dead on the field of battle. There was now a brief pause in the war; but the purpose of vengeance against the murderer of their brother did not depart from the hearts of Joab and of Abishai.

When Abner had come again to Mahanaim to Ish-bosheth, he took to him in marriage one of Saul's concubines, whose name was Rizpah. This bold step was construed, and certainly not without reason, as indicating that he himself aspired to the crown of Israel, since the successors of the king were wont, according to a perverse custom, to obtain as an inheritance his wives also. This arrogance of Abner provoked Ish-bosheth himself against his ambitious counselor. He did not fail to pour upon him the sternest reproaches. Abner, in his rash manner, wrathfully replied: "Am I a dog's head, which

against Judah do show kindness this day unto the house of Saul thy
father, to his brethren and to his friends, and have not delivered thee
into the hand of David, that thou chargest me today with a fault concerning this woman? So do God to Abner, and more also, except, as
the Lord hath sworn to David, even so I do to him; to translate the
kingdom from the house of Saul, and to set up the throne of David
over Israel, and over Judah, from Dan even to Beer-sheba!" Thus
spoke the tyrant. An outburst of anger such as this the feeble Ish-
bosheth could not withstand. He trembled with fear, his speech went
from him, and he could not answer Abner a word again.

And as for Abner, how did he act? He kept by his purpose. He had
never meant to be faithful to Ish-bosheth, but in fellowship with him
pursued only his own selfish ends. He sent messengers to David, and
made offer of his service to him. "Whose is the land?" he directed it
to be said to him. His meaning was, "Whose should it be? I give it
unto thee." "Make thy league with me," he further said, in making
his proposal, "and, behold, my hand shall be with thee, to bring
about all Israel unto thee." Abner recognized now most distinctly in
David the rising star in Israel and however haughtily his words might
sound, he only sought to conceal behind them his despair of Ish-
bosheth's cause.

David believed that in this offer of Abner a divine providence was
to be observed, which would make, as he hoped, a full end to the
unhappy civil war. He declared himself ready to enter into the proposed league. He made this condition, however, that Abner was not
to appear again before his face unless he brought to him his lawful
wife Michal, Saul's daughter, whom her father had, against all law
and right, taken from him and married to Phaltiel. He sent a similar
message to Ish-bosheth. The hand of the king's son must atone for
the injustice he had received from his father Saul, that the restitu-
tion might thereby assume a legitimate character. Besides, it is
conceivable, leaving out of view his love for Michal, that it would be
to David a matter of consequence, for the sake of his authority among
the people, that the king's daughter should be again united with him.

Ish-bosheth, the good-natured man, who without doubt had also
gradually arrived at the conviction that he had no legitimate claim
to the throne of his father, complied with the desire of David. The
commission was given to Abner to dissolve the unrighteous marriage
with Phaltiel. An affecting scene now presented itself. Phaltiel, also

called Phalti, "went with his wife along weeping behind her," till at
Bahurim Abner commanded him to return. Deeply bowed down,
Phaltiel submitted himself to the sad necessity, and many tears
dropped from his eyes during his homeward journey. From this occurrence it is clear that, among the wild briars of unsettled family
relationships by which Israel was then overgrown, here and there also
the flowers of a true genuine love and fidelity were to be met with.
They bloomed, indeed, in the house of David, but their growth was
not unhindered, and he did not remain untouched by the curse
which the Lord had attached to the crime of polygamy in Israel.

After Abner had accompanied Michal to Hebron, he went away
to induce the elders of the so-called kingdom of Ish-bosheth to come
over to the side of David. "Ye sought for David in times past," said he
to them, "to be king over you." And this was indeed the case. "Now
then do it," he added, with a show of piety: "for the Lord hath spoken of David, saying, By the hand of my servant David I will save my
people Israel out of the hand of the Philistines, and out of the hand
of all their enemies."

Then Abner passed through the land of Benjamin, whose inhabitants, beyond all others, had stood fast by the house of Saul, and
spoke to them similar words. After these journeyings, he returned to
Hebron with twenty men, and announced to David with what favorable results his endeavors had hitherto been crowned. David,
rejoicing greatly to see the end of the civil war drawing near, caused
a royal feast to be made for Abner and those who were with him.
After this, Abner again departed, to carry forward, as he said, his
work of peace in the other districts of the land that were as yet under
Ish-bosheth. "I will arise and go," said he, "and will gather all Israel
unto my lord the king, that they may make a league with thee, and
that thou mayest reign over all that thine heart desireth." And David
dismissed him with the salutation of peace.

But immediately thereafter there occurred another scene at
Hebron. Joab returned in triumph with the host entrusted to him,
laden with spoil, from a successful expedition against the Philistines,
and when he received information that Abner had been with the
king, and had been graciously received by him, and in like manner
sent away again, he burned with fierce anger. He rushed into the
king's chamber, and said to him, with less reverence than was befitting, "What hast thou done? behold, Abner came unto thee; why is

it that thou hast sent him away, and he is quite gone? Knowest thou not Abner the son of Ner? He came to deceive thee, and to know thy going out and thy coming in, and all that thou doest!" David heard him in silence; but Joab had formed his own plan. Without David's knowledge, he sent messengers after Abner, who, under pretense of acting in the king's name, were to bring him back again to Hebron. At the well of Sirah, not far from Hebron, the messengers overtook Abner. He believed what they said to him, returned with them, and was received by Joab in an apparently friendly manner.

But before accompanying him into the king's chamber, Joab led him under the gate, where his brother Abishai joined him as an associate, with the pretense of having something to confide to him in secret. He began his conversation with him with the appearance of unfeigned sincerity, and then unexpectedly smote him with his spear, piercing him through, as Abner had once done his brother Asahel, so that he fell in the agonies of death at Joab's feet. Thus the vow of vengeance which he had sworn against Abner was satisfied. But who can describe the anger and astonishment with which David heard of this murder? "I and my kingdom," he cried out, "are guiltless before the Lord forever from the blood of Abner the son of Ner." Then he thundered out (in the spirit of the Old Testament, it is true) the fearful imprecation on Joab, on whose head the crime rested, that there might never fail from the house of Joab, as a terrible warning to all assassins, one "that leaneth on a staff, or that falleth on the sword, or that lacketh bread." And, after this outbreak of anger, he prescribed a national mourning for the slain, while he, with Joab and all the people, rent their clothes and covered themselves with sackcloth and ashes. At the burial of the dead, he did not satisfy himself with personally following the bier, but at the grave of the murdered man he shed a flood of tears, and drew the people that stood around into sympathy with him, so that they all wept with him. Lamenting for the dead, he testified, "Abner has not died as a fool" (as an evil-doer) "dies"; and then he departed from Abner's grave, uttering these words: "Thy hands are not bound, nor thy feet" (as the feet of a murderer) "put into fetters: as a man falleth before wicked men, so fellest thou!" And, believing this testimony of their king, all the people wept again over the departed.

Having returned from the grave, David altogether refused to partake of the burial-feast which, according to Jewish custom, had been prepared, saying, "So do God to me, and more also, if I taste bread, or ought else, till the sun be down" (it was as yet midday). "And all the people took notice of it, and it pleased them" that the king so truly and deeply mourned for one of his servants: "as whatsoever the king did" (so says the history) "pleased all the people." Every one was fully convinced that the king was altogether free from participation in the bloody deed. David honored the dead with that beautiful testimony, which has since so frequently been repeated at the graves of distinguished men: "Know ye not that there is a prince and a great man fallen this day in Israel?"

In speaking thus he did not say too much. Abner was a powerful man, who would have been a mighty support to David, particularly in the field, in the establishment of his kingdom. He was consumed, it is true, as has already been remarked, by a burning thirst for authority and honor—a thirst which sooner or later would have been more dangerous to the king than he himself yet imagined. David knew well that Abner was at one time not the last among Saul's mighty men who had stirred him up against him, in whom the observant captain had detected sooner than all others the future king. Yet David, who experienced such joy in the consciousness of forgiveness, which had been so abundantly extended to him by God, remembered this no more against him; and therefore his unfeigned sorrow for Abner could only be to his honor. Indeed, it bore witness that there was in him a kingly disposition.

But why did David allow Joab to go unpunished? Had he not manifestly made himself guilty of a great crime, since it was not revenge for the shedding of blood which he had executed, but pure murder, since Abner had not slain Asahel like an assassin, but in the midst of the battle, and, moreover, only in the last extremity? Let us hear the king himself. He said to those around him: "I am this day weak" (i.e., scarcely yet have I reached the throne), "though anointed king" (a prince only over Judah, but who had yet to subdue his kingdom); "and these men, the sons of Zeruiah, are too mighty for me" (literally, they are harder, more inflexible, and sterner than I am). What was the meaning of these words? He meant to say, "I have need of such resolute, strong men for my warlike enterprises, which must now be undertaken." At the same time, in his words David gave it to be distinctly understood that he would not have the beginning of his reign signalized by a sentence of death against one of the most heroic and most honored captains of his host; and this so much the less, because it was love toward his slain brother which had placed in Joab's hands the weapon against Abner. The king concluded his address in these words: "The Lord shall reward the doer of evil according to his wickedness." He placed judgment in this matter wholly in the hands of the Almighty, and therefore stood guiltless and justified before his people.

3. Two years had passed away since Ish-bosheth was proclaimed rival king at Mahanaim. The war between his adherents and David had continued, even after the death of Abner, without much bloodshed, indeed, and always favorably to the cause of the rightful ruler. "David," it is said, "waxed stronger and stronger, and the house of Saul" (through the enforced as well as through the willing subjection of the tribes) "waxed weaker and weaker. In the First Book of Chronicles we read a long list of men skilled in arms, who, particularly after Abner's death (and in consequence of this event Ish-bosheth's courage also had failed him), poured in from all quarters of the land to Hebron to testify their submission to David.[2] A way, however, was made for the first time for the general submission of the people, by a new occurrence, which was by none so truly and so deeply lamented and condemned as it was by the man who might have hailed it as the most desirable thing that could have happened in his interest.

Among Ish-bosheth's partisans were two men who were captains of bands, Baanah and Rechab, sons of Rimmon, a man from one of the towns of the small Hivite free states of Gibeon, which formerly, at the time of the conquest of Canaan, had entered by means of an artifice into a covenant with the Israelites. After the discovery of their pious fraud, they were, however, pardoned by Joshua, and, because they promised truly to renounce the service of idols, were received under the protection of Israel, and were employed in all manner of service, particularly about the holy tabernacle. Three of their towns, among which was Beeroth, the birthplace of the above-named captains of bands, were reckoned to the tribe of Benjamin. Four hundred years after Joshua, it came into Saul's tyrannical mind, without any cause, utterly to destroy the Gibeonites, who lived as a peaceful and pious people in his land. Many of them fled to the dis-

---

2. 1 Chronicles 13.

tant town of Gittaim. Among these was Rimmon, whose sons must
have found favor in the eyes of Saul, because we find them as lead-
ers in his army. Yet it is to be supposed that, in the remembrance of
the injury inflicted on their race, they rendered only half-hearted service to the house of Saul. What may have embittered them
particularly against Saul's son is not announced. It must have, however, been soon apparent to them that Ish-bosheth's cause was
irremediably lost. The hope of finding under the new government a
more splendid place than had hitherto been granted to them, may
also have been among the motives which led to their criminal plot.

They come to Mahanaim with the pretense of obtaining provisions—in particular, wheat for their army. It was about midday, and
the sun shone at its brightest, when Ish-bosheth had retired into a
cool chamber, that he might there enjoy his noonday rest.
Concealing the murderous weapons under their garments, the two
traitors came stealthily up to him, fell upon the couch of their lord,
to whom they had sworn fidelity, and smote him through while he
slept. After they had separated his head from his body, they hastened
with it, through the whole night, to the residence of the newly
crowned king of Judah, full of joyful expectation of the triumph with
which they would be welcomed at Hebron. Having arrived there,
they appeared before David, unveiled in his presence their bloody
trophy, and said to him, "Behold the head of Ish-bosheth the son of
Saul thine enemy, which sought thy life; and the Lord hath
avenged my lord the king this day of Saul and of his seed."

David stood paralyzed with astonishment and terror. For the second time such an embassy as this must have made his heart
tremble within him! Yet he did not need to consider long what was
to be done. With holy indignation he looked upon the murderers,
and then, turning to those around him, said, "As the Lord liveth,
who hath redeemed my soul out of all adversity, when one told me,
saying, Behold, Saul is dead (thinking to have brought good tidings),
I took hold of him, and slew him in Ziklag, who thought that I would
have given him a reward for his tidings: how much more, when
wicked men have slain a righteous person in his own house upon his
bed? shall I" (looking toward the strangers) "not therefore now
require his blood of your hand, and take you away from the earth?"
And when he had said this, he commanded some of his soldiers who
stood around him, and they led away the murderers from his pres-

ence, smote them to the ground with the edge of the sword, cut off their hands and their feet, and hung them up as a terrible spectacle and warning by the pool at Hebron. But they took the head of the murdered son of Saul and buried it honorably, according to the command of David, in the sepulcher of Abner in Hebron.

By such conduct as this on the part of David, the respect as well as the hope with which the people regarded him could not but be greatly increased. Every one felt that his sorrow for the fate of Ish-bosheth was as pure as his indignation against his murderers was stern. Evidence was again afforded that he knew how to temper the strict execution of justice; yea, even to use gentleness when the matter respected injuries which had been done to himself personally, and even to keep his eye open to the discovery of the better sides of the character of his sworn enemies. Before all the people he honored the rival king Ish-bosheth with the name of a "righteous person," and thereby indicated that he had been goaded on to rebellion against him whom God had chosen by those around him, who were lusting for power and covetous of honor. These things also open up to us a most pleasing and encouraging glance into the future of the government of the new ruler over the people of God. The bloody acts to which he had found himself shut up were not a reproach to him, but became him as the representative and guardian of the inviolable law of God in Israel.

Psalm 25 belongs to the first period of David's kingly reign. He opens it by calling upon the Lord for His mercy and His gracious presence. "Let none that wait on Thee be ashamed," we hear him saying, "let them be ashamed who transgress without cause." Thereupon he prays the Lord that He would show him His way, and lead him in His truth. "Thou," he adds with confidence, "art the God of my salvation; on Thee do I wait all the day." The words that follow move us with their sorrowful tone: "Remember not the sins of my youth, nor my transgressions: according to Thy mercy remember Thou me for Thy goodness' sake, O Lord." But again he lifts up his voice in praise to God as one who is "good and upright, and therefore will teach sinners in the way; yea, all whose paths are mercy and truth unto such as keep His covenant and His testimonies."

After this, the psalmist describes the blessed lot of him who fears the Lord. The Lord will teach him the way wherein he should walk. "His soul shall dwell at ease; and his seed shall inherit the earth." It is true there were many of the enemies of the psalmist yet within the land; and the Philistines were again threatening the borders. Moreover, the impetuous men around him showed a disposition that was little in accordance with his. He often felt himself lonely and miserable, but his eyes were ever toward the Lord. He knew that the Lord would pluck his feet out of every net. He concludes with the beautiful saying, "Let integrity and uprightness preserve me; for I wait on Thee"; and adds the prayer, "Redeem Israel, O God, out of all his troubles."

And how shall we conclude this day's meditation? With the prayerful wish that this saying of David's might not only be truly uttered by all the great and mighty ones of the earth, but also that it might more and more become our own. For this accompanies it: "God sends prosperity to the upright," and "He is a buckler to all them that walk uprightly."

16

David, King Over Israel

It was a solemn and ever memorable moment in which the old patriarch Jacob, from his deathbed in Egypt, bestowed upon his sons his parting blessings, and in prophetic intimations unveiled to them their future. After he had blessed his first-born, Reuben, and then the two that followed, Simeon and Levi, he beckoned to Judah (not his favorite son, since he had brought upon him much grief and sorrow) to draw near to his couch. The heart and the tongue of the old man were no longer in his own power; but the Spirit of God was upon him, and, overcoming within him his human predilection for the sons of Rachel, namely for Joseph and Benjamin, put into his lips these words, the grandeur and far-reaching significance of whose meaning remained in part perhaps to himself a secret: "Judah, thou art he," he said to him, "whom thy brethren shall praise: thy hand shall be in the neck of thine enemies; thy father's children shall bow down before thee. Judah is a lion's whelp: from the prey, my son, thou art gone up: he stooped down, he couched" (namely, after victorious battles) "as a lion, and as an old lion; who shall rouse him up? The scepter" (the symbol of royalty) "shall not depart from Judah, nor a lawgiver from between his feet, until Shiloh (the Prince of Peace) come; and unto Him shall the gathering of the people be."[1]

History has long ago affixed its seal of ratification, word for word, on this prophecy. Already, when the beloved land was conquered, it was the tribe of Judah which laid its hand on the enemy with the courage and strength of the young lion. We know, however, who it is in whom that ancient Word has found, and will yet further find, its final and exhausting realization. This complete fulfillment was pre-

---

1. Genesis 49:8–10.

figured in the person and life-course of the man whom we shall this day salute as he sits upon the throne, ruler over all Israel. It is pleasant to see how the seed-corn, apparently insignificant, which was cast into the earth a thousand years before, in the remote land of Egypt, is continually springing up and always sending out new branches, till at last it majestically unfolds itself, covering with its shadow all the ends of the earth.

2 Samuel 5:1, 7

> Then came all the tribes of Israel to David unto Hebron, and spake, saying, Behold, we are thy bone and thy flesh. And David took the stronghold of Zion: the same is the city of David.

"The word of the Lord is right; and all His works are done in truth."[2] Thus spoke David in the thirty-third Psalm. He had already richly experienced all this, and felt his soul sustained and elevated by this truth till this day, when we again meet with him. (1) The homage of all the people, and (2) the subjugation of the stronghold of Zion, are the two facts to which at present we confine our attention.

1. Joy prevails in Israel. The division which tore the people is healed. Every doubt as to David's divine call to occupy the throne of the king has disappeared. The house of Saul lies in ruins under the hand of the Almighty. His son Ish-bosheth is dead, and Mephibosheth, Saul's last surviving descendant, is incapable of succeeding to the throne, having been incurably lamed when a child, due to a fall. And who could deny that David, the deliverer of the fatherland from the power of the Philistines, the subduer of the Amalekites, who, with his widespread fame as a hero, united in himself also the renown of an unsullied love of righteousness, rooting itself in the fear of God, a wonderful magnanimity and generosity, an affability and gentleness which gained everyone, and altogether the rarest excellences of heart and spirit—who could deny that this David had already for a long time borne on his brow the impress of one divinely called to be sole ruler over Israel?

So there came unto him representatives of all the tribes, from Dan to Beer-sheba, after the last seditious convulsions in the provinces had been suppressed, penitent on account of their opposition, and now fully reconciled to him, to do homage to him as their king at

---

2. Psalm 33:4.

Hebron. "Behold," said they, "we are thy bone and thy flesh" (i.e., related to thee by blood). "Also in time past, when Saul was king over us, thou wast he that leddest out and broughtest in Israel: and the Lord said to thee, Thou shalt be a captain over Israel." From the last words we again see that the prophetic sayings which had heretofore been uttered concerning David, beginning with the prophecy of old Samuel, had been widely spread abroad among the whole people. Full of thanks to his God, who had so graciously brought him hitherto, David entered into a holy covenant with the elders, the representatives of Israel, and, solemnly praising Him, vowed to them before the Lord, in perfect honesty of heart, that he would govern only in the name of the Lord, and in accordance with the word and direction of the Lord alone.

Thus Israel, after long division, was again one kingdom. It had cost David not less than seven years continuous labor, partly in subduing the rebels, partly in wisely governing that portion of the land of Judah which had submitted to him from the beginning, to reconcile and unite to himself all the tribes. The hope for the future of Israel long appeared like a dead tree. Now it sent forth fresh new branches rich with promise. Seldom, perhaps, has any prince ascended a throne with a better conscience than did David. No reproach, either of a human intrigue or of improper conduct toward the house of Saul could be laid at his door. And how fortunate is it for a people when he who is called to be the director of their affairs is a man with conscience void of offense! This is what Solomon means when he says, "Blessed art thou, O land, when thy king is the son of nobles"; and in another place, "Mercy and truth preserve the king."

Yet one thing we find occasion ever anew to lament in the case of David, namely this, that he has not yet gained enlightenment and strength enough to shake himself free from the heathenish abomination of polygamy, which was then, indeed, deeply rooted in the habits of society, and particularly prevailed at royal courts. He had, as we are already aware, several wives, and, according to the custom of the times, those who were left behind by his predecessor fell to him by inheritance. Yet it must not be overlooked that the latter were reckoned more as belonging to the household of the prince than to his family, and held a place corresponding to that of "ladies of honor" in the present day. But the original divine law of marriage, which had then so greatly disappeared even from the knowledge of the chosen people, was always grossly violated, although this indeed took place with a certain unconsciousness of guilt, on account of which this violation was regarded meanwhile with divine forbearance. Nevertheless in the case of none, not even of David, was it passed by wholly unpunished.

When David became ruler over the whole of Israel, in the year 1050 before the birth of Christ, he was thirty years of age; and he reigned forty years, including the seven years and six months during which he bore the scepter of Hebron exclusively over the tribe of Judah. Of the children who were born to him at Hebron, the three eldest were Amnon, Chileab (or Daniel), and Absalom, who were followed by three other sons. He did not experience much joy in his children. This he might indeed attribute to the unlawful married relationships from which even he, the man of God, had not kept himself.

2. The first royal act of David after his coronation was a warlike one, which had for its object the obtaining possession, by conquest, of the stronghold of Zion. He chose as the place of his residence this cluster of hills, only partly built upon at first, from which there was an extensive view far into the interior of the land, and on which already, from ancient times, a holy consecration rested.

One of these eminences had become forever glorious by an act of faith, a thousand years before, more wonderful than any other the world has to the present hour yet seen. It was the hill of Moriah, from which in those ancient days the word of Jehovah commanded the patriarch Abraham to proceed, that he might there offer up as a burnt-sacrifice his only son, who was dear to him as his own heart. The test to which he was thereby subjected did not concern Abraham's paternal love. That would have been the case if it had been demanded of him to substitute his own life for that of his son. As little did it concern his love to God, as a trial whether it was able to overcome in power and strength his natural affection for his first born.

A test of this kind many a one has stood, with the victorious self-renouncing cry of Job, "The Lord gave, and the Lord hath taken away; blessed be the name of the Lord!" Rather it was a test of his faith, that it might be seen whether Abraham would truly honor God the Lord as the Holy One who keeps His word and covenant, and can never lie.

The divine promise had been given to the patriarch, "In Isaac shall thy seed be called, and I will make of thee a great nation as the

stars of heaven, and in thee shall all families of the earth be blessed."
To Isaac he thus saw that there was united, according to the word of
Jehovah, not only the future of his own house, but also the future of
the salvation of the world. And now he must, so it appeared to him,
forever put an end to the one and to the other in the person of his
son. Would not at the same time the truth and fidelity of God by this
act be destroyed? Abraham in his heart resolutely and with composure said "No!" "It is impossible," he thought, "that the Lord should
not stand to His word. If I put my son to death, God both can and
must and will raise him up again from the dead!"

Sustained by such thoughts as these, he erected, with a bleeding
heart, it is true, but nevertheless with a firm hand, an altar, and laid
the wood thereon, and laid his son upon it. Already he held the knife
over him, when He, who from that time forth with justice bore the
honored name of the "father of the faithful," heard the voice sounding from heaven, "Lay not thine hand upon the lad: for now I know
that thou fearest God." And when he lifted up his eyes, he saw
behind him a ram caught in a thicket, which he took and offered up
for a burnt-offering in the stead of his son. We know that in this
transaction something unspeakably greater in the future was foreshadowed, which in its deepest import was to him as yet a sealed
mystery.

At that place of sacrifice, so full of meaning, there occurred at the
same time another incident. When Abraham returned, crowned with
victory, from the battle against Chedorlaomer, a mysterious man here
met him, brought forth bread and wine, and blessed him with the
solemn words, "Blessed be Abraham of the most high God, possessor of heaven and earth and blessed be the most high God which
hath delivered thine enemies into thy hand!" With what elevated
feelings must the patriarch have heard this surprising and unwonted salutation at such a time! With the exception of his house, faith
in the one living God had died out of the wide world, to give place
to a blind worship of nature. Then suddenly this precise, full, comprehensive confession struck upon his ear. And from whose mouth
did the words sound forth to him? He who uttered the blessing was
Melchisedec, i.e., "the king of righteousness." He was the ruler of
Salem, i.e., "Peace," and united in his person at the same time both
the dignity of the monarch and the sacredness of a priest of the Most
High.

Did Abraham now realize whose shadow and type it was
which stood before him in this man? Certainly he did not apprehend it so distinctly as David afterward did, and much less did he
perceive it in the clearness and comprehensiveness with which the
apostle at a later period did, who testified, "Melchisedec is like unto
the Son of God," and who then brings expressly forward and
explains the several typical facts in the appearance of this mysterious man.[3] Perhaps something of this may have also hovered dimly
before the soul of the old patriarch, of whom the Lord says that he
rejoiced to see "his day," the day of Christ, and who, moved by
magnificent, though at the same time dim contemplations, testified
his submission to Melchisedec, by giving him the tenth of all that
he had.

This place Salem, at the time of Joshua's taking possession of the
land, changed its ancient name into that of Jebus. The tribes of Judah
and Simeon took the fortress, which was built on the Hill of Zion,
and burnt it, after they had put to death the heathen who dwelt
there. Yet there was not at that time a complete rooting out of the
Canaanitish tribe of the Jebusites. On the contrary, at the time of the
judges, they had built up their rocky fortress "Jebus" only more strongly than before; and, in the Book of the Judges, we meet with Jebus
under the title of "The city of a stranger that is not of the children
of Israel."[4]

Such a place also existed in David's day. So he undertook to complete the work of his fathers. The remnant of the outlawed heathen
tribe must—such was the command of God—leave the hallowed
places, and the old mountain stronghold must resume its original significant name, and be transformed into the royal dwelling of the
kings of Israel. Therefore David proceeded with his men of war
against Jebus and besieged it; but the dwellers there felt themselves
perfectly protected in their stronghold, surrounded by defiles,
strong walls and ramparts, and in their presumptuousness received
the besiegers that came against them with mockery and scorn.
"Except thou take away," they said insolently to David, "the blind and
the lame" (as ye disdainfully name our gods), "thou shalt not come in
hither." Now in this war the matter concerned not only the subjugation of the haughty Jebusites, but at the same time, and before all

3. Hebrews 7.
4. Judges 19:12.

other things, the preserving the honor of the God of Israel. It was necessary that a decisive proof should be given that Jehovah was the only true God, and that all other gods were as nothing.

David gave the word to his men, "Whosoever getteth up to the gutter, and smiteth the lame and the blind" (the idol gods that are there), "that are hated of David's soul, he" here David's words are terminated; but whoever has taken notice of them up to this point can have no difficulty in completing them with the following clause, "He shall be chief and captain in my army." Joab offered himself for the execution of the difficult undertaking. The storm began. The battle was hot and bloody. But David's men took fort after fort, mounted the gigantic battlements, and at length also climbed over the walls and threw down whatever opposed them. A glorious victory was gained. Jebus fell into David's hands, and the name of Jehovah was exalted before the heathen. After that heroic exploit, these words became proverbial in Israel: "The blind and the lame shall not come into the house"; which means, "Keep thy house free from idols, and seek elsewhere shelter and protection."

After David had restored the old name to the place, with the prefix "Jeru" (i.e., citadel or town), and had called it "Jerusalem," which means, "The dwelling-place of peace," he caused it to be built and extended on a large scale, and then came from Hebron and dwelt there. "He built," it is said, "round about, from Millo and inward"; which words are to be understood as meaning that he surrounded the fort, or the higher part of the city on Mount Zion, destined as his residence, which was also called the city of David, with a strong wall round about from the castle Millo, and adorned the spacious enclosure with numerous stately houses. Within this space thus enclosed by a wall he also built his royal palace, while the lower half of the district, being more level, was gradually covered over with private houses.

The fame of David's name, and the report of his noble undertakings, had already spread so wide, that the prince of the rich city of Tyre, famous for its arts and commerce, sent ambassadors to him to be witnesses of his magnificent works, and at the same time to convey to him a present of cedar trees, even placing at his disposal experienced carpenters and masons. What was now seen openly before the eyes of the whole world, the history announces in these words: "And David went on and grew great; and the Lord God of hosts was with him. And David," it is further witnessed, "perceived" (i.e., found himself anew strengthened in the conviction) "that the Lord had established him king over Israel, and that He had exalted his kingdom for His people Israel's sake."

O how important a thing it is, and worthy of being most earnestly desired, that such a seal of divine approbation should be granted to one seeking to discharge the duties of his office in the name of the Lord! Not all, however faithfully they walk before God, and however conscientiously they wait on their calling, are so fortunate in this respect as David was. How many rulers, preachers, and teachers of the people have often, to the end of their lives, had occasion to complain, as once did Isaiah, "I have labored in vain, I have spent my strength for nought, and in vain yet surely my judgment is with the Lord, and my work with my God!" There have been noble princes, who have been all their lives through mistaken by their people; faithful sowers, who have sown in the spiritual field, and have seen their good seed fall into stony places, where it grew not; unwearied teachers of youth, who have earned only ingratitude for their labor. Heavy, sorrowful trials these, fitted gradually to crush the spirit of the laborer in his earnest efforts, and to fill his heart with dejection and longing for death!

But how frequently has it been experienced that the seeds which these men have committed to the furrows of the field assigned to them, and which they have watered with their tears, were yet so far from being lost, that they have suddenly begun, though the sowers may have before that gone to their graves, powerfully to bud and spring up, and to unfold in the blossoms of a spring rich with promises. Names apparently forgotten are then with grateful thanks celebrated as those of benefactors, worthy of everlasting remembrance. Rulers, mistaken by the men of their own time, have become illustrious in the eyes of posterity as the very models of shepherds of the people. Some have wished them back again, and men have made pilgrimages to their sepulchers. May such experiences encourage all those who know what it is to sigh over faithfulness in labor that has been misunderstood, and over efforts in the services of brethren as fruitless and wasted!

Yet from no work which is done in the name of the Lord has the Lord withheld a reward and a blessing even for the time that now is; and will the joy of His servants be the less on that account, that

they first see from heaven the seeds they sowed springing up, growing green and flourishing! That word of the psalm shall forever
verify itself: "They that sow in tears shall reap in joy. He that goeth
forth and weepeth, bearing precious seed, shall doubtless come again
with rejoicing, bringing his sheaves with him."

David now took up his residence on Mount Zion, the glory of the
land. From this time begins the history of Jerusalem as that of a city
without an equal for magnificence, for the vicissitudes through which
it passed, and for the importance of its relations to the whole world.
During more than 2,000 years, this city, the capital of a narrow strip
of territory, lying remote from the great highways of the nations, saw
almost all the kingdoms of the world rising up in arms against each
other around its walls. Sometimes raised up to heaven, sometimes
cast down to hell, thrice over thrown to its very foundations, and
always rising up again out of its ruins—now abandoned to the heathen, plundered, covered with disgrace, and again covered with the
highest honor—the city stands on its seven hills among the cities of
the earth as a candlestick with seven branches, from which with
equal splendor and power the consuming flame of the holiness and
justice of God, as well as the mild, blissful light of the divine, long-
suffering, and love, mercy, and covenant-keeping faithfulness,
shines forth over the world.

Jerusalem was the center and the place from which came the revelations of God—the highly honored city which saw the infallible
interpreters of the Most High walk through its streets—the city
which listened to the testimonies of an Isaiah, a Jeremiah, and many
others of the prophets, till at length the time looked forward to for
a thousand years arrived, when the cry was heard: "Rejoice greatly,
O daughter of Zion behold, thy King cometh unto thee: He is just,
and having salvation!"

Jerusalem may be regarded as the standard erected in the sight of
all the nations of the earth, toward which has marched a peaceful,
glorious band of pilgrims. For the past 2,000 years, what is there that
has blessed, cheered, or made truly happy the lot of mankind, which
has not emanated from the hill on which the cross was erected? But
there also waved the victorious banner of the Conqueror of death,
and there, from the opened heaven, the Pentecostal fire-stream of the
Holy Spirit poured down over all flesh; and to the present hour the
city of the earthly David appears encompassed by the light of great

promises. And how sweetly to our ears does the name Jerusalem sound; for it reminds us of the "city which hath foundations, whose builder and maker is God," the Jerusalem which is above, toward which we, as we hope, are making our way, and of which the poet sings—

> Jerusalem, my glorious home,
>   Name ever dear to me!
> When shall my labors have an end,
>   In peace and joy in thee?
>
> When shall these eyes thy heaven-built walls
>   And pearly gates behold,
> Thy bulwarks with salvation strong,
>   And streets of shining gold?
>
> There happier bowers than Eden's bloom,
>   Nor sin nor sorrow know;
> Bless'd seats! through rude and stormy scenes
>   I onward press to you.
>
> Jerusalem, my happy home!
>   My soul still pants for thee;
> Then shall my labors have an end,
>   When I thy joys shall see.
>
> —J. T. Hermes

Yes, we also, as many of us as believe, may repeat with the singer of Psalm 137, "If I forget thee, O Jerusalem, let my right hand forget her cunning!"

After David had become ruler over the whole of Israel, and had erected his throne on Mount Zion, he sang, animated by the Spirit of God, that imperishable song, Psalm 101, in which he presents not only before his own eyes, but also before the eyes of all his successors, and all who wear crowns on earth, that eternally valid law for the guidance of those who rule. "I will sing," he begins, "of mercy and judgment: unto Thee, O Lord, will I sing." And then he continues: "I will behave myself wisely in a perfect way. Oh, when wilt Thou come unto me? I will walk within my house with a perfect heart. I will set no wicked thing before mine eyes: I hate the work of them that turn aside; it shall not cleave to me. A froward heart shall depart from me; I will not know a wicked person. Whoso privily slandereth his neighbor, him will I cut off: him that hath an high look and a proud heart will not I suffer. Mine eye shall be upon the faithful of the land, that they may dwell with me: he that walketh in a perfect way, he shall serve me. He that worketh deceit shall not dwell within my house: he that telleth lies shall not tarry in my sight. I will early destroy all the wicked of the land; that I may cut off all wicked doers from the city of the Lord."

We entreat it for all the great and the mighty ones of earth, that the Spirit from above may write the essential principles and truths of this rule, for those who govern, on their very hearts, as with letters of fire. How well would it then be with themselves! How well with the people, whose direction has been entrusted into their hands by God the Lord!

17

The King in the Field

There will be no end to wars and rumors of wars in the world till the longed-for time arrives, when, according to the prophecy of Zechariah, "there shall be upon the bells of the horses, Holiness unto the Lord, and there shall be no more the Canaanites in the house of the Lord of hosts." War stands in manifest opposition to the original order established by the Creator, for God does not wish that His children, "created in His image," should tear and destroy one another, but that they should help one another with the hands of love. The "angels of peace" may well weep bitterly, when they look down from their blessed heights on our battlefields, while we, perhaps in the very sight of them, weave laurel-wreaths and sing songs of triumph. These blood-red fields of battle are witnesses how dreadful is yet the power which sin, the mother of war, exercises on the earth.

Nevertheless the Lord shows patience and forbearance, and instead of saying concerning the degenerate race, "The end of all flesh is come before me for the earth is filled with violence through them; and, behold, I will destroy them with the earth," He condescends to interpose, guiding and governing men amid the storms of battle, and making them subserve the purposes of His kingdom. By means of them He executes His judgments, He awakens the spiritually dead out of their torpor, commands the inconsiderate to pause, and purifies the atmosphere from dangerous elements. So much has this been the case, that His servant, Moses, says of Him, "The Lord is a man of war."[1] And He is so; and the victory to Him is always certain.

---

1. Exodus 15:3.

However confusedly the threads of the world's history may seem to cross each other, the day will not fail to come, when, as with the voice of many thunders, the cry shall be heard sounding over the circle of the earth, "Hallelujah! for the Lord God omnipotent reigneth." Therefore it is well with all those who stand by His cause, and who rejoice in covenant fellowship with Him. They shall triumph with Him. But, on the contrary, woe to them who, under the banner of the "prince of this world," oppose the interests of the kingdom of heaven, while at the same time, though unconsciously and against their will, they are compelled to do it service. These will one day find associating itself with the positive punishment inflicted upon them, the dejecting and painful consciousness that their whole life has been like a wave of the sea, which has in vain tried and expended its might against an immovable rock.

Oh, happy is the man to whose heart there is nothing closer than the wish that in all his actions he may be with God, and God with him! We shall today meet anew with such a man, and he no other than King David.

2 Samuel 5:19

> And David inquired of the Lord, saying, Shall I go up to the Philistines?

David is scarcely crowned king over the whole of Israel, and has retired, from amid his people doing homage to him, to his city of Zion, when once more the trumpet of war summons him forth from his repose again to the battlefield.

This is the first time such a thing has happened to him as king; but it is only that he might be blessed for the strengthening of his faith by three experiences, on account of which every prince and general may well envy him. Let us fix our attention now upon these.

1. The old enemy of Israel stands again in battle array upon the plain. God the Lord always knows how to blend with the encouragements which He permits His people to experience as many discouragements as that this result shall be obtained, that they shall be guarded against the danger of losing their balance. The Philistines, who had not yet been wholly driven out from all corners of the land, had burst again into Judah with a powerful army, and had penetrated as far as the valley of Rephaim, a fruitful plain spreading itself out to

the southwest of Jerusalem, through which ran the boundaries of the tribes of Judah and Benjamin. They heard of the homage which the people joyfully rendered to David at Hebron, and of the elevation to the throne of Saul of the man who once slew the pride of their nation, the hero Goliath, and they conceived that it was a fitting time to oppose, with all the forces they could put in array, him whom they believed not yet sufficiently equipped for war.

But is it not conceivable to suppose that God meant to make use of them also as a rod of correction against David for the false steps he had taken when in the midst of them? In addition to this, the rec-ollection of the hospitality which the Philistines had once extended to him when he was a fugitive, would make it very difficult for him to go to war against those who had been his deliverers. It is true they had, by making an incursion into his fatherland, wickedly broken asunder all the bonds of peace. But might it not, however, seem advisable that David should at least make an attempt to avert the necessity of bloodshed by negotiations of peace? Indeed, the king needed, in order to his entering upon the war with full resolution and freedom of soul, an unambiguous direction from on high; and there-fore, after he had left his city, and, along with his army, had taken up a position strongly fortified by nature over against the army of the Philistines, which was pressing forward, he turned himself with this humble inquiry to the Lord, whether made directly or through the mediation of the priest is not announced: "Shall I go up against the Philistines? Wilt Thou deliver them into mine hand?" And the Lord answered His servant with adorable condescension: "Go up: for I will doubtless deliver the Philistines into thine hand."

From this moment David was himself again, full of courage, vig-orous in action, and confident of victory. Animated anew by the word of the Lord, he gave the signal for battle. The armies rushed against each other. The Philistines did not long hold their ground, but soon gave way, and fled from the Israelites. David gave to the Lord the honor that was His due, saying, "The Lord hath broken forth upon mine enemies before me, as the breach of waters." The meaning of these words was: The Lord has made them like a stream which, break-ing through its embankments, rushes wildly foaming into the open field. Perhaps it may be the case also that in this expression David had before his mind the waves of the Red Sea, which at the command of God divided and gave to His people an open passage.

The place where this victorious battle was fought was called from
that time Baal-perazim, i.e., "The Lord hath scattered them."
Here we are to notice that the word "Baal," i.e., "lord," was not at
that time used, as it was at a later period, to denote only the god of
the Phoenicians, but it was employed to designate the true living
God of Israel. How complete the terror was that assailed the
Philistines, is evident by this circumstance among others, that they
left behind them, as spoil for the conquerors, their images, which
they regarded as most precious, and for which their life and blood
would have been in their esteem but a small price. The conquerors
knew what to do with them! They hastily piled up a heap of wood
and burnt them, praising the one true and living God, the God of
Abraham, Isaac, and Jacob, who had stood so wonderfully and so
gloriously by their side. This was the first of the three faith-
strengthening experiences which befell the king in that war. We are
anew strengthened in the conviction that all the wars of the children
of Israel were in their deepest import religious wars; but as such they
had not for their object the compulsory spreading of their faith, but
only the warding off from their borders of heathen darkness, and
therefore they might rejoice in the approbation of God, the
Disposer of battles.

2. The Philistines soon reassembled after their hasty flight, and
filled up by new accessions to their number the breaches that had
been made in their army. Once more they pressed forward to the former battlefield in the valley of Rephaim. Then there occurred the
events which are afterward described in the twenty-third chapter of
our book.[2] The Philistines took possession of Bethlehem. David
pitched his camp not far from them, in a natural mountain fastness.
The well-known cave of Adullam served him and his generals as a
tent. His people carried their heads loftily. And why should they not?
There were many things which served to raise their self-confidence.
They regarded themselves specially as the banner-bearers and the
armor-bearers of him who was at their head, not by human authority, but by the appointment of the Most High. They served in the
most direct manner by their work one who was the representative of
the divine government on the earth.

They formed, in their combined character as an army, the living

2. 2 Samuel 23.

mirror in which, clearer than anywhere else, the rays of the
majesty and glory of the royal throne of a vicegerent of God were
reflected. As an organized body, in their implicit and yet free obedience, and in the punctuality and discipline of their service, they
present before the world a noble ideal, which corresponds to a law
having its origin not from any human source, but from above, and
which claims in every conscience the authority of an unlimited
power; it is the ideal of the inviolable divinely ordained moral government of the world. And higher than this, another thing yet
encourages their hearts. It is not that they know themselves to be the
blossom and marrow and strength of their people, but that they recognized themselves as the divinely appointed guardians and
protectors, not only of the homes, the throne, and the altar, but especially of the noblest and most inalienable possessions of their people
against assaults both from without and from within. As the armed
manhood of the land, they formed the brazen wall of protection
around the kingdom of God, and the hedge of defense around the
territory on which their people must grow up to the accomplishment,
both spiritually and temporally, of the national destiny appointed for
them by God. Such deep convictions as these could not but
impart a peculiar elevation of mind to David's warriors. It gave them
the right knightly spirit which, to the present hour, imparts to the
profession of a soldier its true nobility.

David stands on an advantageous elevation, as on a watch-tower,
and waits for reinforcements out of Judah, in order that he might
then again attack the enemy in the valley of Rephaim. After long
marching from place to place, yet always crowned with victory, he
rejoices in a brief moment of repose. Surrounded by several of his
generals, he looks out into the distance. His eye especially rests on
the little town which was his birthplace, which for a long time he
had not visited nor even seen. A thousand images from those days
when he, an innocent, happy boy, there tended his father's flocks, rise
up in his memory and hover before his soul.

The day is hot and sultry. Then he feels a longing for a drink of
the precious water, even to this day celebrated, which welled up at
the gate of Bethlehem, and which had so often refreshed him in his
youth. Involuntarily these words escaped from his lips: "Oh, that one
would give me drink of the water of the well of Bethlehem, which is
by the gate!" Scarcely had the words been uttered, when three of his

mighty men—the Tachmonite, Eleazar, and Shammah—in whose ears they sounded, rushed forth. "They brake," says the history, "through the host of the Philistines"; and before the heathen sentinels recovered from their surprise, and had regained breath to sound the alarm, these mighty men had already drawn water from the well, and were returning with it to their lord.

A knightly act this! But was it not foolhardiness rather, if it was not even "servility"? and should we not call it folly to trifle thus with courage, and lavishly to deal with life? This question resembles that with which Judas Iscariot once presumed to do dishonor to Mary's anointing of her Lord at Bethany. Pure love has its measure in itself, and disregards in its outward expression every critic. Mary indeed consecrated there the most precious thing in her possession, not to any mortal prince, but to the Savior of the world, her own Savior. Also this exploit of these three heroes was a sacrifice offered, not so much to the man David, as rather in him to the "anointed of the Lord," and therefore to the Lord Himself. Had any wish or command of their human ruler and leader in war stood in opposition to any commandment of God, they would without doubt have said, "We ought to obey God rather than men"; but at the same moment they would have laid down their swords, yea, even their heads, at the king's feet.

The three valiant men of war, whose exploit the history celebrates with the simple but significant words, "These things did these three mighty men," returned again unhurt to the cave of Adullam, and presented the vessel, with the refreshing water from the well of Bethlehem, to the king. He graciously received the cup out of the hands of the faithful men, but instead of raising it to his lips, "he poured it out unto the Lord," and said, "Be it far from me, O Lord, that I should do this: is not this the blood of the men that went in jeopardy of their lives?"

Here we have also a beautiful trace of knightly magnanimity. The king desired in the field to fare no better than his soldiers. He wished to share with them all their hardships and wants. Besides, the drink-offering was in Israel chiefly the sign of repentance. David bowed himself down, by means of that symbolical action, penitently before the Lord, because he had inconsiderately said to his brave men around him, "Oh, that one would give me drink of the water of the well of Bethlehem!" and had, without necessity, exposed to danger the lives of three of his noblest officers; but at the same time he silently, yet with deep feeling, thereby testified his thanks to the Lord that He had given him such true, devoted, and obedient servants. Thus there was generosity on all sides.

From that camp-scene there shine dimly out to us many typical truths. We also know of an open well of Bethlehem, whose water quenches forever the thirst of the soul. Grace, forgiveness, justification, and sanctifying strength is the water which is here drawn, and the effect of this water is the peace of God, which passes all understanding. This well, also, was once in the custody of the Philistines. The three heroes who burst through to make it again accessible to us, who does not know them? Luther, Calvin, Zwingle are the three names. Repentance, prayer, and faith are the three which today bring the water to our mouths. We indeed drink of it; and there happens to us what was once said to the Samaritan woman, "Whosoever drinketh of the water that I shall give him shall never thirst; but the water that I shall give him shall be in him a well of water springing up into everlasting life." For that wherewith we are refreshed pours itself forth again in an inexhaustible stream of love and thankfulness toward Him who is the personal source of all life; and thus at the same moment in which the son of Jesse poured out the drink-offering before the Lord, and to the praise of the Lord, we also come near to Him whose type he was.

May we all long for the spiritual well under the gate of Bethlehem, as David at that time did for the water which can refresh the body! Amid the busy scenes of this world's frivolities, this thirst is but seldom felt. It is felt burning within us first in the cave Adullam, where all manner of people assemble: "Every one that is in distress, and every one that is in debt, and every one that is discontented."

3. Let us return to the scene of battle! The heroic exploit of the three mighty men who broke through the Philistines' host at Bethlehem was only a knightly interlude in a stern drama. The Philistines had placed themselves in battle array over against the army of Israel, and at that time were superior to them in the number of their active forces in the field. But this was David's watchword, "In God is the rock of my strength!" He inquired at the Lord whether it was His will that he should engage in battle, and received the answer: "Thou shalt not go up; but fetch a compass behind them, and come upon them over against the mulberry trees. And let it be, when thou hearest the sound of a going in the tops of the mulberry trees, that

then thou shalt bestir thyself" (i.e., join battle): "for then shall the Lord go out before thee, to smite the host of the Philistines."

This was a remarkable occurrence. But one need not be surprised at it when one remembers that it happened not only for the advantage and benefit of the people of Israel, but of the whole world, that the Lord of all lords was pleased, once for all, to show Himself to His chosen people in a manifest and palpable manner as the living God, as the all-disposing Protector, Leader, and Governor of men. It must now indeed be manifest, in the department of sensible experience, how far His condescension to mortal men will go, and what they who approached Him with confidence might expect from His kindness. It must be written in history with a distinctness which will make it readable by the dimmest eye, that He will always be found of those who seek Him, and that He thinks it not beneath His dignity to commune with sincere suppliants, though it may be without audible words, as a "man with his friend."

We have therefore to consider events such as those before which we now stand, as belonging to God's book of living examples, in which, for the strengthening of our weak faith, He had in view the making manifest to us, once for all, in the outer world, that which constantly goes on in reality in the world of spirits, which is hidden from our view. These self-revelations, coming forth in human form, are not descents of God to the human level, but symbolical actions of God, which the Lord might have prefaced in some such manner as the following: "That ye for all times may know how I stand toward you, the children of the dust, and shall always testify to you according to the measure of your conduct toward me, I will unveil before you for once, in sensible and living forms, my government upon the earth; and this I will do in my care over my people Israel."

David had, according to the divine command, taken up the position assigned to him. He waited with anxious expectation for the signs that had been announced. Suddenly they appear. There is a rustling among the tops of the mulberry trees, as if an invisible host were passing over them. We know what these signs indicated to him—nothing less than that which was once presented before the mind of Jacob, in his dream of the ladder let down from heaven; and which was signified to Moses in the bush, which burned and was not consumed; to Elijah, in the still small voice at Horeb; and to Saul of Tarsus, in the light which shone around him from heaven. The Lord was near, and was going forth in his behalf. Full of the most joyful faith, David now gives the word, "Forward!" In clear echo the word is repeated by the generals among all the ranks of the army. The storm of battle breaks loose; and the issue is, that the Philistines are vanquished, and are pursued with great loss from Geba in Judah even unto the Caananite town of Gazer.

The words of the Lord, "When thou hearest the sound of a going in the tops of the mulberry trees then thou shalt bestir thyself," are important for us also, in a figurative sense, in our warfare with the children of unbelief in this world. They teach us that in our own strength, and merely with the human weapons of reason and science, we are not to make war against the adversary. Success can only be counted upon when the conflict is undertaken under the influence of the Holy Spirit of God, breathed forth and in the immediate blessed experience of the gracious presence of the Lord, and of the truth of His word. Then there breaks forth from our hearts that which we call "testimony"—a speaking from the present enjoyment of salvation; a speaking arising from a comprehensive, vital, powerful conception of the infallibility of that for which the undertaking has been begun; a speaking of the whole animated personality. This breaks through the enemy. No bulwark of science, falsely so called, withstands this. We may compare Luther, the hero of the faith in the conference at Marburg, with the same Luther in his answer at Worms, in vindicating himself before the emperor and the empire. What a difference is manifest between the one and the other, although his confession at both places was the same! At Marburg he spoke from his own spirit. At Worms there was above him "the sound of a going in the mulberry trees," and the old Romish gigantic superstructure trembled under the weight of his word.

After his two victories over the Philistines in the valley of Rephaim, and particularly after the latter, which was the more complete and decisive, David sang one of his songs of victory and of triumph. Probably it was Psalm 29. After he has here, with a loud voice, challenged everything that has breath, even the angels of heaven not excluded, to join with him in giving honor to the name of Jehovah, he praises "the voice of the Lord," which was in that "sound of a going in the tops of the mulberry trees," and which, typically giving assurance of victory, called unto him, "Now bestir thyself!" and he compares it to the voice of the thunder which follows the lightning, rolling among the clouds. "The voice of the Lord," he sings, "is powerful; the voice of the Lord is full of majesty. The voice of the Lord breaketh the cedars; yea, the Lord breaketh the cedars of Lebanon. He maketh them also to skip like a calf; Lebanon and Sirion" (i.e., Hermon) "like a young unicorn. The voice of the Lord divideth the flames of fire. The voice of the Lord shaketh the wilderness; the Lord shaketh the wilderness of Kadesh. The voice of the Lord maketh the hinds" (from terror) "to calve, and discovereth the forests; and in His temple doth every one speak of His glory. The Lord sitteth upon the flood" (which once swept away sinners from the earth); "yea, the Lord sitteth King forever," for the destruction of the ungodly. "The Lord," the singer concludes, "will give strength unto His people; the Lord will bless His people with peace." Oh, may the Lord deal thus also with our people! This happens whenever the people, in respectful submission, will hear His voice.

18

The Bringing Up of the Ark of the Covenant

One of the most stirring scenes presented to us in the history of Israel was that which occurred in the days of Eli the high priest, when the messenger who had escaped from the bloody battle with the Philistines came with evil tidings to Shiloh. He told not only of the entire overthrow of Israel, but he also brought the yet sadder intelligence, that the ark of the covenant had fallen into the hands of the heathen, and that Eli's two sons, Hophni and Phinehas, had perished on the field of battle. For Eli, an old man of 98 years, this distressing report was too much. As if struck by lightning, he fell backward from his seat and broke his neck. His daughter-in-law, the wife of Phinehas, when she heard the evil tidings, "bowed herself and travailed," and at the moment of giving birth to her son, the agonies of death came upon her, and with her last breath she named him Ichabod, and herself interpreted the word in the heart-breaking cry, "The glory is departed from Israel: because the ark of God is taken."[1] Echoed by many thousands of voices, this lamentation of the poor woman sounded throughout the whole land, in a cry of woe piercing even to the heavens.

A more sorrowful day than this Israel never had experienced. The blood of their young men fruitlessly shed in battle; the triumph of the uncircumcised; and, in addition to that, the loss of their most precious treasure, the ark of the covenant, which was of infinitely greater significance to the Israelites than was their Palladium to the

---

1. 1 Samuel 4.

Greeks—what an accumulation of misfortune! The ark of the covenant was to the children of Israel the visible symbol and pledge of the gracious presence of their God. Jehovah Himself had instituted it as such by His servant Moses. We regard this as not beneath the dignity of God. Great is the Lord when He unveils before us His majesty, whereby He shows us the immeasurable distance which separates Him from all His creatures; but His greatness is not the less manifest when He familiarly condescends to hold fellowship with men, accommodates Himself to the necessities of their weakness, and, to use the words of Solomon, "rejoicing in the habitable part of His earth," reveals Himself to them, and makes Himself understood by means of pictures and sensible signs. The holy ark was a sign of this kind; and as such it served as a bond, and, as it were, a chain to hold Israel together as one people. What wonder, then, that the joy with which the people hailed the event, which we shall this day witness, perfectly corresponded in its power and depth to the sorrow with which the whole people at that time echoed the cry of the wife of Phinehas—"Ichabod!"

2 Samuel 6:15

> So David and all the house of Israel brought up the ark of the Lord with shouting, and with the sound of the trumpet.

David stands on the pinnacle as well of his royal power as of his spiritual life. The Lord has, as he himself joyfully sings, "made his mountain to stand strong." He mounts up with wings as eagles. The important celebration which we are this day to consider is the bringing up of the ark of the covenant. We see this, indeed, at first in an astonishing manner (1) interrupted, but afterward (2) brought to a successful conclusion, amid the unclouded joy of the people with loud voice praising their God.

1. The enemies of Israel are vanquished. From the lofty summit of Zion's tower waves the banner of victory. Peaceful thoughts fill the soul of David. That which has long lain upon his heart shall now be accomplished. The religious life of the people, which, in spite of the days of fasting and prayer which were celebrated with many tears under Samuel at Mizpeh, had continually declined since the time of Eli, must now be awakened. The Levitical ordinances of divine worship, which had been completely broken in upon, must be again

restored. Already for sixty-five years the ark of the covenant had remained neglected in Kirjath-jearim, the City of the Wood, lying on the borders between Judah and Benjamin, and then under the roof of Abinadab, the Levite, of Gibeah. Abinadab's son Eleazar was consecrated as the guardian of the ark. "But no one," it is said, "had inquired any more after it," and least of all had Saul the king himself done so. The tabernacle, with the altar burnt-offering, had meanwhile remained separated in the ark, first at Nob, and then at Gibeon, under the care of Zadok the priest. For it, also, little concern is felt by the people of Israel.

David knew the prophecy which had been uttered by Moses, when dying, regarding the tribe of Benjamin: "The beloved of the Lord shall dwell in safety by Him; and the Lord shall cover him all the day long, and he shall dwell between His shoulders." He doubted not but that these mysterious words indicated that Jehovah would choose that tribe before all the rest as the scene of his revelations of Himself. That this prophecy pointed to Jerusalem, which was the glory of that tribe, seemed to him to be denoted by the ancient type of the altar erected by Abraham, and by the sacrifice which he had offered up upon Mount Moriah. His soul was elevated within him by the thought that for the future the house of his God would stand near to his own. He was indeed conscious that Jehovah "dwelt not in temples made with hands," but that "the heaven was His throne, and the earth His footstool"; yet he also knew the adorable condescension of his God, that He had particularly chosen one place on the earth where He would be found by His people, and where He wished His own to gather together around Him, as on the steps of His throne, that He might bless them.

It becomes not those, it is true, who bear earthly authority and exercise lordship in this world, to hold in their hands both the sword and the censer, nor to say in what ways God should be worshiped. But if it lies near the heart of any prince, it then did to the heart of David, to build "as the swallow her nest" his palace, in a spiritual sense, near the temple, and to show himself, according to the words of the prophet, as a "nursing father" to the Church of God, then all that are pious in the land will rejoice and say, "God speed the king!" though the children of the world should shake their heads and mock.

David gathered together a great assembly of the captains of his host and the chief men of the tribes, priests and Levites, to

Jerusalem, in number 30,000 men, and informed them of the thoughts which filled his soul. Among other things, he said to them, "If it seem good unto you that it be of the Lord our God, let us send abroad unto our brethren everywhere that are left in all the land of Israel; . . . and let us bring again the ark of our God to us: for we inquired not at it in the days of Saul." "And all the congregation," it is recorded, "said that they would do so." They approved of his proposal, as without doubt agreeable to the will of God.

After the preparations for this important celebration had been made, the king went forth, in company with the great multitude which had assembled around him from all corners of the land, to Kirjath-jearim, "to bring up from thence the ark of God the Lord of hosts, that dwelleth between the cherubims." It is known that the ark, according to the command of God, was made of the durable shittim or acacia wood, and was covered over, both outside and inside, with plates of gold, and that the two tables of the law were laid up within it (on which account it was called the "ark of the covenant"), along with Aaron's rod that budded,[2] and the pot of manna, which corrupted not, from the wilderness. A heavy golden plate, called the "propitiatory," or mercy-seat, served as a lid to the ark. Two cherubim of gold, with their faces one toward another, were raised up at each end of the "mercy-seat," and overshadowed it, looking down with outspread wings, in devotional attitude, to the ark. They represented the majesty of Jehovah watching over the law and the people of Israel, and ruling in the midst of them.

The whole symbolically represented the throne of the God of Israel as the eternally Holy One, but also as the God rich in mercy and reconciled to the world. The law with its commands and threatenings appeared covered—a prophetic indication this of the future redemption and the cherubims stood there representing those who, as the Apostle Peter afterward expresses it, desire to look into the mysteries of redemption. Once every year, on the great day of atonement, the high priest drew near to the holy ark, yet not without the blood of sacrifice that had been offered—a shadow of that which, typically represented in the holy of holies of the temple, would one day find its realization. God then revealed Himself to the high priest, as we read of Moses and Samuel, that Jehovah spoke to

---

2. Hebrews 4.

them "from between the cherubim." Whether He always revealed Himself to the priest after the same manner, is uncertain. But the mercy-seat was in itself a divine pledge that the Lord was with His people, and that He would remain faithful to His word and covenant to the end.

After David and the people had reached Gibeah, a new cart, constructed for this special purpose, was brought, and the ark of God, covered with a curtain, was brought out of the house of Abinadab and placed upon it. Then there followed a solemn offering up of sacrifice, after which the immense procession was set in motion and followed the ark. Harpers, trumpeters, and a great band of other players on diverse kinds of instruments of music, went before the procession. Psalms which David himself had composed for this celebration, and which he had probably also provided with their music, were sung by many thousands of voices in harmonious accord. The king himself, clothed in simple robes, without any of the insignia of his royal dignity, followed immediately behind the wagon drawn by the oxen, joining in the choir with an animation which displayed itself not only in his countenance, radiant with joy, and in his powerful ringing voice, but also in his whole deportment. Thus they went on, in undisturbed jubilee, till they came to Nachon's thrashing-floor, not far from Jerusalem, when the solemnity was suddenly interrupted. The oxen, which were driven by Uzzah and Ahio, the sons of Abinadab, which drew the cart, stepped aside, perhaps enticed by the grain on the neighboring-thrashing floor. This caused the cart to shake and rock to and fro, so that the ark appeared to be in danger of falling from it. Then Uzzah sprang forward and seized hold of it, with the well-meant intention of saving it, and in that same moment, smitten by the anger of God, he sank down dead to the ground.

One may conceive the surprise and terror which now took possession of all. The procession is arrested. The instruments and the song are silent. We share in the terror of the people. But the surprise which at the same time that event raises within us, is greater than that which the children of Israel experienced. One must look somewhat deeper for the cause of it. The Mosaic law, known to every Israelite, ordained expressly that the "holy thing," i.e., the ark, should be borne on staves, and that no one should directly touch it, "lest he die." This commandment was forgotten at the bringing up of the holy thing. They were negligent about this law, and had followed the manner in which the Philistines had once brought back the holy treasure, rather than kept before their eyes the Mosaic order. The ark must be carried, and not borne on a conveyance; and, moreover, carried by priests, and not, as it at this time happened, by two youths, who, besides, were not even of the tribe of Aaron. Thus by this solemnity there was again brought to view the general neglect of religious observances which prevailed in Israel; and it showed the necessity of raising again before the eye of the people, in a very distinct manner, the law which had so deeply sunk out of view.

Through the familiarity of daily observation of that old ark in the house of their father Abinadab, the sons had apparently lost all reverence for it, so that they saw no longer anything in it particular; and this sinful indifference toward the mysterious treasure was the cause of Uzzah's thoughtlessly laying hold of it—an act which he must atone for with his life, according to the divine threatening, as a lesson and a warning to the whole people. A similar judgment from God once fell upon Nadab and Abihu, the sons of the high priest Aaron himself, when they, as wantonly as Uzzah, instead of the holy fire from the altar of burnt-offering, presented strange fire with the frankincense before the Lord. Fire from the Lord destroyed them also. If they had, by an unseasonable and immoderate partaking of wine and strong drink, as seems indeed to have been the case, deprived themselves of that presence of mind and sobriety appropriate to the service of the tabernacle, they were certainly doubly guilty and worthy of punishment.

If the occurrence at the thrashing-floor of Nachon may be regarded as having a spiritual import, it is also a solemn warning. It teaches us that we tread upon the honor of God, if we allow ourselves to be anxiously afraid about the triumph and the progress of His cause; and that we overstep in a suspicious manner the limits of modesty befitting us, as often as we entertain the presumptuous thought that it lies upon us to save from destruction the ark of the covenant, when at any time the cart (Church) on which it is carried appears as if about to be overthrown, through the negligence and unfaithfulness of those who are appointed for its direction.

Indeed, in our own days, there are not lacking men like Uzzah, who act as if it were all over with Christianity, if they did not maintain it against the power of modern negations. Then, at one time, we see them with strange blindness busy themselves about bringing it into concord with the ruling public taste, whatever that may cost, heedless that in doing so they themselves surrender it to a process of decomposition, by which it is stripped of its essential qualities, and goes forth as something altogether different from what it originally was and must be. Again, we find them in the sweat of their brow laboring to overcome the unbelief that is around them, perhaps also their own; or, in default of the Holy Spirit, striving by all manner of means chosen by themselves—sometimes oratorical, sometimes artistic, sometimes liturgic—to support the kingdom of God and save it from destruction.

This zeal, notwithstanding its good intention, is yet unholy, because it is as faint-hearted as it is presumptuous. Perhaps they may experience meanwhile a divine forbearance, which would not have corresponded with the spirit and character of the Old Testament; yet they will scarcely be spared the sorrows of sanctifying trials that will come upon them. The Lord does not need such helpers.

"The breach," as our history expresses it, which the Lord made upon Uzzah, filled the whole of Israel with not a little alarm. The king himself trembled at such a manifestation of the divine anger. "How shall the ark of the Lord," he cried with a sorrowful heart, "come to me?" He feared lest in bringing it up he had taken an arbitrary step, and therefore one displeasing to the Lord, and he could not find courage to carry it farther forward. He therefore left it by the way, in the house of a Levite named Obed-edom, and returned home without it, in deep dejection of spirit, along with his trembling people. This interruption of a joyful festival was to everyone a new admonition that the kindness and grace of God are never alone, but are always accompanied by His holiness. God never permits that anyone should sin, and yet, sinning, should rejoice and be glad before Him.

If His benevolence tends to draw us aside to levity and presumption, we will soon see Him exchange gentleness for severity, though He thereby embitter to us the fairest day of our lives. In educating us, God cares more that we should fear Him (with the more of a childlike spirit the better) as the Holy One, and as demanding holiness in us, than that we should always prosecute our pilgrimage-journey here below with unclouded joy. He therefore causes it frequently to happen that we are compelled, in the midst of the superabundance of our prosperity and of our joy, suddenly to join in the lamentation of Job: "Thou art become cruel to me; with Thy strong hand Thou opposest thyself against me." But how speaks the prophet: "Wherefore doth a living man complain; a man for the punishment of his sins?" The Lord may for a time withdraw His countenance, but He is always faithful in His purposes toward His people, and after the storm He always brings them at His own fitting time into the sunshine again. However sorely He may chastise them, He yet remains faithful by His word of promise. "Can a woman forget her sucking child, that she should not have compassion on the son of her womb; yea, they may forget, yet will I not forget thee. Behold, I have graven thee upon the palms of my hands."

2. For an everlasting memorial that the Lord is a "jealous God," who will not suffer the least violation of any one of His commandments, David called the place where the death-stroke fell down on Uzzah's head, Perez-uzzah (i.e., the "rent of Uzzah"). Obed-edom the Levite, of Gad-rimmon, in the tribe of Manasseh, reverently, and in strict accordance with the divine direction, received the ark into his house From that day forth the house of this pious man presented a bright contrast to the terrible judgment that had come upon Uzzah.

God is ever the same; He changes not through all ages; yet He loaded with manifold blessings the keeper of the ark. Among other blessings, God increased to Obed-edom in the course of time the number of his children and of his children's children, till there were amongst them sixty-two vigorous men held in repute among the people, and also richly blessed. He himself was afterward entrusted with the honorable office of keeper of the door of the tabernacle, in which the ark was at a later period deposited. Three months had passed away, when David believed that he recognized, in the blessings with which the Lord had crowned the house of Obed-edom, an unambiguous intimation from God that he might now venture to bring up that holy thing to Jerusalem. What happened to him is frequently experienced in the sphere of the spiritual life by souls troubled on account of the burden of their guilt, namely, that first through seeing the consolation with which other sinners like themselves have been comforted by the Lord, they gain courage to lay hold for themselves on the promises of divine grace.

With a good conscience the king therefore now gave directions to renew the celebration of bringing up the ark, which had been once interrupted in a very wonderful manner, and to conduct the affair with great splendor, but now in all respects in strict accordance with the divine law. Once more he summoned the representatives of all the people to Jerusalem, and said to them, "None ought to carry the ark of God but the Levites; for them hath the Lord chosen to carry the ark of God, and to minister unto Him forever." But to the priests and Levites of the house of Aaron he said, "Ye are the chief of the fathers of the Levites: sanctify yourselves, both ye and your brethren, that ye may bring up the ark of the Lord God of Israel unto the place that I have prepared for it. For because ye did it not at first, the Lord our God made a breach upon us, for that we sought Him not after the due order."

With these words, in the presence of all the people, he gave the honor that was due to the priests. Their reputation, so deeply obscured among the people since the days of Eli, had received new confirmation through the breach that had come upon Uzzah. Then the king placed himself, as he had done before, at the head of the multitude forming the procession, and went forward to the house of Obed-edom. There the ark was lifted up by the priests with the greatest care, and the procession again set in order. When they who bore the ark had gone six paces forward, the celebration was hallowed by the sacrifice of an ox and a sheep. Then the singers lifted up their voices in harmony with the players on instruments. And higher and higher rose their hearts than before, in more solemn, but at the same time more real and hallowed joy.

Such a procession of worshipers as this, of such grand significance, had never before been seen in Israel. What wonder that Jerusalem should be then adorned as the bride on her marriage day! With this emblem of His presence, Jehovah Himself in person that day entered the city of David, and those days when "the candle of God" was over the head of His people again returned in greater brightness. But listen! The melody of Psalm 24 strikes on the ear. They first praise Jehovah: "The earth is the Lord's, and the fullness thereof; the world, and they that dwell therein!" They then ask earnestly in their own hearts, "Who shall ascend into the hill of the Lord? and who shall stand in His holy place?" The answer is, "He that hath clean hands, and a pure heart; who hath not lifted up his soul unto vanity, nor sworn deceitfully. He shall receive" (the choir exultingly sings) "the blessing from the Lord, and righteousness from the God of his salvation. This is the generation of them that seek Him, that seek Thy face, O Jacob."

At length a loud jubilee-sound echoes on Mount Zion: "Lift up your heads, O ye gates; and be ye lift up, ye everlasting doors" (the doors of the ancient Salem, the type of the everlasting city of God); "and the King of glory shall come in. Who is this King of glory? The Lord strong and mighty, the Lord mighty in battle. Lift up your heads, O ye gates; even lift them up, ye everlasting doors; and the King of glory shall come in. Who is this King of glory? The Lord of hosts, he is the King of glory. Selah."

David had specially composed this song for this festal procession to Jerusalem; and who sang it more joyfully than he did? Who is able to describe his inward emotions during the singing of this "Song of Degrees"? O the holy feelings which then flowed through his soul! the flame of lofty devotion and thankfulness which rose up to heaven from the altar of his heart! On this day there came up once more in the brightest colors before his memory all the great things which the Lord had done to him—how He had from his childhood revealed to him His name; guided and guarded him in his youth; given into his hand the wonderful victory over the Philistine; taken him under His gracious protection against the rage of his persecutors; and then had raised him, the poor shepherd boy, from tending his flocks, even to the throne of His chosen people, and had overcome all his enemies before him; and now, in the glorious events of this day, so rich in promise, had placed the crown on all the remaining days of his life!

How his heart melted in humiliation and shame before the Lord; but how again it mounted upward on the wings of purest delight! But what above all other things filled him with joy, was the consciousness that God the Lord was gracious and kind and favorable toward him. He felt himself freed from the burden of guilt in the enjoyment of divine forgiveness. He tasted only love and mercy; he reveled as if the whole glory of the New Testament already surrounded him with its rays, in the most lively consciousness that he was a child of God. It was in the very nature of these blessed experiences that they must make themselves manifest in outward action. But words of exultation reached not to the full measure of their manifestation.

In his whole outward behavior and appearance, in the radiant splendor of his countenance, and in the harmonious movements of his body, the feelings that were within him were revealed. The history says, "David danced before the Lord with all his might"; that is, he gave expression in outward movements, and in a rhythmic action of his body, to the feelings which filled him. Singing and gesticulating, he went on before the ark.

The conception which the world of the present day associates with the word dance is here not at all appropriate. In Israel the dance was a form of divine worship, in which the highest and holiest inspiration oftentimes expressed itself, as, for example, in the case of Miriam and her companions after the passage through the Red Sea. If it had not been so how would the Spirit of prophecy have said to Israel by the prophet Jeremiah, "Again I will build, and thou shalt be built, O virgin of Israel: thou shalt again be adorned, and shalt go forth in the dances of them that make merry?" And how would the singer of Psalm 150 have exhorted the pious, "Praise ye the Lord; praise Him with timbrel and dance?"

The festal procession, amid the jubilant shouts of the people, poured through the gates of Jerusalem. But after it had arrived at the royal residence on Mount Zion, how was the holy harmony of joy interrupted by a discordant note! And, alas! it was Michal, David's own wife, the daughter of Saul, who gave utterance to it. This woman, who had formerly loved David more as the youthful hero crowned with victory than as the pious servant of Jehovah, and who had perhaps been made more thoroughly worldly through her union with Phaltiel, stood, as the procession came up toward the royal palace, at an opened window; and when she saw her husband divested of all the signs of his royal dignity, clothed in a plain coat such as was worn by the Levites, in the midst of the common people, as if he had been one of them, come forward singing and gesticulating, she almost went beside herself with shame and indignation.

Had her husband been guilty of a crime, she could scarcely have been more violently excited than she was now by this his supposed self-humiliation. The holy angels looked with delight on this celebration. Jehovah Himself could only be well pleased at the holy feelings, in harmony with those of the "man after His own heart," which flowed through the hearts of His people, who had been so long estranged from Him. Since the time of Joshua, there had not appeared in Israel a day of such universal animated offering of homage before the throne of the Almighty as this was—a day which bore on its brow a ray of heaven's own glory, and which opened up a most cheering prospect into Israel's future.

While among young and old everyone was more or less excited by the spirit which moved over this festival, Michal was the only being who looked upon it with spiteful countenance, and profaned that most holy scene with the discord of her scorn. We pity the poor woman, who, completely consumed by the vanity of lofty imaginations, seems scarcely to be any longer capable of pious elevation. It is sad that there are not lacking among the men of the present day persons of the same character. Such persons see, in the pure fire kindled by the Spirit from on high, only a morbid fanaticism; in the animated expression of holy elevation of heart, only a display of self-righteous cant.

Yes, the lovely reflection of the life from God, which only deserves the name of life, appears to them as hypocrisy and a pretense. The region in which faith presents to the Lord its spiritual burnt-offerings, meat-offerings, and drink-offerings, where love anoints His head and His feet with its most precious ointment, and where hope in the apprehension of an invisible and an imperishable inheritance soars away above the earth, is to them an altogether concealed and unknown world. We may therefore well feel compassion for such persons, thus, rather than burn with anger against them. According to the Scriptures, the "natural man receiveth not the things of the Spirit of God, because they are spiritually discerned." The life which is from God and in God, is and remains to everyone a mystery, till, by his own experience of it, it is unsealed to him by the Spirit of God.

David had, in passing, perhaps perceived the ill-humor and bitter discord of his wife; but he remained master of his spirit, and went on farther joyfully singing psalms. Having arrived at the place on Mount Zion where he had prepared a new tabernacle for the ark (the old one remained in ruins at Nob, where Saul had directed it to be taken), he commanded the holy thing, which had as it were been raised out of the grave, the refuge and the "heart" of Israel, to be carried amidst songs of praise into the tent. After this was done, and the priests had offered burnt-offerings and thank offerings, and had in the name of all the people made confession of sin, and also had renewed the promise of implicit allegiance to the Lord, the important festival was brought to a close by David blessing the assembled people in the name of the Lord, and thereafter commanding that there should be dealt out amongst them, to every one, man and woman, a cake of bread, a piece of flesh, and a flagon of wine, that they might keep the feast of joy; or, in case they had come from a distance, that they might be refreshed for the homeward journey.

After this, David himself went home to his own house, to consecrate it anew with praise and thanks to God. But what a discordance there jarred upon his mind! Michal greeted him bitterly, with an angry tone of scorn saying, among other things, "How glorious was the king of Israel today, who uncovered himself today" (degraded himself by his attire and by his behavior) "in the eyes of the handmaids of his servants" (i.e., before the lowest of the people), "as one of the vain fellows" (the common people) "shamelessly uncovereth himself!" A hateful side-glance this to simple, humble Levites, the servants of the tabernacle! That the king, the lord of the land, should come hither in one company with the lowliest artisans and laborers, clothed in plain attire like them, joining with them in singing psalms, and, instead of restraining his feelings in a way corresponding to his high position and courtly manners, giving free expression to them in his actions and motions before all the people— that was an unwonted spectacle, and could only cause offense in a soul such as that of Michal, to whom the enthusiasm of faith and a genuine modesty and humiliation before God were strange things, and appeared as an unpardonable breach of propriety.

But how frequently does one meet such ill-temper as that of Michal even at the present day! It displays itself when at any time one belonging to the higher ranks of life, who has been brought, through the grace of God, from the "broad way," salutes in the time of his "first love" every companion in the faith as a brother, and is happiest among those who, whether they be distinguished in rank or lowly, rejoice like himself in the Lord. He worships in the same fellowship, and joins with them in spiritual songs, meeting familiarly with the lowliest among them, as if birth, position, rank, and social etiquette were the most indifferent things in the world.

How frequently does one also see relations and friends change their demeanor toward such as disregard the conventional boundaries, and convert it into hateful mockery! That Prussian king himself did not escape such scorn whom history has adorned with the name of the "Confessor," and who once, when in the presence of an assembly of believing preachers, gave free expression in high excitement to the feelings of his heart, glowing with love to Christ. "I know well," he said, "it is not politic for me to say what I now utter in your presence"; but he did not on that account for a moment check the flow of his thoughts and feelings.

But this state of pious elevation of mind never continues long. It soon gives place to the accustomed calm and uniform course of thought. David is not always so lofty in his experience as he was on that day of festal joy. But he is deserving of pity who understands not the flapping of the eagle's wings, by which souls consecrated to God are in times of particular visitations of grace lifted up above all the boundaries of their common life, and placed in a condition where, in the emotions that fill them, they rise above all earthly things.

The feeling which flooded David's heart in opposition to Michal's malicious attack, was rather that of compassion and sorrowful pity than of anger and irritation. With the mild tone of perfect presence of mind and composure he answered her, "It was before the Lord, who chose me before thy father, and before all his house, to appoint me ruler over the people of the Lord, over Israel: therefore will I play before the Lord. And I will yet be more vile than thus, and will be base in mine own sight: and of the maid-servants which thou hast spoken of, of them shall I be had in honor." How incomparable is this heart-effusion! In the words there lay along with grief on account of the misapprehension he had experienced on the part of his wife, at the same time a certain boldness—yea, pride—which was hallowed because rooted in the deepest humility.

David boasted of the great things God had done for him when He raised him so high before Saul and his house; but he testified this only to the praise of God. He granted it to Michal in his reply, that he had abased himself; but not before men, but before Him who dwells in the heavens. He feels himself all unworthy of the high dignity of bringing home the ark of God, and appears to himself incomparably lower than he does to his scornful wife. He will, however, become yet more abased (namely, in his humiliation before God), and will covet no higher honor than that which he could share with the pious handmaids of whom she spoke.

Is there not something precious in this disclosure of the heart of the king of Israel? Might not one almost believe himself transported from the days of the Old Covenant into those of the New, in which the Apostle Paul poured forth these words: "I count all things but loss for the excellency of the knowledge of Christ Jesus my Lord; for whom I have suffered the loss of all things, and do count them but dung, that I may win Christ"? Indeed, David himself predicted in these words, "I will yet become more vile than thus," something of which he then had no apprehension. He would, indeed, in a most sorrowful manner, "be yet more vile" on account of an event which, at the moment of his uttering this language, he would have thought an impossibility. Michal did not escape divine chastisement for the hateful slander by which she had so sorely grieved her husband in one of the holiest moments of his life. In inheriting her father's disposition, she also therein shared her father's fate in that, remaining childless to the end of her days, she gave no heir to the throne of Israel.

Unmistakably the "Song of Degrees," whose festal tones we hear in the Psalm 122, relates to the bringing up of the ark of the covenant to Zion. "I was glad," David begins, "when they said unto me, Let us go into the house of the Lord. Our feet shall stand within thy gates, O Jerusalem." Then he praises Jerusalem, builded as a city compact together; as the city "whither the tribes go up, the tribes of the Lord, unto the testimony of Israel, to give thanks unto the name of the Lord. For there are set thrones of judgment, the thrones of the house of David." Then he addresses to the people the summons to seek the salvation of Jerusalem, and to pray to the Lord that He would prosper all who love the holy city, and that peace might dwell within her walls, and prosperity within her palaces. Then, addressing Jerusalem herself, he concludes with the solemn promise, "For my brethren and companions' sakes, I will now say, Peace be within thee. Because of the house of the Lord our God, I will seek thy good."

We join joyfully in this festal song, while we think of the Jerusalem of which the apostle speaks when he says, "The Jerusalem which is above, which is free, is the mother of us all." With reference to this city of God, we also give ear to the cry of the prophet, "Let Jerusalem be in your hearts"; and we renew our vows in the words of Psalm 137, "If I forget thee, O Jerusalem, let my right hand forget her cunning!"

19

A Retrospect

It was an enviable testimony with which the Lord blessed His disciples when He said to them, "Ye are not of the world, but I have chosen you out of the world."[1] Happy is he who is entitled to appropriate these words with confidence as applicable to his own case! There are many who are of such a mind who are seeking after the infallible marks of the child of God. But these everyone must seek for in the depths of his own soul. "The Spirit," says the apostle, "beareth witness with our spirit, that we are the children of God." This "witness of the Spirit" will attest its genuineness, however, in the prevailing moral aims of the inward man. The "Yea, Lord; but yet" of the woman of Caanan; the humble sorrow for sin, accompanied by a decided renunciation of it; the consciousness of guilt before God losing itself in the believing appropriation of the grace of God in Christ—form the essence of that character the possession of which entitles us to reckon ourselves among the elect of God.

But that holy nature which is created within us carries in it the impulse to make itself manifest in outward life by word and deed; and thus there is furnished another recognizable mark whereby we may prove that we "are no more of the world, but that He hath chosen us out of the world." That the conduct of such an one must be in conformity with the divine commandments, follows as a necessary consequence. But the evidence of the outward conduct is not to be wholly relied on; for though two persons may perform the same action, yet the act of both may not therefore be the same. Even so, false steps, infirmities, and imperfections by no means warrant any one to entertain the suspicion that he is not "chosen out of the

1. John 15:19.

237

world," if he is at the same time engaged in a holy warfare against them, for he may obtain, through repentance, forgiveness from God. There are, however, characteristics which unmistakably distinguish those who have indeed escaped from the world; and on a retrospect of the celebration of the bringing up of the ark, of which we were witnesses, we shall discover several of these, in the person and conduct of King David.

2 Samuel 6:14–15

> And David danced before the Lord with all his might; and David was girded with a linen ephod. So David and all the house of Israel brought up the ark of the Lord with shouting, and with the sound of the trumpet.

In the portrait of David, as it here appears to our view, several essential marks of a true state of grace unveil themselves before us. There are these five. We may describe them thus, in the language of the New Testament: (1) joy in Christ; (2) separation from the world; (3) the open confession of the crucified one; (4) love to the people of God; and (5) bearing willingly the shame of the cross. Let us consider these in succession.

1. With high animation David accompanied to Mount Zion the holy ark, the symbol of God condescending to manifest mercy and grace to sinners; and the first characteristic of those who have attained to life in God is their hearty joy in Christ. Esteem for Him, or having a delight in Him, is not that which is here meant. As little is it the joy which being occupied with Him as with an object of scientific or artistic interest affords, and which may even possibly be associated at the same time with a secret hatred of Him. Rather there is intended by it the holy delight and the inward love to the Son of God, as to Him in whom is found not only the salvation of others, but our own salvation both for time and for eternity. There are many, indeed, who intelligently and truly know how to bear witness of the great things for which the world is indebted to the Lord Christ. But no ray of joy beams from their countenance thereat, and no secret little current of more inward emotion glides perceptibly under their words. Perhaps such testimonies are given forth in a highly oratorical manner; yet to every one of a finely organized ear, the presence of the sounding-board is missed. The freshness of the spring is lacking; the breath of the heart is lacking—in a word, the fresh, warm life.

"But are there not," it is asked, on the contrary, "among true Christians such as stand in anxiety and are of an oppressed, troubled spirit? Are they only the children of God who are able to triumph and shout for joy as David did before the ark of the covenant?" One may indeed acknowledge what is here implied. The joy in Christ wrought by the Spirit of God has its different degrees and steps, as also its manifold forms of outward expression. The wearied wanderer, when from a distance the end of the journey toward which he strives becomes visible, rejoices, and not he only who has already reached it, and with delight has laid aside his pilgrim-staff. The prisoner to whom the tidings is first brought that one is at hand to set him free, already rejoices, although the joy of him who sees himself already set free will be purer, and fuller, and more unmingled. So there is a joy in Christ of desire and of hope, as well as a joy of perfected satisfaction and blessed enjoyment of Him. But wherever neither the one nor the other exists—whether it be only as a little spark and a glimmering light, or as a clear burning flame—there we cannot speak at all of a life of faith, yea, not even of a tender germ of it.

Here let me say, that though you may present an appearance of sorrow, may hang your head like a bulrush, tremble like a leaf at the thought of death, eternity, and judgment, yet on that account it does not become me to declare you destitute of the divine life. But if I name to you the name of Christ as that of the Savior, or lead you into the circle where they are truly comforted in Him, and if then I see not once a twilight of joy, though it were only the joy of a trembling hope shooting through the dark cloud which covers your brow, how dare I, by this indifference toward the only Savior of your soul, count you among His flock? Your sorrow is certainly not "godly sorrow," wrought by the Holy Spirit, which "worketh repentance not to be repented of." Heartfelt joy in Jesus, in whatever measure it may be possessed—delight in the assemblies where His honor dwells, and where His love to sinners is celebrated in songs of praise—belong essentially to the character of those who are "chosen out of the world."

2. The position which any human being holds in relation to the world lying in wickedness is the second thing which must be referred to, in coming to a conclusion as to whether his Christianity be a reality or only a pretense and a mask. David separated himself with decision, both in disposition and in action, from the multitude in Israel,

and swam with all his might against the stream of the godless spirit of
the time, which had gained such wide sway since the days of Saul.

Thus will it be with true Christians, Everything that is called pal-
try straining at a gnat and Pharisaic conformity to law, should
certainly be far from them. What they may eat and drink, how they
may clothe themselves, and what should be their manner of life or
their mode of speaking—for such things the children of the New
Covenant have given to them no directions. Even the joke and the
laugh are not denied to them; only to the latter there must not be
any occasion to say, "Laughter, thou art mad." Still less is it denied
to them to rejoice in the beauties of nature, which indeed to them
rather first disclose their magnificence, as well as in the works of pure
art, or to mingle in honorable society, particularly when they understand how to consecrate and season all this with the spiritual.

Here it is said to them, "All things are yours, for ye are Christ's." But
whoever can sit with pleasure where "the sinner sits," and is contented
in circles where the tone and manners forbid that the name of Jesus
should be lovingly named; whoever finds "green pastures" in amusements which are only fitted to please the senses, but make no provision
for the spirit; whoever finds himself drawn to society in which vain,
foolish talk takes the place of friendly edifying conversation—in short,
he can make no pretension to the Christian's name whose heart is not
oppressed by the stifling atmosphere of libertine, worldly society, however respectable be the appearance in which it clothes itself.

To those who are truly Christ's own it has been said, "Come out
from among them" who are worshipers of the idols of this world,
"that ye be not partakers of their sins"; and they are certainly obedient to the inner impulse of such divine directions. Perhaps on that
account they appear to those who are wandering on the broad way
as peculiar persons. But what do they care for that? They go forth
with a steadfast step along their path, which alone is the way of
peace. "They think it strange, says Peter, "that ye run not with them
to the same excess of riot, speaking evil of you."

But how strange does it seem to the disciples of the Lord that anyone is capable of wasting the short span of life in such a vain,
frivolous, ungodly manner! Oh, happy are all to whom the word of
the Lord is applicable: "Ye are not of the world." Such hear also with
composed mind when the Lord further says to them, "Therefore the
world hateth you!" At the same time they take notice also of the

conclusion of that discourse of their Master: "The servant is not greater than his lord. If they have persecuted me, they will also persecute you. But all these things will they do unto you for my name's sake, because they know not Him that sent me." And how they feel themselves elevated by the words of the apostle: "If ye be reproached for the name of Christ, happy are ye; for the Spirit of glory and of God resteth upon you: on their part He is evil spoken of, but on your part He is glorified!"

3. That which further designates the true Christian is his open, frank confession. Not as though everyone making confession as such is already a Christian; but he who does not make confession is not a Christian. The word of the Lord places this beyond question: "whosoever shall confess me before men, him will I confess also before my Father which is in heaven." And to the same effect that word of the apostle: "With the heart man believeth unto righteousness; and with the mouth confession is made unto salvation." Let one look upon David the king, clothed in the plain dress of a Levite, how he goes singing and playing before the holy ark of the covenant! He allows himself to be restrained by no laws of social manners which unbelief dictated to him. He follows the impulse of his own heart, moved by holy emotions. All the world shall know that the consciousness that God is kind and gracious toward him is his highest honor, his most precious jewel—more precious than crown and scepter, and whatever else of the coveted things of earth may be named.

But do you who read these words freely and frankly keep David before your eye as he makes his confession? Does it constrain you, as often as opportunity is given you, also openly and loudly to bear witness that in Christ you have found your one thing and your all? It is nowhere, indeed, commanded by the Lord to be extravagant with your confession. Rather He warns you against this in one of His sayings, according to which you must not give that which is holy unto the dogs, nor cast the pearls before swine. But has not this word become to you plainly a favorite expression? Are you not accustomed, if you apprehend that your honest confession will give rise to mockery and ridicule among your neighbors, to use that saying as a cloak for cowardly silence? Do you not make use of it with dishonest mind as a shield against the accusations of your awakened conscience, when your Savior is drawn down to the dust, and you "art," to use the words of Calvin, "put to shame by every dog which at least barks when it sees its master laid hold of?" Do you not take care, at least before you make confession to review the circle in which you find yourself and are a hero only among friends and persons like-minded with yourself; but, on the contrary, among opponents are you a cowardly deserter of your standard? If you must answer these questions in the affirmative, then how can you call yourself a disciple of Him who said, "Whosoever shall deny me before men, him will I also deny before my Father which is in heaven"? Whoever is ashamed of the gospel of Christ has not yet experienced it as the power of God which brings salvation. All true life of faith shows itself as a "city set on an hill," and is like a "candle placed on a candlestick." A joyful going forth under the standard of the cross, especially where it brings reproach, is the third of the indispensable marks of those who "are chosen out of the world."

4. But like this, love to the people of God is also of decisive importance. We were witnesses how much David felt himself at home at Ramah with Samuel, and at Naioth among the sons of the prophets. Among his most confidential friends were the pious Abiathar and the prophet Gad, and all those whom, at the festival of the bringing up of the ark, he especially blessed in his heart, and as such preferred, with whom he hoped "to be had in honor." They were lowly people, but "quiet in the land," unknown to the world, though known in heaven. And there are also at the present day those consecrated to the Lord, no matter to what social rank they belong, to whom true believers are the most closely related. Whoever finds no trace within him of congenial attraction for such fellowship, even feels himself more at home in the circles of the children of this world than in those of the children of the kingdom of heavens, may feel assured that he is numbered among those who will one day hear these words out of the mouth of the Lord, "I never knew you!"

A holy partiality for them whom St. John had in his eye when he said, "As many as received Him, to them gave He power to become the sons of God," and whom the Lord describes as "the salt of the earth," Paul as "of the household of God," and Peter as "the chosen generation and royal priesthood," takes an essential place among the marks by which a true Christian standing is known. Everywhere in Scripture preference for those with whom one feels himself a brother in the Lord, and with whom he meets the distinct echo of that which moves himself most deeply, and which lies before all other things nearest to his heart, is presented as such. Thus, for example, we read in the First Epistle of John: "Whosoever believeth that Jesus is the Christ, is born of God: and every one that loveth Him that begat loveth Him also that is begotten of Him"; and in another place: "We know that we have passed from death unto life, because we love the brethren."

5. Yet another characteristic of the true Christian, to which we have already in passing made allusion, must be mentioned. It shines forth with special brightness in the example of David, It is the joyful readiness to bear reproach for the sake of Christ—a feature which is too frequently missed, particularly among the so-called "upper ranks," among those who wish to be regarded as living Christians. It is true that it is not an easy thing to feel that we are regarded in the eyes of a supposed enlightened world, if not as hypocrites, yet as simpletons who have fallen behind the education of the times. Hence, with so many of those "advanced Christians," the zealous endeavor in their so-called confessions to break off in some way the point from the fundamental articles of the faith, to divest the doctrine of the cross of its foolishness, to preserve the honor of a certain "reasonableness" in the gospel by "spiritualizing," that is, evaporating interpretations, and to obtain for themselves the recognition that they do not belong to the "blindly believing" pietists, but hope to show that their faith will endure also the test of philosophy.

Hence also an assiduous accommodating of themselves to the manner of speaking and to the form of life prevalent among the children of this world, a going along with them in the spirit and tone which prevail in their circles of society, and a prudently calculated participation in their amusements up to that limit at least beyond which one cannot go without incurring the reproach of an open falling away from the rule according to which all are called upon to act who wish to belong to Christ.

Indeed, there is scarcely a more lamentable sight than is presented by the half-heartedness and the cowardice of those persons to whom certainly the threatening is applicable which has been spoken by the Lord, "I will spue thee out of my mouth." Every noble-minded man disdains to receive honor from those who withhold it from a mere human friend whom he esteems and loves, and can one be ashamed of the heavenly Friend, and deny Him in order that he may only preserve the favor of His enemies?

What a bright contrast to such miserable conduct does the example of David present to us! He found his honor directly in the dishonor which on account of his joyful confession of the covenant God of Israel, those who were estranged from God heaped upon him, and which he would have avoided had they been able at all to recognize him as one of their own class. What manliness and nobility in these words of David: "I will yet be more vile than thus, and will be base in mine own sight" (unmoved by what the blinded world may say regarding him): "and of the maid-servants which thou hast spoken of, of them shall I be had in honor."

At that time the king of Israel stood worthily by the side of Moses, of whom the Scripture says, "By faith he esteemed the reproach of Christ greater riches than all the treasures of Egypt; for he had respect unto the recompense of the reward." The apostle calls unto Christians, "Let us go forth therefore unto Him" (the crucified One) "without the camp" (the world hostile to the faith), "bearing His reproach. For here we have no continuing city, but we seek one to come." He who attempts to escape at any cost from this duty to which we are called, instead of looking upon "the reproach of Christ" (provided it be unmerited reproach, and not willfully brought upon himself) as a distinguished mark of honor, cannot boast himself that he has been in earnest with his Christianity. So long as the world remains what it now is, it is impossible for those who are actuated by a true and decided faith to pass through it without incurring reproach.

Our retrospect is concluded. The lessons we have gathered, however, may for many be not the most comforting. Yet if the result is only self-condemnation and shame, the effort we have made is richly enough rewarded. But to those who are alarmed we address this message of encouragement, that there are not only those who have become Christians, but who are becoming such, and that there are as well "babes and sucklings" in Christ as youths and fathers in the Lord. To every such one let this announcement be made for his comfort, that it is already a great thing, and rich with promise, when it can be said of him, as it once was said of Saul to Ananias, "Behold, he prayeth!" Let us rejoice in the words of the prophecy, "A bruised reed shall He not break, and smoking flax shall He not quench, till He send forth judgment unto victory."

20

The Great Promise

Among the more pleasing signs of our times, in general manifesting so little of a favorable inclination to the faith, must be noticed the undeniable progress which theological science has made. From the mere philosophical and speculative contemplation of the miracles, it has moved to a historical consideration and critical judgment of them. Men are accustomed now to inquire no longer first into the possibility, but, before all other things, into the historical credibility of the miracles recorded in the Bible. It is asked, Are they borne witness to by credible persons who report them—by ear and eye—witnesses whose honesty, discretion, and conscientiousness lie under no suspicion? And thus evermore conclusively is the testimony strengthened, that we have in truth to do with men of this sort in the evangelists and apostles. It is granted that miracles have been wrought; but from this point there is a divergence in the view entertained both as to the nature of a miracle and as to the power by which it has been brought about. While one seeks to trace it to an elevated human ability, another ascribes it to natural means and processes, which as such were, to the generation that then was, still a mystery; and thus again the immediate emergence of divine omnipotence is called in question, is even directly denied, and the old unbelief maintains itself in its stronghold.

The luminous chain of miracles which is unveiled before us in the Holy Scriptures is elongated through thousands of years, link after link. It does not belong by any means to a dark ignorant age, but in great part to one when, not only in Rome and Greece, science and art flourished, but when also among the Jews a sober intelligence allowed no room for fantastic myths. The reality and truthfulness par-

245

ticularly of the miracles of Jesus and His apostles, were so little doubt-ed either by Jews or Gentiles, that the former, to avoid the conclusions forced upon them by an acknowledgment of them, were under the necessity of resorting to the feigned supposition that the miracles were wrought through demoniacal power; and that the Gentiles, in the second century after Christ, imputed to their magi-cian Apollonius of Tyana, in contrast to the miracles of the Lord, yet greater works (though unmistakably bearing a resemblance to them) than Christ did, in order that the people might be prevented from embracing Christianity, having no longer occasion to envy the Jews their Worker of miracles.

Why now arises the aversion of so many in our days to belief in the miracles, but from this cause, that the separation between heav-en and earth is immeasurably great, and they no longer recognize the Creator of the world as a living, personal, and free agent? But, keep-ing in view the attributes which appertain to Him, which enter into our conception of deity, how natural then is it for us to think that the high and exalted One would not be bound by the laws which He has imposed on His creation? Rather would He remain, unrestrained and free, Lord in His own great house, while He left Himself room, in the organization of the materials of the world, for operating with higher powers than originally dwelt within them. He gave to nature a direction by virtue of which, always serviceable to His wisdom or His love, it might be able to bear deviations from its accustomed course, and this without doing injury to the law according to which we see it move itself, and to which must be attributed an elasticity or ductility arising from the will of God! He who, because "He doeth according to His will in the army of heaven and among the inhab-itants of the earth," will at some time perfectly change and transfigure the world which now is, and then it will no longer be to anyone a question whether He is a God who can work miracles. This work of renovation, which we wait for, will stand side by side with the most astonishing of His miracles, namely, the first creation of the world out of nothing, as the mere expression of His almighty will; yes, even louder then than over the work of the beginning, will "the morning stars sing together, and all the sons of God shout for joy."

These explanatory words may serve to strengthen our faith in the event of which we shall hear today. The condescension of God to us poor mortal men is our salvation—is our life. We shall anew be witnesses of this while we meet with a miracle in the world of the human mind, a protest of the living God, the reality of which is by its consequences raised above all doubt.

2 Samuel 7:11

And the Lord telleth thee that He will make thee an house.

The Star announcing salvation, which Balaam once saw arising out of Jacob, after that the Lord had opened his inner eye, had since those olden times not come much nearer to the circle of the spiritual vision of the children of Israel. It formed, indeed, the center of all their national hopes. Israel recognized it, though veiled in all the types and symbols of their worship of God. But now the hour has struck in which He will withdraw from a portion of it the veil which covered it; and David was chosen by the Lord partly as a personal type, partly as the bearer of new revelations, to perform this work of the unveiling. Today we see him honored by having communicated to him a most important and significant divine revelation. Let us consider (1) the contents of this revelation, and then (2) the influences which flowed from it.

1. David has ceaselessly and most honorably made use of those days of peace which the Lord granted to him in building and adorning Jerusalem, in restoring the orders of the priests, which had been almost lost, providing singers and musicians for the public worship of the sanctuary, and setting over them men endowed with eminent gifts, such as Asaph, Heman, Ethan, and others, as chief musicians. Besides these things, he had busied himself with the organization of the army, and directed his attention, with paternal solicitude, to the administration of justice throughout the land. He had also completed the erection of his royal residence on Mount Zion, and had made all the arrangements about it, both internally and externally, corresponding to his royal dignity.

Today we enter his palace. There he sits alone, deeply engaged in the contemplation of all the grace wherewith the Lord to this day had crowned his life. His soul overflows with thankfulness. Only one thing troubles him. He is constrained to reveal it to the prophet Nathan, his friend and counselor. For the first time today we meet this man of God. Many a time after this, in the life of David, we shall meet Nathan by his side. It was this prophet who wrote, at a later period, a history of the reign of David, and also of Solomon, which, however, has not come down to us. He had an essential part in the revival and improvement of the public worship of God under David.

Nathan having been sent for by the king, appears before him, and is received by him with these words: "See now I dwell in an house of cedar, but the ark of God dwelleth within curtains" (in a mere tent). He spoke thus with visible sorrow; and what do we wish for more than that David's thoughts about the spiritual house of God, the Church, were those of all the great ones of the earth! Nathan soon discovered what moved the heart of his royal friend; and the idea of a temple worthy to be a dwelling-place of the Most High finds a lively echo in his soul. "Go," said he to the king, "and do all that is in thine heart; for the Lord is with thee." He could not but believe this, because his intention had as its object only the glorifying of the Lord.

Yet what took place? In the following night the word of the Lord came in a vision to Nathan. And what was its import? A declining of David's plan, and a denial of the prophet's approbation given to it. Here there presents itself to us a striking testimony of the reality of immediate divine revelations. David and Nathan united, according to their best knowledge and conscience, in a truly pious and holy work, and suddenly they renounce their cherished purpose, whose execution everything appeared to counsel. Why did they give up the noble intention? Not certainly of their own accord, but rather because God the Lord spoke regarding it, and interposed immediately His veto.

And how should the living personal God, who has given to man the power of speech, not Himself be able to speak to the children of men? No argument that can stand the test can be urged to the contrary. But if it is asked why God refused His consent to an undertaking which only proved honorable to David's heart, let us hear what the Lord says to David in the First Book of Chronicles: "Thou shalt not build an house for my name, because thou hast been a man of war, and hast shed blood."[1] There is not the least foundation for any suspicion that, in the darling project of the king, there mingled human vanity or love of show; but the time was not suitable for works of peace, and especially for the building of a temple, while yet great and fierce wars were in immediate prospect against the sur-

---

1.   1 Chronicles 30:29.

rounding heathen nations, But let us consider what the Lord revealed to the prophet in that vision of the night. It has also for us the highest significance.

Early in the morning Nathan appeared again before David, and informed him of what had occurred in the night, and of the communication he had received from the Lord. "Go and tell my servant David, Thus saith the Lord, Shalt thou build me an house for me to dwell in?" Nathan further announced to him that the Lord had directed him to say to the king that He did not need an house. Since He led the children of Israel out of Egypt, He had been among them, leading and helping them, and had revealed Himself to them in the humble tent, and had never said to any of the tribes of Israel, "Why do you not build me an house of cedar?" He had been also at all times with His servant David, without first requiring him to build Him an house. He had taken him from the sheepfolds and set him as prince over His people, and He would be thus still with him.

He would also appoint a place for His people Israel, and plant them that they might dwell in a settled place of their own, and no longer wander or be made to tremble on account of their enemies. The children of wickedness would no longer afflict them as before. "Also the Lord telleth thee," continued Nathan with an elevated voice and with great emotion of heart, "that He will make thee an house." With much excitement the king hears these last words, for already the secret thought of their import rose dimly before his soul.

Nathan says, "The Lord telleth thee, When thy days be fulfilled, and thou shalt sleep with thy fathers, I will set up thy seed after thee, which shall proceed out of thy bowels, and I will establish his kingdom. He shall build an house for my name; and I will establish the throne of his kingdom forever. I will be his Father, and he shall be my son. If he commit iniquity, I will chasten him with the rod of men, and with the stripes of the children of men: but my mercy shall not depart away from him, as I took it from Saul, whom I put away before thee. And thine house and thy kingdom shall be established forever before thee: thy throne shall be established forever."

The double sense of these words of the Lord is soon apprehended by David, even without mentioning that the expression, "If he commit iniquity," is capable also of the translation: "If I will make him sin." First, the words especially contain a promise of the establishment of the dynasty of the royal house of David. His kingdom would be hereditary; and his son Solomon, who was not yet born, would be his first successor on the throne. Him Jehovah had chosen that he should build an house, i.e., a temple, to the Lord. He would be a Father to the king; and that kingdom would consequently be His kingdom, the kingdom of God. This latter part of the promise opens up a wide and magnificent prospect into times then remote. It points to a kingdom which is not of this world; while all the kingdoms of this world are subjected to decay, and to a King who, although sprung from the seed of David according to the flesh, nevertheless belongs to another and a higher rank and sphere of being than that of man.

2.   How was David now affected by this revelation of the prophet? With great agitation of soul he listened to it. What words were these: "I the Lord will build thee an house"—"Thy throne shall be established forever"—"Thy kingdom shall have no end"—"I the Lord will be Father of the future King, the everlasting Ruler, thy successor, and he shall be my son!" Yes, David understands it. The most important and the most surprising moment of his life has come. There he sits silent and absorbed in deep thought. The veil which concealed the distant future has been raised before him.

Suddenly he sees the promise which already had been given to the patriarch Abraham all at once connected with his own house. Abraham's seed, the great One who was to come, in whom "all the nations of the earth would be blessed," rises up before his inward eye as a descendant of his house. He must relieve his deeply agitated heart. Having dismissed Nathan, he rises from his seat and hurries to the holy tabernacle, in order that there, before the ark of the covenant, that symbol of the throne and of the presence of Jehovah, he might pour out before the Lord all the thoughts that filled his soul.

We hear his prayer. "Who am I," he begins, "O Lord God? and what is my house, that Thou hast brought me hitherto? And this was yet a small thing in Thy sight, O Lord God; but Thou hast spoken also of Thy servant's house for a great while to come." "This" (the future establishment of my kingdom) "is the manner" (law or ordinance) "of a man who is God the Lord"—not of a mortal man, but of one who is God-man. Some interpreters regard this passage as an exclamation of surprise, and translate it, "And this is the law of man, O Lord Jehovah," i.e., You appoint such a law to a man and his house, that You open up to him a view into eternal ages! But according to the more accurate interpretation we have put upon the words, the expression means, "It cannot be a mortal man of whom You have spoken such great things. He must come from above." Altogether, unmistakably a vision of the Messiah, the promised Son of God, now hovered before the eyes of David. Something further, as we shall immediately see, places this beyond question.

Let us bend our ears further to the prayer of the king: "Thou Lord God knowest Thy servant," i.e., he needed here not many words. "For Thy word's sake, and according to Thine own heart, hast Thou done all these great things, to make Thy servant know them." Hereupon David gives animated expression to his feelings in praising God, who had constantly overshadowed His people with His favor, and continues to bless them. "What nation in the earth," he cries out, "is like Thy people, even like Israel, whom God went to redeem for a people to Himself, and to make Him a name, and to do for you great things and terrible, for Thy land, before Thy people, which Thou redeemedst to Thee from Egypt, from the nations and their gods? For Thou hast confirmed to Thyself Thy people Israel to be a people unto Thee forever: and Thou, Lord, art become their God."

Then with a beating heart David again returns to the distant future which the Lord had personally opened up before his sight. "And now, O Lord God," he prays, "the word that Thou hast spoken concerning Thy servant, and concerning his house, establish it forever, and do as Thou hast said. And let Thy name be magnified forever, saying, The Lord of hosts is the God over Israel: and let the house of Thy servant David be established before Thee. For Thou, O Lord of hosts, God of Israel, hast revealed to Thy servant, saying, I will build thee an house: therefore hath Thy servant found in his heart" (i.e., felt it deeply pressed in upon his mind) "to pray this prayer unto Thee. And now, O Lord God, Thou art that God, and Thy words be true, and Thou hast promised this goodness unto Thy servant: therefore now let it please Thee to bless the house of Thy servant, that it may continue forever before Thee: for Thou, O Lord God, hast spoken it: and with Thy blessing let the house of Thy servant be blessed forever."

Such was the king's prayer. As it streamed forth from his heart he subsequently recorded it. Never afterward did he forget what the Lord had revealed to him. It echoed through the whole of his future life; and the mystery it contained unfolded itself more and more under increasing enlightenment. The glorious image of the King, his great

successor, who was ordained to rule forever, presented itself in con-
tinuous revelations more distinctly on all sides before his soul. In
Psalm 110, Him who, according to the flesh, would be his descen-
dant, he calls, in regard to His majesty, his "Lord" when he says, "The
Lord said unto my Lord, Sit Thou at my right hand, until I make
Thine enemies Thy footstool."

Near the end of his days, that divine message which had been
brought to him by Nathan again rises up within his soul, filling him
with comfort. It blesses the time of his departure from the earth. In his
dying song, with joyful elevation of feeling, he breaks out in these words:

> The God of Israel said,
> The Rock of Israel spake to me;
> He that ruleth over men, just
> A ruler in the fear of God.
> And as light of the morning when the sun rises,
> As morning without clouds;
> The tender grass springeth out of the earth
>   by clear shining after rain.

That is, His government will, in ever-widening circumference,
spread life, and blessings, and prosperity around it. And from what
house will He go forth as the Son of man, who is the great Prince of
life and Prince of peace? David says—

> My house is established by God,
> For He hath made with me an everlasting covenant.

Thus David did not fail to apprehend the mighty import of that
great promise which had been communicated to him; and how widely did its influence beyond him extend! From that time forth,
throughout the whole of Israel, the longed-for and expected Founder
of an everlasting kingdom of peace was called the "Son of David." All
the prophets from that time knew of Him as the "Branch out of the root
of Jesse" bringing salvation. The hope of the people now clung to the
line of David. The eye of their longing desire rested on Bethlehem. A
knowledge of the heavenly descent of this Son of David, and of His
essential oneness with God, became always the more unambiguous;
and His "goings forth from of old, from everlasting" held a place in the
contemplation of the enlightened in Israel with the same clarity as did
His human descent. And when at last the time of His appearing drew

nigh, the message of the heavenly herald came to Mary, the daughter of David, saying, "Thou shalt bear a son, and He shall be great, and shall be called the Son of the Highest; and the Lord God shall give unto Him the throne of His father David." And soon after that we hear the old priest Zacharias, "full of the Holy Ghost," exultingly cry out, "Blessed be the Lord God of Israel; for He hath visited and redeemed His people, and hath raised up an horn of salvation for us in the house of His servant David." And when He drew near to Jerusalem, there sounded forth from the excited multitudes around Him that cry of homage, "Hosanna to the Son of David! Blessed is He that cometh in the name of the Lord." At a later period, also, we hear that cry of distress repeatedly from the lips of those who are suppliants for deliverance and help, "Lord Jesus, Thou Son of David, have mercy on me!"

In all this we distinctly hear the echoes of that revelation which was once communicated to David by means of Nathan the prophet, only more and more, as time advanced, unfolded, enlarged, and perfected by the Spirit of God.

Thus Christ already for hundreds, yea, for thousands of years before His appearance, lived in the expectation of the friends of God. Adam, Abraham, Moses, and many more after them, had already received tidings concerning Him, and comforted themselves therein with their whole hearts. "Many prophets and kings," said the Son of David Himself when He appeared, "have desired to see those things which ye see, and have not seen them." A longing expectation of His coming was felt throughout all Israel, and passed over even to many of the heathen tribes.

The Sun whose rising David in spirit had hailed, has now for nearly 2,000 years shone in the firmament of the world; and who may express the fullness of salvation and of blessings wherewith to this day it has enriched and made glad this poor earth? It is true that it forms clouds as well as scatters clouds; but in undimmed splendor it holds on its way, and remains pure and spotless even then, when, under its rays, because they fall upon moor and marsh, only poisonous vapors arise. Yet how many even among those who, destitute of faith, turn their back upon it, participate in its beneficent influence even far more richly than they themselves know or wish to know! All the best things which the world enjoys in civilization, in social progress, in a well-ordered national and family life, together with the hopes which shine into the night of the grave, it owes to the "Sun of righteousness with healing in His wings," which diffuses its blissful light over the ungodly as well as over the righteous. O that everyone would come within the circle of its radiance, and join himself to the holy band of pilgrims which at all times, in calm and joyful faith, has been marching through the great wilderness of this world, and whose watchword is, "Hosanna to the Son of David!"

Psalm 89, composed by Ethan the Ezrahite, but in the spirit of David, has undoubtedly a reference to that remarkable prayer in which David poured out his heart before the Lord in the holy taber-nacle at the time of his receiving the great promise. The author of it desires to sing of the grace of the Lord, and with his mouth to make known His faithfulness to all generations. "Mercy shall be built up," thus he sings, "forever: Thy faithfulness shalt Thou establish in the very heavens. I have made a covenant with my chosen, I have sworn unto David my servant, Thy seed will I establish forever, and build up thy throne to all generations. And the heavens shall praise Thy wonders, O Lord: Thy faithfulness also in the congregation of the saints."

The singer after this adores the power and holiness of Jehovah, and proclaims that they are a blessed people who walk in the light of His countenance. "In Thy name," he says, "shall they rejoice all the day; and in Thy righteousness shall they be exalted. For Thou art the glory of their strength; and in Thy favor our horn shall be exalted." Then returning to David, he continues, "Then" (that is when You gave to him the great promise) "Thou spakest in vision to Thy Holy One, and saidst, I have laid help upon one that is mighty; I have exalted one chosen out of the people. I have found David my servant: with my holy oil have I anointed him: with whom my hand shall be established; mine arm also shall strengthen him. The enemy shall not exact upon him; nor the son of wickedness afflict him. And I will beat down his foes before his face, and plague them that hate him. But my faithfulness and my mercy shall be with him; and in my name shall his horn be exalted. I will set his hand also in the sea, and his right hand in the rivers. He shall cry unto me, Thou art my Father, my God, and the Rock of my salvation. Also I will make him my first-born, higher than the kings of the earth" (in the person of the Messiah). "My mercy will I keep for him forevermore, and my covenant shall stand fast with him. His seed also will I make to endure forever, and his throne as the days of heaven."

In the following verses the singer recalls to mind that which the

Lord, in the revelation which He had entrusted to Nathan, had promised to David in the event of his seed (i.e., his immediate successor) being guilty of a transgression (i.e., if he broke his covenant, for instance), that notwithstanding this He would not change anything of the great and rich promise that He had made. "O Lord, Thou hast said," he continues, "Once have I sworn by my holiness, that I will not lie unto David. His seed shall endure forever, and his throne as the sun before me. It shall be established forever as the moon, and as a faithful witness in heaven." But now he thinks of the contradiction which appeared to exist between the time so full of manifold threatenings and oppressions at which he composed his psalms, and this glorious promise which was given to David and to his seed.

"O Lord, where are Thy former loving-kindnesses," he cries out, "which Thou swarest unto David in Thy truth?" He prays to the Lord that He would remove this appearance of contradiction. Yet he leans confidently on an immovable rock, God's word, and concludes in faith with the doxology, "Blessed be the Lord forevermore. Amen, and Amen."

Ethan the Levite composed this psalm in his advanced age, when the kingdom of David had been defeated under Rehoboam, and much ungodliness prevailed on every hand, and threatened in yet greater measure, as the consequence of manifold disorders, to spread among the people. Ethan, however, gives us himself a remarkable and elevating example of how the promise given to David still lived among the people, and how the pious found in it their consolation. The prospect into the heavenly kingdom was, as we know, to them yet darkened by thick clouds; but on this very account their hope was directed with all the greater animation toward the appearing of the Messiah's kingdom in this world. To this hope they clung under all circumstances, because it had founded itself on the word of the living God.

Truly those old saints may put us to shame, who now see the sun shining with splendor on these divine promises, of which they had scarcely as yet an apprehension. May we tread in the footsteps of their faith, and may our hearts also appreciate the prayer of Psalm 119: "O Lord, order my steps in Thy word; for Thy word is true from the beginning: and every one of Thy righteous judgments endureth forever!"

21

Mephibosheth

David was not only the ancestor of Christ according to the flesh, but also the type and personal prefiguration of the future Messiah. In the contemplation of Israel, he became so with a degree of clarity which led them without hesitation to designate the promised Savior directly by the name of David, which the Lord approved of and confirmed. Thus we meet with a confirmation of this in the prophecies of Jeremiah: "It shall come to pass in that day, saith the Lord of hosts, that I will break his yoke from off thy neck, and will burst thy bonds, and strangers shall no more serve themselves of him: but they shall serve the Lord their God, and David their king, whom I will raise up unto them."[1]

That which was typical in David was not limited to the general outline of his appearance as the theocratic king over Israel, and consequently the head of the most prominent of all the nations of the earth, and the conqueror at whose feet the heathen round about did homage. But it extended even to his individual actions, circumstances, situations, and experiences. Consciously or unconsciously, David, in his triumphs, in his zeal for the house of the Lord, in his concern for the revival of the constitution of the kingdom of Israel, as well as in the persecutions and injuries which he endured, and in the experiences of help with which he saw his life crowned, foreshadowed in unmistakable features the appearance of his future glorious Descendant.

Not a few also of David's psalms (and we may here only name the twenty-second, the forty-first, and the sixty-ninth, in which, under

---

1. Jeremiah 30:8, 9.

distress and threatening danger, he expresses himself in complaints before the Lord, but at the same time praises Him as his Comforter, Helper, and Deliverer) shape themselves under the secret influence of the Holy Spirit, word for word, into complete representations of the history of the sufferings of Christ, and thereby become true Messianic prophecies. The enemies of the Lord at a later time verified these, when they, for example, in giving to Him who was athirst on the cross drink mingled with vinegar and gall, in piercing His hands and feet, in the mockery which they heaped upon Him, etc., literally fulfilled all that David described as experienced by himself.

When suffering and dying, Christ clothed His feelings in words borrowed from one of the psalms, and thereby set His seal upon its contents as prophetic. Let us only call to remembrance the words, "My God, my God, why hast Thou forsaken me?" and the cry, "I thirst," which, as the evangelist remarks, the Lord made use of "that the Scriptures might be fulfilled." He makes the same remark regarding the dividing of His raiment under the cross, and therein points to the eighteenth verse of Psalm 22.

We come today to a scene in the life of David which is likewise rich in typical features. We do not maintain that that scene is recorded with the conscious intention of presenting to us a prophetic prefiguration, yet we are justified in contemplating it as such, and in so interpreting it. We will make use of it as seen from this point of view.

2 Samuel 9:7

> And David said unto him (Mephibosheth), Fear not: for I will surely show thee kindness for Jonathan thy father's sake.

As the type of the divine Prince of peace distributing grace, David comes for the present before us. He appears as such (1) in the call of Mephibosheth, (2) in the condescension with which he favored him, and (3) in the elevation to which he raised him.

1. In an inhospitable district of the country on the east of Jordan lay a little town, which owed its name, Lo-debar (i.e., without pasture), to the desert waste lying around it. It was for the most part inhabited by heathen; yet, since the last war in Judah, many Israelite fugitives, adherents of Saul, had settled in it. Among these, in the house of the husbandman Machir, we meet with a young man maimed and lame on his feet. No one took any notice now of his dis-

tinguished descent. As the first-born of Jonathan, the eldest son of
King Saul, he was for a long time presumptive heir to the throne of
Israel. His name is Mephibosheth. When, after the disastrous battle
at Mount Gilboa, which cost Saul and Jonathan their lives, his nurse
fled with him, then a child not yet five years old, among the mountains of Gilead, she let the poor boy (whom she carried in her arms,
because, being wearied, he could not go farther) fall, so that he
became incurably lame.

May we not here now recognize in Mephibosheth our own image?
If he lost his right to the earthly crown in consequence of the overthrow of his people in the plains of Jezreel, so we also have lost our
right to the crown of heaven by the ruinous fall in paradise. Did he
walk thenceforth halting on his feet? Who of us can boast that in his
natural condition he takes firm steps in the ways of the Lord, and
who could exclude himself from the number of those to whom that
word of the prophet refers: "How can ye do good that are accustomed
to do evil?" Did he live in Lo-debar, the desert pastureless wilderness?
And Lo-debar is, keeping out of view the gracious helps that are
granted, also our present dwelling-place. It is the field which, smitten with the ban and oppressed by the curse, can bring forth to us
only thorns and thistles—a vale of tears, even a valley of death,
where no herb grows which can cure our deep wounds, and no flower
of consolation which can truly refresh our hearts and eyes.

After the murder of Ish-bosheth, Mephibosheth also with terror
saw in spirit the sword hanging over his own head. Over our heads,
before that event took place on account of which the world still
stands, the sword of the justice of the almighty God was suspended,
and trembling we read on our wall the "Mene, Tekel," "Thou art
weighed in the balance and found wanting!"

But what happened to Mephibosheth, our living mirror, at Lo-
debar? Hopelessly lame, he halted about his desert dwelling-place,
while David, victorious from a new battle against the Philistines, in
which he thoroughly routed the ancient enemy of his people, and
took "Metheg-ammah" (i.e., the fortress and metropolis of the
Philistines, Gath) out of their hands, returned to Jerusalem with a
multitude of prisoners, and great spoil of golden shields and conquered banners. Thus the prince of Israel again stood there as a living
type of the divine Conqueror, who "spoiled principalities and
powers, and made a show of them openly, triumphing over them."

After that campaign there was again granted to David a brief cessation of war, and an opportunity was afforded him, who was so greatly blessed by God, to scatter also on his part benefactions and blessings around him. Looking out for those who might need help, whose necessities he might be able to mitigate, he first directed the inquiry to those around him—an inquiry which did honor to his heart, and proved the continuance of his love for the friend of his youth—"Is there yet any that is left of the house of Saul, that I may show him kindness for Jonathan's sake?" Ziba, formerly a steward in Saul's household, now a devoted servant of David's, replied, "Jonathan has yet a son, who is lame on his feet."

"Where is he?" asked the king. Ziba answered, "Behold, he is in the house of Machir the son of Ammiel, in Lo-debar." Immediately the king sent for him. Who does not see at once rise up before his eyes out of this historical incident the great Antitype? As David stood there, so stands David's Son on the heights of the spiritual Zion, and invites to come to Him all who by sin have become estranged from the house of their heavenly Father, and who mourn over their misery, and "labor and are heavy laden," longing for a return to the state of peace and honor, in fellowship with God, which they have lost, that He might bestow upon them the mercy of God. And whether they dwell at Lo-debar, or have lost them at Zeboim and Admah, they are welcome to come; for His standard is free grace. He entreats also to come to Him, with the same purpose of saving them, even those from whose eyes it is yet concealed how deeply they are already sunk, and who, at the brink of the gulf in which the "fire" burns that shall never be quenched, may yet dream of bright and happy days.

Besides His word, He sends after the wanderers messengers, like fishermen and hunters, clothed sometimes with tribulation and with the cross, and sometimes with help and blessings, that they might rescue them if possible even from the dens of robbers and of murderers, and bring them back. If it is asked, Whereby shall it be known when these His messengers come? Let them know, that if the false peace in which one has heretofore been contented begins to forsake him, and he begins to complain to his friends that something oppresses and burdens him which he is not himself able to name; if he can no longer remain in the circle where scorners sit, and in which till now he has found his element, but feels himself distressed even in the assemblies of the pious, as if there he stood before invisible judgment-seats: then let him perceive herein the first gentle footsteps of the messengers who have been sent out after him by the King of the heavenly Zion.

When sometimes here and sometimes there a word of divine truth, like an arrow from a concealed bow, strikes him, and spiritual lightning flashes over him, filling him with the apprehension that he is not on the way which can be called the way of life; and when at any time the sight of a coffin carried past makes him think as if he heard a spirit whispering to him, "O eternity, thou word of terror!" and he feels a cold shivering run through his limbs: then have the messengers of God already opened their mouths to him.

And if it now becomes to him ever clearer and clearer that he must no longer continue in his present course and if he finds, as often as he makes the trial to return to his former companionships, that the way is as if covered with thorns, and he is constrained to say to himself, The tree of life grows not to thee there on the way along which the multitude go: lo, then the moment has come when the messengers are saying to him, "Go from Lo-debar; for King David has sent for thee to come to him!" Now he begins his journey to Jerusalem, and the way of return to his old companions is barred against him, while the thorns behind him rise up strong as a palisade, and he finds himself irresistibly constrained to prosecute his course.

2. Mephibosheth at length reached the royal city. Having been brought in before David, trembling with fear, "he fell on his face, and did reverence," thus doing homage to the king, and testifying his subjection to him—a distinct picture of the first bowing down of a sinner awakened out of his death-sleep, before the Lord of all lords. Until that time he knew Him only as an object of thought from the report of others, but he is now personally and immediately acquainted with Him as the true, living Governor of the world as well as of the saints in Israel, and also as his own Ruler and Judge. His knowledge, derived from an acquaintance with the Catechism, of the Lord of all lords, remains with him only as a phantom or as a dogma, until he makes an advancement to a truly personal contemplation and experience of Him.

The first impression which an actual meeting with Him as a general rule produces, will, because of the consciousness of an entire

estrangement from Him, be one that awakens uneasiness. It will find
its expression in the words of Daniel, "How can I talk with this my
Lord? for as for me, there remaineth no strength in me, neither is
there breath left in me," rather than in that cry of the church-father,
suddenly removed from amid the commotion of the world before the
face of the heavenly King of glory: "I have loved Thee too late, O
Beloved!" But the relation in which he stands to the Lord soon
changes, and a like thing happens to him as once happened to the
prophet just named, when "One like the appearance of a man
touched" him, and thereby strengthening him said, "O man, greatly beloved, fear not: peace be unto thee; be strong, yea, be strong."

While Mephibosheth was lying prostrate and silent at his feet,
David looked down at him and said, "Mephibosheth!" Then at the
hearing of his name he ventured to speak, and replied, "Here I am,
thy servant." "The king," he begins to think, with joyful surprise,
"will act with condescension toward me." The repentance of a sinner generally takes such a course. Perhaps he stands at the first with
an oppressed soul before the Majesty on the throne of the universe.
There is as yet established no relationship between him and the
exalted One. He thinks that the heavenly Judge will overlook him,
the worm in the dust. But then it happens to him as if he heard
himself undoubtedly called by name by the Lord.

When is this? Then, if His law, as if it were above all others given
to you, follows after you, condemning you at every step, and when
you hope to escape from it in the whirlpool of worldly dissipations,
it only doubles its threatenings and curses against you; if, when you
endeavor to drive out of your mind care for the future of your life, yet
now only so much the louder it thunders through your soul the cry,
"Awake, O man, out of your sleep of death!" if you know not where
to find rest till you have confessed all your guilt to the Judge of the
living and the dead; and if you find yourself constrained to place first
in the light of His eyes that which you would most of all conceal
from Him, or even perhaps palliate before Him; yea, if, as generally
it happens to sinners, it comes to you, the individual, with the most
special and most indubitable reference, and changes the "Ye,"
addressed as if to mortal men in the mass, into the "You" from the
mouth of the Lord, thrilling with deepest emotion your soul—behold,
then you hear yourself personally addressed by the Lord from amid the
crowd, and then to you also the call is, "Mephibosheth!

Mephibosheth!" The Lord calls you by name; and while the relation
in which you have hitherto stood to Him, and in which He has stood
to you, was a relation of estrangement, between Him and you there
has begun a momentous confrontation. You stand before His bar.
What will you choose? You can no longer think of escape. Rather
there remains for you now nothing else than to fall down at His feet,
as Mephibosheth did, and to resign yourself wholly up to His grace
or His displeasure, with the humble cry, "Here am I, Your servant!"

David addressed with friendly words the man who was still prostrate before him in the dust, and said to him, "Fear not: for I will
surely show you kindness for Jonathan you father's sake, and will
restore you all the land of Saul your father; and you shall eat bread
at my table continually." What magnanimous condescension and
goodness! Who does not share in the happiness of this maimed and
sorrowful man at this unexpected fortunate change in his situation?
His soul, one would think, would now express loudly its triumphant joy at these kingly words. But no; the weight of the grace
thus experienced wholly crushed him. The history relates that he
"bowed himself, and said, What is your servant, that you should look
upon such a dead dog as I am?"

Also here many a sinner who has found grace will see as in a mirror a picture of his own experience. To such an one there is the
consciousness that the grace of God humbles even more than His
wrath. He cannot comprehend how he should be made partaker of
so great a thing. And if he has before cried till he is almost hoarse, "O
Son of David, have mercy on me!" he would now, when the mercy
which, while lying in the dust, he prayed for, has been inwardly
sealed to him by His Spirit, rather cry with Peter, "Depart from me,
for I am a sinful man, O Lord!"

How copiously now for the first time do his tears fall at the feet of
Immanuel! How deeply he now presses his face in the dust! "What
is Your servant," he now says to Him, "that You should look upon
such a dead dog as I am?" After the banner of free grace has unfolded itself over the penitent sinner, for the first time he gains
courage to speak out the whole sentence of condemnation over his
own condition, while hitherto his anguish made him hesitate fully to
express himself before the Lord. Willingly he places himself now in
the lowest room among the company of those who have with him
been made partakers of grace, and there is fulfilled that which the

Lord said by the mouth of the prophet Ezekiel, "I will establish my covenant with thee; and thou shalt know that I am the Lord; that thou mayest remember, and be confounded, and never open thy mouth any more because of thy shame, when I am pacified toward thee for all that thou hast done, saith the Lord God."[2]

3. What now further happened to Mephibosheth? Something noble and great beyond all expectation. The moment of his deepest humiliation was also to him that of his highest elevation. David, who once himself had lain before Saul as Mephibosheth now did before him, and had also called himself a "dead dog" (and who does not think here of the divine Son of David whom we also once met with in a situation in which the complaint of Psalm 22, pointing prophetically to the Lamb of God, "I am a worm and no man!" lay near His holy lips)—David called Ziba to him, and said, "I have given unto thy master's son all that pertained to Saul and to all his house" (as family possessions). Truly a kingly act!

How highly was Mephibosheth here suddenly raised up again from the dust of deepest abasement! He who had sunk down among the lowest in Israel now saw himself set among princes. But does there not mirror itself in his elevation, though it may be even in faint and dim outline, that which awaits all who fall down before the feet of the heavenly Son of David, doing Him homage? Also to them it is said, "All that appertained to Adam your father, and to his house, shall again become yours"; and what your ancestor once lost for those who were his seed, shall be received back in? What was Adam's relationship with God when compared with the relation of children, in which we can utter our "Abba, Father!" and call the Son of God our Brother? What was Adam's tree of life in paradise compared with that spiritual Tree of Life under whose shadow we trust, and with deepest satisfaction can say with the bride in the song, "His fruit was sweet to my taste?" What was Adam's safety in comparison with that which we are entitled to comfort ourselves in the assurance of—we who are "kept by the power of God unto salvation"? And what, finally, was the earthly Eden in which Adam walked when compared with that in which the tabernacles of a Sabbath of eternal rest await us? O the incomparable restoration of all that we lost by the fatal fall of our ancestor! The apostle is fully justified in representing, as he does, in

---

2. Ezekiel 16:62–63.

Romans 5, the grace by which we are made partakers in Christ as so great, that it infinitely outweighs the loss which we have sustained through Adam's transgression.

Let us hear what was further commanded to Ziba: "Thou therefore, and thy sons," says David, "and thy servants, shall till the land for him, and thou shalt bring in the fruits, that thy master's son may have food to eat; but Mephibosheth thy master's son shall eat bread always at my table." By these words Ziba was thus given back to the son of Jonathan as steward to manage his affairs.

But did not the divine Descendant of David speak in behalf of His chosen to the Holy Ghost in a manner similar to that in which David then did to Ziba (whose name, interpreted, means "planter")? Did He not, with the same careful consideration for the hereditary lameness and weakness of His disciples, entrust to the Comforter from on high the management and oversight of the field of their hearts and lives? And is it not truly He who plows and cultivates this field, scatters in the torn furrows the precious seed, and watches over it that the birds may not consume it, and cares for it, that, at the right time, dew and rain and sunshine may render fruitful the spiritual husbandry? This blessed work He carries forward partly by His direct and immediate operation in all manner of secret ways, partly and principally by the Word and sacraments. For the same end those who are already saved must work together with Him. Our fellow-pilgrims to the Jerusalem above, in their knowledge and experience point out to us the way, and dig for us wells in the wilderness, and as pastors and preachers lead us in the green pastures of the gospel.

David had yet further directions to give to Ziba. "Thou shalt," he continued, "bring in to Mephibosheth what thou sowest, that it may be his bread wherewith he may sustain himself." In the further interpretation of this historical picture, this feature indicates that the seed which God's sower, the Holy Spirit, sows in our field, and whatever noble thing He plants there, is wholly His own, the Spirit's own. Yet, by grace, it shall be reckoned to us as if it were the produce of our own labor and had sprung from our own seed, sown by ourselves. Our works, although they are His, "follow us into eternity, and go with us before the judgment-throne of God"; so that, according to the expression of Isaiah, "we eat the fruit thereof." The heavenly David has so willed it, made it possible, and brought it about. Who can fathom the riches of the mercy which God in Christ has destined for us?

After the king had finished speaking to Ziba, the latter replied: "According to all that my lord the king hath commanded his servant, so shall thy servant do. As for Mephibosheth, said the king, he shall eat at my table, as one of the king's sons. And Ziba kept his word. His whole household, consisting of fifteen sons and twenty servants, served Mephibosheth and his son, whose name was Micha. From that time Mephibosheth tarried for the most part at Jerusalem," and "did eat continually at the king's table," who was as little ashamed of his maimed guest as his great heavenly Antitype is ashamed to assign to us who are not the less lame, after He has gathered us together here below around His royal table, a place at His great marriage-feast.

At the time when David showed to Mephibosheth "the mercy of God," he may have sung for himself and Israel the song which we read as Psalm 131. Through all the kindness with which the Lord had overshadowed him, particularly in his call to the throne, and in the glorious victories which He had given into his hand, David felt himself in the same measure humbled as he was exalted, and truly prospered. Thus he sings: "My heart is not haughty, nor mine eyes lofty: neither do I exercise myself in great matters, or in things too high for me" (i.e., reaching far beyond my strength and my knowledge). David indeed knew that he himself, as well as his people Israel, were called to great things by God. Yet he will not wait for these things with impatience, nor impetuously of his own will grasp after them; but unassumingly, and confining himself to things that are lowly, he will leave it to the Lord to determine further regarding him as He may. Thus he had done, and thus he intends to continue still to act. "Surely," he continues, "I have behaved and quieted myself" (I suppress within my soul the stirrings of self-boasting and of pride), "as a child that is weaned of his mother: my soul is even as a weaned child" (like a child free from care and unassuming, wholly resigned to his mother).

"Let Israel hope in the Lord," he thus concludes this short, lovely song, "from henceforth and forever." In this song David stands before his God as once Mephibosheth stood before him, the king of Israel. O, may his psalm find an echo in every heart! "They that put their trust in the Lord shall never be forsaken but He scattereth the proud in the imagination of their hearts!"

22

David on the Pinnacle of His Greatness

The last assault of the tempter on the Son of God in the wilderness—an assault more of despair than of any hope of success—was to show Him all the kingdoms of the world, and the glory of them; and in extravagant self-boasting he said, "All these things will I give Thee, if Thou wilt fall down and worship me." Satan by this proposed to enter into an alliance with Him. The meaning of his promise, we know well, was this: he would be helpful to Him in subduing the world within a short time, by means of compliances and concessions to the habits of thought, the inclinations, the tastes and lusts of the natural man, and thus would verify His word of the one fold under the one Shepherd. Moreover, the tempter took into account the wide scope which the worldly power, the riches, and the glory of the children of men are wont to afford to him for all his arts of seduction.

How he was dismissed by the Lord with the proposal by which he only defeated himself is well known to us. He retreated for the present before the sword of the Word of God by which the wicked one is always vanquished, however subtle or however coarse be his temptation.

Today we shall see the son of Jesse raised to great power and glory; not, however, by any human means, but by the arm of his God. But here, also, over him who is raised to greatness, "the old serpent" is wont to reckon on triumphs. Can we therefore be free from solicitude regarding David, the man of God?

266

2 Samuel 8:15

> And David reigned over all Israel; and David executed judgment and justice unto all his people.

These words form the conclusion of a record of a succession of triumphs with which David's wars had hitherto been crowned. In the tenth chapter of this book of Samuel we have presented to us a register of a new series of victories. Let us on the present occasion direct our attention (1) to David's *victories*; and (2) to his *triumphal songs*.

1. In the time of David, the Holy Land was surrounded by heathen tribes who were for the most part hostile to the people of God. With justice might the king of Israel say, "They compassed me about like bees." On the southwest, the Philistines inhabited a strip of land lying along the shores of the Mediterranean. In the south, in the wildernesses of Sin and Paran, dwelt the wild Bedouin race of the Amalekites and the warlike tribe of the Edomites. To the southeast, on the farther side of the Dead Sea, we find the Moabites, the worshipers of the monstrous idol-god Baal-Peor; farther to the north we meet with the Ammonites, the devoted servants of Moloch; and in the north the Syrians, who were divided into several kingdoms.

David did not of his own accord begin any war, but on every occasion waited for the intimation from God, and only then did he take up arms when he was attacked. However, he always had to be prepared for war, and standing always on his watchtower. Himself a hero accustomed to war from his youth, he had command, with the general obligation of the people to the use of arms, over an army of almost 300,000 men fit for war. In times of peace, every twelfth part of this army, changing each month, was assembled for the purpose of engaging in military exercises. Besides, a numerous body-guard surrounded the king, to which both Cherethites and Pelethites belonged—Philistines who were partly prisoners of war, partly had come of their own accord, and partly were born in Israel. The Cherethites belonged to the tribe inhabiting the south of Philistia, and gradually had become melted into *one* tribe with the Philistines. They had originally come from the island of Crete. The name Pelethites was derived from "Pelishti" (*Heb.* for Philistine), signifying the original inhabitants of the seacoast. David appointed Joab as commander-in-chief over the whole army, while he gave him as adjutants his brother Abishai, and Ittai the Gathite.

The first campaign, after the total subjugation of the Philistines, was against the Moabites. The occasion of this war against that people, to which Ruth, the great-grandmother of David belonged, and which had at one time granted a hospitable shelter to David and his family, is not known. In any case, it was not David who was the guilty cause of this bloody war. To this time he had never violated the obligations of thankfulness under which he lay to that people. Hatred against the Israelites was deeply rooted among the Moabites, who were sunk in the lowest debasements of idol-worship.

The foundation of this enmity was laid even in the days of Moses. They had, it is true, at a later period, through the hatred which they bore to Saul, been disposed to extend greater kindness to David when he was persecuted by Saul; but when David mounted the throne, the old hatred arose again in all its fierceness. They burst over the eastern borders of the Holy Land with a formidable army, as soon as they heard of the march thither of the Syrian legions for the complete destruction of the kingdom of Israel. This invasion was, however, only the means of bringing about their own overthrow and their perpetual subjugation. Two-thirds of the people of Moab were destroyed. This was a dreadful judgment; but the measure of their iniquity was full, and "wheresoever the carcass is," says the Lord, "there will the eagles be gathered together." And not Moses alone, but also the apostle of Jesus Christ says, "Our God is a consuming fire."

The inroad of the Syrian hosts from Lebanon and from the banks of the Orontes and Euphrates, prepared for the Israelites incomparably heavier work than the invasion of the Moabites did. The occasion of that war was the following: Among the Syrian princes, Hadadezer was then the most powerful. He was king of Zoba, a region lying between the above-named rivers and the borders of Canaan. At the time of Saul, after his victory over the Hagarites, the neighboring tribe of Reuben extended its territory into that land, even as far as the Euphrates. On the armed revolt of Hadadezer, his first effort was to recover the provinces which had then been taken from him. For that purpose several Syrian nobles entered into an alliance with him. He marched against that tribe with a powerful armament. David placed against him a no less powerful veteran army. But the Syrians, when about to begin the battle with the certainty of victory, saw themselves, to their surprise, suddenly surrounded and assailed at the same time both in front and rear. Nothing remained for them but to lay down their arms and submit.

The spoil which fell into the hands of the conquerors was immense. Of prisoners they numbered about 1700 horsemen, whose horses were "houghed," and so rendered unfit for the service of war, if not for every other purpose, together with 20,000 footmen; and among the spoil were many shields of gold. David consecrated them all to the Lord, and set them apart for the purpose of adorning the tabernacle, and afterward for aiding in the erection of the temple. The Syrians after this became tributary to the king of Israel, and manifested their subjection by rich presents to him. "Thus the Lord," as the history records, "preserved David whithersoever he went." David also experienced further joy when the Syrian prince Toi, the king of Hamath, an ancient town situated on the banks of the Orontes, and existing even to the present day, sent his son Hadoram to him, to congratulate him on his victory over Hadadezer, with whom Toi maintained hostile relations, and to present to him "all manner of vessels of gold and silver and brass." These presents David dedicated in like manner unto the Lord and to His sanctuary, and then returned in triumph to Jerusalem. After a brief repose, he was however again called forth to war.

The Edomites took advantage of this opportunity, when they believed that Israel would be obstructed by the Syrian war, to wreak their anger against their old hereditary enemies; and for this purpose had already crossed in great multitudes the boundaries of Judah. But it was only to their own ruin. They were driven back to the Valley of Salt, lying to the south of the Dead Sea, toward Mount Seir, and were there overthrown in a bloody battle. The whole of Edom then became subject to David, and was occupied by Israelite garrisons. The history says that by this victory David "gat him a name," and repeats the remark, that the Lord preserved him whithersoever he went.

All these wars, however, were only the prelude to one incomparably more threatening and alarming which soon afterward broke out. It happened that Nahash, king of the Ammonites, to whom David felt that thanks were due, probably because of help which he had rendered to him in the days of his distress, was now dead, and his crown was inherited by his son Hanun. When David received tidings of this, he said, "I will show kindness unto Hanun the son of Nahash, as his father showed kindness unto me"; and he sent messengers to him, enjoining them to convey to him his expressions of sympathy at the loss of his father, and in his name to comfort him. When they arrived at the residence of the Ammonite prince, the nobles of the land, who, since that well-merited humiliation which their people had experienced in the time of Saul, had nourished in their hearts a burning spirit of revenge against Israel, said to Hanun their lord, "Thinkest thou that David doth honor thy father, that he hath sent comforters unto thee? Hath not David rather sent his servants unto thee, to search the city, and to spy it out, and to overthrow it?" Hanun lent an ear to these malicious whispers, and commanded his servants, that, to mock and disgrace the messengers, they should shave off the one-half of their beards, cut off their garments in the middle, and thus send them back to Jerusalem. The command was executed.

When David heard of this outrage he was angered, and gave charge, for the purpose of doing honor to the messengers who had been so shamefully treated, to some of the men of rank who were around him to go to them with a friendly salutation, and at the same time to say to them, "Tarry at Jericho until your beards be grown, and then return." This saying of David's has become a widespread proverb, which is often addressed to persons who presumptuously venture to intermeddle with anything for which they are not competent. Equally suitable is it to whisper these words to those spirits who are distinguished by an exaggerated estimate of themselves, who, after the bitterest humiliation which they have already experienced, have the confidence soon again, with incredible forgetfulness, to resume their old boastful tone. How many conceited reformers, or youthful politicians, or forward critics in our days, might be advised to tarry at Jericho till their beards be grown! May the advice always meet with the same compliance as that which was shown by David's messengers!

The Ammonites soon enough perceived how their presumptuous trick would be regarded by David. They therefore judged it advisable to look around them for allies. For that purpose they turned to the Syrians, who were thirsting for revenge against Israel, who dwelt at Beth-rehob, the high valley lying between the Lebanon and the Anti-Lebanon, and at Zoba, over which Hadadezer ruled, and at Maacah lying to the east. From these places a host of allies came to them, who altogether numbered more than 30,000 footmen. David

sent forth Joab with a not less considerable army to meet them. The
Ammonites took up their position close by their strongly fortified
chief town of Rabbah. The Syrians placed themselves at a little distance in battle array, and hoped thus to cause a division, and, as a
consequence, a weakening of the Israelites. They indeed so far gained
the first of these objects named, when Joab with the one half of his
army confronted them, while he directed the other half under the
command of his brother Abishai to march against the Ammonites.
"If the Syrians be too strong for me," he said to Abishai, "then thou
shalt help me; but if the children of Ammon be too strong for thee,
then I will come and help thee. Be of good courage," he added, "and
let us play the men for our people, and for the cities of our God: and
the Lord do that which seemeth Him good." We see from this order
of the day that Joab did not underestimate the danger which threatened Israel. It refreshes us to perceive the confidence in God which
again animated Israel.

Joab began the battle. The conflict was impetuous and bloody.
The Syrians were overthrown. When the Ammonites perceived this
there fell upon them "the terror of God." They fled in confusion from
before the face of Abishai back to their fortified city, and closed the
gates behind them. Joab returned amid the triumph of the people to
Jerusalem. The war was, however, not yet ended. The Syrians burned
to re-establish their warlike renown. Hadadezer strengthened his
army by a large reinforcement, consisting for the most part of cavalry,
whom he had brought from the distant Mesopotamia, and placed
under the command of Shobach, his brave and experienced captain.
When David heard of this he perceived that the fatherland was in
danger, and he called to arms the whole military strength of Israel. At
Helam, on the other side of Jordan, they encountered the Syrian
host. God was with his people. The Syrians were vanquished. Seven
thousand of them remained dead on the battlefield; and among these
was Shobach, the commander-in-chief.

The result of the war was that the Syrian kingdom concluded a
treaty of peace with Israel, and paid tribute to King David. The
Ammonite city, Rabbah, was afterward taken by storm, and a terrible court-martial was held on its garrison. The few words which refer
to it are ambiguous, and have been interpreted by some as meaning
only that the Ammonites were compelled to work as slaves for Israel.
But more probably the words are to be read as pointing out a more

severe condemnation, a putting of them to death by iron saws, and harrows, and axes, and by casting them into burning brick-kilns. According to an ancient reading, instead of "brick-kiln," is found the expression, "brazen image of Moloch," in whose glowing arms the prisoners breathed out their life, in the same manner as thousands of their own children whom that deeply degraded people had hitherto offered up in sacrifice to this cruel god.

This terrible punishment was inflicted on that most depraved and most cruel of all the heathen tribes, consequently only as a requital; and a guilt crying to heaven as with many thousand voices, was expiated—a guilt made all the greater on this account, that the Ammonites had once carried their barbarity to such an extent as to put out the eyes of the Jabeshites, a peaceful people, and had dismembered and slain their women at Gilead with savage fierceness.

The partial destruction of the Ammonites, whose iniquity also "was full," was at the same time an act of judgment inflicted by the Almighty God, who will not be mocked, as the putting of the Canaanites under the ban also was. Not David, however, but rather Joab, his stern captain, was answerable for the choice of the horrible punishment inflicted upon them. It must also never be forgotten that the history of David, which we are now contemplating, is that of one who lived in the time of the Old Covenant, the Economy of the Law, and not in the age or which it is said, "After that the kindness and love of God our Savior toward man appeared." In it other laws prevail.

Thus David had vanquished all his enemies, and that divine promise already given to Abraham, "Unto thy seed have I given this land, from the river of Egypt unto the great river, the river Euphrates," had reached its fulfillment. David stood on the pinnacle of his greatness, and could now devote his whole solicitude for the welfare of his country to the regulation of the internal affairs of his kingdom, a duty in which he did not fail. "He executed judgment and justice unto all his people." He set in order the business of his government; he appointed Jehoshaphat, the son of Ahilud, as "recorder," that is, writer of the chronicles of the kingdom, Seraiah as "scribe," and Benaiah, the son of Jehoiada, as chief over the Cherethites and the Pelethites.

He took special interest, however, in the further carrying forward of the arrangements connected with the worship of God. He

appointed the priest Zadok to the charge of the old tabernacle at
Gibeon, and Abimelech, the son of the high priest Abiathar, who
was then still living, to officiate in the sacred services at the new
tabernacle on Mount Zion. David's sons were appointed to the highest offices of state. They "stood before the king," that is, they had
direct access into his presence, and they who sought an audience of
the king must do so through them.

2. Our Psalter contains several songs which betray an undeniable
reference to the last wars and victories of David. These are songs of
victory, which have served as models for all later hymns of a like
kind, not only in Israel but in the whole of Christendom. Even to
this day every hymn of praise, every "Song of Degrees," which would
stir and elevate the heart, must extract its tone, its harmonies, its
imagery, and its very thoughts from the book of Psalms.

To these psalms belongs in the first place, the sixtieth, which bears
the inscription, "To the chief musician" (it was composed for the
congregation of Israel). "On the Lily of Testimony" (on the loveliest subject in the Law, namely, the gracious promise). "A mystery" (a
song of deep meaning). "By David. To be learnt" (namely, by the
people). "When he" (i.e., David) "conquered Aram" (the Syrians) "of
the two rivers" (Orontes and Euphrates), "together with the
Syrians of Zobah; and Joab returned, and smote Edom in the Valley
of Salt twelve thousand men." Here the time of the composition of
the psalm is distinctly indicated. David sang it after the successful termination of the first war against Hadadezer, and after his victory over
the Edomites in the Valley of Salt, before he was, however, the lord
of the whole land.

He begins by looking back on the very threatening invasion of the
Syrians, in which his army had to lament sad losses, and on all the
terrors of war which had spread over his land. "O God, Thou hast
cast us off, Thou hast scattered us, Thou hast been displeased. Thou
hast made the earth to tremble" (as by an earthquake); "Thou hast
broken it: heal the breaches thereof; for it shaketh. Thou hast showed
thy people hard things; Thou hast made us to drink the wine of
astonishment" (thy judgments). "Thou hast given a banner to them
that fear Thee, that it may be displayed because of the truth" (i.e.,
Thou didst give them deliverance, and didst raise up that before
them like an encouraging banner; for it sealed the truth of Thy
promises and Thy faithfulness toward Thy covenant people). "That

Thy beloved may be delivered, save with Thy right hand" (then the singer continues, regarding himself as identified with the people of Israel); "and hear me. God hath spoken in His holiness" (glorious promises has He given to me); "therefore" (i.e., on the ground of them) "I will rejoice; I will divide" (to Israel) "Shechem" (the land on this side of Jordan), "and mete out the valley of Succoth" (the land on the farther side of Jordan). The whole land David regards as his possession. But why does he name only these two places? He names them as denoting the two portions of the land, with a retrospective reference to the patriarch Jacob, who, after his return from Mesopotamia, settled first in Succoth, and then afterward in Shechem, and there built an altar, thus foreshadowing the possession of the land at a later period.

The congregation, which the psalmist here represents, further sings in triumph: "Gilead is mine, and Manasseh is mine; Ephraim also is the strength of mine head" (as being a particularly powerful and numerous tribe); "Judah is my lawgiver" (the tribe which ruled, with an allusion to Jacob's prophecy, "The scepter shall not depart from Judah, nor a lawgiver from between his feet"); "Moab is my washpot" (brought by me to the deepest humiliation); "over Edom will I cast out my shoe" (as one, when about to wash his feet, casts his shoe to a slave). These words breathe the most confident assurance of a perfect subjugation of the Edomites. "Philistia" (the psalmist further sings), "triumph thou because of me" (i.e., do homage to me as ruler). After this he expresses hope, trusting to the promise of God, that the war prosecuted against the Edomites would be terminated according to his wish. "Who," he says, "will bring me into the strong city?" (the city of the rock Petra). "Wilt not Thou, O God, which hadst cast us off?" (and once Thou didst so, namely, at the beginning of the Syrian war, as we were compelled on that occasion to say, "But Thou hast cast us off, and put us to shame; and goest not forth with our armies"[1]). Then follows the sigh, "Give us help from trouble; for vain is the help of man"; and then the attestation of the most joyful courage, "Through God we shall do valiantly: for He it is that shall tread down our enemies."

Psalm 108 presents a peculiar character. It is a combination of the sixtieth and the fifty-seventh blended into one, and repeats even sin-

---

1. Psalm 44:9.

gle thoughts and words contained in them both, with changes inten-
tionally interposed. The origin of this psalm is plainly to be traced to
the same period as that of the sixtieth. What led the psalmist to this
union of two psalms appears plainly from the changes made on the
sixtieth. David sang the fifty-seventh Psalm in a very sorrowful situation; when, fleeing before Saul, he regarded his life as nowhere
safe, and was full of grief also on account of others. Yet he did not
then lose his courage, but clung fast to his God and His infallible
promises.

The confidence which animated him in those days, so full of anxiety and of distress, he gives expression to in the fifty-seventh Psalm.
And now, when he is on the sunny heights of his life, he recalls to
memory those bygone times, and repeats the old psalm, naturally
with the omission of all that those days of distress then drew forth
from him. Commencing at the seventh verse of that psalm, he sings:
"My heart is fixed, O God, my heart is fixed; I will sing and give
praise. Awake up, my glory" (soul); "awake, psaltery and harp: I
myself will awake early" (with my song of praise). "I will praise Thee,
O Lord, among the people; I will sing unto Thee among the nations:
for Thy mercy is great unto the heavens, and Thy truth unto the
clouds. Be Thou exalted, O God, above the heavens: let Thy glory
be above all the earth." With these last words he now passes over
from that psalm of his youth to the sixtieth, only changing the
expression, "Philistia, triumph thou because of me," into "Over
Philistia will I triumph."

Psalm 20 is a Davidic war-song, belonging to the same days as
those above named. This psalm puts into the mouths of the people
the intercession for their king when pressed by his enemies, that the
Lord would hear him in his distress, protect and strengthen him, and,
accepting his meat-offering, would send him help out of His sanctuary. "Grant thee" (thus they address the king) "according to thine
own heart, and fulfill all thy counsel. We will rejoice in thy salvation,
and in the name of our God we will set up our banners: the Lord fulfill all thy petitions!" Confidently certain that their intercessions
would be heard, the congregation of Israel continues: "Now know I
that the Lord saveth His anointed; He will hear him from His holy
heaven with the saving strength of His right hand. Some" (the enemies) "trust in chariots, and some in horses: but we will remember
the name of the Lord our God. They are brought down and fallen:

but we are risen, and stand upright. Save, Lord: let the King" (of all kings) "hear us when we call." It is well for those princes who are accompanied in their enterprises by their people offering such prayers on their behalf; and it is well also for the people who can with the same reason boast, as when the Israelites did, "The Lord of hosts is with us, and our confidence is in Him!"

We have before us, in Psalm 68, an animated song of triumph, which has reference, with its whole contents, to the issue, so glorious for Israel, of that most fearful of all their wars, the Syro-Ammonitish. The psalmist begins it with joyful expressions of praise to Jehovah as the Protector of the righteous, and the inflexible Judge of the wicked. Then he recalls the mighty deeds by which God had made Himself glorious to Israel during their marchings in the wilderness, and the peaceful days which He had granted to His people after the conquest of Canaan till the erection of the tabernacle on Mount Zion.

After a description of the glory of God, who, as the King of all kings, sat enthroned in majesty on His holy Hill of Zion, and had again shown Himself, in the subjugation of all the enemies of His people, that he was the God of Israel, the psalmist describes the festal procession in which the holy thing, the ark of the covenant, which had accompanied the army into the field during the Ammonite war, was brought back again to Jerusalem. He names several tribes, among others those of Benjamin and Judah, Zebulon and Naphtali, which took part in this procession, as representatives of the whole nation.[2] Then he sees in spirit the veil raised from the most distant future, and all the nations of the earth bending under the scepter of the God of Israel. Then the song becomes Messianic, and closes with these words: "Ascribe ye strength unto God: His excellency is over Israel, and His strength is in the clouds. O God, Thou art terrible out of Thy holy places: the God of Israel is He that giveth strength and power unto His people. Blessed be God!"

Who that is intimately acquainted with the psalms is not forced, as he reads them, to pause and consider whether it be true that between him the reader and the birthdays of those songs almost 3,000 years intervene? Do they not all breathe the same freshness of life as if they had been composed but yesterday? It seems to us with

---

2. Psalm 68:25–27.

them as if we dwelt in our own homes and beside our own altars, and this thought rests on no delusion. How strange the songs of other nations sound to us, while in the psalms of Israel we everywhere meet with our own God, and with the whole range of our own personal feelings and experiences! Is it not clear from this that it was He who knows the hearts whose throne is in the heavens, who Himself loosed the tongue of the sacred singer that he might sing His songs for all ages, and give expression to all the diverse moods of feeling which move about in the world of hallowed human thought?

"The Psalter," says Luther, "is a little book for all saints, in which each may find, in whatever circumstances he is placed, words which accord with these circumstances, and which are to him so appropriate as if they were set in order specially for his sake alone, that he cannot himself find better words nor does he desire to find them. And it may well be affirmed that, if such words please anyone, he is certain that he is in the community of the saints, for they all sing with him one hymn, and particularly so if he can utter the same words toward God as they have done, which can only be done in faith; for unbelievers have no relish for them."

May God grant that everywhere the "taste" for these imperishable hymns may be increased, and that, in ever wider circles, that apostolic word may receive attention, and may awaken corresponding feelings: "Teach and admonish one another in psalms and hymns and spiritual songs, singing with grace in your hearts to the Lord!"

23

David's Fall

If the Old Testament history needed for its confirmation yet further support than the numerous testimonies of Christ and His apostles, this may be found in that holy simplicity and that outspokenness, free from every calculation, whose unmistakable seal is imprinted on all its narratives. In its histories we meet also with no trace of any other intention than that of faithfully presenting a record of that which has happened in its actual circumstances.

There are many things in the Bible histories which fill us with true astonishment: the fine tact, which everywhere seizes on the most perfect forms of expression; the unadorned simplicity and purity of its whole manner of representation; and the noble art of delineating, with a few traces of the pen, not only whole scenes and circumstances, but also the persons moving and acting in them, so fully and vividly before us, that we seem as if living and acting in the midst of them; and there is secured for them henceforth an enduring place in the world of our recollections as familiar forms. But that which above all other things convincingly commends to us these old historians, is the honesty which conveys to us everywhere in their annals the quieting feeling that we stand on sure historic ground, on the ground of a "sure word of prophecy"; but which, if the matter were considered as secular, might easily bring upon the sacred analysts the reproach that, as authors, they little apprehended their own advantage, inasmuch as not seldom, when they present before us human models, at the very moment when our highest interest and delight are awakened toward them, they suddenly again, as with one stroke of a hammer, dash them to pieces.

What a noble image rises up before us in the patriarch Abraham at the beginning of his journey! He stands before us as a man of God without an equal. With hopeful animation we accompany him on his farther life-course. But suddenly the overwhelming discovery surprises us that this sun also has its spots, and that even "the father of the faithful," though it was only temporarily, turned aside from the path of faith in hours of weakness more than once into eager impatience, or into open violations of exact truth.

How the patriarch Jacob comes to our view commanding our reverence! Only let a few individual incidents in his life be passed over in silence, and Jacob would stand before us as the pure ideal of most submissive resignation to the command and will of God. But even here arises the danger that suddenly a strong ingredient of most sorrowful lamentation over the imperfection of all human greatness will—not secretly, but with unveiled openness—mingle with and mar our animation.

Moses, of whom the honorable testimony is borne that he was found "faithful in all God's house," is so little on that account raised above the rank of sinners needing free grace, that rather it is announced concerning him that he was prohibited from entering the promised land on account of his disobedience to the Lord.

And now the "man according to God's own heart," David—who could be preferred to him, as presenting a pattern to the eyes of Israel and of the world of every manly and princely virtue, almost beyond the reach of imitation, if only a single event in his life had been covered with the mantle of charity, or at least been placed in a milder light? But the unsparing style of the sacred history tears away relentlessly all coverings from the unhappy event, so that one is compelled to utter a cry of surprise, and to express aloud the lamentation, "How art thou fallen from heaven, thou beautiful star of the morning!" But what do the sacred writers of God care for this? They narrate facts, and write what is truth, as they are commanded; and if any other aim influences them, it is only this, to show to the world, for a warning to all who would deify the creature, that God alone is good, and that all men are sinners.

2 Samuel 11:27

> And David sent and fetched her [the wife of Uriah] to his house, and she became his wife. But the thing that David had done displeased the Lord.

(1) What is this that came to pass? and (2) How was it possible? Let us consider the answer to these two questions.

1. We return to the royal palace. Great triumphs are there being celebrated. It is still splendid in the rich festal ornaments with which the excited population have adorned it. Proudly waves the banner of Judah from its lofty tower; and glittering pyramids of spoil, built up of armor, shields, standards, and other materials of war, proclaim the glory of the conqueror. But our first step into the interior startles us. There we find it no longer as it was yesterday or the day before. We look around in vain for bright unclouded countenances. Everything here betrays a sudden interruption of the joy. Perhaps the servants busy themselves as before in their accustomed duties but we miss in them the former festal order, in place of which a certain negligence and lawless confusion is manifest.

Something must have happened which has brought about this change in their previously respectful demeanor. Evidently they carry about with them some dark secret. They whisper to one another with signs of great inward agitation: here, melancholy and truly sorrowing; there, as if with scarcely concealed satisfaction they felt themselves free from some burdensome interdict. Outside the palace also suspicious rumors are circulated; while the people about the court maintain a reserve, and seek cautiously to avoid questions of idle curiosity. Especially those standing nearest to the throne endeavor as far as possible to put to dead silence, through feigned equanimity, the event that has occurred, though many will scarcely succeed in altogether concealing the secret satisfaction at meeting their pious lord and master, whose godliness had restrained them, now on a moral equality with themselves.

The children of the king are filled with shame and bowed down; but deepest is the shame and sorrow of the pious, faithful Abigail, who saw what was her highest glory and her pride brought to nought by one blow, and the walls of her own chamber heard her sorrow.

The king himself comes forward. No, he is no longer himself as we have hitherto known him! We miss in him the wonted freedom and firmness of step in which his conscience, free from reproach, formerly reflected itself. His friendliness, formerly so natural to him, now betrays itself as affected and restrained. His look, once so open and clear, has become unsteady. So also have become his demeanor and his language. His inborn dignity is broken. He is like a man who anx-

iously labors to hold together the threads of his honor which are parting from each other, that he might not appear altogether uncovered.
Whoever listens at the door of his bedchamber will hear coming
forth from it many half-suppressed sighs; but, alas, they are no longer
sighs to God! Ah! how has the Lord departed so far from the man,
and how has the man himself departed so far from the Lord!

What is it that has produced this most surprising change?
Something scarcely credible. The tongue hesitates to speak of it. A
most atrocious crime has been committed. A twofold heavy guilt rests
upon David's head. He, the most pious among thousands, whom we
have just seen raised above the earth, on the wings of divine inspiration, to a height which no common emotion can reach, and in
whom not only the human ancestor of the future Savior of the world,
but also His personal type, stands before us, meets us suddenly—we
tremble while we proclaim it—as an adulterer and as a murderer.

Let us lift the veil. While the royal army was besieging the yet
unconquered and strongly fortified capital of the Ammonites,
David, who for this time had preferred to remain at Jerusalem, while
his valiant captain and faithful friend Uriah was with the host, was
inflamed with adulterous passion for Uriah's wife Bathsheba, and
wickedly beguiled her to unfaithfulness. A craftily contrived
attempt to conceal this crime, by sending for Uriah from the camp,
was frustrated; and therefore he contrived a more godless plan still,
whereby Bathsheba, as a widow, might become his with the appearance of entire compliance with the law.

He sent back the unsuspicious warrior to Rabbah to Joab, the
commander-in-chief of his army, with a letter, which, under the name
of "Uriah's Letter," has become notorious throughout the world. It
was written with the same pen with which the sweet psalmist had
written his psalms. The contents of this well-sealed, treacherous letter was as follows: "Set ye Uriah in the forefront of the hottest battle,
and retire ye from him, that he may be smitten, and die." Scarcely
did Joab venture to trust his eyes when he read this order; but how
could he not but suspect that something strange had happened at
Jerusalem? Besides, the prospect of being freed, in the person of
Uriah, of a dangerous rival in the ranks of the army might be welcome to the ambitious man.

Willingly he undertook, without conscience as he was, the
secret commission of his royal master, whose "too pious ways" had

been to him long since a scandal, against whom also he bore a grudge, because he had once not only compelled him to put on the accustomed signs of mourning for Abner, who had fallen by Joab's own hand, and to accompany him to the grave, but had also done him the disgrace of calling down the righteous vengeance of God before all the people upon him, the murderer of Abner.

On the occasion of a new sally of the enemy from their strong-hold, Joab placed Uriah, in consequence of the command that was given him, in the foremost ranks of his host, against which the first assault of the furious Ammonites broke, and the base plot was suc-cessfully carried out. Uriah, the noble warrior, was left dead on the field, and many of his brave companions in arms fell by his side.

Joab had thus far to lament a sensible defeat; but to the messen-ger whom he sent to Jerusalem, with tidings regarding the bloody outcome of the battle, he gave the cunningly devised instruction, that he should first in general announce to the king the mournful result of the battle, and show to him how his brave army had pressed forward triumphantly, "even unto the entering of the gate"; but that here it happened, like as once it did in the days of the judges, before the fortified town of Thebez, to Abimelech the captain, upon whose head a woman cast down from the wall a piece of a millstone; so also the enemy, pressed back into the fortress, after they had barred the gates behind them, had thrown pieces of rock down from the top of the walls upon these the heroes of Israel, and had thereby crushed to death many of the brave men. If the messenger should think that he saw the king's wrath arising, he was then to say, in addition, that Uriah was among the slain.

The herald hastened away, and began, as soon as he arrived at the royal palace, punctually to fulfill his commission. But when he thought that he perceived, in the eagerness and excitement with which the king listened to him, only the prognostics of an approaching storm of anger and indignation, he hastened on, in his alarm, with the report, and said, "And thy servant Uriah the Hittite is dead also." But how it surprised him when David now answered him with an incomprehensible mildness, "Thus shalt thou say unto Joab, Let not this thing displease thee; for the sword devoureth one as well as another: make thy battle more strong against the city, and overthrow it; and encourage thou him!"

Unhappy David, how deep you have fallen! And the first sinful act how constantly it propagates others! Murder comes after the adultery, and after the murder a sad web of dissimulation, hypocrisy, and lies. And no mention of the living God! Only an appeal to a blind fate, which, according to some, sometimes takes away this one, sometimes that one. O how that word of the Lord here again verifies itself: "He who commits sin is the servant of sin"; and that word of Peter: "Of whom a man is overcome, of the same is he brought in bondage!"

When Bathsheba received news of the death of her husband, "she mourned," the history informs us, "for her husband"; and without doubt her sorrow was deeper and more genuine than was that of David, although he did not neglect to appoint for his own house, as well as for the army, mourning for the fallen hero. Scarcely were the accustomed days of mourning over, when he sent and fetched the deceived woman to his house, "and she became his wife," under the appearance of perfect rectitude. O David! Pride and ornament of Israel, what a course you are following!

Well he knew that which the history records, that "the thing that David had done displeased the Lord." But with all his might he strove against the consciousness of guilt which was awakening within him. He persuaded himself that the death of Uriah had at least covered his disgrace from the eye of the world; but he did not consider that Joab, in whom he had never possessed a true and genuine friend, and many others besides him, had it in their hands at any moment, as it had even already happened, to unveil the dark secret. In spite of all that has happened, David wishes yet to stand where he has stood before. O the deceitfulness of sin! It happens to the king according to the expression of the apostle: "Their conscience also bearing witness, and their thoughts the meanwhile accusing or else excusing one another."[1] Shame and frowardness strive together within him for the mastery; and according as the one or the other gains the victory, the man is saved or eternally lost. A fearful danger this in which he is placed! That which alone can save him from the awful shipwreck which he has suffered, is self-condemnation, repentance.

2. But how can it be explained that a man of God, such as David, could forget himself so far as to stumble into such a depth of sin? This

---

1. Romans 2:15.

circumstance may serve as a certain mitigation of the sentence pronounced against him on account of his fall, that he lived under the economy of the law, in which there was not at the command of the pious a treasury rich in the means of protection and defense against the assaults of the devil, the world, and the flesh, such as afterward was provided those who are baptized with the Spirit of Christ. By this Spirit, in a sense and a measure of which they who lived in those times could scarcely form any conception, the children of the New Testament are made partakers of the divine nature.

This also may be said in favor of David, that however high in every respect he stood above his time, yet he breathed the air of his own century, and inherited the opinions then prevailing regarding polygamy—a sad and God-displeasing family portion. But there ever stood both the word of Moses, "God made one man and one woman," and the command of God, "Thou shalt not commit adultery," written by the finger of God, before the eyes of the Israelites, so clearly and unambiguously, that a violation of it under any circumstances merited the curse and condemnation.

David had without all contradiction, forfeited life, according to the divine order of the kingdom. He was guilty of death, even though, to the disgraceful betrayal of friendship, and the web of lies and dissimulation, there had not been added, aggravating and filling up the measure of his iniquity, the terrible murder, and the many other sins which that one deed, made fruitful of hell, brought forth from its prolific heart.

David's fall appears, indeed, at first view to be an inexplicable mystery. An approach, however, is made to our comprehending it, when in thought we place ourselves in the situation in which David was at that time. He had reached, as we know, the summit of his fame and his glory as a ruler. Abundantly crowned with laurels, he looked back from the high elevation to which he had ascended upon his past life, in which he had gained victory after victory, and which made him appear as a favorite of God, raised to high eminence before thousands. All that he had taken in hand had prospered, often beyond his expectation. His enemies lay subdued at his feet. Kings of vanquished nations paid tribute to him as his vassals. His kingdom, grown to a mighty power, stretched itself, as had been shown in a prophetic vision to the patriarch Abraham, from the river of Egypt to the Euphrates, and from the Mediterranean Sea to the country on the east of Jordan. A glory surrounded him, which sent forth its rays even into the remotest regions, and filled the people far and near with amazement.

David was renowned not only as the most distinguished hero, but also as the greatest saint of his times. Never yet had any reproach as to his morality been uttered, and everyone regarded it as an honor to be able to come near to him to do him homage, and to be favored with his friendly look. He saw himself, indeed, at the goal of the boldest wishes which can be cherished by a human heart; and whatever of comfort or of pleasure the earth had to bestow was poured in unlimited fullness at his feet.

The thought now presents itself to our minds, that one overloaded to such an abundant measure with blessings would surely overflow with gratitude to his heavenly Benefactor, and that his whole thoughts and endeavors would be directed to the preserving and administering and employing, in a manner pleasing to God, the gifts that had been bestowed upon him. But a superabundance of earthly prosperity and worldly honor is at all times a dangerous dowry. Wherever men celebrate their triumphs, it will never fail that the "enemy," "who goes about like a roaring lion, seeking whom he may devour," will mix himself up among the guests.

How frequently does it happen that the prosperous, before they can perceive it, are seized by a mental giddiness, so that they are no longer masters of their steps! They deal with that which they have obtained in the most inconsiderate manner, as if it were an inalienable possession. How frequently, also, in a sudden fit of passion, do they take steps which lead them on unobserved from the summit of their glory down to headlong ruin! They act as if some mysterious voice whispered to them, "Thou art come to so lofty a station, and seest thy renown so much established in the world, that without danger thou canst permit to thyself many things which are certainly prohibited to others. Thou art not to be touched. Whatever thou undertakest, to thee it will only be interpreted for the best. The mantle of honor in which thou shinest covers in thee all that would in others be reckoned a fault. That high consideration which thou enjoyest serves thee as a shield against every suspicion. Especially thou hast, in thy rank, thine own measure, and mayest permit to thyself many a thing which is denied to those whom thou seest beneath thee."

Whose voice is this but that of the old serpent, of whom it is written that he was "more subtle than all the beasts of the field," yea, of the father of lies? He finds favorable ground there, where everything goes according to our wish, and where there is prosperity and success in worldly things, for the unfolding of his destructive delusions! How often is it experienced that even noble natures cannot bear elevation to one of the lowest steps of that height on which we see David standing, without being seized with the demoniacal giddiness we have spoken of. Some princely favor and respect with which they see themselves honored, deprives them suddenly of their self-command and composure; and before one thinks of it, they enter on the ways of frivolity and self-forgetfulness, which only a short time before they were heard condemning with the most decisive earnestness. And if such things happen, as, alas! is often the case, even to men whose office it is to defend religion and the Church, this is so much the more to be lamented, because that thereby the moral character of the whole order to which they belong is suspected, and, besides that, the name of God is exposed to blasphemy.

Notwithstanding all we have above remarked, the enigma remains scarcely to be explained, how a man so spiritually advanced, and coming forth so brilliantly from the severest trials, such as David, could have become intoxicated by the enchantment of worldly glory to the neglecting of a divine prohibition the most unambiguous, and uttered in the most positive manner. If the infernal fascinations of Satan ever gained a splendid victory, then they did so in the overthrow of that leader of the chorus of the saints of his time. More expressively than every other example, that of David gives emphasis to the apostolic warning: "Let him that thinketh he standeth, take heed lest he fall." O that the king on this occasion also, instead of remaining inactive at Jerusalem, had gone out with his army to the field against the Ammonites, and had exchanged the temptation of idleness for the hard toils of war! Or that, instead of that self-pleasing look from the roof of his house, by which he was led to sink himself, he had once more been composedly reflecting on the way in which the Lord had hitherto led him, and then had tried to measure the relation in which his dignity stood to those blessings which had been poured down upon him from above!

It has been supposed that a sign of estrangement from the divine life is to be seen in David, in that he took too much to heart the insult offered to him by the Ammonites in the persons of his ambassadors, and undertook the campaign against the offenders solely to expiate his wounded honor as a king. But this is an unwarrantable opinion. What put the weapons against the Ammonites into his hands was rather his zeal for the glory of God, which he believed to have been touched in the disgrace experienced by his messengers, associates of the covenant people. The cruelty he committed on the finally conquered enemy, and his placing the crown of the vanquished Ammonite king on his own head, instead of consecrating it to the Lord, and his not praising God for the victory, have been referred to also as proofs of a spiritual falling away having already begun in David. But the storming of Rabbah took place after David's fall, and not before it, and in that case it cannot be concluded from the silence of the history that David did not give the honor to the Lord. No. The temptation came suddenly upon him like an armed man. In a moment, when he beheld himself in his magnificence, Satan, that "liar and murderer from the beginning," surprised him, and brought him to ruin.

O let no one, however far advanced in holiness he may think himself to be, imagine himself set free from taking to heart that watchman's cry of Christ, "Watch and pray," and that of the apostle, "Be sober and watch." Protection and safety are only found in cleaving by a steadfast faith to God and to the grace of God. But particularly, when anyone blessed with worldly goods thinks himself strong enough to continue with firm step in the straight way, let him take heed to what may come upon him. May God only not let the snare which awaits him be too strong, nor the pit to which he is hastening be too deep! How many have glided down the slippery path of uninterrupted worldly prosperity to an abyss out of which they never again arose, and learned to estimate that saying of Eliphaz to Job, "Happy is the man whom God correcteth, therefore despise not thou the chastening of the Lord!"

What appears to us yet more incomprehensible than David's fall, is the stubbornness with which for months he, the fallen one, fought against confessing in the sight of God the heavy guilt which lay upon him. Deceiving both God and himself, he would be neither an adulterer nor a murderer; for if he had acknowledged that, then he would be such an one (he could not conceal it from himself), that a destiny would certainly await him like that which had fallen upon Saul and his house. The crown might then no longer rest on the head of one worthy of being stoned. If he had acknowledged himself guilty of the crimes with which he was chargeable, he would have seen himself under the absolute necessity of saying to God, whose name he had caused to be blasphemed, "Judge me, O Lord, and save Thine honor while Thou destroyest me!" From this he shrank back with horror; and so much the more, since he would have been under the necessity of attesting the sincerity of his self-condemnation first, and before all things, by the dismissal of Bathsheba. Therefore with vehement haste he hunted after excuses, and, as he imagined, not unsuccessfully.

He had, indeed, not searched for the sin; but his offense appeared more as a sad fate than as a willfully committed transgression. He had not, indeed, put Uriah to death with his own hand, but he had exposed him only, like every other soldier, to the accidents of war. Besides, the event screened him in respect of the former sin; for the customs of the greater part of Eastern kings numbered such vile actions as that which brought guilt upon David among the privileges of princes; and their royal position was regarded as securing to them freedom for many things which would have been considered as culpable if committed by those in the lower ranks of society. Nevertheless, his conscience raised a decided protest against all these palliations of his fall. Inexorably it named it by its right name. Yet, by sweeping together all the possible armor of lies and self-deceit, he made one attempt after another to come to terms with the judge within his breast. Then came to him sorrowful days and nights, full of anxiety and terror.

What he suffered during this time of lying and concealment, he afterward himself gave expression to in few but striking words, which are preserved to us in Psalm 32. Let us hear him. "When I kept silence," says he, "my bones waxed old through my roaring all the day long. For day and night Thy hand was heavy upon me: my moisture is turned into the drought of summer." O how intelligible this is! In spite of all the false grounds of justification which, like fig-leaves, he had laboriously sewed together as a covering for his nakedness, the consciousness of guilt within him, which separated him from his God, still maintained its authority. How could he feel otherwise toward the thrice Holy One than as his angry Judge? How was it possible for him to look up to Him, even with any degree of childlike confidence?

The lively and fervent expressions with which he naturally commences that psalm, composed after his reconciliation with God, throws a still clearer light than the words just quoted on the misery he then endured: "Blessed is he whose transgression is forgiven, whose sin is covered. Blessed is the man unto whom the Lord imputeth not iniquity, and in whose spirit there is no guile." Not the less clearly do we perceive the distress of mind which he at that time felt, in the earnest call, resting on his own most sorrowful experience, which he addresses to all sinners: "Be ye not as the horse, or as the mule, which have no understanding; whose mouth must be held in with bit and bridle, lest they come near unto thee"; and then the sentence: "Many sorrows shall be to the wicked," connected with the instructing and at the same time encouraging addition: "But he that trusteth in the Lord, mercy shall compass him about."

We mourn over the sudden fall of the man who was the crown and clear-shining pole-star of his people, and to whom, with greater justice, and in a yet more sorrowful sense, may be given back the words which he himself once pronounced on the death of Abner, who fell pierced by the swords of Joab and Abishai, "Know ye not that there is a prince and a great man fallen this day in Israel?" We lament the dark eclipse of that ideal of royalty, shining in such incomparable brightness, which the world looked up to in David before his fall. But we do not overlook it, also, that by men who, like David, are once rooted in God, the words of Israel recorded by the prophet Micah may fittingly be uttered: "Rejoice not against me, O mine enemy: when I fall I shall arise." He has, indeed, again arisen, the man of God and what his portrait has lost in ideal splendor, it has gained in comforting significance.

Of David's fall it may be said, in a certain measure, also that "it has become the riches of the world." If his fall was to conduce only to his own deep humiliation, then therein the Lord found occasion for the unfolding, in the most glorious manner, of His grace and His unchangeable faithfulness. But David was not the "man after God's own heart" he had been before. Much rather he now truly, for the first time, became so; and how many of his most heart-stirring psalms would never have been heard in the Church if he had walked on continually to the end along the lofty path of cloudless holiness, unmoved and without wavering! Living ideals of virtue would have been of less use to us than portraits of poor sinners on whom mercy had been bestowed.

24

David's Repentance

We are accustomed to associate with the word "repentance," so frequently occurring in our translation of the Bible, exclusively the idea of mourning over past sins. Because of this many are misled into a hasty and unwarrantable assumption that they have obtained the forgiveness promised to penitents; others, on the contrary, because they do not shed tears over their demerits, are led unnecessarily to despond of divine mercy. To the former it may seem as a warning—to the latter, on the contrary, as an encouragement—to know that our word "repentance," as it is commonly understood, does not fully represent the meaning of the word in the original. The fundamental meaning represents, according to the import of the Greek, less a matter of feeling than an act of the moral will. It would be accurately translated by the expression, "A change of mind." Among other texts, these words of the apostle make this unambiguously clear, "For godly sorrow worketh repentance to salvation not to be repented of: but the sorrow of the world worketh death."[1]

Here Paul certainly speaks of sorrow on account of sin as an indispensable condition to salvation. He represents the sorrow which he means as "godly," in opposition to a "sorrow of the world," which latter has its foundation only in a selfish concern for the consequences of sin, instead of love to God. But he represents the sorrow of which he speaks not by the same word which Luther translated "repentance" ("Busse"). Literally, the passage stands thus: "The godly sorrow worketh

---

1. 2 Corinthians 7:10.

for salvation." Even further "Repentance not to be repented of." Thus Luther interprets the verse.

But the godly sorrow is itself the repentance; how then can it work that which it already is? According to the original text, the sorrow toward God rather works "a change of mind which no one repents of," while sorrow toward the world results in death. John the Baptist begins his work, preparing the way for Christ, with the cry, "Repent" (i.e., "change your mind"). It is obvious that this change of mind cannot but be accompanied by grief and humiliation before God on account of the guilt-laden condition in which men find themselves. In so far the common idea attached to the word "repent" is always vindicated. Yet it abridges the full meaning of the original expression, according to which a stronger emphasis is laid on the resolute rupture with sin than on the sorrow on account of it.

The degree of strength which the latter must reach is nowhere expressed in Scripture. Whether that feeling of guilt pours itself forth in tears, or shows itself in the silent bending down of the broken heart before God, it is all the same, provided it is strong enough to drive us irresistibly into the arms of the Lord Jesus as our only Mediator and help in time of need. Today we shall have occasion to contemplate the turning-point of salvation, which is designated by the word "repentance," in its most genuine manifestation.

2 Samuel 12:13

> And David said unto Nathan, I have sinned against the Lord. And Nathan said unto David, The Lord also hath put away thy sin; thou shalt not die.

A much more joyful spectacle presents itself this time to our view than that which, with burdened hearts, we last contemplated. We again breathe freely. The ban which lay upon David is removed. Let us thoughtfully consider this event, so blessed and full of significance. Let us see (1) who was the preacher of repentance whom the Lord sent; and (2) what was the effect of his sermon.

1. Since our last visit to the royal palace at Jerusalem, the agitation and confusion have only increased. That further act which the king had added to his first wickedness, thereby aggravating it, had become notorious. The commander-in-chief Joab found no personal interest in keeping that unhappy "Uriah's Letter" a secret. It must

already have become widely known who it was that was guilty of the death of the noble hero who had fallen in battle. Not the less extensively, also, was the report spread abroad of all that had passed between David and the messenger who had been sent to him from the camp, as well of the king's hypocritical language to the messenger.

What wonder that, under the influence of such news among the servants at the court, the bands of respectful reserve were completely dissolved? Their high lord must thank them even if they did not proclaim from the housetop that which was spoken in the ear. The king himself, however, appeared to be calm. He imagined that his disgrace was concealed at least from the eyes of his people. But in this delusion he was like a man who, while his house over his head is in flames, mistakes the glare of the fire which lights up his chamber for the morning rays of a peaceful day. The image of his heaven-crying sins became fainter and fainter, retiring into the background from before his conscience; and so he would have fallen gradually into a condition of the most dangerous security, had he not, as often as he ventured to draw near unto God the Lord again in his former manner, found the way to the throne barred against him. If he had recourse to prayer, he felt himself refused and driven back.

Heaven had shut itself against David, and his harp stood silent and covered with dust in a corner. We tremble for him. Yet over him He kept watch, whom Moses heard proclaimed from heaven as a God who is "merciful and gracious, long-suffering, and abundant in goodness and truth." He never forsakes those who once in sincerity have given to Him their heart and hand. "He knows," as David himself has sung, "our frame, and remembers that we are dust." If those who are His have gone astray to the very brink of hell, yet He goes after them to rescue them from the snares of Satan. Let us watch the steps of this God in David's life. The eternally faithful God has already, as Job says, "numbered the steps of His erring servant, and watched over his sins."

For a long time we have heard nothing of Nathan, the friend and counselor of the king. This need not surprise us. The sad events that had happened were not kept a secret from him. What Nathan's soul experienced on account of them we may conjecture. Yet he hesitated, without a summons from his royal master, and without divine direction, to approach the palace. He gave vent, in the stillness of his own chamber, to his burdened heart in earnest intercession for the fallen one. Suddenly there came to him, in the way of an immediate revelation, a commission from God. In obedience he went to the palace, was announced to the king, and admission was granted to him.

But what were his feelings at the appearance of his exalted lord? He must do violence to himself in endeavoring to conceal the humbling impression which was produced on his mind by the entire change that had passed over the king. After the accustomed respectful salutation, he opened his mouth, and, with hardly restrained equanimity, laid before him, as the supreme judge in the land, a case for his decision. "There were two men," he said, "in one city; the one rich, and the other poor. The rich man had exceeding many flocks and herds: but the poor man had nothing, save one little ewe-lamb, which he had bought and nourished up: and it grew up together with him, and with his children; it did eat of his own meat, and drank of his own cup, and lay in his bosom, and was unto him as a daughter. And there came a traveler unto the rich man, and he spared to take of his own flock, and of his own herd, to dress for the wayfaring man that was come unto him; but took the poor man's lamb, and dressed it for the man that was come to him."

Thus spoke Nathan. It was a parable. Its simplicity, as well as the gentle, forbearing manner of the prophet, might appear strange to us. Scarcely does he distantly refer to the weight of the double sin of which the king was guilty. But let us hear him further. He discharges his commission with a delicate tact, and thinks, what Solomon afterward said, that "surely in vain the net is spread in the sight of any bird."

First, he only aims, unnoticed by David, to uncover the source of his great sin in his contemptuous unthankfulness toward God, who had continually loaded him with blessings, as well as the insatiableness of his desire after miserable earthly vanities; and then he would give him occasion, in the verdict which he would pronounce against an offense incomparably smaller than his own, unconsciously to pronounce against himself a tenfold stronger condemnation. The object was gained. David went "with simplicity" into the snare that was laid for him. Scarcely had he listened to Nathan's report, when, perhaps to bribe his own conscience by this stern pronouncing of judgment, he broke out with flaming anger in these words, "As the Lord liveth, the man that hath done this thing shall surely die." Thus the rich man must die according to his sentence, after that he had restored fourfold the lamb that was taken away by the most culpable abuse of his authority and power.

What do we say to the blindness in which King David now stands before us? But is it not a circumstance of everyday occurrence, that a sinner should see his own image in the lost son of the well-known parable, or in the priest who without compassion "passed by on the other side," avoiding the man who had fallen among thieves; or in the heartless, selfish man who said, "Soul, thou hast much goods laid up for many years; take thine ease, eat, drink, and be merry"; or in any other worthless person, without imagining that while he utters his sentence of condemnation against these miserable persons, he only pronounces sentence of death upon himself, and makes true the apostolic sentence, "Wherein thou judgest another, thou condemnest thyself"?

How frequently does one hear the avaricious violently declaim against the abomination of Mammon-worship, the backbiter against the ruling passion for slander, and even dissolute persons against the prevalence of sins against the seventh commandment, as if they stood pure as angels before evil-doers whom they so boldly summon before their tribunal. That is the "deceitfulness of sin." The phantom of holiness in which men vaunt is exchanged for the reality. Yes, men regard themselves as virtuous because they perceive and unsparingly pronounce sentence against the lack of virtue in others. And if the awakening conscience raises its protest against anyone's venturing to absolve himself of that of which it accuses him, then he persuades himself that the moral indignation with which he burns against the iniquities of others makes amends and atones for all the sins with which he must charge himself.

None of the similitudes of our Lord is more frequently verified in daily experience than that of the blinded man who does not see the beam that is in his own eye, while he manifests a scornful displeasure at the mote he sees in his neighbor's eye. The Pharisaic spirit, which never wearies to increase the burden lying on others, which they themselves "will not move with one of their little fingers," has, unfortunately, not died out from the midst of Christendom! The severe masters who sit in Moses' seat are truly not the persons who give occasion to a favorable opinion on the part of others of their own state. Whoever arrives at a thorough knowledge of himself will always have forbearance and mildness toward his companions, and will on all occasions be much more inclined to leave the final decision with Him whose "eyes are as a flame of fire," than to pronounce sentence by his own presumptuous authority with the important mien of a judge over his fallen brother.

The king has spoken. According to his sentence, the transgressor who took away his only ewe-lamb from the poor man must atone for his crime with his life. If the king reckoned his moral indignation as a virtue in some respect atoning for his own sin, he forgot that, as the Scripture says, "The law is not of faith" (i.e., it was not given that men should call it good, and be zealous for it), but "that it should be obeyed."

Nathan believed that the moment had now come in which he should remove from the eyes of his royal master without reserve the blinding spell of the father of lies. With solemn earnestness he looks at him and says, with all becoming respect, but not the less firmly and fearlessly, "Thou art the man!" If ever a word from human lips fell with crushing weight, and with the illuminating power of a gleam of lightning, it was this. The judgment just pronounced pealed like a trumpet-note into the inmost soul of the king, making him tremble. A prophet had spoken it, and the mouth of the seer is that of Jehovah. Stripped of all his veils, David sees himself in a moment haled before the judgment-seat of Him who "will bring to light the hidden things of darkness, and will make manifest the counsels of the heart." And it is David himself who is the accursed criminal, yet in an incomparably higher degree of guilt than the man whom he has just pronounced worthy of death.

The ban which has so long lain upon his soul is broken, and it happens to him according to the words of Isaiah: "The sinners in Zion are afraid fearfulness hath surprised the hypocrite." Nathan had difficulty in restraining the feelings of regret which moved him, on account of the bold words he had spoken, when he saw the countenance of the king grow pale with amazement. But it became him, the servant of Jehovah, to do violence to himself, whatever it might cost him, and to speak out to the very last iota the commission that had been given to him. He therefore continues to say, "Thus saith the Lord God of Israel, I anointed thee king over Israel, and I delivered thee out of the hand of Saul; and I gave thee thy master's house, and thy master's wives into thy bosom, and gave thee the house of Israel and of Judah; and if that had been too little, I would moreover have given unto thee such and such things. Wherefore hast thou despised the commandment of the Lord, to do evil in His sight? Thou hast killed Uriah the Hittite with the sword, and hast taken his wife to be thy wife, and hast slain him with the sword of the children of Ammon" (against whom he so faithfully helped you). "Now therefore the sword shall never depart from thine house; because thou hast despised me, and hast taken the wife of Uriah the Hittite to be thy wife. Thus saith the Lord, Behold, I will raise up evil against thee out of thine own house, and I will take thy wives before thine eyes, and give them unto thy neighbor. For thou didst it secretly: but I will do this thing before all Israel, and before the sun."

Thus Nathan spoke to the king. In the last words he pointed prophetically to the terrible things which he would experience at the hands of one of his own sons, and on his account. Nathan's announcement of the punishment in a remarkable way reminds us of the Mosaic sentence, "An eye for an eye, a tooth for a tooth," as well as of that word of the apostle, "He that soweth to the flesh shall of the flesh reap corruption." How rich is history, and not sacred history alone, in examples which confirm that word of the Book of Wisdom, "Wherewith any one sins, therewith also shall he be plagued!" Yet this is not to be considered as an irrevocable sentence. Let us rejoice that God the Lord in Christ knows the way for Him to substitute, without any injury to His holiness and truth, a free pardon in the place of merited judgment!

2. The king is overwhelmed. The earth trembles beneath his feet. He experiences a prelude of the great day of judgment. The veil is raised, and all that was hidden in darkness is brought out to light. He sees in spirit the bloody shade of Uriah accusing him before the throne of the Judge of the world; sees that impious letter, which the wicked one prompted him to write, unsealed, spread out before the Almighty, and feels as if forced with Job to cry out, "Thine eyes are upon me, O God, and I am not" (i.e., I can live no longer); he would have given way to despair, had he not discovered, amid all the dreadful things which Nathan had said to him in discharging his commission from God, yet one thing which sustained him. It was this—the remembrance of the grace with which the Lord has previously accompanied him. That compassionate question was, "Wherefore hast thou despised the commandment of the Lord, to do evil in His sight?"

That overwhelming sentence, "Thou art the man!" struck him with all the force of a flash of lightning; this "wherefore" pierced through his soul, inflaming, dissolving, melting it. It seemed to him as if, instead of anger, compassion and love were uttered in it; and therefore it came to pass that his heart, instead of being benumbed, was only softened in deepest humiliation and shame, and encouraged him to an open confession. The fire of repentance, which had been long kindling within him, but which he violently suppressed, now broke forth into a clear flame; and with inexpressible emotion agitating his contrite spirit, which was now set free from the phantom by which it had so long been bound, and from the cunningly contrived deadly falsehoods by which he had endeavored to weaken the complaints of his conscience, he broke out aloud in the frank confession, "I have sinned against the Lord."

Scarcely has he uttered this confession, with which he casts himself without reserve on the grace and the wrath of the righteousness of God, against whom he had done evil, when there is returned to him, like a blissful echo, from the mouth of the seer, the absolving word, "The Lord also hath put away thy sin; thou shalt not die."

How is it with the king when he hears this message? Does he hear aright? Such a sudden change from the terror of judgment to the joy of pardon! He is like one who dreamed. At the very moment when he believed that he was delivered up to the awful kingdom of the lost, the fearful abyss at his feet closes; and instead of the lightning which he expected to break forth for his destruction, there shines around him the morning light of a new heavenly day of peace.

O the blessedness of repentance toward God, when it completes itself in a decided breach with sin. It is the golden bridge, though also wet with tears, which leads into the arms of everlasting mercy, into the paradise of reconciliation with God. The cry, when it is sincere and bathed in godly sorrow, "I have sinned," how it releases the burdened heart! That perpetually enduring fruit and consequence of such a genuine humbling of the heart before the Lord, the pardon of sins, is the most worthy to be desired of all the possessions of life.

Nathan's comforting words were followed, it is true, by a sentence of wrath. Because the king, by his wicked deeds, had given occasion to the enemies of Jehovah in Israel—and of such persons there were many since the days of Saul's misrule—to blaspheme, God's glory did not permit that he should wholly escape well-merited punishment. In the name of the Lord he announced to him chastisements by which he would have been utterly destroyed, had not the announcement of them been preceded by that word of grace from the lips of Nathan.

Yet that message of grace was not sufficient to bring perfect peace to the sinner. He thirsted after a yet more unambiguous assurance of his reconciliation with God. After he had honestly thanked the prophet for the courage and faithfulness with which, as a bright example to all who minister in holy things to the great ones of the earth, he had discharged his sacred office toward him, he dismissed him, and went to the retirement and solemn stillness of the holy tabernacle. What passed in the inner exercises of his soul as he stood there before the ark of the covenant, that symbol of Jehovah's presence, and how he poured out his heart before the Lord, he has recorded in Psalm 51, which he has left behind as an evidence of his genuine conversion, and as an example to the Church of God of penitential prayer. Let us examine this precious legacy, and may the Lord create in our souls a clear and continuous echo of its contents!

"O God," he begins. He had not yet found full confidence to say, "My God." Yet he knows God his Father; and if he trembles, still he is far from despair. He prays, "O God, have mercy upon me, according to Thy loving-kindness: according unto the multitude of Thy tender mercies blot out my transgressions." The suppliant urges his petition first of all by an appeal to the earnestness of his repentance: "I acknowledge my transgressions: and my sin is ever before me. Against Thee, Thee only, have I sinned, and done this evil in Thy sight: that Thou mightest be justified when Thou speakest, and be clear when Thou judgest."

Laying claim to God's mercy, he supports his petition further by referring to the universality of human corruption: certainly not, however, as if thereby the guilt of individuals was lessened: "Behold, I was shapen in iniquity; and in sin did my mother conceive me. Behold," he continues, "Thou desirest truth in the inward parts" (i.e., true rectitude of the innermost disposition and aim). But whence is this obtained? The suppliant says, "In the hidden part Thou shalt make me to know wisdom" (i.e., in the depth of my soul). But how shall this be done? By pardon of sin and the communication of the Holy Spirit.

With a fundamental comprehension of the types and symbols appertaining to the holy tabernacle and the Levitical ordinances of divine worship, as adumbrating the atoning work of the future great Mediator and High Priest, the psalmist prays, "Purge me with hyssop" (i.e., do in reality to me what is typically done by the priest for those who are, according to the Levitical law, impure, when he sprinkles on them, by means of a branch of hyssop, water in which has been mixed the ashes of a red heifer)—"purge me with hyssop, and I shall be clean; wash me, and I shall be whiter than snow. Make me to hear joy and gladness; that the bones which Thou hast broken may rejoice. Hide Thy face from my sins, and blot out all mine iniquities. Create in me a clean heart, O God; and renew a right spirit within me. Cast me not away from Thy presence; and take not Thy Holy Spirit from me. Then will I teach transgressors Thy ways" (this he does in Psalm 32); "and sinners shall be converted unto Thee. Deliver me from blood-guiltiness, O God, Thou God of my salvation; and my tongue shall sing aloud of Thy righteousness" (i.e., praise the faithfulness with which You verify Your words of promise spoken to penitents). "O Lord" (by Thy gracious sentence), "open Thou my lips; and my mouth shall show forth Thy praise. For Thou desirest not sacrifice, else would I give it; Thou delightest not in burnt-offering. The sacrifices of God are a broken spirit: a broken and a contrite heart, O God, Thou wilt not despise."

Finally, the psalmist promises to the Lord, if He would extend to him mercy rather than justice, the thanks of the whole congregation, on whom the stroke of the sword would also descend, which was drawn against their king. "Do good" (he says) "in Thy good pleasure unto Zion: build Thou the walls of Jerusalem" (instead of overthrowing them). "Then shalt Thou be pleased with the sacrifices of righteousness, with burnt-offering, and whole burnt-offering" (such as shall be offered to Thee in a right spirit): "then shall they offer bullocks" (i.e., sacrifices which are at the same time spiritual) "upon Thine altar."

Thus David, from an inexpressibly deeply moved heart, poured out his supplication. That this penitential prayer, enlightened and full of earnestness, pierced through the clouds and found an audience with God, the king has himself testified in Psalm 32: "I said" (he thus bears record), "I will confess my transgressions unto the Lord; and Thou forgavest the iniquity of my sin." Thus the gracious announcement made by Nathan is sealed to him by God in the holy tabernacle in an immediate manner, and now for the first time, with, fullness of joy, he is able to sing Psalm 103: "Bless the Lord, O my soul; and all that is within me, bless His holy name. Bless the Lord, O my soul, and forget not all His benefits: who forgiveth all thine iniquities; who healeth all thy diseases; who redeemeth thy life from destruction; who crowneth thee with loving-kindness and tender mercies"—and so on, in the words of that incomparable song of praise and thanks.

How blessed the king is now! With what overflowing joy he exclaims, "Blessed is he whose transgression is forgiven, whose sin is covered! Blessed is the man unto whom the Lord imputeth not iniquity, and in whose spirit there is no guile!" Free and unburdened he now again stands before God. Well does he know that he is not holy before Him. To him also may be applied that old tradition regarding the Apostle Peter, that so long as he remained on earth tears were always seen trembling on his cheeks. Humbly David confesses, with the Apostle James, "For in many things do we offend all." He continues to pray, "Cleanse Thou me from secret faults."

But of one thing he is henceforth fully and clearly conscious, namely this, that there is in him a true, holy earnestness of purpose to will only that which his God wills. Thus he comforts himself with the patience and long-suffering of the merciful Lord, who afterward said to His own, by the mouth of one of His prophets, "Hearken unto me, O house of Jacob, and all the remnant of the house of Israel, which are borne by me from the belly, which are carried from the womb: and even to your old age I am He; and even to hoar hairs will I carry you: I have made, and I will bear; even I will carry, and will deliver you."

David is now again wholly "the man according to God's own heart" which he formerly was. He is now so more than ever he was before, after he has come forth freed from all the dross of selfishness and self-love, and seven times purified as gold from the furnace of thorough self-condemnation. But he stands there as a lofty candlestick, from which, with inexpressibly cheering splendor, the free grace of God sends forth its rays, like a holy flame, wide over the world—the grace which brings comfort to all who, like the king of Israel, "are poor and of a contrite spirit, and tremble at God's word."

What do we, I pray, the children of the New Testament, want of the encouragements of the Old Covenant? Do we not, more thoroughly than the saints under the economy of the law, know God, "who will abundantly pardon"? Indeed, to the very end of life, that saying of the Apostle John holds true: "If we say that we have no sin, we deceive ourselves, and the truth is not in us." Yet, following close after it, there sounds to us not less clearly from the mouth of the same witness the testimony transporting us to the very heavens: "If we confess our sins, He is faithful and just to forgive us our sins, and to cleanse us from all unrighteousness."

25

The Beginning of the Chastisement

I will be jealous for my holy name."[1] Thus the Lord spoke by Ezekiel. It sounds like a human utterance, and yet it is in a high degree worthy of God, and is fitted to bring us to our knees before Him in the dust. It might well, indeed, be a matter of indifference to the All-sufficient whether His exalted name were honored or blasphemed on earth—to Him who, according to the apostle's expression, "is not worshiped with men's hands, as though He needed anything, seeing He giveth to all life, and breath, and all things." Were He to shut the gates and windows of His holy dwelling over the earth, and leave us to go on in our way unnoticed, who would dispute with Him on that account, and maintain that His glory suffered thereby any diminution?

But in how much clearer splendor does His glory beam forth to us, when He, "jealous" for the glory of His name, extorts from us the testimony, as if something important to Him depended on our acknowledgment, "There is none like unto Thee, O Lord; Thou art great, and Thy name is great in might!" For to the glory which belongs to Him as the infinite Ruler over all, there is joined the greater glory of His love, by virtue of which His heart prompts Him to require that the world should bow to Him, doing homage to Him for its salvation. This love proves itself not only in His benefactions and blessings, but also in almost all His chastisements In this adorable character we shall today see Him, in His conduct toward the royal transgressor, "jealous for His holy name."

---

1. Ezekiel 39:25.

2 Samuel 12:14

> Howbeit, because by this deed thou hast given great occasion to the
> enemies of the Lord to blaspheme, the child also that is born unto thee
> shall surely die.

These are the words which immediately follow the announcement
of grace to David. The threatening, "I will raise up evil against thee
out of thine own house," was not removed by the message which
came after it, "The Lord hath put away thy sin." In a high degree
David had made the enemies of the Lord to blaspheme. It was his *fear
of God* which had once opened to him the way to the throne of
Israel. He was required to reestablish the theocracy which had been
so deeply shaken under Saul, and to restrain by his personal example the forgetfulness of God which was prevailing in Israel. The
bringing in of a new time of implicit submission to the holy and inviolable ordinances of Jehovah, was the duty imposed upon him; and
it is not to be denied that he had already, in the happiest manner,
begun to fulfill it.

And now, all at once, so mournful a *fall*! As a matter of course, it
would be said in the circles of apostates and scorners, "These are the
pious, and this is the divine guidance, strength, and preservation of
which they are wont to boast!" And what scorn would the heathen
around pour upon the kingdom of Israel and their God! If a kingdom
of God on earth, therefore, is to be perpetuated, the Almighty must
stop the mouths of blasphemers, and glorify Himself by an impressive
action, as a God who never slumbers nor sleeps, and before whose
eyes sins in every rank, even though found among His own chosen
ones, *must* ever remain guilt and sin, and, as *such*, accursed and liable
to punishment. And it was so. We shall today hear the sound of
God's avenging rod, (1) in *the death of the king's child*, and then (2) in
the permitting of a twofold evil in David's house.

1. According to the law, David had without contradiction forfeited his life. But if the merited sentence of condemnation had been
carried out on him, the people would have been more severely punished than himself. For who would have succeeded him on the
throne that could have prevented the land from becoming immediately again the scene of the wildest civil war, and of renewed
incursions and devastations on the part of the neighboring nations,
who were even now with difficulty restrained? The work of regen-

erating the political and ecclesiastical state of Israel, successfully
begun by the help of God, would not only have been arrested, but
would have fallen to pieces, when near its consummation; and,
besides, it would have deprived the Lord of the opportunity of record-
ing for all the world, in the life of David, the warning, "Be not
deceived, God is not mocked," much more legibly than it could have
been done by his removal from the earth. On these grounds the Lord
forgave to the king the punishment of death, but only, for the same
reasons, to surround him by yet more sensible chastisements.

First, David saw himself touched on one of his most vulnerable
sides. His little son, the child of Bathsheba, was suddenly seized by
a fatal illness. This was an indubitable proof to blasphemers among
the people that the Almighty honored His commandments, and
would let no violation of them pass by unpunished. But how does it
comport with the justice of God, that the innocent child must atone
for the sin of the father? This question certainly borders on human
curiosity. But God the Lord will never be at a loss in such cases for
the answer. No injury on this account was done to the child, that it
must for the time serve as a candlestick for the shining and burning
light of the holy severity of God as a righteous Judge. Indeed, it cuts
deeply into the soul of the father and mother to see their children in
infancy writhe under the sufferings of life. But the Lord is certain to
proceed more gently toward the suffering little one than it may seem
to those for whose chastisement that domestic cross is specially sent.
And if the Lord takes the sick child to Himself, who will complain
that it can be said of him, "His soul was well-pleasing to God, therefore He hastened him away from this sinful life?"

When David saw his darling child lying pale and moaning, what
wonder that his heart was pierced with deepest sorrow! He would
perhaps have exchanged his proud palace for the hut of a poor laborer if he could thereby have purchased the life of his son. But where
will he go in his necessity? That is not to him for a moment a matter
of doubt. The way into the presence of his God is again opened to
him. He betakes himself to his chamber for prayer, and will neither
eat nor drink. He lies with his face upon the earth, and wrestles the
whole night through in supplication before the Lord for the life of his
beloved child.

But no "amen" comes in response to his earliest petitions. He can
no longer conceal it from himself that his child must now be taken

from him. Inexpressibly humbled and ashamed, he confesses himself
the sorrowful cause of this chastisement that has fallen upon him, but
without servile fear and trembling. After the pardon had been granted to him, the punishments with all their bitterness had lost for him
their deadly sting. It is the chastening, fatherly hand of the Most High
which now wounds him and though He cause him to experience that
which is most sorrowful, he will no more wander from his God.

The elders of his house were solicitous regarding the health of
their lord, on account of his grief and sorrow. They approached him
with the request that he would take some food, lest he should do
himself harm. But in vain. As long as his child breathes, in spite of
the words of Nathan, "The child shall surely die," he will not refrain
from urging his supplications before the Lord. The seventh day
(whether from the birth of the child or from the beginning of his
sickness is uncertain) at length dawns. Suddenly there is a solemn
stillness in the palace. With soft steps the servants move through the
halls. Their downcast looks betray what has happened. Yet they cannot take courage to announce it to the king. They said to
themselves, the history remarks, "Behold, while the child was yet
alive, we spake unto him, and he would not hearken unto our voice;
how will he then vex himself, if we tell him that the child is dead?"
Thus they thought and were silent.

At length the king began to apprehend what this solemn stillness
about him signified. "Is the child dead?" he asked. With sadness they
answered, "He is dead," and added not a word further. What are we
now to expect? We anticipate that the sorely tried father will pour
out his heart in loud lamentations, and perhaps, falling into error as
to the power of prayer, will make shipwreck of his faith, and begin to
doubt the foundation of his consciousness that God had taken him
again into favor. Such sorrowful scenes too frequently meet us, under
like circumstances, ever in the "dwellings of the righteous." But in
the house of David a scene of a different kind presents itself, which
greatly surprises us, and holds before us a mirror in which we shall
scarcely be able without shame to look at ourselves, having fellowship
in the privileges of the New Covenant, who are called also, even
under the heaviest cross, to "walk worthy of the gospel." No sooner
did the king receive the sorrowful intelligence than he arose from the
earth, washed and anointed himself; and after he had changed his
apparel, as if he had been going to a joyful festival, hastened back to

the holy tabernacle to adore the decision of God, as in every form, and under all circumstances, holy and worthy to be praised.

The sacred tent had not for a long time been the scene of a holier act of worship than this. Here the sacrifice was offered to the Lord which alone is to Him well pleasing. What the king here laid down at His feet was his own wisdom: "The foolishness of God is wiser than men"; his own righteousness: "Enter not into judgment with Thy servant; for in Thy sight shall no man living be justified"; his own will: "Not as I will, but as Thou wilt"; yea, his body and his life. "If the glory of Thy name require it, O my God, destroy and spare not; only let not Thy grace turn away from me." Wholly devoted to God, he desires only this one thing, that the Lord would glorify Himself and defend the honor of His name. It sufficed for him that his sin was forgiven. This consciousness is his crown as well as the armor in which he now felt himself able successfully to meet all that might happen to him.

In an elevated frame of mind he now returns from the sanctuary to the palace. When he had came in, he commanded that bread should be set before him, and he begain to eat. His attendants were astonished, and said to him, "What thing is this that thou hast done? thou didst fast and weep for the child while it was alive; but when the child was dead, thou didst rise and eat bread." Hear now what the king says to them in reply: "While the child was yet alive, I fasted and wept: for I said, Who can tell whether God will be gracious to me, that the child may live?" Thus not only from paternal tenderness toward the beloved child, but also, and more especially, from longing after a new seal of divine favor, he had so earnestly prayed for his preservation. He continues: "But now when he is dead, wherefore should I fast? Can I bring him back again? I shall go to him, but he shall not return to me.

In these last words David obviously gives expression to the hope of again meeting with his beloved son in that future world to which he had gone. It may be inquired, Where did he think that place of meeting would be? Was it in the grave? Impossible! How in that case could he express what he had in his mind as a hope? Was it in Hades, or the kingdom of the dead? He could scarcely have thought with so joyful an elevation of mind of his son as there.

It is true we know that to the saints under the Old Covenant the land beyond the grave was veiled in deep darkness, and was more to them the object of dim anticipation than of a clear penetrating faith.

But we are persuaded that to them also moments of special illumi-
nation were not rare, in which they saw opened before them clear
prospects into the future world. Such a moment of clear spiritual
vision was now given to David when he uttered these words of hope.
The world of the blessed, of the "just made perfect," rose up before
him, though only in dim outline, and he felt himself richly comforted
at the death of his beloved child.

With the consolation with which he himself was cheered, he also
comforted "Bathsheba his wife." She too, who without doubt
shared not only the repentance and humiliation of her husband over
the sin of the past, but also his sorrow at the loss of the child, needed in a high degree the assurance that God had forgiven, and was
again gracious. And this assurance was granted to her. The mercy of
God extended so far that He even condescended to purify and hal-
low a bond which had been formed in sin, and to give to them, now
united together in His fear and in walking before His countenance,
at a later period, after the return of the king from the final subjugation of the Ammonites, a second son, in the place of the one He had
taken away. To this son David gave the beautifully significant name
of "Solomon," that is, Kingdom of Peace, as a memorial of the peace
again restored between him and the Lord, whose commandments he
had so grossly trodden under foot.

The removal by death also of that first child from the earth must
have served to prevent many future, difficult, and complicated ques-
tionings as to the right of succession to the throne, and therefore
perfectly set at rest the anxiety of the parents, since no doubt could
arise as to the legitimacy of little Solomon. What now remains for us,
but in the dust to adore the exceeding riches of the grace of God, as
He made it manifest in this providence, and to praise the amazing
influence of the blood of the Lamb, which, already dispensing its efficacy, was able so perfectly to wash away sins!

2. Before the history proceeds to record the further trials which
came upon David, it mentions the final termination of the bloody
war against the Ammonites, the last of the enemies of Israel who had
not been completely subdued. Joab was still engaged in besieging
Rabbah, the strongly fortified chief town of the Ammonites. After
he had taken the "water city," a strong outwork from which the place
was usually supplied with water to drink, he sent messengers to David
to inform him of the fact, and to say that the fortress itself could not

now long hold out against the army, and therefore that the king might come at the head of a reinforcement, so that he, the commander-in-chief, and not Joab, his captain, might have the glory of the conquest ascribed to Him. David obeyed the apparently noble-minded proposal of Joab, and made his appearance accordingly. The town was taken by storm; and, among the rich spoil which fell to the conquerors, there was the royal crown of the Ammonite prince, all set round about with precious stones, which was valued at more than 85 pounds weight of gold.

Not without horror we read of the revenge which was practiced against the now completely vanquished enemy. With iron saws and harrows, and with brazen statues, they put to death all those at least who were found with arms in their hands; they threw some of them, even alive, into the glowing furnace of brick-kilns. According to another reading of the text, the conqueror dealt with them according to a terrible law of retaliation, as the heathen, in their idolatrous fanaticism, had numberless times dealt with their own children, when they laid them as offerings in the red-hot arms of the brazen images of their gods Moloch and Milcom. We shudder at such heathenish cruelty; and it astonishes us to see Israel, "the people of God," taking vengeance in such a manner on their enemies who had fallen into their hands.

It is true that there was not a more depraved, and at the same time a more arrogant, nation among all that were around them, than the Ammonites were. None, moreover, manifested such malicious and obstinate enmity against the people of God as they did, although they were in some degree related to the seed of Abraham, inasmuch as they were descendants of the younger daughter of Lot. During the journeyings of the Israelites through the wilderness, they were among the number of those who encouraged and bribed Balaam to curse the chosen people. At a later time, they perpetrated unspeakable horrors in Gilead, to which the prophet Amos refers, and laid waste the land on the east of Jordan.[2]

The Israelites needed to be constantly on their guard against their plundering armed invasions. In their obduracy they were now fully ripe for the judgments of God, and Israel was chosen by God as the instrument of their infliction. But certainly the Lord did not

---

2. Amos 1:13.

appoint the kind of judgment which was to fall upon them, and as little can it be believed that David had any share in it. It may be true
that he gave, in Jehovah's name, the command that they were not to
be spared; but the inhuman cruelties that were perpetrated were
doubtless suggested by Joab, the stern captain, who believed that he
must follow the same Eastern practices of war as the barbarians themselves adopted.

Let us now hear the further strokes of the rod of chastisement with
which David was smitten. It is not difficult to bear the adversities
which one experiences without, if one can only look back to his home
as to a beloved peaceful dwelling in which are found harmony and
love, yea, as to a "tabernacle of God with the children of men." A
"house-cross" is the heaviest of all earthly crosses. The gall which is
mingled in our cup by those who are nearest to us surpasses all other
in bitterness. David must, through God's appointment, and through
His righteous permisson, abundantly experience this.

The trial of this character which first came upon him was the
accursed conduct of Amnon, David's first-born son by Ahinoam, toward
Tamar, the sister of Absalom and step-sister of the criminal himself.
David was overpowered with distress when the tidings of this was
brought to him. The infamy which thereby rests upon his house he is
no longer able to bear. Yet his depressing consciousness of his own guilt,
pardoned though not forgotten, will not allow him to punish his guilty
son according as he deserves. The crime of his son awakened him only
to a new self-condemnation. How could he meet the degenerate
Amnon, without feeling his own cheeks burning with shame?

The cloudless domestic happiness which once cheered the circle
of his home, where was it now? What mitigated in some degree
David's grief at the sin of Amnon and Tamar was the genuine penitence which he found in the latter. Tamar immediately laid aside,
and indeed forever, her royal ornaments, retired into a lonely and private sphere, and devoted herself only to pious exercises, consecrating
to them her whole life.

While David failed to punish Amnon with the punishment due to
him for his crime against Tamar, her brother Absalom undertook the
work of revenge. For two whole years, according to the spiteful character of Oriental natures, he brooded over his dark purpose before he
carried it out. At length the fitting moment seemed to him to have
arrived. Absalom invited to a feast of sheep-shearing his royal father,

and all his brothers and sisters, to his estate Baal-hazor, lying not far
from the town of Ephraim. The king declined the invitation both for
himself and for his son Amnon. Absalom pressed his father, however,
that at least he would permit his brother Amnon to accept of it, lest
it should grieve him to be separate from the rest of his brothers. The
king replied, "Why should Amnon go with thee? Let him remain
beside me." But as Absalom did not cease to press his case, the father
at length overcame his dark forebodings, and granted the request.

After all those who had been invited, with the exception of the
king, had arrived at Baal-hazor, Absalom took certain of his servants
aside, and commanded them, saying, "Mark ye now when Amnon's
heart is merry with wine, and when I say unto you, Smite Amnon;
then kill him, and fear not: have I not commanded you? Be courageous, and be valiant." The command was punctually obeyed. Before
it was observed by anyone, Amnon lay on the ground weltering in his
blood, struck down by the murderous hand of the servants. Who can
describe the consternation that overpowered all who were there present? The king's children hastily arose, "and every man gat him upon
his mule and fled." But an exaggerated report of the awful occurrence
went before them. To David it was told that all the king's sons were
slain; and forthwith the palace at Jerusalem echoed with loud cries
of mourning. David tore his garments, and, moaning with sorrow, lay
with his face in the earth.

Then Jonadab his brother's son came up to him, who was himself
concerned in the crime of that murder, inasmuch as he had once
assisted Amnon in carrying out his shameful wickedness. With
feigned sympathy he conveyed to the deeply moved father the intelligence which preserved him at least from perfect despair, that
Amnon only was slain, and no other member of the royal family
besides. "By the appointment of Absalom," said he, "this has been
determined from the day of that sorrowful transgression. Now therefore let not my lord the king take the thing to his heart, to think that
all the king's sons are dead." Yet that one calamity that had fallen
upon his house seemed to the king to be ground enough for his expe-
riencing the deepest sorrow.

Suddenly the cry of the watchman from the watchtower sounded
forth: "The king's children approach!" And it was indeed they who
appeared. But when at their entrance into the palace they saw the
head of their father bowed down with sorrow, they lifted up their

voices and wept aloud; "and the king and all his servants wept very sore." And why should not the tears of David flow? Alas, to adultery and incest there was now added blood-guiltiness, so that the dreadful trio of accursed crimes in the heart of his family was now full! The king's house, which formerly shone so gloriously, is now wholly covered with disgrace and shame and the king was loudly charged by his own conscience with the guilt of bringing, by his own unhappy conduct, all these evils that followed.

Among the psalms we find none which contains special reference to these terrible domestic events. Nevertheless there are notes sounding out from many of them, which without doubt derive their character from the circumstances in which the singer was at that time placed. To this class belongs that sigh breathed forth in Psalm 6: "O Lord, rebuke me not in Thine anger, neither chasten me in Thy hot displeasure. Have mercy upon me, O Lord; for I am weak: O Lord, heal me; for my bones are vexed. My soul is also sore vexed: but Thou, O Lord, how long? Return, O Lord, deliver my soul: O save me for Thy mercies' sake. I am weary with my groaning; all the night make I my bed to swim; I water my couch with my tears."

Such is also the character of these words of Psalm 38: "I am ready to halt, and my sorrow is continually before me. For I will declare mine iniquity; I will be sorry for my sin." The king would at that time have perished in his afflictions, had he not maintained a firm faith in the free, boundless grace of his God. O that he might now cling closely and with yet firmer hold to that support, for he will feel yet heavier strokes of God's avenging rod, as we shall immediately see— to his own humiliation and to the glorifying of God, and presenting to us and to all the world a warning that "he that soweth to the flesh shall of the flesh reap corruption."

26

The Rebellion

The sacred history unfolds to us, along with numerous examples of true and enduring piety, also dark pictures of sin, in connection with which are illustrated the gracious purposes of God. Among the ten commandments there is not one which we do not there see transgressed in a more open or more subtle manner. But what meets us within the narrow boundaries of a single people, the Jews, is only a specimen of the moral portraiture of the whole of the human race. The history of the world, through which runs an unbroken, continuous chain of sins, is the fearful "handwriting" which "witnesseth against us." In so far it is certainly the "judgment of the world," as it describes and condemns the world as lying in "wickedness.

The continuance of the world in being would lead us to err as to the being of a holy and righteous Governor of the world, if we did not know of the God-man who has become security, with the honor of His name, for the regeneration and the renovation of the world, and its deliverance from sin. Christ became the Rock against which broke the waves of a new flood which threatened the earth; and His cross the place over which the clouds, charged with the lightning of God's wrath for our destruction, were divided. It is true that sometimes, judging from appearances, one is led to conclude that a sentence pronounced against man, such as that just referred to, is too hard, or altogether unjust. Sometimes our race appears like a volcano, which, because it has continued for a long time silent, and has clothed itself all around with flowers, presents the appearance of a peaceful mountain, where one may find a hospitable dwelling. But before one is aware of it, the deceitful fire, which meanwhile, as if

311

imprisoned, had rolled through the bowels of the apparently peaceful mountain, breaks forth, roaring and thundering from its depths, so as to fill all around it with amazement and terror. In the course of our meditations today, we come to the outburst of a moral volcano which has subsequently had many parallels, and in which, on this occasion, we shall see verified also that proverb of Solomon: "The beginning of strife is as when one maketh a breach in a dam for the waters" (of sin to flow forth).[1]

2 Samuel 15:10

> But Absalom sent spies throughout all the tribes of Israel, saying, As soon as ye hear the sound of the trumpet, then ye shall say, Absalom reigneth in Hebron.

We present these few words from the further unfolding of the history, because they show us the starting-point of all the horrors of which we shall further be witnesses. (1) Israel's situation; (2) the traitorous conspiracy, and (3) David's conduct. These are the three particulars which shall occupy our attention at this time.

1. The relation which a great part of the people sustained to their king, meanwhile, no longer corresponded to that unclouded relation in which David stood to his God and Lord after he had become again the object of His grace. The mournful fall by which, according to the letter of the law, David had made himself guilty of death, had, as we know, greatly injured his reputation. In the eyes of many of his subjects, he continued to be the adulterer and the murderer, worthy of the condemnation of both God and man. His pious actions, his attention to the public ordinances of worship—perhaps even his psalms—had for the time lost their credit and their sacredness. Not everyone was capable of estimating properly the repentance of the fallen man, and his humiliation before the Almighty.

That open confession of guilt which he bore about with him rather provoked those who were estranged from God to mockery and scorn, than raised again their reverence for him. He appeared to them as a weakling; for the blinded world, indeed, knows nothing of the courage which lies at the foundation of and accompanies true humility, and nothing at all of the greatness of a man who again comes

---

1. Proverbs 17:14.

forth from the crucible of a genuine and thorough self-condemnation before God, adorned with the crown of the gracious pardon of God. A stain such as that which adhered to David was only, in their judgment, to be atoned for with the blood of the guilty. Of any other washing and purification, especially of that effected by the blood of the Lamb of God, and by means of the fire-baptism of the Holy Spirit, they had no conception. The holiness of communion with God was to them a deeply hidden mystery.

The forbearance which the king showed toward the depraved children of his house was by no means fitted to strengthen the estimation of the people for him. They thought that he should without mercy drown his daughter Tamar, and that Ammon his first-born should also be destroyed from among the people. And how did David act toward Absalom, the murderer of his brother? It is true that the report of his bloody act kindled within him a violent and holy indignation. He even commanded that for some time the criminal, who had fled to Talmai, the king of Geshur, his grandfather by his mother's side, should be pursued; but, after a lapse of three years, during which he had been searched for in vain, he became again reconciled to him through the mediation of Joab.

"And the soul of David," the history records, "longed to go forth unto Absalom: for he was comforted concerning Ammon seeing he was dead." Joab, encouraged by this, in order to protect himself from the punishment of the murder he had himself committed, by the pardon and reconciliation of Absalom, the avenger of his much-wronged sister, and to secure for himself his own position in the event of Absalom's ever succeeding to the throne, had artfully contrived the matter in the following manner.

At Tekoah, a town lying at the distance of five hours from Jerusalem, in the neighborhood of which once lived Amos the herdsman, when he was called to be a prophet, lived a "wise woman," fit for any intrigue, with whom Joab was acquainted, and through whose cunning he hoped to reach his object. The plan devised was that, having put on mourning apparel, the woman should go to the king and say to him, "I am indeed a widow woman, and mine husband is dead. And thy handmaid had two sons, and they two strove together in the field, and there was none to part them, but the one smote the other, and slew him. And, behold, the whole family" (armed for revenge) "is risen against thine handmaid, and they said, Deliver him that smote his brother, that we may kill him, for the life of his brother whom he slew and so they shall quench any coal which is left, and shall not leave to my husband either name or remainder upon the earth." This was Joab's plot: and the woman did as she was directed.

She went accordingly to the king, and with the cry, "Help, O king!" fell on her face to the ground, and did obeisance, addressing to the king the words which Joab had put into her mouth. And when she believed that she saw that her words had touched and moved the king's heart, and had even received the king's gracious promise, "As the Lord liveth, there shall not one hair of thy son fall to the earth," she carried forward her plot with dexterity, and sought with tact and adroitness to turn the compassion she had awakened within the king toward his own son Absalom. She gently pointed out to the king that he would be guilty of sin against God, and against the people of God, if he should so far deny his paternal heart as not to call back again from his banishment his obdurate child. God the Lord, she said, does not act so unmercifully toward His fallen children, thereby gently referring to David's own experience; then flatteringly she adds: "The word of my lord the king shall now be comfortable: for as an angel of God, so is my lord the king, to discern good and bad: therefore the Lord thy God will be with thee."

David perceived, from the words of the woman, a strangeness about them, leading him to suspect that they had been suggested to her, and he replied, "Is not the hand of Joab with thee in all this?" The woman answered with a delicate, courtly indirectness, "My lord is wise, according to the wisdom of an angel of God, to know all things that are in the earth"; and then she openly confessed that in the whole matter and form of her humble petition she certainly was assisted by the counsel of his chief captain Joab. But David, caught in the decision already expressed to the woman in the case of her son, believed that he dare not refuse to grant also the request urged, as earnestly as it was respectfully, in behalf of Absalom. He commanded that Joab should be brought to him, and he said to him, "Behold, now, I have done this" (i.e., promised to this suppliant woman shelter and protection for her son): "go, therefore bring the young man Absalom again." Then Joab fell to the ground on his face, and bowed himself, and thanked the king, and said, "Today thy servant knoweth that I have found grace in thy sight, my lord, O king, in that the king hath fulfilled the request of his servant."

Thus the plan he had formed was successful; it is true it was at the cost of justice, with which the pardon which David extended to Absalom did not least harmonize. David did not distinguish with requisite precision between the two cases submitted to his judgment. Absalom's murder of his brother could only be atoned for, according to the law of God, with the blood of the murderer, because it was an act committed, not in the heat of strife, but with all deliberation; while to the son of the widow the sanctuary as yet stood open as a refuge to him from the avenger of blood. Yet the heart of the father prevented the right exercise of the functions of a judge in the case of the former, and this might excuse in some degree the sentence quite too hastily uttered.

But by a great part of the people David's conduct could not be excused. Rather, the severer their condemnation of it, so much the less did they show themselves capable of respecting the deep reason actuating the royal judge humbly conscious of his own guilt. There was seen by them in David's forbearance only a new proof of his weakness and of his paternal partiality, and, along with all the favor entertained for Absalom, at least by a certain class of the people, his being pardoned contributed also to weaken yet more the feelings of veneration with which they regarded David's government. Thus the bold and resolute revolutionist found the ground in Israel already prepared for his plan of overturning the throne.

2. After three years' banishment, Absalom returned, in company with Joab, from Geshur to Jerusalem. The king yet hesitated, however, to see his face. That satisfaction might yet in some measure be done to justice, all entrance into the palace was for two years longer, for his humiliation, denied to the murderer of his brother. This, however, only served the more thoroughly to embitter the heart of the hardened Absalom against his own father. At last Joab succeeded in bringing about a reconciliation, though it was only on one side that the feelings of reconciliation existed. David granted permission to his apparently penitent, humbled son to come into his presence, pardoned him fully, and sealed the new covenant of affection with a kiss. But he did not kiss the ill-will out of the heart of his son. Absalom's heart remained embittered with hatred against his father, and he planned revenge.

Absalom was a man beautiful in his person. He was esteemed the most handsome man in Israel. But the idea that in a fair body there must necessarily live a beautiful soul was falsified in his case. He seems to have valued very greatly the carefully cherished ornament of unusually long and luxuriant hair. With his vanity there was associated a burning ambition, and he had long flattered himself with the hope of at some time ascending the throne of Israel. But that he should attain to this, in the way of peacefully succeeding to it as his father's heir, was now, after all that had happened, greatly doubted by him. It only remained for him to force open some other path to the glittering prize which hovered before his eyes; and what wonder is it that, in the many troubles that had come upon his royal father, from the disaffected state of the people's minds toward him, he thought the favorable moment had come?

It could not be difficult for him who charmed the people by his engaging exterior to gain a following, at least among a certain class of the people—the frivolous, and those who were forgetful of God. He already arrogated to himself princely authority, while he surrounded himself not only with splendid horses and carriages, but also with a troop of fifty life-guardsmen. To the people on whose support his hopes must be built he condescended most graciously, accommodating himself to them in all things, even in their supposed religious enlightenment, and in their neglect of the traditional ordinances and manners; and he presented before them a golden age, which he said would come when his father's crown would descend to him by inheritance.

When they who sought an audience with the king came to Jerusalem, it was he who received them, early in the morning, outside before the gates, and inquired in a most friendly manner regarding their homes and their petitions. If they answered thus: "Thy servant is of one of the tribes of Israel, and this and that is the matter which concerns him"; then he answered, with feigned sympathy and pity, "See, thy matters are good and right; but there is no man deputed of the king to hear thee. O that I were made judge in the land, that every man which hath any suit or cause might come unto me, and I would do him justice!" It happened now that if one addressed in so courteous and comforting a manner felt himself constrained, with thankful emotion, to render him royal homage, he put forth his hand and took him in his arms, and, declining the homage, kissed the man, whoever he might be. What wonder that by such acts he stole away not a few hearts in Israel! Is it not to this hour the chosen way of those who, in whatever form, cherish Absalom's desire, to flatter the multitude, and to delude them by pretenses and by phantom images of a golden future?

When Absalom, now in the fourth year after his reconciliation with his father, believed that there was a numerous faction which he might regard as securely attached to him, he appeared one day before the king with the request that he would grant him permission to go to Hebron, his birth-place, and the place which was hallowed by the graves of the patriarchs, that he might there perform a vow unto the Lord; "for thy servant vowed a vow," said he, "while I abode at Geshur in Syria, saying, If the Lord shall bring me again indeed to Jerusalem, then I will serve the Lord." Without suspicion the king granted to the dissembler the desired permission, and sent him away affectionately, saying, "Go in peace." And Absalom went away, after he had secretly sent spies throughout all the tribes of Israel to sound the people, and say to those who might show themselves favorable to his plan, "As soon as ye hear the sound of the trumpet, then ye shall say, Absalom reigneth in Hebron."

Among those who were associated with the king's son in his traitorous project, and as one of the most prominent, was Ahithophel, of the town of Giloh, Bathsheba's grandfather and David's counselor, a man famous among all the people on account of his knowledge and wisdom, but who had for a long time secretly longed for the opportunity to avenge on the king the lost honors of his family. Because of his remarkable intelligence, Ahithophel was held in such esteem among the people, that his "word was regarded by them as almost like a decree of God; and this contributed even more extensively to the torch of insurrection. The history informs us that "the conspiracy was strong; for the people increased continually with Absalom." That which happens at every insurrection, happened also here—only the ringleaders knew what was aimed at, while the great mass, who had nothing to lose, but hoped only to gain, were drawn almost blindfold into the whirlpool. Partly the ennui which came upon the people after those glorious days of victory and of triumphs, rich with spoil, were over; partly the discontent on account of the pressure of taxation, the many limitations of freedom, and other burdens by which a rightly constituted monarchical government is conditioned—these things were all conducive to the rebellion.

At all events, that mutinous plot opens up to us an altogether sad view of the condition into which, after a brief religious awakening, a considerable portion of the chosen people had again fallen back. It was almost forgotten by the people that David was their king "by the grace of God." Not the less had they forgotten the rich fullness of incomparable blessings which the Lord had heaped upon them through him. In general, that commandment, so unambiguous, which inculcated, along with obedience to father and mother, at the same time a like obedience to the divinely appointed authorities, appeared to have altogether vanished from before their eyes. Their revolt against David comprehended in it a like resistance to Jehovah Himself. And that they permitted themselves to be encouraged, by the example and call of the king's degenerate son, to raise their standard, instead of being thereby only inflamed to a yet deeper abhorrence of the traitorous undertaking, only showed more manifestly the infamous character of their crime.

3. Soon enough the king was made aware of what was in progress, and how in Absalom he had only nourished a serpent in his bosom. The tidings of what was happening, threatened utterly to crush him to the ground; and so much the more did it oppress him, as in this calamity he was constrained to recognize a new chastisement measured out to him by the Almighty. For this reason, the state of mind into which he was brought by the dreadful tidings was not so much one of anger and revenge, as rather of humiliation and contrition of heart. When he heard that "the heart of the men of Israel was after Absalom," and that the waves of revolution had already rolled up to Jerusalem, his capital, and the place of his residence, he deemed it advisable to leave the latter, especially as he believed that there were grounds for fear that, through the treachery of conspirators in their midst, it would be delivered into the hands of the rebels. He hoped also, by his departure, to cause a sifting of the people, and to be able to assemble around him those who remained faithful to him. "Arise, let us flee," he said to his friends; "for there will be no escape for us from Absalom: make speed to depart, lest he overtake us suddenly, and bring evil upon us, and smite the city with the edge of the sword." The men were obedient to their royal master, and, as with one mouth, replied, "Behold, thy servants are ready to do whatsoever my lord the king shall appoint."

And now we are called to look upon a heartrending spectacle. Leaving behind him some of the "women" (who are to be distinguished from his wives, and are rather to be regarded as ladies of honor belonging to his court), the king fled on foot, accompanied by all his household, along with his chief captains and his life-guard, "the Cherethites and the Pelethites." A Philistine, who was a worshiper of the true God, who had just come from Gath to Jerusalem—Ittai was his name—joined him at this time with 600 horsemen. Thinking that this man might find himself in an error, David declined his company at the beginning, saying to him, "Wherefore goest thou also with us? I am perhaps not the king to whom thou hast bound thyself; it will be another." He meant Absalom, without naming him. "Return," David continued, "and take back thy brethren: mercy and truth be with thee." But Ittai replied, to the deepest disgrace of the rebellious sons of Israel, "As the lord liveth, and as my lord the king liveth, surely in what place my lord the king shall be, whether in death or life, even there also will thy servant be." Moved by such magnanimity, David answered, "Go and pass over." This unexpected meeting, immediately before the gates of the city which he had just left, appeared to the royal fugitive almost like a friendly salutation from his God, and applied the first healing drops of balsam to the wounds of his heart, torn with sorrow.

Thus he wandered forth. He who was once the pride of Israel and the terror of the surrounding nations is now a poor exile. Wherever he comes, all the people weep with a loud voice, and many of them eagerly entreat him, saying, "Let us go with thee, that for thee, or with thee, we may die." On his path of sorrow, presenting for the first time a genuine type of the great future King who was promised to him, he passes over the brook Kidron, with his head covered, and weeping, and then goes on "by the ascent of Mount Olivet, toward the way of the wilderness." After he had thus passed on for a space, absorbed in thought, he raised the veil with which he had covered his countenance, and looked up with eyes still moistened with tears. Then he perceived, to his surprise, in the procession, the two high priests Zadok and Abiathar, and behind them the Levites carrying the ark of the covenant. But thinking this retinue not worthy of the holy thing, he commanded those who bore it, saying, "Carry back the ark of God into the city: if I shall find favor in the eyes of the Lord, He will bring me again, and show me both it and His habitation. But if He say thus, I have no delight in thee; behold, here am I, let Him do to me as seemeth good unto Him."

This entire resignation of his own will, in which the king

showed his repentance and humiliation before the Lord, as it could not be more thorough and genuine, fills us with wonder. David is prepared from the heart to submit to all the consequences of his sin, though they were the most destructive, provided only that God would not withdraw from him His favor and His grace. Asaph's words, "Whom have I in heaven but Thee? and there is none upon earth that I desire besides Thee," expressed altogether the feelings of David's heart. Meanwhile, he did not forget that he was the king, and that, as such, it was his duty to turn away from his people and his kingdom the evil to which he was prepared personally with resignation to submit.

Therefore he directed the priests to return to Jerusalem with the ark of the covenant, and there carefully to find out the state of matters, and then by credible messengers, who would faithfully keep it secret, to send him information thereof. A similar direction he gave to his aged, sagacious friend, Hushai the Archite, who came to him on the top of the mount, at the place where, with their faces turned toward the temple and its holy of holies, they frequently prayed. He came with all the tokens of deepest sorrow, with his garments rent and with earth upon his head, and desired him that he would grant him permission to share with him in his future fortune. David, however, represented to Hushai that, owing to his advanced age, he would only be a burden to him but that, on the contrary, he would do him more advantageous service if he would return to Jerusalem, seek to gain the confidence of Absalom, and at the same time endeavor to penetrate, and, where possible, to frustrate, the plans of Ahithophel, of whose apostasy David had, not without surprise, received information, and against whom he had invoked the arm of the Almighty with the sigh, "O Lord, I pray Thee, turn the counsel of Ahithophel into foolishness!" What Hushai might learn of the conspirators was only to be entrusted to the two high priests, who would convey it to the king by their sons Ahimaaz and Jonathan. The old man entered into the proposal of his royal friend, and returned to Jerusalem, which had by this time been taken possession of by Absalom and his accomplices.

When the king, with the company of his faithful followers which appeared like an escort to a funeral procession, as they went along with downcast head and in silence, had gone a little distance farther, he saw Ziba, the servant of Mephibosheth, whom, as we know, he had entrusted with the management of the possessions left by Saul, that he might administer them for his surviving son, coming toward him driving before him a couple of asses, saddled and loaded with bread, raisins, figs, and wine. And the king said unto Ziba, "What meanest thou by these?" Ziba answered, "The asses be for the king's household to ride on; and the bread and summer fruit for the young men to eat; and the wine, that such as be faint in the wilderness may drink." Again a cheering surprise for the king! But the joy was very soon indeed embittered with the gall of a disheartening discovery. To the question addressed to Ziba, where Mephibosheth the son of his friend Jonathan was, he received the sorrowful answer, "Behold, he abideth at Jerusalem: for he said. Today shall the house of Israel restore me the kingdom of my father!" Thus Mephibosheth also seemed to have gone astray, and to be faithless.

With deep indignation, and yet not without precipitancy, the king said, "Behold, thine are all that pertained unto Mephibosheth." Ziba bowed himself with affected emotion to the earth, and said, "I humbly beseech thee that I may find grace in thy sight, my lord, O king!" He saw the object of his unworthy calumny gained; for indeed his report was nothing else than a slander. Perhaps it is true that even Mephibosheth, in the tumult of rebellion which raged around him, may have for the moment wavered, and may have suffered the thought to occur to him, that the party kept under by the hand of power, which in secret always still adhered to the house of Saul and his government, might yet gain the mastery. But he had not formally rallied the conspirators to his standard, and therefore David was not spared at a later period the experience of bitter repentance because of his sentence of condemnation pronounced altogether too hastily. Perhaps the numerous sorrowful experiences which he had had of the treachery of friends for whose fidelity he could have pledged his life, may seem as some apology for his suspicion. The overpowering and bridling of his easily excitable and quickly roused temperament was a task the discharge of which gave him much to do, even to the end of his days.

As if the heart-sorrow which was experienced by the king had not yet been sufficient, he was soon overtaken by a new trying humiliation at the Benjamite hamlet of Bahurim. A man of the race of Saul, whose name was Shimei, came forth from this place just named, and began to curse him whom he now believed to be forsaken by

God as well as by the whole people, and to cast stones and clods at him and all his servants. "Come out, come out, thou bloody man, and thou man of Belial," he cried furiously after him: "the Lord hath returned upon thee all the blood of the house of Saul, in whose stead thou hast reigned; and the Lord hath delivered the kingdom into the hand of Absalom thy son: and, behold, thou art taken in thy mis-chief, because thou art a bloody man." This grief, piercing his heart as with a poisoned sting, David might perhaps have had in recol-lection, when, at a later period, by the inward operation of the Holy Spirit, he wrote that Messianic psalm which forms, as it were, a pro-gram of the crucifixion of Christ, where he breaks out in these words, "I am a worm, and no man; a reproach of men, and despised of the people."[2]

While Shimei raged against him, Abishai the son of Zeruiah became highly excited, and, grasping the hilt of his sword, said, "Why should this dead dog curse my lord the king? Let me go over, I pray thee, and take off his head." But what did the king answer? Let us hear. He is here master of his own spirit, and therefore "is better than he that taketh a city." To Abishai and his brother Joab, who had expressed himself similarly, he said, "What have I to do with you, ye sons of Zeruiah? So let him curse, because the Lord hath said unto him, Curse David. Who shall then say, Wherefore hast thou done so? Behold, my son, which came forth of my bowels, seeketh my life: how much more now may this Benjamite do it? Let him alone, and let him curse; for the Lord hath bidden him." These words need no explanation. They are the direct expressions of the deepest humili-ty and lowliness before God. He was constrained to bow to the sentence of Shimei, who called him a "bloody man" and a "man of Belial," as too well founded, and discerned in it, because the mouth of him who cursed was not closed by the hand of God, only an echo of Jehovah's sentence, and a new and deserved punishment decreed against him by God.

Without contradiction and murmuring he bore the insults; yet, in the words which follow the decided "halt" which he commanded to his two enraged companions, he gave evidence that, in spite of all the distress that had come upon him, his faith in the grace of God had by no means suffered shipwreck. "It may be that the Lord," said

2. Psalm 22.

he, "will look on mine affliction, and that the Lord will requite me good for his cursing" (i.e., of the Benjamite) "this day." So Shimei continued unhindered, going along on the hill's side over against him, "and cursed as he went, and threw stones at him, and cast dust." The patience of his captains, always prepared for war, was sorely tried, till the king with his whole company reached the town of Bahurim. The greater part of the inhabitants of that place had not renounced their fidelity to him; and there, after the long and sorrowful journey, he found rest and refreshment among friends. The king with his train afterward moved to the wilderness of Judah.

At Jerusalem, meanwhile, the rebels held a council of war, and considered how they might most securely bar the way against the fugitive king and his adherents. Hushai had insinuated himself among the traitors, and, under the appearance of being of Absalom's party, had approached with the loyal cry, "God save the king!" But when Absalom addressed to him the double question, whether that was the fidelity which he had sworn to his friend David, and why he had not joined himself to his band, he received the double answer, "Whom the Lord, and this people, and all the men of Israel, choose, his will I be, and with him will I abide. Whom should I serve? Should I not serve in the presence of his son? As I have served in thy father's presence, so will I be in thy presence." Absalom, indeed, allowed himself to be deceived. These words of Hushai, spoken ambiguously, were understood by him as meaning that Hushai too had deserted from David, and had joined the standard of revolt.

From that time the rebel thought that no secret should any longer be kept hid from him. Thus Hushai was initiated into the infamous plan which Ahithophel had suggested to Absalom, viz. that he should take possession of David's women who had been left behind, appropriate them to himself, and thereby, in the eyes of the people, break down behind him the bridge to every possible return to reconciliation with his royal father, and at the same time designate himself as in fact the heir to his father's crown and royal state. According to the agreement, tidings of all this was now, by means of Hushai, conveyed in a safe way to David.

Absalom closely followed the impious counsel of Ahithophel, and hoped thereby to make his adherents only the bolder and more decided. The history informs us that "the counsel of Ahithophel, which he counseled in those days, was as if a man had inquired at the oracle of God: so was all the counsel of Ahithophel, both with David and with Absalom." Thus it was also at one time with David. That was a matter of regret; for Ahithophel was, in his innermost spirit, essentially a godless and cunning man, who always sought only his own interest. He knew, however, how to clothe himself in an appearance of piety, through which even David had in his innocence allowed himself to be deceived. In the circle of David's friends, Ahithophel was the Judas Iscariot. But at how many royal courts, from those days down to the present time, has there been met with, in the person of some one of the most highly favored and most richly decorated with honors, the copy of Ahithophel!

The feelings of David's mind, in the days of his flight from Absalom, have found their expression in Psalm 3, among others. According to all appearance, it was in the first night after his departure from Jerusalem that his heart poured itself forth in this song: "O Lord," the singer begins, "how are they increased that trouble me! Many are they that rise up against me. Many there be which say of my soul, There is no help for him in God" (and would thus rob me of my last and only consolation). "But," he continues, raising himself up again in childlike confidence—"But Thou, O Lord, art a shield for me; my glory, and the lifter up of mine head. I cried unto the Lord with my voice, and He heard me out of His holy hill" (the Mount Zion, where the ark of the covenant stood, the pledge that the Lord would dwell among His people). "I laid me down and slept; I awaked; for the Lord sustained me" (This psalm is an evening song, sounding out to us from the camp in the wilderness). "I will not be afraid of ten thousands of people, that have set themselves against me round about." Hereupon now follows the prayer originating in the quickening recollection of formerly experienced help: "Arise, O Lord; save me, O my God: for Thou hast smitten all mine enemies upon the cheek bone; Thou hast broken the teeth of the ungodly." Finally, the singer closes with the confession: "Salvation belongeth unto the Lord"; and with the intercession for Israel (although Israel in its blindness had heaped upon him all the evil he was then enduring): "Upon Thy people, O Lord, be Thy blessing!" A noble triumph of David's this over himself, over his old man. The Lord will not forsake him, nor neglect him.

27

The Approaching Deliverance

The Lord hath made everything beautiful in His time."[1] May all who are authorized as believers to appropriate the divine promises, take more earnestly to heart these words of Solomon than generally happens! How often does one hear in their circles the complaint that one in vain waits for the fulfillment of this or that promise of the Lord!—a complaint to which there easily clings the doubt as to the genuineness of the state of grace of which it was believed they might boast, or even as to the truth of the whole written word. They do not then consider that if the Lord brings sufferings upon those who are His own, His purpose is to glorify in them not only His power to help, but also, and more particularly, His wisdom, educating them in the way of trial and of sanctification, and that after He has accomplished in them this holy purpose, the hour for the extending to them outward and temporal help has then for the first time struck.

It is well with those who have learned to be "still, and wait on the help of the Lord." They need not be afraid for the sorrow of disappointed hopes. They will see "the glory of the Lord," though in a different form from that of which they dreamt. It certainly remains true, as Solomon in another place says, that "hope deferred maketh the heart sick"; but also not the less true what he adds, "But when the desire cometh, it is a tree of life."[2] The life of David will bring this anew under our contemplation. The morning dawn of the day of his deliverance and restoration begins to break.

1. Ecclesiastes 3:2.
2. Proverbs 13:12.

2 Samuel 17:1–3

> Moreover, Ahithophel said unto Absalom, Let me now choose out
> twelve thousand men, and I will arise and pursue after David this night:
> and I will come upon him while he is weary and weak-handed, and will
> make him afraid: and all the people that are with him shall flee; and I
> will smite the king only. And I will bring back all the people unto thee.

The king finds himself in great personal danger. Let us, in spirit,
again join ourselves to his company. What at this time awakens our
most lively interest is: (1) a new *heart effusion* of the oppressed one;
(2) an *answer to prayer* with which he is favored; and (3) the *gathering
around him* of friends, whose coming cheers his heart.

1. Where we last left the king, there we must again seek for him.
We meet with him in the wilderness of Judah, and at a somewhat later
period than on that occasion. After midnight, when the dawn of
morning was near, we stand in spirit before the door of his tent. He is
awake, and holds communion with his God.

Psalm 63 streams forth from his agitated heart: "O God, Thou art
my God; early will I seek Thee: my soul thirsteth for Thee, my flesh
longeth for Thee in a dry and thirsty land, where no water is." His
outward situation in the inhospitable desert is to him an image of the
condition of his soul. He longs for a gracious look from his God. "To
see Thy power and Thy glory," he continues, "so as I have seen Thee
in the sanctuary. Because Thy loving-kindness is better than life, my
lips shall praise Thee. Thus will I bless Thee if Thou givest me back
my life" (his present condition seemed to him to be like unto death).
"My soul shall be satisfied as with marrow and fatness, and my mouth
shall praise Thee with joyful lips: when I remember Thee upon my
bed, and meditate on Thee in the night watches. Because Thou hast
been my help, therefore in the shadow of Thy wings will I rejoice. My
soul followeth hard after Thee: Thy right hand upholdeth me. But
those" (Thine enemies and mine) "that seek my soul, to destroy it,
shall go into the lower parts of the earth. They shall fall by the sword:
they shall be a portion for foxes. But the king shall rejoice in God;
every one that sweareth by Him" (the Lord) "shall glory: but the
mouth of them that speak lies shall be stopped!"

We see how again in David's soul hope and confidence have
begun to gain ground. He clings to his God, and He will not forsake
His deeply humbled servant in his misery. "The Lord killeth and

maketh alive: He bringeth down to the grave, and bringeth up," sang the pious Hannah, and thereby she described the experience of all God's children. As in David's heart light began to dawn, so outwardly there now appear the first signs of approaching help.

2. While that song in the night, breathing confidence, streamed from David's heart in the lonely wilderness, significant transactions, but of an altogether different character, are being carried forward in Jerusalem, where also sleep is not thought of. The council of war is assembled. They are consulting how most securely they may lay hold of David and put him aside. It is Ahithophel who then again, at least first, carries off the prize of wisdom. He makes the proposal that they should without delay follow after David when he was weary and weak-handed, and fall upon his followers, experienced in war indeed, but for the time not less desponding than the king himself. They should scatter them at one stroke, and then take prisoner their forsaken and deserted chief. If this were done by means of a quick blow, and it could be easily done, then it would not fail that the whole people would join themselves to Absalom, and do homage to him as their divinely appointed king.

Ahithophel's advice pleased Absalom and his counselors; yet it was thought necessary to hear also the old, experienced Hushai. He was called in accordingly, when Absalom informed him of Ahithophel's counsel. "Ahithophel," said he, "hath spoken after this manner: shall we do after his saying? If not, speak thou." Hushai replied, "The counsel that Ahithophel hath given is not good at this time. For thou knowest thy father and his men, that they be mighty men, and they be chafed in their minds, as a bear robbed of her whelps in the field: and thy father is a man of war, and will not lodge with the people. Behold, he is hid now in some pit, or in some other place: and it will come to pass, when some of them be overthrown at the first, that whosoever heareth it will say, There is a slaughter among the people that follow Absalom. And he also that is valiant, whose heart is as the heart of a lion, shall utterly melt: for all Israel knoweth that thy father is a mighty man, and they which be with him are valiant men. Therefore I counsel that all Israel be generally gathered unto thee, from Dan even to Beer-sheba, as the sand that is by the sea for multitude; and that thou go to battle in thine own person. So shall we come upon him in some place where he shall be found, and we will light upon him as the dew falleth on the ground: and of him and of all the men that are with him there shall not be left so much as one. Moreover, if he be gotten into a city, then shall all Israel bring ropes to that city, and we will draw it into the river, until there be not one small stone found there."

Thus Hushai gave his advice. What wonder that his plan seemed more acceptable to the ambitious and fickle youth Absalom than Ahithophel's proposal was? It placed before him the prospect of more certain success and of greater glory. He did not, therefore, delay to let the people know that he preferred the counsel of Hushai to that of Ahithophel. The history remarks, that "the Lord had appointed to defeat the good counsel of Ahithophel" (which certainly was the wiser of the two), "to the intent that the Lord might bring evil upon Absalom."

Hushai hastened, according to the agreement made with him, to inform David, by means of the priest's sons, Jonathan and Ahimaaz. They were sent to say to David, "Lodge not this night in the plains of the wilderness, but speedily pass over; lest the king be swallowed up, and all the people that are with him." Hushai manifestly apprehended that Ahithophel's counsel might even yet prevail with the rebels over his. Therefore this warning to David.

The two messengers stayed outside the city, by the well Rogel, waiting for the communication from Hushai. After it had been brought to them by a maid, who seemed to have been initiated into the matter, they went forward on their errand. But a young man met them, and gave information of this meeting on his arriving at Jerusalem, because the urgent haste with which the well-known sons of the priests passed on had awakened his suspicion. Absalom immediately sent several officers after the messengers. They were made aware of this at the moment when they entered into the house of a friendly family at Bahurim to rest for a little. But the master of that house was acquainted with their purpose. He directed his guests to descend into a cistern, at that time dry, which was in his court, and his wife spread a covering over the opening into it, and scattered ground corn over it, so that it would occur to no one that the messengers were hidden there.

Absalom's servants soon appeared. "Where is Ahimaaz and Jonathan?" they asked angrily at the woman of the house. She, deceiving them, answered, "They be gone over the brook of water." The spies went forward in the direction indicated, sought right and left, but did not find them, and at length returned to Jerusalem without having gained their object. Hushai's two messengers now left their hiding-place, thanked their faithful and prudent host, and departed on their way, and soon reached their destination—the tent of the king, in the lonely wilderness. "Hushai sends us," they said to their lord, "and directed us to say, Arise, and pass quickly over the water: for thus hath Ahithophel counseled against you. Then David arose, and all the people that were with him, and they passed over Jordan: by the morning light there lacked not one of them that was not gone over Jordan."

In this information, sent to him so opportunely, David believed that he had reason to recognize a new sign that the Lord still thought upon him in love, and cared for his deliverance. His heart melted in thankfulness to his ever-faithful God. Yet soon more indubitable signs were granted that God had not forgotten him, but was his God now as He had been before. What took place at Jerusalem?

When Ahithophel saw, perhaps for the first time in his life, that his counsel did not prevail, he felt himself not only dishonored, but he concluded that now Absalom's cause, which he had with the fairest hopes for his own future made wholly his own, was absolutely lost. He did not doubt that the people, before one could be aware of it, would, by the delay that had occurred, soon recover from their blind enthusiasm; and that, on the other hand, David's party would recover from their first dejection, and by new accessions would be considerably strengthened. A more bitter enmity and a darker gloom spread itself over the soul of the ambitious man, who had long ago ceased to make inquiry regarding the commandments of God. He hastily saddled his ass, and, with flaming anger, left the camp of the rebels, rode home to his own city, put his household in order, and in a fit of despair put an end to his life. What besides his wounded sense of honor may have driven him to take this step can only be conjectured. The arousing earnestness with which the judge in his own breast, the awakening conscience, held before him the crime of his breach of fidelity to his king and friend, may have certainly contributed to this result. Enough: the people of his house found, to their horror, that he had hanged himself; and after they had loosed him— the dark shadow of the future traitor Judas Iscariot—from the gallows chosen by himself and which was too well deserved, they buried him in his father's grave.

With what a deeply moved heart may not David have bowed himself down before the Lord, when he heard of the "end with terror" to which the most dangerous of his enemies had come! It must have been to him like a new evidence that the eye of God was yet open in mercy over him, and that the ear of God was yet gracious to his prayer. Had he indeed prayed, "O Lord, turn the counsel of Ahithophel to foolishness!" and in how surprising a manner did he see that prayer now answered!

David remembers Ahithophel often in his psalms. Thus, in the forty-first, where he says: "An evil disease, say they, cleaveth fast unto him: and now that he lieth, he shall rise up no more. Yea, mine own familiar friend, in whom I trusted, which did eat of my bread, hath lifted up his heel against me." And in Psalm 55 he says: "For it was not an enemy that reproached me; then I could have borne it: neither was it he that hated me that did magnify himself against me; then I would have hid myself from him: but it was thou" (Ahithophel), "a man mine equal, my guide, and mine acquaintance. We took sweet counsel together, and walked unto the house of God in company." Besides, we meet with undoubted allusions to Ahithophel, his treachery and his dreadful end, in Psalms 69 and 109. It is true that in these judgments the person of the betrayer of Jesus Christ did not appear before the psalmist's eye; but the Holy Spirit put into his mouth the words which he employed in these psalms, in such an order and form that they become at the same time a prophecy of the accursed forerunner and chief of all traitors and suicides.

3. The Lord still evidently remembers in mercy and grace His servant David. The help he longed for becomes always the more complete. Of this we have been already witnesses. A new sun-ray, which falls upon him, will strengthen us in this conviction. By Hushai's advice, the king had gone over Jordan, and had come with his followers to Mahanaim, on the borders of Gad and Manasseh. Suddenly all manner of people, from near and remote districts around, come to him. They were for the most part rural proprietors, among whom was Machir, the son of Ammiel of Lo-debar, and the aged Barzillai, a Gileadite of Rogelim, of whom we shall afterward hear further, and even a royal prince also, Shobi of Rabbah, the son of Nahash, the Ammonite king whom David had made to pass under the yoke. And what did they bring with them to David? The heavily laden beasts of burden which they drove before them will direct

us to the answer. They brought presents of many kinds—"beds, and basins, and earthen vessels, and wheat, and barley, and flour, and parched corn, and beans, and lentils, and parched pulse, and honey, and butter, and sheep, and cheese of kine," and other kinds of provisions and vessels that might be necessary. What moved them to this? "They thought," the history informs us, "the people will be hungry, and weary, and thirsty in the wilderness," therefore let us go and refresh them. Who had put it into their hearts to act thus? David soon perceived this, and accepted the kindly gifts with deep thankfulness, as from the hands of God his Lord.

How highly the fidelity of subjects is valued in times of revolution, and how, beyond description, it comforts rulers who are then surrounded by traitors, we ourselves once were witnesses. Fidelity ennobles, in the eyes of the prince against whom the waves of civil commotion are rolling, at once the humblest peasant and laborer with a higher dignity than that of the most prominent of the dignitaries around his throne who may have already begun to waver. The faithful there at Mahanaim secured for themselves, beyond doubt, in the recollection of the oppressed king, as this was at a later time manifested, a perpetual memorial. And this they did so much the more, as they furnished so important a reason for it, viz. by announcing, as the constant addition of armed bands to the king's host had indeed already done, that a grateful change of mind had begun to force its way among the people.

The moment of decision came ever nearer. Absalom, at the head of his army of conspirators, had marched out of Jerusalem, and was encamped in the land of Gilead, not far from David's camp. In the stead of Joab, who had again joined David's standard, his cousin Amasa had been appointed to the chief command of the army under Absalom. He was a man equal to Joab in warlike impetuosity and bravery. On him Absalom placed his whole confidence. At a later period, however, we again find him among the chief captains of David.

David knew his position, and that the decisive moment had arrived. The tidings of Ahithophel's end had not then reached him. His heart was not a little agitated. Psalm 4 acquaints us with the thoughts and feelings which moved within him at that time, in his camp at Mahanaim. "Hear me," he cries, "when I call, O God of my righteousness: Thou hast enlarged me when I was in distress; have mercy upon me, and hear my prayer." A cry of distress; a cry for help!

It does not surprise us. It is true, as an interpreter of that psalm remarks, the children of the world appear to us to be more composed and more sparing in their expressions of sorrow, under the distresses by which they are assailed, than the friends of God. But what wonder, when for the latter the sufferings which pass over them have an entirely different meaning from that which they have for the former!

While the children of the world see in them only unfortunate accidents, to which they are to accommodate themselves as well as possible, because they cannot now be changed, sufferings appear to believers, on the other hand, as divine chastisements, which they have willfully brought upon themselves by their sins. How can they, therefore, assume an attitude of indifference toward them? Furthermore, they know that they have a Helper in heaven, and are therefore, less disposed to deny their human nature, and by force to suppress their sorrow, than they are who are without God in the world. Such say, Myself being lost, all is lost! seek to protect themselves in the noisy whirlpool of dissipation from despair. Against this they who fear God are secured.

Then "the souls of those living in the fellowship of God are altogether different, and tuned with incomparably greater delicacy than are the souls of those who are estranged from God." To the latter it is easy, for example, to bear with patience the hatred of men, because they themselves hate, and to reconcile themselves to the hatred of others, because they breathe the air of the same sphere; while the pious, more sensitively organized than they, feel themselves most deeply wounded thereby, and in them the well-known proverb is verified, "The tender heart, the keener smart."

Finally, we appropriate to ourselves the remark that the God-fearing have no ground to conceal from themselves and others their human weakness, for they seek their strength not in themselves but in God; while the children of the world, even then, when they are near to despair, endeavor to give themselves externally the appearance of freedom from pain, because their pride struggles against their becoming objects of compassion.

Many burdens, however, pressed heavily on the spirit of the king. To grief at the misfortune which had come upon himself personally, and at the faithlessness of so many of those in whom he once had unbounded confidence, there was united anxiety of mind for the immortal soul of his poor lost son; grief, because of the loss of the love of his people, and bitter sorrow that his efforts for the elevation of religious life in Israel should bear such mournful fruits; and, above all, grief on account of his own great transgression, which gnawed continually at his heart, and was the chief cause of his present wretchedness. Deeply humbled, we see him, in Psalm 4, lying in the dust before his God. Yes, he knew how to find the way out of his distress, to a renewal of his confidence in the grace of God, and to faith in the efficacy of prayer!

There are three strong pillars on which the golden spiritual bridge is supported, over which he presses forward to such confidence. The first consists of the remembrance that it was the Lord from whom he had received in trust the crown of which they now wished to rob him. He speaks to his enemies in spirit, and thus addresses them: "O ye sons of men, how long will ye turn my glory into shame? how long will ye love vanity, and seek after leasing?" He meant that it was vain for them to fight against the ordinances of God; and as that former pretense of the rebels, that they only wished to hold a sacrificial festival at Hebron, from which the whole rebellion had emanated, was a lie, even so also was their presumptuous claim, which they endeavored to make good, that the self-government of the people was a divine right. "But know," continues the psalmist, "that the Lord hath set apart him that is godly for Himself," namely me, His friend, that I should be your prince. The consciousness that he bore the scepter by divine appointment gave him courage to add, "The Lord will hear me when I call unto Him."

"Be ye angry," he further says, "and sin not," as ye do at present. In his humility, David grants that there might be grounds for their raging against him; only he teaches them that their anger should be restrained within just limits. It ought to be a holy indignation. He gives them the counsel, "Commune with your own heart on your bed, and be still." This he himself does in this his song in the night. In the stillness, and not amid the raging assemblies of the people, wildly excited, as an interpreter of this psalm to whom we have already referred here remarks, they ought composedly to commune with themselves, and to reflect upon what they had undertaken and perhaps they might become temperate and of a different mind.

A second thing which keeps the king upright in his distress, is the certainty that the way of the rebels can only be abhorrent to God. He calls unto them, "Offer the sacrifices of righteousness, and put your trust in the Lord." In these words he alludes unmistakably to the hypocritical sacrifice with which they had inaugurated their rebellion, while at the same time he reminds them of the words of Samuel, "To obey is better than sacrifice." He also by these words points out to them that the hopes which, renouncing God, they built on their human might and on their earthly means of war, were altogether vain; while the indispensable condition of all prosperity and of all divine help consisted in the resignation of perfect confidence in the Lord, as He Himself has said, "I will be found of you, if ye seek me with your whole heart."

Finally, the third thing which does not allow the king to despair, is the consciousness that that essential condition to which all help of divine grace is united, namely, a childlike confidence in the Lord, was not lacking in him. "There be many who say" (in the despair of unbelief), "Who will show us any good? Lord, lift Thou up the light of Thy countenance upon us!" Who does not see in these words the allusion to the Aaronic blessing with which the congregation of the Lord is to the present day blessed? The psalmist gives renewed expression to his hope in the grace of God, and affords occasion for us to remark how greatly he is comforted through the grace of the Lord.

"Thou hast put gladness in my heart," he says, "more than in the time that their corn" (namely, of the enemy) "and wine abounded." Undeniably in these words he had before his mind the friendly gifts with which the faithful men who had just come to him from a distance had surprised him and filled him with great joy; for in this occurrence he perceived only a hope-strengthening, friendly salutation of his God—a salutation for which the enemy possessed no ear. O how the king becomes the longer the more joyful of heart! "I will both lay me down," he thus concludes his night-song, "in peace, and sleep: for Thou, Lord, only makest me dwell in safety." Comforted, he lays down his head to rest and sleeps, calmly and free from care, like a child on the heart of his God.

We depart from his tent with these words, from a psalm of one of kindred spirit with David: "He that keepeth thee will not slumber. Behold, He that keepeth Israel shall neither slumber nor sleep. The Lord is thy Keeper; the Lord is thy Shade upon thy right hand."

28

The Restoration

I know how to be abased, and I know how to abound."[1] Thus spoke the Apostle Paul—an utterance of great import. What does it imply, but that he knew himself to be strong to overcome the temptation to self-boasting when he was on the heights of reputation and of honor, as well as to master the temptation to despondency and murmuring when he was in the depths of humiliation and of suffering? With like truth and comprehensiveness of meaning, no saint under the Old Covenant could repeat these words, because none of them could add as he did, "I can do all things through Christ, which strengtheneth me." The revelation of God in Christ was "hailed from afar" by those of old as only something in the future, and the Holy Spirit was, according to the saying of the evangelist John, "not yet given" as a spirit of adoption. There was also lacking the living consciousness of most intimate fellowship with the living God which is communicated through this Spirit.

What wonder, therefore, that a man of the piety of a David, at the pinnacle of royal greatness, should, for a time at least, be overcome by the power of his flesh, and fall back again under the spirit of the world, and, when the storm of tribulation discharged itself over him, should pour forth utterances of sorrow, which almost seem as if they were the sounds of despair!

Yet it excites our astonishment that the mournful matter of Uriah was the only gross sin with which, during the long space of forty years, his life as a monarch was stained; and that his faith always came forth victorious and uninjured, even purified and strengthened,

---

1. Philippians 4:12.

from all the fearful temptations and commotions by which it was
tried, in spite of the comparatively only small measure of the means
of salvation and of grace which was within his reach. So, in spite of
all the weaknesses which he manifested. he must continue to be the
"man after God's own heart," chiefly because never did a sinner, in
more genuine and thorough repentance, break with the sin which in
an unguarded hour overcame him, than he did. God could not forsake nor neglect His servant so sincerely devoted to Him, but must
always bring him again out of all distresses and difficulties, and "set
his feet in a large room."

Today we shall see the Almighty once more, in a most adorable
manner, stretch His helping arm over him. The civil war stirred up
by Absalom terminates in the re-elevation of the humbled monarch.

2 Samuel 18:31

> And, behold, Cushi came; and Cushi said, Tidings, my lord the king:
> for the Lord hath avenged thee this day of all them that rose up against
> thee.

2 Samuel 19:14–15

> And he bowed the heart of all the men of Judah, even as the heart of
> one man; so that they sent this word unto the king, Return thou, and
> all thy servants. So the king returned.

(1) David's victory, and (2) his return to the throne, are the two facts
which on the present occasion will engage our attention. It is true
that the former appears arrayed in the garb of mourning, and the latter comes to pass not without offense; so that we shall find
occasion rather to adore the grace and faithfulness of God than to
admire the victory. To us sinners this can only be consoling and joyful, especially since that which we might find in some degree reason
to reprove in the conduct of the hero of our history will by no means
make any breach in our love to him.

1. The rebel army advanced from Gilead in close array. At its
head, as commander-in-chief under Absalom, was Amasa, the
courageous and resolute son of a half-sister of David's, who was
appointed by Absalom to be successor to Joab, his uncle, who had
now deserted from the rebels. When the news of the advance of the
rebels reached David's camp, he also commanded his men to

move forward, after he had arranged into three bands the people who crowded around him in reinforcements continually arriving, and had given command over them to Joab, Abishai (Joab's brother), and to the valiant and God-fearing Philistine, Ittai of Gath. At the same time, he informed the army that he was resolved to go forth with them in person.

The captains were opposed to this, apparently from fear lest tender regard for his son, the chief of the conspirators, might dispose the king, in the course of the battle, to unreasonable forbearance and mildness. Yet they presented as the ground of their dissuasive counsel this consideration, that if the king perished in battle, his fall would be esteemed in Israel as equal to the death of 10,000 men, and that, in the event of their taking flight, yea, that even though the half of them should die, this would not be considered as a defeat, so long as he, the royal leader, yet remained in the midst of the remnant of his army. It would be more prudent, they thought, that he should continue in the city of Mahanaim, with a reserve, so that, if necessity should arise, he would be prepared to come to their help at the fitting moment. David yielded to their advice without opposition. "What seemeth you best," said he, "I will do." The army then marched forward. The king, however, had one thing which he sought to impress on the hearts of the captains. With a loud voice, and repeatedly, that all who were marching past him might hear it, he said, "Deal gently with the young man, even with Absalom." Who could be offended at this command, coming from a father's heart?

The trumpets sounded, and the battle commenced. In diverse places the hosts encountered each other. In the wood of Ephraim, a part of the mountain range of the same name, the battle raged most fiercely. And as always, so also here, the combatants acted all unconscious of the invisible threads which were in the hands of Him who, as director of the battle, moves upon the clouds above the tumult, and alone determines the result. Thus, He moves behind the scenes to carry out His purposes.

There, in the wood of Ephraim, the battle did not long remain doubtful. On all hands the victory inclined to the side of those who were faithful to the king. The army of the rebels was soon disorganized, and fled in wild confusion. Whatever of the squadrons was not devoured by the sword, perished miserably in the marshes and chasms of the wood. Absalom, hastening away on a foaming horse, had gained the start of his fleeing troops, and thought that he was already saved, when, deprived of all foresight by the confusion into which his anguish and perplexity had brought him, he was suddenly caught in the forked branch of an oak-tree growing in the ancient forest, not by his hair alone, which only contributed to hold him more firmly, but by the head, and remained hanging thereon, while his horse, released from the bridle, flew from under him—an execution which God Himself wrought on the violator of the commandment, which has accompanying "the promise" also the threatening, "Whoso curseth his father or his mother, his lamp shall be put out in obscure darkness."

A soldier of the royal army, who had, in pursuit of the fugitive, penetrated into the thicket, found, to his horror, the king's son hanging on the branch, and hastened back with great speed to announce to Joab his mournful discovery. "Behold, I saw Absalom," said he, "hanged in an oak." "And, behold, thou sawest him," replied Joab, "and why didst thou not smite him there to the ground? and I would have given thee ten shekels of silver, and a girdle." The soldier, of nobler mind than his superior was, replied, "Though I should receive a thousand shekels of silver in mine hand, yet would I not put forth thine hand against the king's son: for in our hearing the king charged thee, and Abishai, and Ittai, saying, Beware that none touch the young man Absalom. Otherwise I should have wrought falsehood against mine own life: for there is no matter hid from the king; and thou thyself " (he knew Joab) "wouldest have set thyself against me." Joab, in his impatience, said, "I may not tarry thus with thee. Where hangs the rebel?" The soldier led him to the hanging tree, and Joab took three darts in his hand, and thrust them through the heart of Absalom. Streaming with blood, the unhappy fugitive fell down to the ground. Then Joab's armor-bearers, ten in number, surrounded and smote Absalom and slew him.

A complete victory was gained. That there might be no unnecessary shedding of blood, Joab directed the trumpet to be blown, as a signal to the people to cease from fighting, and return from pursuing after Israel. But the body of Absalom was thrown into a grave near to the place where he was found hanging, and a heap of stones was piled upon it. Not far from that place, in the so-called King's Dale, Absalom had, after the death of his three sons, chosen out for himself a burying-place, and had erected upon it a magnificent pil-

lar, which is called "Absalom's Place." He had thought that he would
be there, some time or other, buried as king; but he is now buried as
an outlawed evil-doer, as an outcast from among men.

Till this hour that grave speaks to us with a loud awakening voice.
Violations of the commandment, "Honor thy father and thy mother," for the most part, indeed, escape the judgment of human
authorities; but the Almighty has reserved it to Himself to inflict
punishment with His own hand, and for the most part even on this
side of eternity, as He has promised for this world also a gracious
reward to those who keep it holy, according to the promise annexed
to the commandment, "That it may go well with thee." Let anyone
follow the life-course of such as in their youth despise their parents,
the visible representatives of the invisible God, and bring them to
their graves in sorrow, and it will be perceived that even a subsequent
repentance does not secure them against the painful experience that
evil for evil fastens itself to their heels. In the history of the world,
there have been thousands who have followed the example of
Absalom, and have come to a like fearful end. In not a few degenerate sons and daughters has that well-known proverb of Solomon's
been even literally fulfilled, "The eye that mocketh at his father, and
despiseth to obey his mother, the ravens of the valley shall pick it
out, and the young eagles shall eat it."

While the battle raged in the wood of Ephraim, David sat
"between the two gates" at Mahanaim, waiting, in extreme anxiety,
the issue of the conflict. No Israelite city was without such gates. The
space between the outer and the inner gate was occupied as the place
where the magistrates publicly dispensed justice. On the tower of the
outer gate stood the watchman, who looked out in the direction
which led to the scene of battle. In Joab's camp, it was meanwhile
under deliberation who should be appointed to convey the tidings of
the victory to the king. Ahimaaz, the son of Zadok, offered himself
for this service. "Let me now run," said he, "and bear the king tidings,
how that the Lord hath avenged him of his enemies." Joab, however,
declined his offer, from prudential consideration. He regarded the
young man, perhaps, as too tender-hearted to be entrusted with conveying to the king in the right manner the fearful tidings of
Absalom's death. He must also take care lest Ahimaaz should appear
before David as an accuser of those who had put Absalom to death,
contrary to the king's express command.

Perhaps Joab also did not wish to expose the brave youth to an outbreak of the king's anger, which was certainly to be expected; and therefore he chose as his messenger, instead of him, the Ethiopian Cushi, who had come over to Israel and had embraced Israel's faith, and with whom he supposed that there was a great measure of cool manliness. "Go," said he to Cushi, "tell the king what thou hast seen." Cushi bowed himself respectfully and ran. But afterward Ahimaaz begged once more for permission to hasten after him. In vain. "Wherefore wilt thou run, my son," said Joab, "seeing that thou hast no tidings ready for which thou mayest hope for a gracious reward? Another time thou shalt be my herald; but not today, since the king's son is dead." Ahimaaz replied, entreating for the third time, almost with tears, for permission, "Let me run." "Run!" said Joab, in an irritated tone. And the youth ran, and outstripped Cushi.

David kept his eyes steadfastly directed to the sentinel on the watchtower, who at length called out, "I see someone in the distance hastening toward the city." David replied, "If he be alone, there is good tidings in his mouth." He concluded that if his army had been beaten, the highways would have been crowded with fugitives. The watchman called again, "Behold, another man running alone." "Well!" David replied, regarding this again as a favorable token. In a few minutes thereafter the watchman announced, "Me thinketh the running of the foremost is like the running of Ahimaaz, the son of Zadok." The king said, "He is a good man, and cometh with good tidings." A few moments more pass, and Ahimaaz crosses the threshold of the gate, with the joyful exclamation, "Peace, peace, my lord king!" When he came into the king's presence, he fell down to the earth upon his face, and said, "Blessed be the Lord thy God, which hath delivered up the men that lifted up their hand against my lord the king!"

Before the king, however, can respond to the triumphal tone of the messenger, he addresses to him the anxious question, "Is the young man Absalom safe?" Ahimaaz, who was convinced that at that moment the sorrowful tidings would have quite crushed the king, withheld it, and pretended that he had seen, just at the time when Joab sent him forth, a great tumult, but that he did not know what it meant. The king is struck at this, and expects nothing good. In visible excitement, he bids Ahimaaz turn aside and stand near him. Then, in breathless haste, Cushi the Ethiopian comes running up to the gate, and cries, "Good tidings, my lord the king: for the Lord hath avenged thee this day of all them that rose up against thee." But the king had no ear for this tidings, and addressed also this question to Cushi: "Is the young man Absalom safe?" And what answer must he hear! Joab had not erred in thinking that the Ethiopian was less tender-hearted and compassionate than Ahimaaz. The Moor replied to the king: "The enemies of my lord the king, and all that rise against thee to do thee hurt, be as that young man." The king is utterly overwhelmed by these words. Much moved, he hastens up to the chamber over the gate, and begins to sob aloud. Like one in despair, wringing his hands and walking to and fro, the tears running in streams down his cheeks, he cries out again and again, "O my son Absalom! my son, my son Absalom! would God I had died for thee, O Absalom, my son, my son!"

What do we say to this conduct on the part of David? Are we willing to justify him for this weakness? There were not lacking, as we shall immediately see, those in Israel who censured his conduct. Perhaps it might be said to his reproach that he allowed the consciousness of the king to retire too far into the background behind the feelings of the head of a family. In view of the general welfare of the land, he ought at least to have moderated the sorrow of his heart as a father, and to have subordinated his grief to thankful joy on account of the help from God again experienced by the land. He ought to have joined also with his people in praising the name of the Lord, and not to have withheld the recognition which was due to the fidelity and devotion of his soldiers, who so cheerfully and courageously had exposed themselves to death. Yet under all the insignia of royalty he still remained a father, and not only a tender and loving father, but one who walked uprightly before God.

And under what circumstances did he see his son so suddenly taken away, and where might he now expect his immortal soul to be? Is not his wish that he who knew himself as saved by the grace of God had died in the stead of his lost child, perfectly justified, especially as the voice of his conscience had never been altogether silent which whispered to him, "It is thy sin, David, which has incurred all this evil"? Under all these considerations, how can we bring ourselves to condemn the man of God, and to cherish any other feelings than those of deepest sympathy with him, when he utters his mournful cry, "My son, my son!" If he was in that dreadful moment truly weaker than he ought to have been, yet it is a consolation to us to know that soon thereafter "the strength of God is made perfect in such weakness."

The excessive sorrow of David did not fail, it is true, in the first moments, coming as it did immediately after the glorious victory that had been gained, to exercise a depressing and discouraging influence over the spirits of the faithful in Israel. "The victory that day," says the history, "was turned into mourning unto all the people: for the people heard that day how the king was grieved for his son." To the army, to whom the rebel Absalom had become an object of deepest abhorrence, and who saw in his death nothing less than a glorifying of the retributive justice of Jehovah, the sorrow to which the king abandoned himself seemed unmanly, and a forgetting of God; and when they perceived that their commander-in-chief refrained not, with his head covered, from ever and anon murmuring out his sorrowful "Ah, my son Absalom, my son, my son" they became at length weary of the everlasting lamentation, and were on the point of quitting the field and scattering, every man to his home. "The people," it is said, "gat them by stealth that day into the city, as people being ashamed steal away in battle."

Joab's patience also at length became exhausted. Straightway he went to his royal master, and shunned not, in his own harsh and rough way, to represent his untimely and unsuitable behavior. "Thou hast today," he said to him, "shamed the faces of all thy servants, which this day have saved thy life, and the lives of thy wives, and the lives of thy concubines; in that thou lovest thine enemies, and hatest thy friends: for thou hast declared this day, that thou regardest neither princes nor servants: for this day I perceive, that if Absalom had lived, and all we had died this day, then it had pleased thee well." After this bold and rude speech, he gave the king the advice which was certainly prudent—that he should restrain himself, go out to the soldiers and speak to them in an encouraging manner, recognizing their services; and he added, with strong emphasis, "For I swear by the Lord, if thou go not forth, there will not tarry one with thee this night; and that will be worse unto thee than all the evil that befell thee from thy youth up."

Thus spoke Joab, with that culpable haughtiness which distinguished him from his youth—a haughtiness which David's weakness on the present occasion only increased. Joab's words produced the wished-for consequence. David awoke out of his oppressive, sad dream, and saw the unsuitableness of his conduct. He strengthened himself and went out, and soon the news spread among the people: "Behold, the king sits on his seat before the gate to hold a review!" Immediately the soldiers, who had already begun to disperse, were themselves again, and they marched before the king in rank-and-file. He graciously saluted them, rejoicing with them apparently over the victory, and everyone was satisfied and encouraged.

Throughout the whole land the movement in favor of David continued to increase, even though not in every instance in the purest and most genuine manner. It was so, however, with a great part of the people, and with increasing frequency they were heard saying, "The king saved us out of the hand of our enemies, and he delivered us out of the hand of the Philistines; and now he is fled out of the land for Absalom. And Absalom, whom we anointed over us, is dead in battle. Now therefore why speak ye not a word of bringing the king back?" These proposals found an echo.

To the king himself it was a matter of importance that the heart of the tribe of Judah, the tribe of his fathers, in which the rebellion had broken out, should be turned again to him. He therefore charged the priests Zadok and Abiathar to do their part in bringing about this result. "Speak," said he, "unto the elders of Judah, saying, Why are ye the last to bring the king back to his house? seeing the speech of all Israel is come to the king, even to his house. Ye are my brethren, ye are my bones and my flesh." A solemn bringing back of the king by the people would necessarily be regarded by him as an open and actual retraction of the anointing of Absalom. And such a restoration did take place. The history records that "the Lord bowed the heart of all the men of Judah, even as the heart of one man; so that they sent this word unto the king, Return thou, and all thy servants." And so David set forth on his way back to Jerusalem, accompanied by a multitude of people, which continually increased as he moved from place to place. The company, swelling in number from hour to hour, formed itself into a triumphal procession returning with victory.

Thus the king now saw answered the prayer of Psalm 43, in which, before the news of the victory had yet reached him, he had poured out his heart before God in his camp at Mahanaim. "Judge me, O God," he had said, "and plead my cause against an ungodly nation:

O deliver me from the deceitful and unjust man. For Thou art the God of my strength: why dost Thou cast me off? why go I mourning because of the oppression of the enemy?" God's hour had not yet struck. "O send out Thy light and Thy truth" (i.e., Thy grace and Thy faithfulness): "let them lead me; let them bring me unto Thy holy hill, and to Thy tabernacles. Then will I go unto the altar of God, unto God my exceeding joy: yea, upon the harp will I praise Thee, O God my God." David now found himself on the way to this longed-for consummation. Encouraging himself, he had then closed his psalm with the words, "Why art thou cast down, O my soul? and why art thou disquieted within me? hope in God; for I shall yet praise Him, who is the health of my countenance, and my God." His confidence had not deceived him. The moment for thanks and praise had now come.

2. Into what an elevated frame of mind must the remembrance of that prayer, now crowned with so glorious and so superabundant an answer, have raised the king on the occasion of his return to the holy city! This thankful and humbly joyful state of mind easily accounts for those deeds of generosity, truly royal, and almost exceeding just bounds, with which he marked his way. First, he pardoned his nephew Amasa, who was the guilty leader of the rebel army; and did not content himself with only remitting to him the punishment he merited, but even promoted him (without doubt now a penitent man), though not for the present by an open public decree, to the rank of commander-in-chief of his army, instead of Joab, against whom David cherished in his heart feelings of dislike, because he had slain Absalom.

When he arrived at Gilgal, on the banks of the Jordan, he saw himself anew saluted by a great multitude of men from Judah, who had come to do him homage as their king, and to conduct him across the river, and escort him farther on his way. With a like intention, a thousand men had also come out of Benjamin, all animated with the same eager desire to be helpful to the king and his numerous band of followers in their passage, and also thereby to testify their subjection to him. Among those not least ready to do service to David were the well-known slanderer of Bahurim, and the mean and false Ziba, with his fifteen sons and twenty servants, by whose presence he expected to produce an impression which would gain for him some esteem. Both men conducted themselves with so much the more humility, that it was of consequence to them that the guilt which rested upon them should be forgotten—a spectacle of the most lamentable kind, which is so frequently to be met with particularly after newly suppressed revolts.

And Shimei threw himself down at the king's feet, and said, "Let not my lord impute iniquity unto me, neither do thou remember that which thy servant did perversely the day that my lord the king went out of Jerusalem." With these mild expressions he designated his base conduct toward the king when he was fleeing, when he reviled him as "a bloody man," and stoned him with stones, and cast dust upon him. "Let not the king," Shimei continued, "take it to heart!" This was a strong demand made upon the king; but it is not merely to us that it seems so, as we shall immediately see. "Thy servant doth know," continued Shimei, "that I have sinned" (would that he had known this earlier!): "therefore, behold, I am come the first this day of all the house of Joseph" (by this name the rest of all the tribes, with the exception of the tribe of Judah, were wont to be designated) "to go down to meet my lord the king!" And this was all the service which the miserable man could boast of!

At the sight of the knave, Abishai, David's nearest companion in arms, feels the blood boil in his veins, and it is difficult for him to hold his anger within bounds when he hears the humble petition of the hypocrite. He breaks out in these words, "Shall not Shimei be put to death for this, because he cursed the Lord's anointed?" But David quickly interrupted Abishai, who was enraged not without cause, and, restraining him, said, as he had before done in the street at Bahurim, "What have I to do with you, ye sons of Zeruiah, that ye should this day be adversaries unto me? shall there any man be put to death this day in Israel? for do not I know that I am this day king over Israel?" Here there is opened to us anew a glance into the depths of the king's heart. In the feeling of his own unworthiness before God, and in his thankfulness for the grace which he had experienced, he was more master of his spirit than Abishai was.

Perhaps also here, however, it might be said to his reproach, that he acted more as a private man than as the theocratic king appointed as guardian of the law. We do not place ourselves, however, among his judges, but rather rejoice at the magnanimity and mildness of the king, as a sign that something of the spirit of the New Covenant, which teaches us to love our enemies and bless them that curse us, already moved within his soul. Turning to Shimei, he said, "Thou shalt not die"; he even swore to him that revenge would not be taken against him. At a later period he saw himself constrained, by the voice of conscience, to charge his successor on the throne to punish Shimei, as a vindication of the majesty of the divine law which had been so grossly violated by him. Yet this was done solely from the force of high considerations, and altogether against his personal inclinations.

After Shimei, Mephibosheth the son of Jonathan appeared in the presence of the king; and in what an attitude did he come before him! Since the day on which the king had left Jerusalem, fleeing from his son Absalom, Mephibosheth had for grief neither washed his feet, nor trimmed his beard, nor attended to his clothes. "Wherefore," said the king to him, "wentest thou not with me, Mephibosheth?" "My lord, O king," he replied, "my servant" (Ziba the steward) "deceived me for thy servant said, I will saddle me an ass, that I may ride thereon, and go to the king; because thy servant is lame. But Ziba refused to obey the command which I gave to him. Besides, he hath slandered thy servant unto my lord the king; but my lord the king is as an angel of God" (i.e., he sees all things just as they really are): "do therefore what is good in thine eyes. For all of my father's house were but dead men" (judged worthy of death) "before my lord the king; yet didst thou set thy servant among them that did eat at thine own table: what right therefore have I yet to cry any more unto the king?" Thus spoke Mephibosheth.

The king replied, not without visible agitation of mind, "Speak no more of these matters. I have said it: thou and Ziba divide the field between you." David had appointed Ziba as steward for Mephibosheth the son of Jonathan, over the fields which had been possessed by Saul, and had promised to him the fruit of a part of these lands, but not a right of possession to them. But afterward, when David too hastily gave credit to the aspersions with which Ziba had calumniated Mephibosheth, he had promised to the slanderer the produce of the whole of the inheritance. The king now acknowledged the unworthy deception which Ziba had practiced at that time upon him; yet the importance of that day of festal joy, as well as the shame which he felt at the mistake he had then fallen into, moved him to exercise grace rather than justice. Instead of bringing the liar to punishment, he reinstated him in his former condition, and confirmed anew his promise of the half of the produce of the inheritance named. Mephibosheth replied to the decision of the king: "Let Ziba take all, forasmuch as my lord the king is come again in peace unto his own house." A noble trait this, which could only strengthen the king in the conviction of the innocence of Mephibosheth, and which perfectly justified the mildness which he had shown toward him!

At last appeared also a man whom we are able to salute with more unmingled joy. It is Barzillai, the old husbandman from Rogelim, "a very aged man, even fourscore years old," who, in company with others of his countrymen, had so joyfully surprised the king by bringing all manner of provisions to him while he lay in the camp at Mahanaim. At that time, when thousands amid the tumult of the rebellion had broken loose from all restraint, Barzillai knew how to preserve sobriety. In his fidelity to the king he had not for a moment wavered.

With a sound, clear perception, he had very soon discovered that the whole movement in favor of Absalom had only impiety as its foundation, the most wicked falsehoods as its armor, and nothing less than the overturn of all the divinely instituted ordinances as its object. Besides, he saw in David not a ruler who had of his own will mounted the throne, but his "king by the grace of God"; and in the rebellion against him he saw a criminal and traitorous opposition to the Almighty Himself. When he now heard of the complete extinction of the revolt, his soul praised the Lord of hosts; for this triumph denoted to him the preservation not only of domestic morality, discipline, and order, but, above all, of the honor of the name of Jehovah. How, therefore, could he fail to be among the foremost heartily and respectfully to bid Godspeed to the king, again so gloriously exalted by the strong arm of the Lord?

After a lengthened, but, in spite of his years, expeditious march, he came forward to the excited multitude in attendance on the king, at the very moment when he was in the act of entering into the boat which was to convey him across the Jordan. Scarcely had David perceived his faithful old friend amid the crowd, when his countenance was brightened by a beam of exalted joy. There could be no more valued or more welcome meeting than with this plain, honest countryman. Without delay he steps up to the "very excellent man," as the history describes him, and most heartily reaches forth to him his right hand—the old man probably saluting him with these words,

"The God of our fathers yet lives, my lord king!" "Come thou over
with me," said David, "and I will feed thee with me in Jerusalem."
Yes, he wished Barzillai to live with him in his palace for the future,
and to eat with him at his table. It might almost appear as if the condescension and grace of the king had overstepped the limits of
propriety. But in times such as then were in Israel, as has already been
remarked, the gold of fidelity grew in value in the same degree in
which all that is called rank, station, and title begins to fade away as
insignificant. Such times are like the "furnace of the goldsmith." In
them the thoughts of many men are made manifest. The husk perishes, the kernel comes to view, and the frock of the well-approved
workman surpasses in brightness the ermine of the man of rank who
has swayed to the wrong side.

How did Barzillai receive the generous invitation of his royal
master? Not otherwise than might have been expected from the
plain, modest, judicious man. The kindness of the king deeply
moved him; but what he proposed made him smile with surprise.
"How long," said he, "have I to live, that I should go up with the
king unto Jerusalem? I am this day fourscore years old. How can I
discern between good and evil" (i.e., what is suitable in the high
circles): "and how," he continues, harmlessly jesting, "can I taste
what I eat or what I drink?" (the skillfully-prepared dishes of the
royal table are not for me, who have my whole satisfaction in my
country, homely fare). "And how can I hear," he says further, "the
voice of the singing-men and the singing-women?" I have no skill
of high and fine art. The birds sing to me among the trees that surround my home. "Wherefore then should thy servant be yet a
burden unto my lord the king? Thy servant will go a little way over
Jordan with the king. Why should the king recompense it me with
such a reward?" I did nothing more than what it was my duty to do.
"Let thy servant, I pray thee, turn back again, that I may die in
mine own city, and be buried by the grave of my father and of my
mother."

Can anything more lovely be heard than these words spoken in
simplicity, and, at the same time, from a sound intelligence? What a
glad and peaceful spirit do they breathe forth, and how this
Barzillai puts to shame so many old men of our day, who, the more
the years perform their dismantling work on them, are so much the
more zealously bent on concealing the decay of their strength behind

the glittering surroundings of vain dignities, titles, and high alliances! They know nothing of the life in God, with a view to which the apostle says, "Though our outward man perish, yet the inward man is renewed day by day." With the natural life their all expires, and they are bankrupt as soon as, for them, "the flesh which is born of flesh" leaves.

Barzillai had his treasure in heaven, the grace of his God was his jewel, and so he counted his days without vexation, yea, with the calm, hopeful joy that he would soon see the face of Him whom he loved, and in whom he firmly trusted. This prospect had a renovating influence over him, and enabled him to look down into his grave as to his bed of rest. He had by faith overcome the world, and he stood above it. Not as if from a mistaken conception of the earnestness of life, he had peevishly despised whatever the earth could yield of pure and hallowed joy—rather with thankfulness he received it; but it was also a small thing for him to be without it. He was, we repeat, what we have already said regarding him, no rude, narrow-hearted rigorist. He did not, in considering the king's proposal, think that, as one of the "quiet in the land," he must anxiously keep himself far away from all the necessary pomp that belongs to a royal court. Indeed he was, like few of his Old Testament fellow-believers, too evangelically free, and too sound in his faith, to be capable of so narrow a judgment.

He knew that nothing was impure which could be enjoyed with childlike, pure thankfulness to God, and also that many things which might be in and of themselves vain and frivolous, could not be lacking to enhance the necessary splendor of a princely throne. But he had no desire after such things. The glory which he found in the throne of the King of all kings eclipsed for him the splendor of all earthly glory. O how the sight of such a man, with his whole heart delivered from the dominion of earth, and raised to the enjoyment of freedom in God, cheers the heart! Through the power of his faith he himself is a king; the world, death, and the grave lie vanquished at his feet; a serenity which defies all storms irradiates his brow like a diadem; an incomparably glorious inheritance awaits him in heaven; and as he has no one here below whom he may envy, so he has no one and nothing to fear, seeing "all things are his," because he himself "is Christ's, and Christ is God's."

David knew how to honor Barzillai. "Thou doest well," he might think, "that thou wishest to remain on thine own farm. A king's palace is no Eden: ah, it is frequently the splendid grave of peace and joy, rather than their temple!" The king gave him to understand how very willing he would be to render him any favor. Then the old man, referring to his son, who stood behind him, said, "Behold thy servant Chimham; let him go over with my lord the king; and do to him what shall seem good unto thee." Thus he consecrated his son to the service of the fatherland, in whatever situation it might seem good to the king to place him. The king answered: "Chimham shall go over with me, and I will do to him that which shall seem good unto me; and whatsoever thou shalt require of me, that will I do for thee." Thus he spoke; and we shall hear how the king kept his word. In the sight of all the people he embraced the old man, and kissed him, and blessed him on departing; and then went forward on his way. Barzillai, with his heart deeply moved, and full of prayers and intercessions for his kind and condescending lord, returned to his own dwelling at Rogelim, where probably he soon afterward fell asleep in peace with God. His meeting with the king at the passage of the Jordan, remained with him to the end of his days one of the most precious memories of his life; as David himself also reckoned it among the most refreshing scenes in his triumphal return to the holy city.

After David had again mounted his throne, in the name of God, amid the joyful shouts of a loyal people, he consecrated his whole energies forthwith to the restoration of the affairs of the kingdom, which in many respects were disorganized; and at the same time set about the most extensive preparations for the building of the temple. The people celebrated the restoration of their king to his throne in Psalm 21, composed by himself, and with most joyful feelings sang it in fellowship with their exalted ruler, who always in spirit identified himself with his people. "The king shall joy in Thy strength, O Lord; and in Thy salvation how greatly shall he rejoice! Thou hast given him his heart's desire, and hast not withholden the request of his lips. For Thou preventest him with the blessings of goodness: Thou settest a crown of pure gold on his head. He asked life" (i.e., the continuance and establishment of his house), "and Thou gavest it him, even length of days forever and ever" (Thou didst promise that the sovereignty of his seed would endure forever, namely in the Messiah[2]).

---

2. 2 Samuel 7:13.

"His glory is great in Thy salvation: honor and majesty hast Thou laid upon him. For Thou hast made him most blessed forever; Thou hast made him exceeding glad with Thy countenance. For the king trusteth in the Lord, and through the mercy of the Most High he shall not be moved. Thine hand" (O David) "shall find out all thine enemies; thy right hand shall find out those that hate thee. Thou shalt make them as a fiery oven" (for shame) "in the time of thine anger; the Lord shall swallow them up in His wrath, and the fire shall devour them. Their fruit" (of the godless) "shalt thou destroy from the earth, and their seed from among the children of men. For they intended evil against thee; they imagined a mischievous device, which they are not able to perform; therefore shalt thou make them turn their back" (i.e., smite them so that, fleeing from thee, they only show their back), "when thou shalt make ready thine arrows" (stopping for them the way) "upon thy strings against the face of them. Be Thou exalted, Lord, in Thine own strength; so will we sing and praise Thy power!"

29

New Difficulties

The second Psalm is full of the majesty of regal power. It is a song of triumph, breathing faith and hope, and the joyful certainty of victory. The royal psalmist sang it in the midst of the wildly tossing billows of revolution which foamed around his throne, but which in truth rose up against the Lord in heaven, whose prerogatives on earth the king of Israel had to maintain, and whose ordinances he had to preserve and guard. Conscious that he was himself the personal shadow and type of the great future King of glory, who was promised to his house, he saw, with eyes enlightened by the Spirit, in the rebellion that raged against him, a dim reflection of that which would at one time rage against the eternally Exalted One. The revolt against the Son of God rose up in vision before his soul as the culmination of the sins of the world—black as night, but also at the same time brightened by the gleams of the fire of God's anger. Thus, under the inward influence of the Holy Spirit, and according to His purpose, the song formed itself, before David was aware, into a Messianic psalm, which is frequently recognized as such by the apostolic authorities.

"Why do the heathen rage," the sacred poet begins, "and the people imagine a vain thing? The kings of the earth set themselves, and the rulers take counsel together, against the Lord, and against His anointed, saying, Let us break their bands asunder, and cast away their cords from us. He that sitteth in the heavens" (as in an inaccessible, secure fortress) "shall laugh: the Lord shall have them in derision. Then shall He speak unto them in His wrath, and vex them in His sore displeasure." And what is it which the Lord says? This: "Yet have I set my King upon my holy hill of Zion" (the essential antitype of the place where God revealed Himself in Israel, and from which goes forth the law and from which the lines of the kingdom of heaven will go forth through all lands[1]). Hereupon He who has been appointed by God heavenly King appears announcing the law of His kingdom, and says, "I will declare the decree" (the unalterable constitution of my kingdom): "The Lord hath said unto me, Thou art my Son; this day" (i.e., the eternal today) "have I begotten Thee. Ask of me, and I shall give Thee the heathen for Thine inheritance, and the uttermost parts of the earth for Thy possession."

David knew that the Lord could never have promised this to a mere human ruler. "Thou shalt break them" (in so far as they obstinately refuse to obey Thee) "with a rod of iron; Thou shalt dash them in pieces like a potter's vessel." These words remind us of what the Judge of the living and the dead will one day say to those on His left hand, "Depart from me, ye cursed, into everlasting fire, prepared for the devil and his angels." The psalmist concludes his song with the impressive warning, "Be wise now therefore, O ye kings; be instructed, ye judges of the earth. Serve the Lord with fear, and rejoice with trembling. Kiss the Son, lest He be angry, and ye perish from the way, when His wrath is kindled but a little. Blessed are all they that put their trust Him." These concluding words show beyond a doubt who it is that is to be understood by the "Son." He is more than a child of man; for to "make flesh our arm"[2] (i.e., to place our confidence in man) is in God's word laid under a curse. Confidence in the Lord and in His grace, through the great Anointed One who was promised, was David's strength and might. New difficulties await the king; but his faith remains unmoved.

2 Samuel 19:41

> And, behold, all the men of Israel came to the king, and said unto the king, Why have our brethren the men of Judah stolen thee away, and have brought the king, and his household, and all David's men with him, over Jordan?

---

1. Psalm 19:4.
2. Jeremiah 17:5.

2 Samuel 20:1

> And there happened to be there a man of Belial, whose name was
> Sheba: and he blew a trumpet, and said, We have no part in David,
> neither have we inheritance in the son of Jesse: every man to his tents,
> O Israel.

2 Samuel 21:1, 18

> Then there was a famine in the days of David three years, year after
> year; and David inquired of the Lord. And it came to pass after this,
> that there was again a battle with the Philistines.

"I have chosen thee in the furnace of affliction!" In whom have
these words of God, spoken by the mouth of Isaiah, viewed as a
promise, been more fully verified than in the son of Jesse? Today we
shall again see the purifying fires blaze up around him (1) in an *insurrection*; (2) in a *famine*; and (3) finally, in another *war* against the old
enemy of Israel—the Philistines.

1. After the unhappy civil war had terminated, and David had
again recovered all his former power, a new most lamentable
event arose. Among the numerous embassies which came to
Jerusalem, were "all the men of Israel," i.e., the representatives of the
ten tribes (of all the tribes except Judah and Benjamin), which for
the most part had followed the standard of Absalom. What brought
them? Did they come to seek for pardon from David? No. They
rather assumed the mien of innocent men, and complained that they
had not been duly informed of the intended bringing back of their
victorious king to the holy city; otherwise their place in the procession would not have been empty; indeed, as the more worthy, they
would have taken the precedence on the occasion. "Why have our
brethren," said they to the king, "the men of Judah, stolen thee away,
and have brought the king and his household and all David's men
with him, over Jordan?"

The men of Judah, instead of the king, took up the word, and
answered the hypocrites: "Because the king is near of kin to us:
wherefore then be ye angry for this matter? have we eaten," they continued, "at all of the king's cost? or hath he given us any gift?" The
men of Israel replied: "*We* have ten parts in the king." They meant
by this that they consisted of ten tribes, and constituted the
greater part of the kingdom; and that the rebellion had not broken

out among them, but in Judah. "Why then," they further said, "did ye despise us? was not our word the first" (i.e., did we not come to you with the proposal) "to fetch back the king?"

They had certainly issued such a proposal, when, as fugitives, they hastened back to their own districts; but only from interested motives, and in hypocrisy, from fear of David's vengeance, and by no means in genuine repentance. They were reproached with this by the men of Judah, of whom the history says, "The words of the men of Judah were fiercer than the words of the men of Israel." Besides this, the men of Judah gave them to understand that even yet they stood greatly in doubt of the genuineness of their loyalty, and that they could entertain no other opinion of those who merely concealed a concern for their own safety under the mask of submission and fidelity. And such they indeed for the most part were.

The proud, haughty conduct of the men of Judah, which was, as it seems, silently allowed by David, could scarcely fail to irritate the men of Israel. Among them was a reprobate man named Sheba, the son of Bichri, of the tribe of Saul. He had been one of the ringleaders of the former bands of rebels. In him the old fire of rebellion suddenly kindled up again out of its ashes. In an angry mood he departed from Jerusalem with his companions, and had scarcely crossed the borders of Judah when he blew a trumpet, and cried out, "We have no part in David, neither have we inheritance in the son of Jesse: every man to his tents, O Israel" (i.e., to arms!). His words kindled a fire here and there. With hatred against the king, Sheba's partisans were also animated by jealousy and by a spirit of revenge against the proud Judah. Within a short time a considerable band of malcontents, and of the enemies of all divine ordinances, had assembled under the banner of rebellion which was again raised.

Before tidings of this had reached the king—who now only concerned himself with peaceful occupations, and, among other things, with building for the women whom, at his flight from Jerusalem, he had left in charge of his house, a separate dwelling, where, in retirement, they were shut up until the day of their death, living in widowhood—the waves of revolt had risen high in the land. Having been informed of it, David immediately, overlooking Joab, directed Amasa, in whom, after the death of Absalom, he could repose more confidence, saying, "Assemble me the men of Judah within three days, and be thou here present." He then intend-

ed formally to entrust to Amasa the chief command over the whole
army.

Amasa obeyed, but not so expeditiously as was commanded him.
David feared that his delay did not betoken good. He then said to
Abishai, the courageous hero, Joab's brother: "Now shall Sheba the
son of Bichri do us more harm than did Absalom: take thou thy lord's
servants, and pursue after him, lest he get him fenced cities, and
escape." Abishai obeyed, and departed with his band of men. He was
soon after joined by his brother Joab, with his portion of the army,
and the "Gibborim" (i.e., "the mighty men"), a chosen troop
belonging to the royal life-guards. When they had come to the great
"stone" (i.e., the rock at Gibeon), Amasa came to meet them there
with the people whom he had gathered around him.

When Joab saw the man whom he had pursued in the forest of
Ephraim as one of the confederates in Absalom's company, and who
now, as he soon suspected, would supplant him, whose services for
David and the kingdom were so great, his ambition and his jealousy
created within him a thirst for revenge which could only be
quenched by the blood of the hated rival. With dissembled friendship, and with the salutation, "Peace be to thee, my brother!" (they
were the sons of sisters) he stepped forward to meet him. At that
moment the sword which hung at his girdle, outside his armor-coat,
unexpectedly fell from its sheath. As it seems, he regarded this as a
sign that now the moment for the accomplishment of his dark purpose of murder had come. After he had quickly snatched up again
with his left hand the weapon that had fallen, he seized Amasa by
the beard with the right hand, as if he would kiss him, and in the
same instant plunged the murderous blade into his body, so that the
bowels of the unhappy man fell out upon the ground; and forthwith
he died. Consternation seized the bystanders. But Joab and his brother Abishai cried out to the army, "Forward, after Sheba and his bands
of rebels!"

Joab directed one of his armor-bearers to remain standing beside
the body of Amasa, and to cry to the men of Judah whom he had
gathered together, "He that favoreth Joab, and he that is for
David, let him go after Joab!" But when the man saw that notwithstanding this many when they came within sight of the corpse stood
still in amazement, fear came upon him lest indignation at Joab's
deed should rise up to a revolt against the murderer himself.

Therefore he took the dead body and removed it out of the highway into the field, where he covered it with a piece of cloth, to hide it from the view of the soldiers as they passed. The whole army now marched forward without further interruption, under the supreme command of Joab (assumed by him, however, contrary to the king's will), whose iron heroism could not be broken or even bent by the guilt of three murders resting on his conscience.

But what must have been the thoughts of the king when he heard of the fearful occurrence at the rock of Gibeon! Heavier than the loss of the brave captain, Amasa, was the thought resting on his heart, that he himself, although undesignedly, must bear the guilt of this bloody deed. In again admitting Amasa, the leader in the rebellion, into his favor, and in at last promoting him to high office in his army, his forbearance had gone beyond all due bounds. But Amasa's repentance, the genuineness of which he did not doubt, had moved him, and made him inclined to a reconciliation. Besides, he hoped that the elevation the man to the place of the rude and imperious Joab, whose character also was stained by many crimes, would not only meet a wish of his army, but would also essentially promote the reconciliation of those in Israel who were unfriendly toward his government.

In perfect simplicity he had given scope to the good intention of his heart; but the necessary wisdom of the serpent he had at the same time disowned, and particularly he had neglected to wait for an intimation from the Almighty of His resolution. It only now remained for him to bend himself, because of this error, in lowly humiliation before the Lord, who kept him at every step under strict discipline, and did not allow him to pass from the straight path of the law uncensored, but who also, to our comfort, always showed that He was ready to receive again the penitent, who never lost confidence in His mercy, and to renew to him the assurance of His grace and favor.

Sheba's rebellion was, by God's help, soon suppressed. The rebels, pressed by the valiant Joab, fled, without encountering his troops, back to the extreme northern borders of the land. Here they threw themselves into Abel, a town lying not far from the sources of the Jordan, on the borders of the Syrian province of Maachah, strongly fortified, and famous throughout the whole land because of the wisdom of its inhabitants. The site of this town is still indicated by the Druse village called Abil or Ibil. The king's army, pursuing after them, suspected that the city sided with Sheba, and accordingly prepared to storm it. Soon trenches were dug, ramparts were thrown up, and the scaling-ladders were placed. But suddenly a female voice was heard sounding from the top of the wall, crying out, "Hear, hear; say, I pray you, unto Joab, Come near hither, that I may speak with thee."

It was the voice of one of the wise women of the city. When the chief captain accordingly came near to the wall, the woman said to him, "Hear the words of thine handmaid! They were wont to speak in old time, saying, They shall surely ask counsel at Abel; and so they ended the matter. I, Abel, am one of the peaceable and faithful cities in Israel: and seekest thou to demolish and lay waste a city which is a mother" (one of the chief cities) "in Israel? Wherefore wilt thou swallow up the inheritance in Israel?" Joab answered that he by no means intended to destroy the city, if they would only deliver up Sheba, the man of Mount Ephraim, who had lifted up his hand against David his king. The woman replied, "It shall be so done; behold, his head shall be thrown to thee over the wall." Hereupon she hastened to make known to the inhabitants of the city the condition on which alone their town could be saved; and after a short time she returned with the head of Sheba, and threw it over the city wall into the camp of the Israelites. The rebels then, deprived of their leader, laid down their arms, and unconditionally gave themselves up.

Joab now gave command to his army to return, and in his own person brought to the king the tidings of the victory. The glory of the victory belonged, it is true, only to Him of whom Moses sang, "The Lord is a man of war"; but Joab was the instrument in Jehovah's hands in gaining it. That he from whom he had withdrawn his favor should bear the palm, had in it for David something fitted to make him deeply ashamed. He had to reckon it among the chastisements which he must recognize with humiliation as well deserved.

2. The sacred history now makes mention of a three years' famine which came upon Israel. Many interpreters of Scripture believe that the narrative refers to what had already occurred in the first years of David's reign. This is possible; but the reasons which are presented for this opinion are by no means such as to constrain us to adopt it.

David recognized in the long-continued famine a divine chastisement, and therefore he frequently sought the face of the Lord. At last a revelation was made to him, and it contained a ban, i.e., a sentence of unatoned guilt which was still resting upon Israel. "It is for Saul," said the Lord, "and for his bloody house, because he slew the Gibeonites." The history of that slaughter is as follows: While Joshua was yet engaged in the conquest of Canaan, there came one day to his camp at Gilgal a little band of strange looking people. They appeared in worn-out clothes, covered with dust, and with "old shoes, worn and clouted, upon their feet." The bread in their sacks was hard and moldy, and their wine-bottles were "old and rent, and covered up." To Joshua's question, as to who they were and whence they came, they replied that they came from a far distant land, and added: "We are come because of the name of the Lord thy God: for we have heard the fame of Him, and all that He did in Egypt, and all that He did to the two kings of the Amorites, that were beyond Jordan. Wherefore our elders, and all the inhabitants of our country, spake to us, saying, Take victuals with you for the journey, and go to meet them, and say unto them, We are your servants: therefore now make ye a league with us."

These words went to the heart of Joshua and of all that were with him. They entered into a league with the strangers, and sware unto them, that because they acknowledged Jehovah, they would be permitted to dwell among the Israelites. But three days thereafter, when they arrived at their cities, Gibeon, Chephirah, Beeroth, and Kirjath-jearim, it became apparent that their statement, at least so far as concerned the starting-point of their journey, was altogether a deception. They were the inhabitants of the above-named heathen cities of the Canaanites, and had been moved, by the terror which the destruction of the neighboring towns of Jericho and Ai had brought upon them, to their daring adventure.

The congregation of Israel were irritated by the trick which had thus been played upon them. Their princes, however, soothed them, and said, "We have sworn unto them by the Lord God of Israel: now therefore we may not touch them; but let them be hewers of wood and drawers of water unto all the congregation." The people agreed to this, and Joshua made known the decision to the Gibeonites in these words: "Wherefore have ye beguiled us, saying, We are very far from you; when ye dwell among us? Now therefore there shall none of you be freed from being bondsmen, and hewers of wood and drawers of water for the house of my God." They answered, "Because it was certainly told thy servants, how that the

Lord thy God commanded His servant Moses to give you all the
land, and to destroy all the inhabitants of the land from before you,
therefore we were sore afraid of our lives because of you, and have
done this thing. And now, behold, we are in thine hand: as it
seemeth good and right unto thee to do unto us, do." And it was
done to them as Joshua had said, and they were content. Living
faith in the God of Israel had certainly put forth some influence
amongst them, as was afterward in the most joyful manner made
manifest.

Four hundred years after this, when Saul had come to the throne
in Israel, the Gibeonites were enrolled among the "children of
Abraham, according to the spirit." A pious and peaceful race, they
lived in Israel as among their own people, and performed in a quiet and
unassuming manner their humble services for the sanctuary. But while
Saul, after his own departure from God, hated all the God-fearing in the
land, he was specially disaffected—we do not hear on what grounds—
toward the Gibeonites. For a long time he provoked and molested
them in all manner of ways. At last he resolved, under the mask of a
holy zeal for the honor of Israel—whom it did not become to live in
fellowship with strangers—altogether to eliminate that guiltless
people. Under the approbation, and with the help of almost all his
royal house, he inflicted upon them a fearful slaughter, such as Nero
did at a later period upon the Christians at Rome—a deed of cruelty
which long waited for public expiation, since it was forgotten neither
in Israel nor among the neighboring heathen nations; and to pass it
by would have cast a shadow on the righteousness of God as well as
on the holiness and inviolability of His law.

Now, when the famine had broken out over the land, which
brought a new burden of care on David, who as king must answer for
all, he was informed, in answer to his persevering prayer, that the
slaughter referred to was the chief cause of the heavy judgment that
had fallen upon the people. He therefore gave directions that all that
remained of the Gibeonites after the massacre of that people by Saul,
who, as it seems, had put them to death in a wanton manner, should
be brought to him at Jerusalem; and he asked them what, according
to their judgment, should be done to atone for the violation of the
treaty which had been made with them, in order that they might be
able "to bless the inheritance of the Lord." That David consulted
them first, manifestly betrayed a feeling of uncertainty about his own

resolutions, and pointed to an inner conflict which his sense of justice had to maintain with the natural gentleness of his heart.

The Gibeonites, well acquainted with the law, answered the king, with distinct reference to the divine ordinance recorded in the book of Numbers: "Ye shall take no satisfaction for the life of a murderer, which is guilty of death; but he shall be surely put to death."[3] David asked, "What shall I, as the guardian of the laws of Israel, do for you?" They replied, "The man" (Saul) "that consumed us, and that devised against us, that we should be destroyed from remaining in any of the coasts of Israel, let seven of his sons" (not the whole of his race that remained) "be delivered unto us, and we will hang them up unto the Lord in Gibeah of Saul, whom the Lord did choose." Gibeah was not only the birthplace of Saul, but also the place where the bloody counsel against the Gibeonites had been carried out.

David consented, and delivered the seven who were demanded into their hands. Mephibosheth as may be supposed, was not one of the number delivered up. There were two sons of Saul by Rizpah, who afterward became the wife of Abner, and five equally degenerate sons of a daughter of Saul, Michal-Merab (so called to distinguish her from Michal, who is known to us as the wife of David). These the Gibeonites put to death as they had said. That it might at the same time be evident to all the world what was the guilt for which they were put to death, they executed the sentence against them with their own hands, and hung them up openly before the face of the sun, as a memorial for a terrible warning to all of the inviolability of the ordinances of Jehovah.

Our feelings, influenced by the gospel, recoil from this proceeding. The implacableness of the Gibeonites astonishes us; and also the compliance of the king appears to us to be in violent contrast to his whole disposition, as well as to the state of mind in which he was at the time. But let it always be remembered that it was the economy of the law under which those things were done, and with the character of which they harmonized; and that the care of God, in His educating of the human race, aimed above all things at this—that He should be recognized and feared as the Holy One and the Just. To this divine purpose David must bend himself and make full account of it, whatever inner conflict it may cost him. The great guilt of the house of Saul—perjury and murder at the same time—demanded blood,

3. Numbers 35:31.

according to the inviolable law of God's kingdom. Already, indeed, that house, laden with sins, had been smitten by many judgments, but yet by none which discovered itself at the first glance to every one among the people as a requital for that most culpable of all their crimes, the murder of the innocent Gibeonites.

This special chastisement must not be omitted. For the prevention of doubtful interpretations in Israel, and for the heightening of esteem for every iota of the divine law, it must follow all that went before; and it truly did follow. The majesty and inexorable rigor of the law, as it was in Israel divinely manifested, was scarcely ever more vividly and in a more alarming manner brought to view than on this occasion. But He who dwells in heaven, and who "will not be mocked," approved of it, and impressed His seal on the sentence of death carried out by the Gibeonites, by opening again soon thereafter the floodgates of the clouds over the famishing land, and putting an end to the general distress that prevailed in Israel.

One may conceive what David must have suffered in his soul on account of that judicial act. That terrible execution ran directly counter to his whole disposition. But to him, who more than once had exercised unseasonable clemency instead of righteousness, it could not but be for his advantage, to see himself confronted by so imposing a display of the righteousness of God. Yet when he heard of the care with which Rizpah had covered with sackcloth the bodies of her five sons, and not less those of the two others who were executed along with them, that they might be protected against the assaults of the birds of heaven and the beasts of the field, the incident was to him very welcome, in so far at least as therein his more tender human feelings found satisfaction.

He openly showed his high gratification with the display of touching maternal faithfulness on the part of Rizpah, and then gave commandment that the bones of Saul, who had been his principal enemy, and those also of his beloved Jonathan, which the men of Jabesh had taken away and buried, should be brought from the places where they were deposited, and buried, along with those seven who were hanged, in the sepulcher he prepared for them in the family grave of Kish their ancestor, at Zela, in the land of Benjamin. Besides, it is worthy of remark that, after that judicial act at Gibeah, there is not again found any express mention made of the Gibeonites in the book of God, the sacred Scriptures; from which it may be concluded that, while in letter and form the demand they made upon David was righteous, yet in its motive and spirit it was not so, nor well-pleasing to God.

3. Another unexpected incursion of the Philistines gave occasion to the king for a new exercise of faith. They had recovered somewhat from the apparently entire overthrow which had come upon them as the result of the last war, and believed that they could now make war against the king of Israel; and all the more confidently, because that at present they were able to bring into the field, in the stead of the Goliath who was formerly slain, several giants, in war equal to Goliath. David, trusting to his God, went out in person with his army to meet them. They soon began battle. The king found himself in the midst of the tumult; and when one of the giants, Ishbi-benob, being girded with a new sword, ran straightway forward, and had already poised his spear, which was almost 300 shekels of brass in weight, wherewith to pierce him through, Abishai the son of Zeruiah sprang forward, defended his royal master, and smote the Philistine, and killed him. David's faithful men now entreated him that he would keep himself at a greater distance from the dangers of the battle, "that thou quench not," said they, "the light of Israel."

The burden of years began now to press heavily upon the king. He listened to the counsel of his heroes, though he did violence thereby to his own feelings. After the victory had been gained, he returned to Jerusalem, and devoted himself, with unwearied zeal, only to those duties of his government that were of a peaceful character.

The war with the Philistines soon broke out anew. Even after their champion, the giant Saph, in whom the enemy had now placed their hope, had been slain by one of David's valiant men—an event which was followed by the dispersion of the Philistines—they did not lay down their arms, but soon after were again gathered in glittering array on the borders of Israel. This time it was Lahmi of Gath on whom their hopes rested. His surname was Goliath. He was a near relation of that Goliath whom David slew, and, like him, a giant, a man of great stature, and was armed with a spear like a weaver's beam.

He came forth, and boastfully challenged the strongest in the king's army to encounter him in single combat; but, under the well-aimed strokes of Elhanan's sword, who was a dexterous warrior, he fell to the ground covered with wounds. A like fate befell the fourth of the race of the giants, Rapha, whom the Philistines had kept till now as their last hope. This man had on each hand six fingers, and on each foot six toes. With boastful words, and heaping scorn upon Israel, he marched in front of the army of his countrymen. He was slain by Jonathan the son of Shimeah, the brother of David. The hosts of the enemy now became altogether discouraged, and there was a universal flight. For a long time after, the Philistines did not try to wage war again with the invincible might of Israel.

Thus David now again sat in peace upon his throne. Unmolested by enemies from without, he carried forward uninterruptedly his work of building up the state and Israel's worship. All his adversaries were completely subdued, and as tributaries lay at his feet, and therefore he now tuned his harp again, after it had long been silent, to animated songs of thanks and praise, such as Psalm 18, which he assigned to the "Chief Musician," and thus appointed for use in the public worship of God. In a somewhat changed form, this psalm is met with once more interwoven with the history, only without its ecclesiastical destination.[4] At all events, the changes with which it there appears were made by David's own hand, and are of the character of brief supplementary and explanatory remarks.

The heart of the singer first gives vent to itself in the ardent effusion: "I will love Thee, O Lord my strength. The Lord is my rock, and my fortress, and my deliverer; my God, my strength, in whom I will trust; my buckler, and the horn of my salvation, and my high tower." That which above all things hovers before his soul is the unbounded and undeserved grace with which the Lord stood by him at all times, ready for his help. In view of the past, the present, and the future, he says, "I will call upon the Lord, who is worthy to be praised: so shall I be saved from mine enemies." After these introductory words, he directs his look first to those distresses amid which, before he mounted the throne, particularly during the persecution he had suffered at the hands of Saul, he had experienced so richly the wonderful help of God. He expressively describes the difficulties which then beset him as "the sorrows of death and of hell" which surrounded him, and as "the floods of ungodly men" that raged around him, and made him afraid. But in his anguish he had cried unto the Lord, who had in the most evident manner heard his voice from His holy temple.

---

4. 2 Samuel 22.

An interpreter of this psalm here excellently and truly remarks: "David must first learn, in large letters, what one may possess in God the Lord in times of trouble, in order that the smaller letters may become legible by him, as they are exhibited to him in more hidden deliverances, helps, and reliefs." The psalmist depicts in vivid colors the wrath of the Almighty and the weight of His punishments against evil-doers on earth, who will not that He should reign over them; and he praises the strength of God with which He delivered him, as once He did Moses, from great waters, and set him always free from his powerful enemies and haters. But why does the Lord perform so great things for him? "He delighted in me," answers the singer; and speaks thus without vain self-boasting of his righteousness. His sin and his weakness he calls to mind but little. In perfect truth and rectitude, however, he may and he must confess, to the praise of divine grace which was with him, "I have kept the ways of the Lord, and have not wickedly departed from my God."

His innermost and deepest longings and strivings and aims were always directed to praise his Lord with every breath, and to serve Him; and it well becomes him to confess, "All His judgments were before me, and I did not put away His statutes from me. I was" (according to my innermost thoughts and endeavors) "also upright before Him, and I kept myself from mine iniquity" (i.e., from that which dwells within me, for I am not a holy creature). "Therefore hath the Lord recompensed me according to my righteousness, according to the cleanness of my hands in His eyesight" (who sees things that are concealed, so that He judges differently from the world). "With the merciful Thou wilt show Thyself merciful; with an upright man Thou wilt show Thyself upright; with the pure Thou wilt show Thyself pure; and with the froward Thou wilt show Thyself froward." David wishes by these words to bring into the remembrance of the congregation to which this psalm is dedicated, to be sung by them, the fact that God deals with men as they deal with Him, and that He will only be kind to those who are, from the bottom of their souls, and with the purest resignation, devoted and submissive to Him.

It is not in the remotest degree self-satisfaction which reveals itself in these words. David knew very well how frequently God the Lord had in his experience shown Himself "froward" to him when he was "froward." The psalmist aimed only at quickening anew in the minds of the people the general truth, that the Lord will only show friendship and grace toward those who, however poor in moral excellence and weak they may be, love Him in sincerity. "Thou wilt save," he cries out, "the afflicted people" (i.e., those who are bowed down) "but wilt bring down high looks." That David, without falling into vain self-exaltation, was justified, in spite of the many false steps of which he knew himself to be guilty, in confidently reckoning himself among the God-fearing, and therefore among such as were well-pleasing to God the Lord, is placed beyond a question by the divine testimony that is borne to him by the mouth of the prophet Ahijah, in these words: "My servant David kept my commandments, and followed me with all his heart, and did that which was right in mine eyes."[5] This testimony is again repeated, but with one express limitation: "David did that which was right in the eyes of the Lord, and turned not aside from anything that He commanded him all the days of his life, save only in the matter of Uriah the Hittite."[6]

In the second part of our psalm (vv. 29–46), the psalmist calls to remembrance the many instances of gracious direction and assistance given to him by God, which blended themselves with the later period of his life, and at the same time also those which stood in prospect for the future in consequence of divine promises. "Thou, Lord," he begins, "wilt light my candle" (or surround me with splendor); "the Lord my God will enlighten my darkness." All his victories and triumphs over hostile nations David attributes to the Lord alone. "By Thee I have run through a troop; and by my God have I leaped over a wall. As for God, His way is perfect: the word of the Lord" (His word of promise) "is tried; He is a buckler to all those that trust in Him."

In the verses next following he continues to praise the strength of the Lord as it was made great in the weakness of His servant, as had been made evident during many a warlike undertaking. One might be confused, on reading the harsh and stern words of the thirty-seventh and thirty-eighth verses: "I have pursued mine enemies, and overtaken them; neither did I turn again till they were consumed. I have wounded them, that they were not able to rise: they are fallen under my feet." But with such utterances we are never to forget that David does not speak here as a private man, but under the impulse of the Holy Spirit, as the theocratic king, who recognizes, in the enemies

---

5. 1 Kings 14:8.
6. 1 Kings 15:5.

who stand up against him, the enemies of God and of His kingdom, whose overthrow and subjugation is to be sought only for the advantage of his kingdom.

In verse 43 he more particularly describes the enemies against whom the Lord had helped him. They were partly domestic, particularly Saul and Sheba. Regarding them he says, "Thou hast delivered me from the strivings of the people" (i.e., from their malevolent enmity). They were partly the neighboring tribes of the Philistines, the Amorites, the Ammonites, etc. These he has in mind when he says, "Thou hast made me the head of the heathen: a people whom I have not known shall serve me." The psalmist concludes his psalm as he had begun it, in the language of joyful praise to the Lord of hosts: "The Lord liveth; and blessed be my Rock; and let the God of my salvation be exalted. It is God that gives me vengeance" (i.e., leaves it to me to avenge the injured honor of His name), "and subdueth the people under me. He delivereth me from mine enemies; yea, Thou liftest me up above those that rise up against me: Thou hast delivered me from the violent man" (Saul, or Absalom, or Sheba). "Therefore will I give thanks unto Thee, O Lord, among the heathen, and sing praises unto Thy name."

He concludes, looking with the eye of an enlightened seer into far-distant future times: "Great deliverance giveth He to His king; and showeth mercy to His anointed, to David, and to His seed forevermore." Here again plainly hovers before the eye of his memory the great promise which was once graciously given to him by the Lord. It is expressed, as we know, in the words, "When thy days be fulfilled, I will set up thy seed after thee, and I will establish his kingdom. He shall build an house for my name; and I will establish the throne of his kingdom forever."[7] Who was the descendant of the house of David of whom such great things could be said? We know Him. Who could it be but the Messiah who was to come, Jesus Christ, blessed forevermore!

---

7. 2 Samuel 7:12–13.

30

The Numbering of the People

The Apostle Paul, in his Epistles, frequently expresses his wish that believers "may have their senses exercised to discern that which is excellent," or "what is that good and acceptable and perfect will of God." Thus there are supposed to be, even among the regenerated, diverse degrees in the development of the moral consciousness. It greatly needed purification, e.g. in John and in his brother James, at the time that they besought the Lord to cause fire from heaven to descend upon the Samaritan hamlet which had refused Him hospitality. A similar lack we find in Simon Peter, when, in the ardor of his erring love, he drew sword against the enemies of the Lord; we find it in all the apostles, when they forbade the mothers who were bringing their infants to Jesus; and, on another occasion, when they wished the Lord to send away the woman of Canaan who was seeking help from Him. They all, indeed, had good intentions; but, from a lack of enlightenment and of moral tact, they acted in opposition to what was right and well-pleasing to God.

After they had received the baptism of Pentecost, they were no more subject to the reproach of having failed in regard to the good-will of God, with the exception of Peter in a single instance. But in their communities they always found occasion to stir up Christians to the cultivation and improvement of their spiritual perceptions. But if even believing children of the New Testament were in lack of such an admonition, how gently ought we to judge the saints of the Old Testament economy in respect of the moral power of distinguishing things that differ! It may well pain us to see them in so many of their views (e.g. regarding marriage, slavery, and often, also, regarding the duty of truthfulness) fall so far short of "the good and acceptable and perfect will of God." We shall today find reason to complain of a false step taken by David, manifesting in him, though his intention may not have been perhaps evil, a very defective power of forming distinct moral judgments. Yet that stands beyond doubt that the saints of the Old Testament, when they speak and write in the name and under the commission of God, for the Church, were animated and guided by the Spirit of God, and guarded by Him from any blending of their perverse weakness and insufficiency with their preaching and writing.

Here it becomes them to say, with the writer of Psalm 45, "My tongue is the pen of a ready writer." What we read in all the psalms, although they welled up from the individual experience of the singer, had as their foundation a divine impulse. While they thought that they were speaking and writing their own thoughts and words, it was still another who formed and stamped them. This explains what Peter says of the sacred writers, that they had often to study and search into the meaning of their own writings.[1] Besides, in general, the moral delicacy of those saints who lived in the times before Christ, even when we meet them in their everyday life, and they are not speaking and acting as the organs of God, for the most part extorts from us a true surprise, and brings often deep shame upon us, who have far behind us those days to which John referred in the expression, "The Holy Ghost was not yet given."

2 Samuel 24:1

And again the anger of the Lord was kindled against Israel, and He moved David against them to say, Go, number Israel and Judah.

Were the faithfulness of God toward us not more unchangeable than ours is toward Him, what would become of us all? With this humbling acknowledgment, let us draw near to the contemplation of a new controversy between Jehovah and the king of Israel, and inquire (1) concerning the subject of it; (2) its progress; and (3) its issue.

1. After trying times of sorrow and humiliation, David again sits on Mount Zion, "under his vine and fig-tree." How heartily do we

---

1. 1 Peter 1:10.

grant to him this time of rest! May it not be to him again, as it has been before, only a snare! The burden and heat of labor came as a curse into the world; but, by the grace of God, it was changed into a great blessing. Let no one wish to leave off working before God permits it to him. When "amusement" is needed, he who is a "murderer from the beginning" mingles only too willingly among the ministering spirits who are ready to lend a helping hand thereto. Even in the aged, and such as have entered upon a condition of rest from active labor, "idleness," the brooding hen, discovers many concealed nests in which there are evil eggs to be hatched.

Many a one deceives himself by thinking that, when the longed-for days of cessation from toil have come, he will spend his life in studying God's Word, and in devotion and prayer. But most will, contrary to their expectation, experience that the "treasure is in earthen vessels," and that the "flesh is weak," however "willing" the "spirit" may be. Besides, it is seen that, for the most part, the trials and the evils of life for the first time attach for us the rope to the bell which summons to prayer; and these words of the prophet are accomplished: "Lord, in trouble have they visited Thee; they poured out a prayer when Thy chastening was upon them."

That which is here said was not in all respects true of David. He has permitted to himself, only for a moment, some cessation from the business of the government. The most difficult problems of his exalted office were solved with the help of God; and therefore he might well now, for once free from care, lay himself down with pleasure upon the pillow of rest at home, which the old Barzillai had refused to share with him. But the short leisure hour speedily brought him danger. One day, along with other guests, the evil one, of whom we before made mention, crept in upon him. The Second Book of Chronicles names him.[2] It was the same to whom the curse adhered, of waging an unsuccessful war of destruction against those who are defended to the last moment of life by God, who will indeed make for them a way of escape. "Satan stood up against Israel," it is said in the passage referred to, and provoked David to number the people. Our text, on the other hand, begins with the words, "And again the anger of the Lord was kindled against Israel; and He moved David against them, to say" (to Joab), "Go number Israel and Judah." The

---

2. Chapter 22.

apparent contradiction which we here meet need not surprise us, for it can be easily explained.

The two historians look at the same thing from different points of view. It is true that it was of Satan to plan the mischief and to bring thereby new evils upon Israel and its kind. God the Lord, who, according to the Apostle James, never tempts anyone to evil,[3] thought it in harmony with the purposes of His wisdom to grant, to a certain extent, permission to the prince of darkness, and by him to open a way for the judgments which must be executed against the people—who form an organic unity with their prince—on account of the new offenses with which they had stained themselves in the revolts under Absalom and Sheba. Besides, the case is not as if Satan first instilled the sinful desires into men. Rather, he only carries the match to the fire always prepared in the children of Adam. It is the business of the wicked one to make opportunity; and never may one believe himself justified, according to the example of Eve, in laying the guilt upon him. The guilt always remains with ourselves, whenever we allow ourselves to be deceived by Satan. "Every one shall bear his own iniquity," says the word of God.

David transgressed in an affair which might easily present itself before him as one which was divinely approved. A numbering of the people was what he intended. Moses once undertook such a thing, and certainly without sinning therein. From this it is again clear, that though two persons perform the same action, yet the actions may not on that account be the same. The numbering of the people which Moses once undertook was, however, in consequence of an express command from God, which was wanting in the case of David. Moreover, a Church object lay at the foundation of what Moses did, namely, the distributing of the temple-tax; and on this account it was performed by Moses and by the high priest, in conjunction with the heads of the tribes; while David, on the other hand, entrusted it only to the soldiers. Finally, the divine order, presented in the Second Book of Moses, was not considered by David—an order which enjoined (lest there might arise from the numbering a temptation to the people to self-boasting) that every Israelite on the occasion should give, as reminding him of his sins, a piece of money, the price of a sin-offering.[4]

---

3. James 1:13.
4. Exodus 3:12–13.

Then there was room for the suspicion that David would either, with self-satisfaction, see his own greatness in the number of his men who were capable of going forth to war, or, through arbitrary limitation of the freedom and rights of the people, would incite them to renewed rebellion, if he would not even seek, by means of his superior army, which had now once more entered on a career of victory, to enlarge, after the manner of other Oriental potentates, the boundaries of his kingdom. This last he might truly have been able to do, if he had changed the attitude of defense, which he had hitherto maintained, into one of attack. Yes, he might for a moment persuade himself that the elevating of a theocratic state, which was bounded by narrow limits, into an imposing world-state, would only tend to the glorifying of God.

But such thoughts were human, not divine, and testified only a momentary darkening of his consciousness as to his true calling. Even Joab, the stern warrior, who had by no means a superabundance of the fear of God, felt that in this matter his lord entertained a purpose which was not approved of in the sight of God. When the king commanded him, "Go now through all the tribes of Israel, from Dan even to Beersheba, and number ye the people, that I may know the number of the people," the man of war shook his head doubtfully, and answered according to his practical instinct, and his own measure of propriety, "Now the Lord thy God add unto the people, how many soever they be, an hundredfold, and that the eyes of my lord the king may see it: but why doth my lord the king delight in this thing?" His meaning was this: "What thou purposest does not befit a king of Israel."

How greatly must David have felt himself, at a later time, put to shame when he remembered that even Joab had presented before him the more righteous course; and he, the king, had to reproach himself that he had not taken to heart the warning of his captain, who, besides, inquired so little after God! In fact, David despised the admonition. "The king's word," it is said, "prevailed against Joab, and against the captains of the host." Even a man of God like David may be overcome by such an enchantment and fascination. "Let not him that girdeth on his harness boast himself as he that putteth it off." If such a counsel as this was addressed to David by so ungodly a man as Joab, it was nevertheless good and wise, like that which was afterward given by the high priest Caiaphas, when he said, "It is expedient for us that one man should die for the people, and that the whole nation perish not."

A uniform holiness, even in the people of God, is in very few instances, if indeed ever at any time, to be met with on this side of eternity, with the exception of that which is found in the innermost exercises of the soul. In spite of all the processes of sanctification which we pass through, there can scarcely be named a sin which, as a temptation, even though it may be victoriously opposed, may not anew arise within us. No Christian is so well approved as to be able to obtain, from a clear conscience, a right to regard himself as now able to be justified on the ground of his own virtue. The blood of Jesus Christ remains for him continually necessary. If our inner life is sound, it happens to us even according to the word of John the Baptist: "We must decrease; but Christ must increase." Free grace becomes ever the more precious to us, and our consolation and our hope, resting in the cross, become the longer the greater therefore, also, so does the peace which "passeth all understanding" become our full and unlimited inheritance.

2. Joab goes forth, in obedience to the royal command, though not without inward reluctance, in company with the captains of the army, and numbers the people, from Dan, in northern Persia and the rocky coasts of Tyre, to Beersheba, i.e., from the extreme northern to the extreme southern borders of the land. After the lapse of nine months and twenty days, he returned to Jerusalem, appeared before his royal master, and briefly and in a fretful mood said to him, "Know then, now, that thou hast in Israel eight hundred thousand valiant men who draw the sword and in Judah five hundred thousand men." After he had made his report, he bowed himself and retired with an accusing conscience, and in sadness of spirit.

"See then, David, thou hast gained thy purpose. What a power is this that is placed at thy disposal! A population of six millions, the inhabitants of the little tribes of Levi and Benjamin not being reckoned. What great things mayest thou now undertake! Who may dare raise his head so loftily as thou mayest; and who is there that may sit on his throne so free from care and so securely as thou dost?" So many in spirit might perhaps say to him. But what happens? Instead of glorying, the king bends his head, descends in silence from his seat, and withdraws into one of his more remote chambers; and now listen!—"I have sinned greatly in that I have done," he cries out with deep emotion of heart: "and now, I beseech Thee, O Lord, take away the iniquity of Thy servant for I have done very foolishly!"

Wonderful! That very thing from which David promised to himself kingly joy, now brings him only bitter sorrow; and that which ought to have added to his dignity, suddenly humbles him in deepest abasement. But this does not surprise us.

As the sun always breaks through the clouds which encompass it, so the conscience, when once it is awakened and enlightened by the Spirit of God, always comes forth again victoriously out of every eclipse, and frees itself from every entanglement, and asserts anew its authority as a judge. Indeed, in believers it constantly increases in tenderness, and becomes more and more like the apple of the eye, to which the smallest mote gives annoyance; nor can there be any rest obtained till it is removed. The world cannot comprehend how so many things which it thinks unimportant fill the children of God with such deep shame and make them so sad. "What is there so serious," it is perhaps said to them, "in examining thy treasures, or in seeking the favor of this or that influential man, or taking a lottery-ticket? Where is there a divine command which thou hast thereby transgressed?"

And, indeed, those who thus speak are not conscious where such a divine precept is. But they know it well who have transgressed it. Their heart has forsaken the Lord, and distrusted His power and love. They have cherished doubt as to the truth of the divine promises. These are transgressions of which, as such, the children of this world have indeed no apprehension. Therefore it happens that they so frequently accuse the faithful of straining at gnats. They know nothing indeed of the tender relation in which a man loving God stands to his Lord. They know only the mere letters of the ten commandments; while to them that finer law which arises for the souls of believers out of their inward fellowship with the Lord, is something quite unknown. More deeply than under these words, thundered forth from Sinai, "Thou shalt," and "Thou shalt not," the people of the Lord bow down their faces in the dust when they hear the question, "Lovest thou me?" With the "written they also know of an unwritten law, which makes the way" strait and narrow for them, and which often makes them water their couch with their secret tears, even where the written law seems to justify them, because they know themselves to be guilty of a violation of the divine economy not understood by the blind world.

David lay again in the dust, and this time with so much the deeper contrition, the quicker this new fall and transgression followed the gracious manifestations he had but just experienced. "O Lord," he might say within himself, "how could I think thus? How greatly did I misunderstand my place as that of one of Thy vassals, and that of Israel Thy people as Thy possession, which Thou hast separated for Thyself for a holy purpose from all the people of the earth? I was not even far from the folly of wickedly crossing Thy counsel concerning this inheritance which Thou hast chosen for Thyself, and arbitrarily removing the boundaries which Thou in Thy wisdom hast established." May the penitence of the king bring him peace!

The snare of Satan is torn asunder, and the prisoner is again free. With all his faults, into which in unwatchful moments he fell, he yet remains (how frequently already have we had occasion to make this remark!) the "man after God's own heart." In his genuine, sorrowful repentance of his plan of numbering the people, what a sweet, fragrant blossom do we see unfolded before us of his hidden life in God! What a beautiful childlike feature on the countenance of his inner man!

We are here reminded of our Lord's parable of the shepherd and the lost sheep. Does it cause us to wonder that the heavenly Shepherd, momentarily neglecting as it were the rest of the sheep, should hasten after the lost, and, after He has found it, should, with loud cries of joy, carry it carefully back on His shoulders to the flock? Not from the virtues of the children of God, but from their tears and their faults, shine out to us the noblest features of their new life. But if anyone thinks that he may therefore sin, that his soul may in repentance and humiliation produce its fairest flowers, such an one is thereby most undoubtedly to be recognized as a child of Belial, whose "damnation would be just."

To the penitent king his sinful deed was forgiven. But the manifestation of divine grace may not obscure the divine righteousness. After David had spent that night in prayer, at the beginning of which his eyes were opened to his error, the word of the Lord came in a divine revelation, early in the following morning, to Gad the seer, who had succeeded Nathan at the court of David in the office of teacher of the youthful Solomon: "Go and say unto David, Thus saith the Lord, I offer thee three things; choose thee one of them, that I may do it unto thee." We shall immediately hear what the prophet was further commanded to say to the king. In the words "choose thee" God manifested great condescension to David, from which the king drew the comforting conclusion that the Lord would again deal with him as His friend, and would act gently toward him. Yet his faith was put to a severe test.

Gad appeared before the king, and delivered to him the message with which he was entrusted: "Thus saith the Lord, Choose thou. What dost thou wish? Shall seven years of famine come unto thee in thy land? or wilt thou flee three months before thine enemies, while they pursue thee? or that there be three days' pestilence in thy land? Now advise, and see what answer I shall return to Him that sent me." We are astonished. This proceeding on the part of God will appear strange to us, even as altogether human. But let us not forget that it was the kind intention of God to prove Himself, once for all, by His actions in Israel, for all times and for all nations, in an unequivocal, palpable manner, as a living God, as the "Preserver of men," who is not far from every one of us. The comfortless contemplation of a Deity who sits enthroned at an immeasurable distance, high above the stars, in inaccessible, eternally quiescent majesty, unconcerned with the insignificant interests of mortals, would forever give the death-blow to all who at any time would long after fellowship with God, and immeasurably increase the burden of their distresses.

Let us rejoice, therefore, at the unbounded kindness of the Most High toward us poor children of Adam, instead of being offended at it. What would a God be to us, who, sufficient in Himself, stood toward us as a stranger, and far away? Let us, with wonder and praise echo the words of Job, in which, when overpowered by the feeling of his weakness and his misery, he exclaimed, "What is man that thou shouldest magnify him? and that thou shouldest set thine heart upon him? and that thou shouldest visit him every morning, and try him every moment?"

One of the three judgments named by the seer must fall upon the land. They were the same as John represented in the book of Revelation, under the figure of the three riders on the red, black, and pale horses. The twofold guilt of the king and of the people challenged the arm of avenging justice. Forbearance on the part of God would at least have silenced the song of the angels around the throne—"Holy, holy, holy is the Lord of hosts!" How did the king decide? The choice was difficult and painful. Will it be famine?—even a seven years' famine?—the fields burnt up, the brooks without water, despair in every dwelling? David contemplated the terrors of this scourge, under which the land had indeed before groaned and languished, and he started at the thought. Will it be three months' flight before pursuing enemies? The images of the flight before the rebels under Absalom stand vividly before the mind of the king—his way to Kedron, the treachery of unfaithful friends, the heart-piercing griefs he suffered at the hands of godless men, the cursing of the slanderer Shimei! The king shuddered at the remembrance of these things. Will it be a three days' pestilence?—the land a field strewn with corpses?—poison to the breath of the inhabitants?—tears their food—and in every place the wailing of widows and orphans? Oh, horror—enough to soften a stone! And must the king open the floodgates to these horrors? Thoughts in wild confusion follow each other through his mind. Oh, that someone might choose for him! But the prophet Gad stands before him, and awaits his answer.

3. Then the resolution rose up in the soul of David. His consciousness of guilt did not allow him to venture on praying for the turning away of the judgments altogether. If then, one of them shall and must fall upon the people, let it be the last! "And who knows," thought David, "whether the Lord in His grace may not repent also even of this?" He says to the seer: "I am in a great strait: let us fall now into the hand of the Lord, for His mercies are great; and let me not fall into the hand of man." What an honorable testimony this is for God, and what an accusation against man!

David thinks what Jeremiah afterward gave utterance to in his Lamentation: "But though the Lord cause grief yet will He have compassion according to the multitude of His mercies. For He doth not afflict willingly, nor grieve the children of men. To crush under His feet all the prisoners of the earth."[5] David is conscious that the Lord "correcteth in measure" those who are His, and that, although He neither can nor may spare to them the cup of His anger, He never offers it to them without mingling in it an ingredient of concealed elements of grace; while men, even when they are only the instruments in inflicting the righteous judgments of God, easily pass from their position as instruments, and overstep the limits of compassionate moderation marked out to them, and give free scope to the spirit of

---

5. Lamentations 3:32–34.

anger and revenge within their own hearts. Thus the Lord reproved the king of Assyria, whom he had chosen as the rod of His anger against an hypocritical nation, that he had forgotten that he was only an instrument in God's hand, and that his stern and insensible heart was only intent on destroying and extirpating the people.[6]

Enough: David gave himself up unreservedly to the Lord, that He might do with him as He pleased. Thus the plague broke in upon the land as an immediate chastisement from His hand, and swept away of that imposing multitude, in which the king sought delight, not fewer than 70,000 men. But when the angel whom Jehovah employed as His instrument in the infliction of this punishment, and also as a herald of His nearness as a Judge, lifted up his hand over the holy city as if he would also smite it, "then"—so the history announces—"the Lord repented Him of the evil, and said to the angel that destroyed the people, It is enough; stay now thine hand." And what then took place? The king, deeply humbled, remained with the elders in his palace, and prepared himself for the moment when the plague would also smite him personally; when suddenly, by the thrashing-floor of Araunah the Jebusite (one of the surviving ancient inhabitants of Zion), he saw the angel with the drawn sword in his right hand standing before him. At the same instant that he saw this heavenly visitant, he cried aloud, "Lo, I have sinned, and I have done wickedly: but these sheep, what have they done? Let Thine hand, I pray Thee," he continued, "be against me, and against my father's house!" Thus also Moses once offered himself, with true royal spirit, as a sacrifice for Israel.

But here there was need for an altogether different expiatory sacrifice, as a type, a shadow of Him who was to come. The prophet Gad went forward to David, and said, "Go up, rear an altar unto the Lord in the thrashing-floor of Araunah the Jebusite." David did according to the word of the prophet. But when Araunah, who had been formerly the prince of the Jebusites, saw the king coming to him, with his retinue, he bowed his head to the earth, after that he also had been honored by seeing the angel, and said, "Wherefore is my lord the king come to his servant?" David replied, "To buy the thrashing-floor of thee, to build an altar unto the Lord, that the plague may be stayed from the people." Araunah, agitated by the sight of the angel,

---

6. Isaiah 10

answered, "Let my lord the king take and offer up what seemeth good unto him: behold, here be oxen for burnt-sacrifice, and thrashing-instruments and other instruments of the oxen for wood. All these things did Araunah, as a king, give unto the king. And Araunah said unto the king, The Lord thy God accept thee."

David, however, answered, "Nay; but I will surely buy it of thee at a price: neither will I offer burnt-offerings unto the Lord my God of that which doth cost me nothing." "It must be my own," he meant to say, "that symbolically it might signify the giving up of myself in sacrifice." David then bought the thrashing-floor, together with the oxen, and offered up a burnt-sacrifice, which was at the same time a sacrifice of thank-offering unto the Lord, which prophetically pointed forward to the true mediatory sacrifice on the cross; yea, also, as the consequence of the divine decree, it had in it even the atoning efficacy of that sacrifice.

The thrashing-floor of Araunah lay on the heights of the mountain of Moriah, on which was once performed the significant act of the offering up of Isaac; and therefore it appeared to the king as the place pointed out by God on which afterward the holy temple should be built. After he had at that place offered up the burnt-sacrifice, and the Lord had given testimony by fire from heaven, which consumed it, that David's act was well-pleasing to Him, the plague left Israel. The tribe of Benjamin, within whose borders Jerusalem lay, and also the portion of Levi, remained altogether untouched by the judgment that had fallen upon the land. David himself (to whom the deep, heart-breaking sorrow which he had suffered on account of the distresses that had come upon his people, was reckoned as a kind of equivalent for the plague, under the judgment of which the land had to atone for its manifold guilt) also remained, for the sake of the people, who so greatly needed him, exempt from the general plague. The angel lowered before him his sword, and retired from the visible world behind the curtains of the invisible.

We know that the so-called "modern" consciousness is wont to take great offense at scenes such as these of a personal interposition of heavenly angels in judicial visitation upon Israel. We recognize, on the contrary, therein adorable grace, and praise the Lord that it has pleased Him, the Eternal, for the strengthening of our faith in the truth and reality of the invisible world, to bring it out into the world of visible appearances, once in the course of ages, so palpably and manifestly, and in connection with His guidance of the chosen people. Henceforth it is to us beyond question that that world is something more than a mere phantom. We hail the testimony of the prophet, "The Lord hath made bare His holy arm in the eyes of all the nations; and all the ends of the earth shall see the salvation of our God," with the joyful exclamation, "For this let the Lord be forever praised!"

What is there incredible in this, that God once announced His presence in the appearance of an angel, who afterward, in the person of His only begotten Son, became man, and went out and in among us as a man? Before this latter miracle, all others of which the sacred history makes mention retire into the background as insignificant. How greatly does it altogether outweigh this incident in the case of David, in which we can only recognize the natural forerunner of that infinitely greater One!

If any of the psalms contains a reference to that judgment which then fell upon David and Israel, it is the ninety-first, which does not, it is true, carry the name of its author on its front, but which we cannot for a moment fail to recognize as Davidic, and which has been by the Septuagint translators ascribed to David. Certainly this psalm, which treats of the safety and comfort of the pious amid the troubles of life, looks back not only to the "rider on the pale horse," who then carried death and destruction around him, scattering them throughout the land, but points at the same time to all other dangers and distresses which the pilgrims to the city of God may meet with here below. This more general reference of the psalm makes it obvious that it was intended as a song to be sung in the stated worship of the temple, which might be sung in every time of difficulty and distress, and which indeed has been sung, times without number, not only by Israel of the Old, but also by the Israel of the New Covenant, in times of war, and pestilence, and famine.

The psalm begins thus: "He that dwelleth in the secret place of the Most High shall abide under the shadow of the Almighty. He says" (literally, "I say." The appropriating and confessing I is exchanged several times with the addressing and demanding thou), "My refuge, and my fortress: my God; in Him will I trust. For He delivered thee from the snare of the fowler, and from the noisome pestilence. He covers thee with His feathers" (this the psalmist had just experienced), "and thy trust will be under His wings. His truth is thy shield and buckler. Thou needst not be afraid for the terror by night: nor for the arrows that fly by day; for the pestilence that walketh in darkness; nor for the destruction that wasteth at noon-day. Though a thousand fall at thy side, and ten thousand at thy right hand; yet it shall not come nigh thee. Only with thine eyes shalt thou behold" (not in thyself experience) "and see the reward of the wicked. Because the Lord is thy confidence; thou" (thou who hast surrendered thyself to Him) "makest the Most High thy habitation. No evil shall befall thee, neither shall any plague come nigh thy dwelling. For He shall give His angels charge over thee, to keep thee in all thy ways. Thou shalt tread upon the lion and adder; the young lion and the dragon shalt thou trample under feet. Because he hath set his love upon me" (the Lord speaks), "therefore will I deliver him: I will set him on high, because he hath known my name. He shall call upon me, and I will answer him: I will be with him in trouble; I will deliver him and honor him. With long life will I satisfy him" (a promise most precious to believers under the Old Covenant, who expected the promised salvation in the future), "and show him my salvation."

In how rich a measure did King David, during his seventy years pilgrimage, see this divine assurance fulfilled in himself! And as a comfort and encouragement to all believers, Psalm 91 stands to this hour, with all the fullness of the precious reversion which it confers, like a fresh fruit-laden tree of life in the garden of the Bible.

31

The National Assembly

"The foundation of God standeth sure" (i.e., the true life of faith planted by the Spirit of God), and bears, according to the words of the apostle, the double inscription, "The Lord knoweth them that are His," and "Let every one that nameth the name of Christ depart from iniquity."[1] Only in so far as we meet with these two "seals" in ourselves, may we consider that we are justified in counting ourselves among those who are born again.

The first of the above-named distinctive marks is the experience (united with the consciousness of walking before God honestly, and without guile and suspicion) that one is the object of God's regard, and, whether chastened or comforted, or preserved or saved by Him, is under His immediate guidance. The other points out the decided inner opposition to all that is called sin and transgression; the pure willingness and resolution to live according to the divine direction alone—the holy aim of the mind submissive to the Lord, which, if it is ever in an unguarded moment disowned, always goes forth anew animated and strengthened from amid the tears of a genuine repentance.

Who among the saints of the Old Covenant ever bore these two spiritual seals of adoption in fuller distinctness than the man whom we shall today see, in the apprehension of the near approach of his departure from the scene of his earthly pilgrimage, setting in order the affairs of his kingdom and its government; and who—when, according to the prophetic vision of Daniel,[2] the "books" of God's universal knowledge shall be opened—shall have no need to

---

1. 2 Timothy 2:19.
2. Daniel 7:10.

be afraid, in so far as they will scarcely be able to accuse him of anything concealed and palliated, as he himself has recorded, as it were
with his own hand in those books his life-course in all its stages, in
his genuine confessions and acknowledgments, his very heart, a book
open before God.

1 Chronicles 28:1

> And David assembled all the princes of Israel, the princes of the tribes,
> and the captains of the companies that ministered to the king by
> course, and the captains over the thousands, and captains over the hun-
> dreds, and the stewards over all the substance and possession of the
> king, and of his sons, with the officers, and with the mighty men, and
> with all the valiant men, unto Jerusalem. Then David the king stood
> up upon his feet, and spake to them.

A solemn national assembly was a worthy close to the government
of David. Let us observe (1) what was the occasion of this assembly;
and (2) how it terminated.

1. The wonderful answer to the prayer with which the king had
approached the righteous God, in the rod which was brandished over
Israel, as well as the divine approbation of his plan of building a temple, which was manifested in this answer, could not but naturally give
a new elevation to David's soul. Psalm 30 opens up to us a glimpse
into his state of mind at that time. "I will extol Thee, O Lord," he
begins the psalm "for Thou hast" (in pardoning to me my transgression) "lifted me up, and hast not made my foes to rejoice over me.
O Lord my God, I cried unto Thee, and Thou hast healed me" (didst
support me). "O Lord, Thou hast brought up my soul from the grave"
(which I felt to be near to me): "Thou hast kept me alive, that I
should not go down to the pit. Sing unto the Lord, O ye saints of His,
and give thanks at the remembrance of His holiness. For His anger
endureth but a moment" (of terror and sorrow); "in His favor is life:
weeping may endure for a night, but joy cometh in the morning."
The three days' pestilence were shortened into a pestilence of one
day, which lasted only from the morning until the time appointed for
the evening sacrifice.[3]

"And in my prosperity I said," continues the singer, "I shall never
be moved. Lord, by Thy favor Thou hast made my mountain" (the

---

3. 2 Samuel 24:15.

seat of my government, my kingdom) "to stand strong: Thou didst
hide Thy face" (in the storm of judgments which broke over me),
"and I was troubled"; and was truly perplexed, because I had, in the
project of numbering the people, presumptuously arrogated to
myself as my own and as self-acquired that which alone was Thine,
and was to me a gift of Thy grace. "I cried to Thee, O Lord; and unto
the Lord I made supplication, saying, What profit is there in my
blood, when I go down to the pit?"

At the sight of the angel by the thrashing-floor of Araunah, as we
know, the king had offered to the Lord his life as a sacrifice for the
people. "Shall the dust praise Thee? shall it declare Thy truth?" (as
I, Thy poor servant, will do if Thou grant me grace instead of justice).
"Hear, O Lord, and have mercy upon me: Lord, be Thou my helper."
Thus David sang with a sorrowful, broken heart. And the Lord heard
him, spared his servant, and commanded, and the devastations of the
plague were averted. "Thou hast turned for me my mourning into
dancing: Thou hast put off my sackcloth" (the clothing of the penitent), "and girded me with gladness; to the end that my glory may
sing praise to Thee, and not be silent. O Lord my God, I will give
thanks unto Thee forever."

After such a blessed experience of the continued grace of his God,
the king went forward with quickened mind to the definitive accomplishment of all his yet unfulfilled designs for the building up of the
domestic affairs of his kingdom. What lay particularly near his heart
were the preparations necessary for the building of the temple. For
this purpose he called in the assistance of strangers, because the people of Israel were more given to pastoral and agricultural affairs.
Particularly he employed the Phoenicians of Tyre, a people skilled in
labor and in the arts, who had for a long time been associated with
the people of God, and had professed their faith, and had settled in
the Holy Land. There were more than 150,000 of them. These he
appointed as quarrymen, bearers of burdens, masons, carpenters, hewers of wood, and certain among them as overseers over these.
Moreover, he dug in the mines of the land, and sent for cedar-trees
from Lebanon, as well as gold and silver and precious stones in great
abundance from Arabia.

Amid these and other peaceful occupations the king was interrupted, though only temporarily, by a new occurrence very grieving
to his heart. Adonijah, his fourth son by Haggith, who was next after

Absalom, and resembled him in stateliness as well as in ambition, suddenly put himself forth as successor to his royal father, while he went about with princely splendor and gained a considerable following among those of rank in the kingdom. Even Joab, who could not get over David's placing him behind Amasa, although he had revenged this by the blood of his rival, and who might also be certain of being visited with punishment, laden as he was with the guilt of his many murders, if ever Solomon should become king—even he passed over to the side of Adonijah. Abiathar the priest also, who had been greatly offended by the elevation of Zadok over him, and who therefore would gladly have seen David's last arrangements as to the succession to the throne set aside, allowed himself to be enticed into joining in the secret plot.

The king, to whom information was brought of all that had happened, did not regard the conspiracy as of a threatening character, and indulged his beloved son with a confidence and a paternal tenderness which passed beyond proper measure. But not so did David's faithful men, to whom, besides his life-guards, belonged the priest Zadok, Benaiah the heroic captain, and the prophet Nathan. When these received information that Adonijah had collected his partisans at the well of Rogel for the purpose of being there formally—on the occasion of a sacrificial festival—proclaimed as heir to the throne, they resolved to crush in the bud, at whatever price, the treasonable undertaking.

Nathan gave information of the conspiracy to the mother of Solomon, whom David had long before chosen as his successor to the throne. "Hast thou not heard," said he, "that Adonijah the son of Haggith doth reign, and David our lord knoweth it not?" He then gave her the advice that she would without delay arouse her husband out of his carelessness, and cause him to go forth vigorously, with the royal forces still subject to his command, in defense of Solomon's rights, which he had sworn to. Bathsheba followed Nathan's counsel. But hardly had she represented the matter in the most respectful manner to the king, when the prophet himself entered the chamber, and energetically confirmed all that she had announced to him. Then the king said, "As the Lord liveth, that hath redeemed my soul out of all distress, even as I sware unto thee, Bathsheba, by the Lord God of Israel, saying, Assuredly Solomon thy son shall reign after me, and he shall sit upon my throne in my stead; so will I do this day."

Bathsheba bowed with her face to the earth, and said, "Let my lord King David live forever."

Without delay the king commanded Zadok, Nathan, and Benaiah, saying, "Go, take with you the servants of your lord, and cause Solomon my son to ride upon mine own mule, and bring him down to Gihon" (a place near Jerusalem, so called from a well springing up at the foot of the hill on which the temple stood, and emptying itself into the pool of Siloah): "there," continued David, "let Zadok the priest, and Nathan the prophet, anoint him king over Israel: and blow ye with the trumpet, and say, God save King Solomon. Then ye shall come up after him, that he may come and sit upon my throne; for he shall be king in my stead: and I have appointed him to be ruler over Israel and over Judah." Thus the king commanded. "Amen," cried Benaiah, the son of Jehoiada: "the Lord God of my lord the king say so too. As the Lord hath been with my lord the king, even so be He with Solomon, and make his throne greater than the throne of my lord King David."

The king's command was obeyed; and the cry was echoed by thousands of the people—"God save King Solomon!" The jubilant shout sounded far and wide, and reached even Adonijah and his traitorous followers. When they understood the meaning of the festal noise, they suddenly dispersed and sought their safety in flight. Adonijah himself hastened to the thrashing-floor of Araunah, and caught hold of the horns of the altar which his royal father had erected there. He hoped to have found there a place of safety from the vengeance of his brother Solomon; but there was no divine statute securing to him such safety. He found it, however, in the conciliatory magnanimity of his brother, who declared to him that, if he "would show himself a worthy man," not an hair of his head would fall to the earth and then, with the words, "Go to thine house," ordered him to withdraw into the quietness of private life.

2. Thus Solomon's succession to the throne was publicly proclaimed in Jerusalem. Nevertheless there yet needed a solemn ratification of what had been done before the people and by them. Among the families of Israel the right of primogeniture, according to the divine ordinance, must under all circumstances be preserved and sacredly maintained. The eldest son was, according to the law, the heir. The conferring of royal dignity, the Lord had, however, reserved to Himself; and it remained for the people only to find

which of the surviving sons of the king the finger of God pointed to as the *chosen one.*[4] Besides, it lay on David's heart to make the matter of the *building of the temple* the common cause of the people, and to animate all Israel for the undertaking. We know, then, the most fundamental reasons by which the king was moved to summon together, before his departure, once more, the representatives of the people of all ranks and orders, to a solemn national assembly.

As soon as those who had been invited were seen assembling on the heights of Zion—courtiers, counselors, chamberlains, overseers over the king's estates, gardens, and flocks, heads of tribes, captains or "princes over thousands and over hundreds," and, besides these, as many from among the people as desired to take part in the assembly—David came forward with a firm step, and with a loud, joyful salutation, into their midst. And when could any of the great ones of the earth salute his people in a more animated frame of mind than he who could point to his kingdom as to his own creation—a kingdom which, in its relation to the nations around, and in its internal order, was then without a parallel in the whole world? Feared as well as justly admired by all the neighboring nations, yes, envied by them, Israel—with the great number of its prosperous towns and villages, with its intelligent and skillful public servants, as well as with its army crowned with victory and always ready for war, and its wise legislation—stood before the eyes of all the world as a true model state. But instead of raising his head proudly on that account, David bowed lowly down before the Almighty, and in purest self-renunciation gave the honor of all to *Him* alone, whose grace was his life and his only glory.

After respectfully saluting the assembled multitude, he addressed them with a loud voice, distinctly heard by them all: "Hear me, my brethren, and my people: As for me, I had in mine heart to build an house of rest for the ark of the covenant of the Lord, and for the footstool of our God, and had made ready for the building: but God said unto me, Thou shalt not build an house for my name, because thou hast been a man of war, and hast shed blood. Howbeit, the Lord God of Israel chose me before all the house of my father to be king over Israel forever: for He hath chosen Judah to be the ruler" (i.e., placed him at the head of all the other tribes); "and of the house of Judah the house of my father; and among the sons of my father He liked

4. Deuteronomy 17:15.

me, to make me king over all Israel: and of all my sons" (for the Lord
hath given me many sons) "He hath chosen Solomon my son to sit
upon the throne of the kingdom of the Lord over Israel. And He said
unto me" (whether by an immediate revelation or by the mouth of
a prophet is not announced), "Solomon thy son, he shall build my
house and my courts: for I have chosen him to be my son, and I will
be his father. Moreover, I will establish his kingdom forever, if he be
constant to do my commandments and my judgments, as at this day.
Now therefore, in the sight of all Israel, the congregation of the Lord,
and in the audience of our God, keep and seek for all the commandments of the Lord your God; that ye may possess this good land,
and leave it for an inheritance for your children. And thou,
Solomon my son, know thou the God of thy father, and serve Him
with a perfect heart, and with a willing mind; for the Lord searche-
th all hearts, and understandeth all the imaginations of the
thoughts: if thou seek Him, He will be found of thee; but if thou forsake Him, He will cast thee off forever." Thus the king spoke, with
deeply moved soul.

After he had uttered these fatherly words, he delivered to his son,
in a solemn manner, a document, the contents of which he thus
described: "All has been given to me by the hand of the Lord, written" (probably by the pen of one of the prophets) "that it may
instruct me in all the works of the pattern," that is, of those works
which were once shown in a divine pattern to Moses the man of
God.[5] The document contained a plan of the future temple in its
details. To it was annexed, next after the courses of the priests, a list
of the precious materials already prepared for the building of the temple. After he had handed it to Solomon, he continued, addressing
him, "Be strong, and of good courage, and do it; fear not, nor be dismayed; for the Lord God, even my God, will be with thee; He will
not fail thee, nor forsake thee, until thou hast finished all the work
for the service of the house of the Lord. And, behold, the courses of
the priests and the Levites, even they shall be with thee for all the
service of the house of God; and there shall be with thee, for all manner
of workmanship, every willing skillful man, for any manner of service; also
the princes and all the people will be wholly at thy commandment."

After these fatherly words to his son, David turned himself to the

_____
5. Exodus 25:9.

people, and said: "Solomon my son, whom alone God hath chosen, is yet young and tender, and the work is great: for the palace is not for man, but for the Lord God." Hereupon he gave the people an account of the valuable materials, gold, silver, precious stones, wood, and stones, which he had gathered for the building; and then he cried out to the multitude, "Who is willing to consecrate his service this day unto the Lord?" Then all the princes and nobles of the kingdom offered themselves willingly. Correspondingly liberal contributions were made.

"The people rejoiced," it is said, "for that they offered willingly, because with perfect heart they offered willingly to the Lord." But particularly David the king rejoiced, and his soul poured itself forth before the whole congregation in the language of prayer and thanksgiving. "Blessed be Thou," he says with loud voice, "Lord God of Israel our father, forever and ever. Thine" (not mine, not ours) "is the greatness, and the power, and the glory, and the victory, and the majesty: for all that is in the heaven and in the earth is Thine; Thine is the kingdom, O Lord, and Thou art exalted as head above all. Both riches and honor come of Thee, and Thou reignest over all; and in Thine hand is power and might; and in Thine hand it is to make great, and to give strength unto all. Now, therefore, our God, we thank Thee, and praise Thy glorious name."

After this utterance of praise, there follows a humble confession of his own nothingness and weakness: "But who am I, and what is my people, that we should be able to offer so willingly after this sort? for all things come of Thee, and of Thine own have we given Thee. For we are strangers before Thee, and sojourners, as were all our fathers; our days on the earth are as a shadow, and there is none abiding. O Lord our God, all this store that we have prepared to build Thee an house for Thine holy name cometh of Thine hand, and is all Thine own. I know also, my God, that Thou triest the heart, and hast pleasure in uprightness. As for me, in the uprightness of mine heart I have willingly offered all these things; and now have I seen with joy Thy people, which are present here, to offer willingly unto Thee."

In the conclusion of his prayer, he presents this earnest petition: "O Lord God of Abraham, Isaac, and of Israel, our fathers, keep this forever in the imagination of the thoughts of the heart of Thy people, and prepare their heart unto Thee; and give unto Solomon my son a perfect heart, to keep Thy commandments, Thy testimonies, and Thy statutes, and to do all these things, and to build the palace, for the which I have made provision."

After this effusion, which was without doubt sealed with the "Amen" of many thousand voices, David challenged the whole congregation to unite with him in praising the Lord their God; and in lofty chorus the voice of praise arose up to the heavens. "All the congregation blessed the Lord God of their fathers, and bowed down their heads, and worshiped the Lord, and the king." There then followed a solemn offering up of sacrifices; then a so-called sacrificial feast, a love-feast, at which Jehovah was regarded as the host; and the food, the flesh of the beasts that had been offered in sacrifice, was eaten with holy joy, as a symbol and pledge of divine grace. The people were in the highest elevation of mind. How could it be otherwise? The radiance of glory which beamed from the countenance of the king could not but tend to elevate and animate the whole multitude.

Solomon was now for the second time, though not anointed by the priests, yet in the most solemn manner proclaimed as heir to the throne and the whole congregation, and "all the princes, and the mighty men, and all the sons likewise of King David," did him homage as their head, and "submitted themselves" unto him as to their future king and ruler, chosen by God Himself.

The Lord could not have more emphatically sealed the perfection of the gracious and unlimited pardon which He had bestowed upon him after his great sin, than by not only elevating the son of Bathsheba to be the heir of the crown of Israel, the most glorious of all earthly crowns, but by placing him, together even with his mother, "the wife of Uriah," among the progenitors in the line of the earthly descent of the great "Son of David," the future Savior of the world. So also the Lord could not give to David a more indubitable evidence of His being well pleased with the whole of his royal government than in that He granted to him to bring it to a close in so significant and glorious a manner by this last national assembly and its proceedings, which were so glorifying to God.

The weighty thoughts which moved the heart of David on that great day, he has given expression to in Psalm 138. The whole chain of divine deliverances, helps, and grace which had passed through his long life lay before him on that day, unconcealed in clearest

brightness; and his eye rested principally on that brightest link in it—
on that great promise penetrating so deeply and so powerfully into
the course of the world's history, which was given to him and to his
house, and the first gentle step toward the fulfillment of which he
believed he saw now already taken, in the holy enthusiasm of the
people for the building of the temple, and in the divine confirmation
of the succession of Solomon to the throne.[6]

As the past, with it thousands of bright footprints of the mercy of
God, so also the future, even to the latest year of his life, opened itself
before him, irradiated by the light of another world. What wonder
that his heart then swelled up with emotion, and that a song of praise
such as this streamed forth from his soul: "I will praise Thee with my
whole heart; before the gods will I sing praise unto Thee. I will worship toward Thy holy temple" (of which the sanctuary to be
erected on Mount Zion would be the earthly image), "and I will
praise Thy name for Thy loving-kindness, and Thy truth: for
above all Thy name" (i.e., above all by which Thou hast heretofore
made Thyself glorious); "Thou hast glorified Thyself by Thy word,"
the word of the promise. "In the day when I cried" (prayed for the
continuance of my house and the honor of Thy name in it) "Thou
answeredst me, and strengthenedst" (by the great promise) "with
strength in my soul. All the kings on the earth shall praise Thee, O
Lord" (i.e., all the nations whose kings are their heads and representatives), "when they hear the words of Thy mouth. Yea, they shall
sing in the ways of the Lord: for great is the glory of the Lord.
Though the Lord be high, yet hath He respect unto the lowly: but
the proud He knoweth afar off" (and will bring him down).
"Though I walk in the midst of trouble, Thou wilt revive me; Thou
shalt stretch forth Thine hand against the wrath of mine enemies,
and Thy right hand shall save me. The Lord will perfect that which
concerneth me (will complete for me what He has begun—the work
whose completion shall be the appearing of the Messiah and of His
kingdom); "Thy mercy, O Lord, endureth forever. Thou wilt not forsake the works of Thine own hands," i.e., Thou wilt infallibly bring
them to a conclusion.

How noble is David, as he stands before us at this national assembly! Not only does he appear, by the grace of God, healed of all his

---

6. 2 Samuel 7.

wounds, and free from all his blemishes, but there is realized in him the image of that mysterious bird which, according to the Egyptian story, when it has become old, throws itself into the flames, that it may come forth out of its own ashes (not only renewed and made young again, but that it may rise to incomparably higher splendor than before) made glorious with shining wings. In David's appearance we see here shadowed forth the transformation which all true believers have undergone, when it can be said of them, "Old things are passed away; behold, all things are become new!"

All the dross that had accompanied the process of his development toward the kingdom of heaven lies behind him, and only the pure gold remains. All his transgressions have disappeared before the grace of the Almighty like a cloud, and only the righteousness, which has been wrought in him by the Holy Spirit, remains before us in fair and symmetrical unfolding, victoriously delivered from all the darkening and disfiguring clouds which it encountered. For this world the divine work of educating David was terminated.

O happy are all they who unreservedly resign themselves to the guidance and discipline and fostering care of the Lord! They may then be free from all care when the waters of affliction flow in unto their souls. He helps them through every difficulty and out of all their distresses, and does not leave them till He has fulfilled His purpose "to the praise of the glory of His grace." It is true, indeed, that, according to the saying of the prophet, as there is around all a glory, so there is around the divine life a veil. But the day tarries not when the shell shall break and the veil fall down, and the noble kernel, silently fostered and ripened to the praise of God and to the admiration of men, shall shine forth in incomparable glory.

32

The Last Days

Everyone knows that there will come one day which will be his last on earth, on which he will have to balance his account with life, and to bid farewell to all that is dear and precious to him in this world. Happy is he who has the shield of a consciousness such as that which animated Paul, who, in the last of his Epistles, could add to the tidings that the "time of his departure was at hand," the joyful exclamation, "I have fought a good fight, I have finished my course, I have kept the faith!"[1] By these words he designated the gain of his earthly life, which super-abundantly sufficed to enable him with peace and equanimity to see fall from around him, like withered leaves, all else of which he might boast, or in which he might rejoice, and which afforded to his soul courage and confidence to add with triumph, "Henceforth there is laid up for me a crown of righteousness, which the Lord, the righteous Judge, shall give me at that day." Great is the man of Tarsus as he there stands before us at the close of his earthly pilgrimage—greater than any of the saints under the Old Covenant. But if any among the latter did come close to the apostle, it was King David, as we shall today be able to witness.

1 Chronicles 29:28

> And he died in a good old age, full of days, riches, and honor.

David's days are numbered. With good reason he might say, in the words of Psalm 69, "The zeal of Thine house hath eaten me up." He meets us today on that path of which, in the fullness of his faith, he

---

1. 2 Timothy 4.

sang in Psalm 23, "Yea, though I walk through the valley of the shadow of death, I will fear no evil: for Thou art with me; Thy rod and Thy staff they comfort me." Thus his faith did not remain without its divine seal. We draw near to the sick-bed, the death bed of the king. (1) David's position before God; (2) his last directions; and (3) his dying songs—are the subjects of our contemplation.

1. We perceive that a great change has taken place when today we enter the palace on Mount Zion. A deep, solemn silence prevails in these halls, once so full of activity. The attendants at the court steal through the chambers silently and with gentle step, and every countenance is clouded with sorrow; but it is another and holier sadness than that which we formerly met with there. It is as if everything that surrounds us, the very pillars and the walls, uttered in our hearing the lamentation of the prophet: "All flesh is grass, and all the goodliness thereof is as the flower of the field: the grass withereth, the flower fadeth." The royal throne stands apart covered with a veil. Instead of the chamberlains and chief men of the palace, there appear now the physicians as rulers in the house. The king lies on his couch gravely ill. "They covered him with clothes," the history records, "but he gat no heat." Some have ascribed this stagnation of the blood in his veins to the terror which overpowered him at the sight of the angel at the thrashing-floor of Araunah, and which never afterward left him. It is questionable whether this opinion is well founded. It is only certain that the confusion into which that sight put him gave him occasion to choose the thrashing-floor of the Jebusite as the place for the sacrifice, because the danger threatening Jerusalem appeared too imminent to afford to him time to undertake a distant journey to the high place at Gibeon, (where the altar of burnt-offering at that time was).[2]

Among those who attend on the sick king, we observe also Abishag the Shunammite, a young healthy damsel, whose presence, according to the opinion of some of the royal servants (which was a widespread superstition among the people of the East at that time), would contribute to revive the sinking strength of the king, and to reinvigorate him. Whether and how far the king himself entered into this foolish counsel of his servants, is not mentioned. But the Scripture expressly and with solemn earnestness removes

---

2. 1 Chronicles 21:29–30.

every unworthy suspicion that might arise to the prejudice of David.

David found himself thus now at that stage of the journey of life where the paths of mortal men, whether they have journeyed along the proud ways of earthly power and greatness, or have wandered along the dark defiles of lowliness and of misery, again meet together. Here, what difference is there between the royal purple and the attire of the humble laborer? What now is that social position, that high consideration, or generally that prosperity which the world in its blindness estimates so highly? Here it all passes out of sight; while that to which God raises, now for the first time comes into full manifestation.

Let us draw nearer to the sick monarch. O how much more glorious is the crown he wears, as he now lies before us, than that golden one with which he was crowned? How infinitely nobler is the adornment in which he leaves this world than the laurel crown of the conqueror which was wreathed around his brow! That which raised him so high above thousands of his fellow-pilgrims was not the royal raiment he wore, the titles of dignity, the applause of the multitude, but the grace which glorified in him its new-creative power.

And to what a degree it changes the whole nature of this sinful son of the dust! Our natural eye, it is true, sees David lying there on the way to eternity, as only a man who, in every sense of the word, might say with Job, "Naked came I out of my mother's womb, and naked shall I return thither"; but to the eye of faith, which knows how to contemplate him in the infallible light of God's Word, in what glory does this son of earth, now stripped of all his worldly splendor, appear before us! There lies before us truly a sinner, against whom the overwhelming sentence of condemnation was with justice uttered, "Thou art the man who must die";[3] but after he again came forth from the fiery crucible of genuine repentance, he is now wholly the Lord's—to Him he wished only to live, thirsting after fellowship with Him. Who will venture now to condemn this man? The exalted One, who in his cause has the last word, knows him (whom the law indeed condemns to death) "no more after the flesh," but has, on the ground of the shedding of the blood of atonement (which was, in the eye of God, who at one view sees the past, the present, and the future

---

3. 2 Samuel 12:7.

already an accomplished fact), spoken out to him the consolation of free and unrestrained grace: "I have blotted out as a thick cloud thy transgressions, and as a cloud thy sins. For mine own name's sake I have blotted them out, and will remember them no more!"

And more yet than even this. On what a couch does the sick monarch rest! The king reposes not only on the bosom of God's pardoning generosity, but, as the object of His divine kindness, in the arms of His love. To what has the happy David to attribute this, but to that robe, white as a lily, which covers his nakedness, and which was not woven or procured by himself but was presented and given to him from above, in the way of a mysterious divine imputation. Therefore threefold salvation is his! Yes, greater still than pardon is the blessing he has obtained. Not as though this was not a treasure of the highest worth. The pardon of sin saves from condemnation and rescues from hell; but it alone affords no assurance of our being brought into the family of God and of our having the privileges of adoption in the kingdom of the Father, but allows the sinner thus forgiven still to stand dejected and trembling at a distance.

Justification is more than absolution. It bestows privileges of the noblest kind, and brings back the sinner into that confidential relationship with God which was formerly enjoyed in paradise, but was forfeited. The favor granted to us would be only partial if we were by it merely pardoned, and not also restored to fellowship with God. Our personal salvation, so long as we are in the body, remains an imperfect work, which can in no way justify any claim in us on Him who "dwelleth in the light" which no man can approach unto, but besides that personal righteousness aimed after by us, and growing up within us, there is provided for us a perfect righteousness—the righteousness of our Head, Jesus Christ, in which all who believe in Him are divinely authorized to glory as their own.

This great and mysterious truth forms the kernel and center of the whole gospel; and never will any objections of the natural reason, which, according to the testimony of Scripture. "understands not the things which are of the Spirit of God," be able to deprive us of it. The regenerated are not only absolved, but also justified—that is, pronounced righteous. Not only are they "washed in the blood of the Lamb," and thereby are free from the curse, but they also therein wash their "robes and make them white," and are in this attire worthy of the crown of glory.

How blessed is the deathbed of a man who is in Christ! What nobler honor, or more to be coveted than this! The wings of everlasting love are stretched out over it! Holy angels stand around as silent guardians. The accusers, whatever they may be, are kept at a distance by the authority of God, and the heavenly Jerusalem opens above him its pearly gates for the reception of his departing soul, dedicated to God. So rest, son of Jesse! Throw every care you upon Him who has made your cause His own, and who stands forth in your behalf. Your pleas are all decided in your favor. Triumph over all your enemies, and rejoice in perfected salvation!

2. Already he rejoiced in it. "How could he, the man of the Old Covenant, who then only 'saw afar off' the promise of the incarnation, do this?" It is true that he did not yet know the full, pure blessedness of a Paul or a John; but in that measure of clarity with which the gospel of Christ shone forth during the economy of the law, the incomparable peace and freedom of the children of God were realized in his consciousness, and indeed in a clearer and more sensible manner than by any other of his Old Testament companions in the faith. The grace of which he felt himself assured made him strong to overcome the king of terrors.

We hear him say to Bathsheba: "As the Lord liveth, that hath redeemed my soul out of all distresses." This word opens up a clear view into his inmost soul. We here see that it is bright day with him. He looks back upon his seventy years' pilgrimage, and what a series of dangers, distresses, and trials, and, alas, also of mistakes, wanderings from the right path, and sins, rises up before his memory! He is overpowered by adoring wonder, as all the pilgrims of God will at last be overpowered at the close of their earthly journey. For how faithful was God, and how he verified that saying: "The gifts and calling of God are without repentance." "He hath delivered me," says David, "out of all distresses."

Without doubt he recalls particularly that anguish of soul which he describes in Psalms 32 and 51, and which among others extorted from him this complaint: "I am weary with my groaning; all the night make I my bed to swim: I water my couch with my tears." And what was he made to experience? God was greater than his heart, and "made him to know wisdom in the hidden part"; yea, "purged him with hyssop" and "washed him," so that he became "whiter than the snow." These expressions indicate that which now especially, above all things, filled his soul; and thus he lay on his couch, ready for his departure to the Canaan on the other side of the clouds, listening to the sound of the New Testament Sabbath bells, coming up to him from out of the distant future.

He sent for his son Solomon to approach his sick-bed, that he might deliver to him his last fatherly counsels and charges. Far from making this solemn act a scene of tender weeping, or showing even a trace of sorrow at the laying aside of the robes of his earthly glory—which he was soon to do—he is calm, cheerful, and trusting in his God, and joyfully prepared to exchange the purple rags which adorned him here below, for the garments of light worn by the harpers before the throne; the fragile scepter of his earthly kingdom, for the palm of triumph of the heavenly conquerors. "I go," said he, "the way of all the earth." One would have thought that, in a moment so earnest and decisive as that which had now come to him, he would have expressed himself more pathetically and more solemnly. But they who, by divine grace, have become free, hate everything that borders on pious display; and how, indeed, could they wish to boast and make a show of their blessed home-going? But they think and feel more than the plain simple words of their lips may lead us to apprehend.

David continued, addressing his son: "Be thou strong, and show thyself a man!"—a brief, explicit, impressive charge, but significant and comprehensive enough for Solomon. "Be strong" (i.e., rely upon God). "Be a man"—that is, walk with God, and take firm and sure steps in His word! "Keep the charge of the Lord thy God," David further says (i.e., hold fast by all that the Lord has commanded, and in His ordinances and institutions see the rule and the bounds of your future government). David concludes: "Walk in the ways of God, and keep His statutes, and His commandments, and His judgments, and His testimonies, as it is written in the law of Moses,[4] that thou mayest prosper in all that thou doest, and whithersoever thou turnest thyself; that the Lord may continue His word, which He spoke concerning me, saying, If thy children take heed to their way, to walk before me in truth with all their heart and with all their soul, there shall not fail thee a man on the throne of Israel." In truth, an admirable farewell charge of a dying prince to the heir of his throne!

---

4. Deuteronomy 15.

O that everywhere, and in all times, similar counsel were addressed to the successors to thrones, when the divine direction strikes on the ear of a ruler, "Put off thy robes, and lay aside thy crown; for thou mayest be no longer king."

After these paternal counsels, David recommended to his son the children of old Barzillai the Gileadite, that he should continue to show to them kindness, and let them continue to be of those who ate at the king's table. "For so," he says, "they came to me when I fled because of Absalom thy brother." But now we hear something from the mouth of David, which we, the children of another than the Old Testament spirit, cannot easily understand. We hear the dying man say to his son: "Thou knowest also what Joab the son of Zeruiah did to me, and what he did to the two captains of the hosts of Israel, unto Abner the son of Ner, and unto Amasa the son of Jether, whom he slew, and shed the blood of war in peace, and put the blood of war upon his girdle that was about his loins, and in his shoes that were on his feet. Do therefore according to thy wisdom, and let not his hoar head go down to the grave in peace. And, behold, thou hast with thee Shimei the son of Gera, a Benjamite of Bahurim, which cursed me with a grievous curse in the day when I went to Mahanaim: but he came down to meet me" (on my return) "at Jordan, and I sware to him by the Lord, saying, I will not put thee to death with the sword. Now therefore, my son Solomon, hold him not guiltless: for thou art a wise man, and knowest what thou oughtest to do unto him; but his hoar head bring thou down to the grave with blood."

Who does not feel himself confused by this charge of David? Does he not now at last thereby bring a stain only upon himself? Both of these men, whom he once made to believe that he would forget their guilt, he commends, while his lips are growing pale, to the vengeance of his successor on the throne! Does this look like a God-fearing man, and particularly a man who had within himself a consciousness, humbling him and counseling him to compassionate mildness, that his guilt, more worthy of condemnation than that which these two men were chargeable with, had been forgiven him by the God of all grace?

There will always be expressions of sorrowful, even of angry, surprise uttered at that feature of the life of David, so far as the times and circumstances are confounded, and David is supposed to be one who is standing on the sunny heights of the faith of such as enjoy the

fully unfolded glory of "the kindness and love of God our Savior,"
after they have entered into that kingdom of peace, where He reigns
who appeared announcing, "I am not come into the world to condemn the world, but that the world through me might be saved."

But notwithstanding all his enlightenment, David yet belonged
to the time when it lay in God's plan of salvation to write, as in letters of inextinguishable fire, on the hearts of the people, before all
other things, the "I am holy, and ye must be also holy," as the first and
chiefest of all the sayings to be remembered. It was, as the Epistle to
the Galatians expresses it, the time of "the covenant from Mount
Sinai," over which was thundered, with a sound louder than all others, that alarming declaration, "I am a jealous God, visiting the
iniquity of the fathers upon the children unto the third and fourth
generations"; and in which, according to the Epistle to the
Hebrews, "the word spoken by angels to Moses was thereby made
firm" (i.e., authenticated) "that every transgression and disobedience
might receive a just recompense of reward."[5] David was a theocratic
king, who had to conduct his government according to the character of that period of his kingdom in which, as a "schoolmaster to
bring us to Christ," the law of temporal rewards and punishments
prevailed.

According to the express command of this law, he was unconditionally bound to avenge the death of his captains Abner and
Amasa—the latter of whom was, besides, his blood-relation—on
Joab, who had treacherously put them both to death, as well as to
give free scope to the course of justice against the Benjamite Shimei,
who in him, the anointed of the Lord, had openly reviled the Lord
Himself. It is true that, at the time of his restoration to the throne,
David for a time subordinated justice to grace. He spared Joab, the
murderer of Abner, because, then just crowned as king, he was,
according to his own expression, "young and tender"; and, amid the
confusions of those times when he ascended the throne, and
which he did not wish to signalize by the shedding of blood, he could
not well carry on his government without so resolute and brave a soldier as Joab was.

After the murder of Amasa by Joab, he could not persuade himself to exercise the commanded severity against him, because he

---

5. Hebrews 2:2.

himself the king, after his own deep fall, had been visited with the exceeding riches of the grace of the Lord his God. The slanderer Shimei he protected against the swords of his captains that were unsheathed against him, because in his cursing and stoning him he recognized only a well-merited chastisement from God upon him as the greater sinner. It is true that he solemnly swore to Shimei at a later period, at the time of his victorious return to Jerusalem, that he would not inflict on him the punishment of death; but this happened in the midst of the overflowing fullness of his thankful joy of heart at the help God had graciously granted to him. He acted then from personal love of an enemy as a private man, and not as king.

Now, however, it had become notorious throughout the whole land that the crimes of Joab and Shimei were unavenged, and this threatened to bring the law into great discredit. And who was to blame for this? David was fully conscious that it lay with him. On his deathbed, the duty still remaining unfulfilled disquieted him greatly; and so he overcame himself and, violently subordinating the feelings of his heart—inclined to pardon—to his conscience and the irrevocable ordinance of God, he directed his son how to act in the words to which we have just listened. Solomon must execute against both of these evil-doers the vengeance which the law demanded, and this so much the more, because they had not as yet manifested the least trace of genuine repentance. To his command, however, David added the somewhat mitigating remark, "Thou art a wise man, and knowest what thou oughtest to do."

Manifestly there lay in that remark the injunction that he ought at all times closely to be on his guard against dangerous men, and ask from God in prayer what was here right and consistent for the king of Israel to do. His fate soon overtook Joab. After he had entered into a new traitorous conspiracy, and "had turned after Adonijah," he was, at the command of Solomon, slain by Benaiah, the son of the high priest Jehoiada, beside the altar of the tabernacle, whither he had fled in the hope of there finding safety. "Slay him," the king commanded, "that thou mayest take away the innocent blood, which Joab shed, from me, and from the house of my father. Their blood shall therefore return upon the head of Joab, and upon the head of his seed forever: but upon David, and upon his seed, and upon his house, and upon his throne, shall there be peace forever from the Lord."

Solomon kept Shimei for some time longer near him, observing him. But when he perceived in him also no change of mind, he devoted him to death, as he had done Joab, on the occasion of an open violation by Shimei of the restriction laid upon him as to his residence in Jerusalem. The king dismissed him from his presence with these words, "Thou knowest all the wickedness which thine heart is privy to, that thou didst to David my father: therefore the Lord shall return thy wickedness upon thine own head; and King Solomon shall be blessed, and the throne of David shall be established before the Lord forever."

We think that which we have now remarked will tend to diminish the astonishment felt at the last charge given by the dying king of Israel to his successor on the throne. That which is sorrowful in it indeed remains; but that is not to be attributed to the disposition of the king, but rather to the economy of the law, which David, as the head of Israel, had to defend and preserve in honor. A king under the gospel economy will certainly in similar circumstances act otherwise. David was indeed an evangelical king, though not according to his outward position, yet in the essential feelings of his heart. Before the judgment-seat of the divine economy of the kingdom under which he lived, his conduct was without reproach. His times were those of the severity of the law, in view of which Paul writes to the Galatians, "Before faith came, we were kept under the law, shut up unto the faith which should afterward be revealed."

3. After David had put his house in order, and had closed his reckoning with life, he turned himself with his whole desire, and with a holy conscience, toward heaven and the glorious visions of the future unfolding of the kingdom of God upon the earth; and the "last words" in which his soul here below poured itself forth show us the "man according to God's own heart" on this side of eternity, as already on a Tabor-height of spiritual transfiguration, which might almost make us forget that a whole thousand years yet separated him from the age of the New Testament. We hear him singing his dying song, which in its commencement plainly accords with the blessing "wherewith Moses blessed the children of Israel before his death," and with that ancient prophecy of the "Star which was to arise out of Jacob." He begins by a reference to himself:

David the son of Jesse said:
The man who was raised up on high,
The anointed of the God of Jacob,
And the sweet psalmist of Israel.
The Spirit of the Lord spake by me,
And His word was in my tongue.
The God of Israel said,
The Rock of Israel has promised me
A Ruler over men, just,
A Ruler in the fear of God.

He who is here described forms the central object of the prophetic part of all his psalms, and consequently the gospel in them. David continues:

And as the light of the morning when the sun rises,
A morning without clouds:
The tender grass springeth out of the earth by clear shining after rain.

(Such would be the appearing of Him who was to come).

For is not my house established by God?
He hath made with me an everlasting covenant,
Ordered in all things, and sure;
That is my salvation and my desire:
Should He then not cause it to grow?
But the godless all of them as thorns thrust away,
For men do not take them in their hands;
But the man that shall touch them
Must fill his hands with iron and spear-shafts,
And they shall be utterly burned with fire.

(i.e., they shall have no place in the kingdom of Him who is to come, and with them there can be no fellowship).

There was here granted to the departing king a grand and glorious view into the distant future. David gives the keynote in his dying song to all the prophecies that were to be uttered after him. They are but variations of his theme which we hear sounding forth from the company of the prophets for 600 years. In richest fullness there was granted to the king what he prayed for in his Penitential Psalm:

"Make me to hear joy and gladness; that the bones which Thou hast broken may rejoice."[6] For how can one with more joyful cheerfulness shake off the dust from his feet in this valley through which he prosecutes his pilgrimage-way, than in the open, unclouded contemplation of the "Sun of Righteousness," with salvation, life, and peace in His wings?

Yet we cannot but notice here the distinction, which ever remains fixed, between the believers of the Old and those of the New Covenant. Christ described it in the highly significant words which we read in the Gospel of John.[7] He there speaks under a solemn asseveration: "Verily, verily, I say unto you" (to His disciples, and in them to all the pious in Israel), "Whatsoever ye shall ask the Father in my name, He will give it you." That was a new thing, as He Himself designated it as such, saying, "Hitherto have ye asked nothing in my name." We poor men have need of a strong support, of a spiritual lever, if we would not merely say prayers, but truly pray, i.e., earnestly, trustfully, confidently talk with God. For who is God, and what are we? What an immeasurable distance between Him, the Highly Exalted One, and us, the creatures of a day on His footstool—between Him, the Most Holy, in His inaccessible light, and us who, in the multitude of worlds, disappear like drops in the ocean, and who are, besides, laden with sins, and therefore in ourselves are unworthy of any regard on the part of the Eternally Holy One! How can we approach Him, and whence do we derive the freedom to venture into His presence? Will not breath fail us at the first words with which we seek to address Him, so that they shall die away?

The pious Israelite joined himself in spirit to Abraham, Isaac, and Jacob, when he wished to draw near to God in prayer, as to those by whom Jehovah had been graciously found. "O God, my Father!" he said; and that gave vent to his heart, though only inadequately, for the suppliant was not himself Abraham. But now comes the Christ, and puts Himself in that place. "Lean on me," He says; "call upon me: pray in my name. "But, Lord," we reply, "Thou Incomparable One, who art Thou, and what are we?" The Lord replies, according to His own word and that of His apostles, "I am He who, obeying in your

---

6. Psalm 51.
7. John 16:23–27.

stead, and bearing upon me that which separates between you and my Father, have removed it out of the way; and in me, the beloved of the Father, ye are made pleasing to God, in so far as in faith ye commit yourselves to me."

In the name of Jesus, therefore, we pray with childlike joy, in living appropriation of that which Jesus the Mediator did for us, as if, being comprehended in Him, we were ourselves Christ—one with Him in His merit, by faith included in His expiation; and this is of wide extent, and is infinitely perfect. Let us hear Him. "I say not unto you," He begins, "that I will pray the Father for you." Let the distinction be observed. The words are not, "I say unto you that I will not pray for you." Without doubt He will do that. How should He not, who bears on His heart those whom He has purchased with His blood? But His disciples must not think that the Father, that He may hear and grant our requests, must always first be appeased by the intercession of Jesus. O no! This has been done once for all. The Lord says, "The Father Himself loveth you, because ye have loved me, and have believed that I came out from God!" What do we wish for more? O this blessed assurance! With Jesus in our hearts and on our hands, we are always welcome before the Father, as often as we draw near, and whatever may be our requests. Not as servants, but as children, we may and should appear before Him, always certain that our prayers will be heard, because for us, who are partakers of the Spirit of God, a holy tact will preserve us from asking that which is unseemly and improper.

The way to this state of childlike confidence and assurance in the heavenly Father was not yet opened to those who expected the "manifestation of God in the flesh" as then only something future. The fear in them was not yet wholly overcome by love before the great atoning work was fully accomplished. It was shown from a distance to the saints of old in mysterious words and figures, and if any one among them understood the way to decipher and explain these hieroglyphics, it was David. But with whatever boldness he knew at times how to cast himself on the heart of his God, he could not say the New Testament "Abba, Father!" We understand the Lord, when, with reference to John the Baptist, He says, "Among them that are born of women there hath not risen a greater prophet than John: notwithstanding, he that is least in the kingdom of heaven is greater than he." To us, the later born children of the New Covenant, it is said, "Blessed are your eyes, for they see; and your ears, for they hear. For verily I say unto you, that many prophets and righteous men have desired to see those things which ye see, and have not seen them; and to hear those things which ye hear, and have not heard them!"

33

David's Death and Legacy

Even the ashes of emperors and kings, of heroes and wise men, we weigh in our hands, and say with the author of Psalm 8, "O Lord, what is man, that Thou art mindful of him? and the son of man, that Thou visitest him?" And yet the transient race of Adam rises in dignity high above all that is great and greatest that is around it in the world. The ashes which man leaves behind him is only the dust of the pilgrimage which the being within him, formed for eternity, shakes off from its feet when it takes its upward flight to the realms of day. His frail and perishing body is only the robe in which he is arrayed for the journey he is prosecuting to his real home, the land of immortality. But in our days it fares with many, in their hopes for a blessed future, as with the miner in a labyrinthine mine, who bends anxiously over his lamp, because, in the midst of the darkness which surrounds him, and the fearful caverns at the brink of which he knows himself to be, it threatens every moment to be extinguished, and inevitably expose him to a dreadful death.

But shame to every one who can so act, after that powerful light from the open grave in Joseph's garden has pierced with its glorious brightness the gloomy darkness of death! How will such a person be put to shame by the dark hopes of many heathen who saw not that light shine, and who, for their hope of immortality, knew no other ground than that which they believed they could find in human nature organized for a higher existence! How, also, will he be put to shame by the men and women of the Old Covenant, who, from the revelations of the future world made known to them, according to the wise counsel of God, only in the form of a faintly rising twilight, knew how to derive the conclusion that to them at least that was

407

beyond all doubt which Solomon the Preacher testified: "Then shall
the dust return to the earth as it was; and the spirit shall return unto
God who gave it!"[1] Yet many among them, as has already been frequently remarked, saw with the eye of faith far beyond this. That to
their class belonged the man whom we shall today see depart from
the scene of his earthly warfare no one will be surprised.

1 Kings 2:10

So David slept with his fathers, and was buried in the city of David.

1 Chronicles 29:28

And he died in a good old age, full of days, riches, and honor.

Thus, with unadorned beauty, and yet with significant and
comprehensive words, the sacred history informs us of the close of
David's life. It unveils to us (1) his death-bed; and then (2) the rich
legacy which he left to the world.

1. It is true that the children of Israel, before the post-Davidic
great prophets, particularly Isaiah, Ezekiel, and Daniel, opened their
mouths, had to maintain a severe inward conflict for the hope, not
indeed of their personal existence after death, but of a blessed life in
the world beyond the grave. The view of most of them did not reach
beyond Sheol, or the kingdom of the dead, which they did not
indeed regard as a state of annihilation, but much less as a blessed
dwelling-place near the throne of God. True, there hovered before
them, as we know, dimly visible in the distant past, the image of
Enoch translated to God, like a bright meteor rich with promise. But
his translation was only an exceptional case, and this blessed lot was
granted to him because, as it is expressly said of him, "he walked with
God"; and who could venture to boast himself of being like him? The
law had marked all as sinners, and the atoning sacrifice of the future
they saw only as a deep unsolved mystery amid the shadows and types
of the holy tabernacle.

We frequently see confirmed among these ancients that which is
declared in the Epistle to the Hebrews, namely, that before the work
of redemption was completed, "through fear of death they were all
their lifetime subject to bondage."[2] Thus we hear the singer of

1. Ecclesiastes 12:7.
2. Hebrews 2:15.

Psalm 88, standing at the gates of death encompassed by many distresses, say to the sons of Korah in his psalm, breathing from
beginning to end the most gloomy sadness: "I am counted with them
that go down into the pit: I am as a man that hath no strength. Free
among the dead, like the slain that lie in the grave, whom Thou
rememberest no more: and they are cut off from Thy hand. Thou hast
laid me in the lowest pit" (i.e., as in the kingdom of the dead), "in darkness, in the deeps. Wilt Thou show wonders to the dead? Shall the
dead arise and praise Thee? Shall Thy loving-kindness be declared
in the grave? or Thy faithfulness in destruction? Shall Thy wonders
be known in the dark? and Thy righteousness in the land of forgetfulness? Lover and friend hast Thou put far from me, and mine
acquaintance into darkness."

Here every hope appears indeed to be extinguished; yet only the
hope of a blessed existence after death—not the hope of existence
generally. In the following psalm, which completes the one just mentioned, the same singer rises up again from his depression to praise
God, "whose arm is mighty, whose throne stands established on justice and judgment, and before whose face mercy and truth go
forth"—and here brighter visions again dawn upon his soul. The
unknown author of Psalm 115 assigns as a reason for the Lord to prolong his life, the circumstance that "the dead praise not the Lord,
neither any that go down into silence." He thus thinks of the kingdom of the dead as a place of silence, and the departed as in a state
of slumber or of waking sleep, but not as therefore robbed of life, or
as having altogether sunk into annihilation.

We once hear, even from the mouth of David, the expression
which at least touches on those dark representations of the state of
the departed—of the righteous as well as of the wicked. In Psalm 6
we hear him say, "In death there is no remembrance of Thee; in the
grave who shall give Thee thanks?" We find similar expressions in
Psalm 30:40. In both places, however, he has in view only to give the
strongest possible expression to his wish, that the Lord would grant
to him that he might yet for a longer time be able to glorify Him on
the earth, and proclaim His name to the sons of men.

In other places we see him raise himself again to far more comfortable and brighter views of the state after death. Thus in Psalm 17:
"As for me, I will behold Thy face in righteousness: I shall be satisfied, when I awake, with Thy likeness." In Psalm 48: "This God is our

God forever and ever: He will be our guide even unto death." In Psalm 52: "I am like a green olive-tree in the house of God: I trust in the mercy of God forever and ever. I will praise Thee forever, because Thou hast done it: and I will wait on Thy name; for it is good before Thy saints." How could a man such as David, to whom, by the Holy Spirit, so clear a light was shed over the greatness, the extent, and the range of the divine plan of salvation, not be able to rise above the dark contemplation of most of his contemporaries, and arrive at loftier and clearer conceptions of the kingdom of the dead? In Psalm 16 he already celebrates a victory over death when he says, "Therefore my heart is glad, and my glory rejoiceth; my flesh also shall rest in hope: for Thou wilt not leave my soul in hell; neither wilt Thou suffer Thine Holy One to see corruption. Thou wilt show me the path of life: in Thy presence is fullness of joy; at Thy right hand there are pleasures forevermore." True, these words are Messianic, but David speaks as the type of the Messiah.

The faithful of the Old Covenant had already the truth in regard to "the last things"; only, according to the wise direction of God, they had not the whole of it. They knew, as the Scripture testifies, that they were "strangers and pilgrims on the earth." They saw the promise not yet fulfilled, it is true, but "were persuaded" of it, and embraced it in hope. Yet the prospect which was opened up to the faith of a few chosen ones among them reached, as we know, much farther than that of the great multitude. What is written in the Epistle to the Hebrews regarding the patriarch Abraham is well known.[3] We meet with David, Psalm 103, on a standpoint which comes very near to the New Testament position. Here he rises on the wings of faith far above the earth, and sees deep beneath him the gloom of the grave and of corruption.

That which awaited the fearers of God on that farther side was, it is true, first revealed in distinct doctrinal form after David and by the prophets. We hear Isaiah, from his watch-tower, sound his trumpet among the people: "The Lord will" (in the time of the Messiah) "swallow up death in victory; and the Lord God will wipe away tears from off all faces."[4] We hear how he utters his notes of triumph in Isaiah 26: "Thy dead men shall live, together with my dead body

---

3. Hebrews 11:10.
4. Isaiah 25:8.

shall they arise. Awake and sing, ye that dwell in dust: for thy dew is as the dew of herbs, and the earth shall cast out the dead." Not less we know how Ezekiel represents the glorious return of the Israelitish people, under imagery which is unmistakably derived from the resurrection of the dead, which is taken for granted as an undoubted fact of the future.[5] Daniel also, in the beginning of the twelfth chapter of his prophecy, is heard saying, "Many of them that sleep in the dust of the earth shall awake, some to everlasting life, and some to shame and everlasting contempt. And they that be wise shall shine as the brightness of the firmament; and they that turn many to righteousness as the stars forever and ever."

The veil was not, indeed, as yet raised for David from the future state of the departed; yet it was sufficiently withdrawn to enable him without fear to lay down his head for his last sleep. We have already heard his last words spoken from his deathbed. They were words of hope, words of most joyful anticipation. His last thoughts on earth were of the "everlasting covenant" which "God the Lord had made with him." The last look of his departing soul rested on the "Star out of Jacob," which, according to Jehovah's infallible promise, would shine upon the world. Thus he departed, "full of days" (i.e., satisfied with life, but also with unclouded consciousness, and in peace), to his home: a poor sinner, yet safely resting in the bosom of the free grace of his God.

His body was buried in the city of David, on the heights of Zion, not far from the hallowed spot on which the temple was afterward built. The inscription over his grave is written in the sacred history in these words: "David did that which was right in the eyes of the Lord, and turned not aside from anything that He commanded him all the days of his life, save only in the matter of Uriah the Hittite."[6] The kings that followed were all estimated according to their resemblance to him as the model king. Thousands of years after his death, pilgrimages were made to his sepulcher; and Peter could say, in his sermon on the day of Pentecost, "His grave is with us to this day." Even to this day they show reverently to pilgrims, on the hill of Zion to the south of the city wall, as the grave of David, a vault over which a Christian church has now been raised.

---

5. Ezekiel 37.
6. 1 Kings 25:5.

2. David died, not only "full of days," according to the remark of the historians, but also "full of riches and honor." His legacy was great and glorious. What he left to his people was, besides a system of government excellently regulated on all sides, an army crowned with fame and experienced in war, and general prosperity prevailing among the inhabitants of town and country, the public worship of God again established according to the divine ordinance, a large number of excellent officers, of pious and zealous servants in the sanctuary, and, in addition, a considerable public treasury, to be expended for the general welfare of the land, and, moreover, a divinely approved plan for the building of the temple, and the richest and most precious material for the carrying out of this plan.

But something greater than all this he left as an inheritance to the whole world—first, in his personal portrait, then in his gracious experiences, and, above all, in his Psalms. In spite of his transgressions, which he always bitterly repented of, and which were therefore blotted out of the book of God, he remains to all princes and rulers of the earth as the noblest pattern. In perfect inward truth he knew and felt himself to be "king by the grace of God." The crown and scepter he bore merely in trust from the King of all kings; and to his latest breath he endeavored with all his earnestness to be found a genuine theocratic king, who in everything must conduct his earthly government according to the ordinances and directions of God. Therefore the Lord made all that he did to prosper; and nothing was clearer to the people than that God the Lord was truly with the king.

David's life-course remains as the most splendid memorial of the free grace of God. Who could number the souls which for almost 3,000 years have comforted, strengthened, and raised themselves up in their conflicts and their heart-anxieties by contemplating it? Whoever seeks a God with whom there is "plenteous redemption"— who hears prayer, who numbers the very hairs on the heads of His people, has an unchangeable love for them, and, as a Protector who neither slumbers nor sleeps, is by their side at every step—will meet with such a God in the experiences of David, the king of Israel. No word of consolation is found in Scripture which was not confirmed in the actual experience of David. The golden chain of divine condescensions and of gracious manifestations, by which his whole life was penetrated, marks it out as an introductory gospel, written in the characters of the actual life. O how did David verify that word of

Psalm 84, "They who pass through the valley of weeping make it rich in springs!"[7]

But the most precious inheritance for which the world has to bless the king of Israel is his Psalms—those immortal songs which, according to the testimony of the singer himself, streamed forth from his heart under the direction and inspiration of the Holy Spirit, and therefore form a constituent part of "the sure word of prophecy."[8] Who does not know that afterward the Lord Christ Himself recognized and solemnly attested the Psalms as belonging to the sacred and infallible canon of the Bible, and that mention is made of them as such in the New Testament altogether about seventy times?[9] In the Psalms the whole life-experience of the psalmist reflects itself, and so also essentially that of all the children of God, whose way, like that of David, leads through sufferings to glory, and under the cross to the crown. There discloses itself to us, in these sacred hymns, the innermost sanctuary of the world of thought of a man of God; with the whole succession of the changing circumstances and dispositions of such an one; with his complaints as well as his thanksgivings; with his sorrows as well as his blessings; with his love, born of God, as well as his hatred not less hallowed; with his sighs piercing through the clouds, as well as his fervent outpourings of thanks.

There sounds forth to us in the Psalms, not merely the heart-utterances of David, but, at the same time, those of the God-consecrated Church of all ages. It is perfectly true, and easily explainable, what an interpreter of Scripture says, when he maintains that there is no Old Testament book which has been so wholly transmitted as an inheritance from the heart and the mouth of the believing Israel, into the heart and the mouth of the Church, as the unequaled Old Testament hymn-book—the Psalter. This, in the fullness of its contents, is, it is true, surpassed by our modern Christian Church-hymns, in so far as the spirit which in the former only knocks at the covering encompassing it around, in the latter has already broken through the shell, and, unbound and joyful, stirs its wings dropping with salvation and with blessings. Redemption, which in the book of Psalms rises up before us as only something then in prospect and eagerly longed for, has long ago been completed; and we sing of the salvation, finished

---

7. Verse 6.
8. 2 Samuel 23:1, 2.
9. Luke 24:44; Matthew 23:43.

by the sacrifice on the cross of the manifested Son of David, and rejoice over the resurrection from the dead of the Prince of peace, and His exaltation to the right hand of the Father.

And yet harmonies from the Psalms sound ever forth to us from the most hallowed of our Christian hymns, as a witness that even our evangelical dispositions and experiences, which are the same, only transfigured under the New Testament, as are expressed in the Psalter, find in them their most suitable embodiment and their most appropriate forms of expression. For the utterance of that which moves our hearts before God, the Psalms appear to us indispensable. More or less embued with them, we will, as often as we need to pour complaints and prayers, thanks-offerings and praises, into the bosom of the Almighty, always, often unconsciously, speak the language of these ancient songs. This language has become the language of the kingdom of the saints of the Lord. Even secular poetry for the most part, when it seeks to elevate itself to the sublime, attempts the bold flight only with words borrowed from the book of Psalms; and thereby actually acknowledges that the Spirit out of which the Psalms were born is altogether different and incomparably higher than the natural human spirit, even in its highest elevation of creative power.

How beneficial it is, and how it elevates the soul, when we find ourselves again, not only in our faith and our confession, but also in our feelings and experiences, in the company of the saints of the Lord who lived thousands of years before; and in their psalms not only meet with the same God to whom we also bend the knee, but see the pious of these times trusting in that grace on which we place all our hopes! How blessed it is to walk in fellowship with those old saints, in the first dawn of the morning rich with promise, in which was announced the glorious rising of the Sun which has now for so long a time in noonday splendor blessed the children of the New Testament! With a swelling heart we hear, in Psalm 2, the challenge: "Kiss the Son, lest He be angry, and ye perish from the way, when His wrath is kindled but a little. Blessed are all they that put their trust in Him." In Psalm 110 we salute Him who is at once David's Son and David's Lord, and to whom these words are addressed by the Eternal Father: "Sit Thou at my right hand, until I make Thine enemies Thy footstool. For Thou art a priest forever, after the order of Melchizedek."

In a whole series of Davidic psalms—6, 16, 22, and 69—we adore Him who is Eternal Love, who humbled Himself to the death for us, yea, the death of the cross. In Psalm 118, where the cry of triumph sounds "in the dwellings of the righteous," "the right hand of the Lord is exalted; the right hand of the Lord doeth valiantly"— we seem already to stand in Joseph's garden and join in the shout of joy: "The stone which the builders refused is become the head stone of the corner. This is the Lord's doing; it is marvelous in our eyes!"

Who does not know Luther's eulogium on the Psalter, itself rising to the elevated strain of a psalm? "The Psalter," says he, "may well be called a little Bible, wherein all that stands in the whole Bible is briefly comprehended and set forth in the noblest manner. In the psalms of praise and thanks, thou lookest into the hearts of all the saints as into a beautiful pleasant garden; yea, as into heaven itself, wherein, like fair beautiful flowers, many joyful and blessed thoughts arise regarding God and His kindness. Again, where dost thou find deeper, sadder words of sorrow than those which are contained in the psalms of mourning? Once more, thou lookest there into the hearts of all the saints; but it is as if into death; yea, as into hell. It is so dark and dismal, because it is distressed by the frown of God's anger! Thus, also, when they speak of fear and hope, they use such words that no painter could thus paint for thee fear or hope, and no Cicero or orator could thus describe them. And the best is, that they use such language about God and in their communion with God as imparts a twofold earnestness to their words.

Therefore, also, it comes to pass that the Psalter is a little book for all saints; and every one, in whatever circumstances he is placed, will therein find words which accord with these circumstances, and are to him just as if they were placed there for his sake alone, so that he himself can neither arrange nor find better words, nor does he wish to find them. Hence it may be concluded that, if such words please anyone, he is certain that he belongs to the community of the saints, since they all sing with him these songs, particularly if he can adopt the same words to God as they have done, which can be done only in faith; for they are not agreeable to an ungodly man. In short, wilt thou see the holy Christian Church depicted within brief compass, in living colors and in a living form, then put up the Psalter before thee, and there thou hast a fine, clear, pure mirror, which will show to thee what Christianity is. Yes, thou wilt therein find thyself, and thy God also, and all creatures."

Only 80 of our 150 psalms can positively be ascribed to David. Nevertheless the whole collection bears with justice the inscription, "The Psalms of David." With the exception of Psalm 90, which was composed by Moses, all the rest were composed after his time, and flow forth, in his spirit and with his melody, from the hearts of singers stirred by him. Next to God, to him we owe our thanks for this won-derful gift.

Thus we take leave of the king of Israel—the man who shows to us the way to heaven in the sincere, unreserved, implicit resignation of himself to the God of all grace. And lo, from a far-distant past, a prophetic trumpet-note strikes on our ear, and voices, born of the Spirit of God, with one accord proclaim the majesty of the Son of Jesse!

Isaiah, the evangelist of the Old Testament, exclaims, "Of the increase of His government and peace there shall be no end upon the throne of David and His kingdom forever." The Lord Himself says, by the mouth of His prophet, "I will make an everlasting covenant with you, even the sure mercies of David." Amos the prophet declares that the Lord has promised, saying, "In that day will I raise up the tabernacle of David that is fallen, and close up the breaches thereof; and I will raise up his ruins, and I will build it as in the days of old." Ezekiel completes the word, when he adds, "I will set up one Shepherd over them, and He shall feed them, even my servant David; He shall feed them, and He shall be their Shepherd. And I the Lord will be their God, and my servant David a prince among them: I the Lord have spoken it."

With elevated hearts we listen to these and similar words, full of promise, sounding forth from the company of the prophets; and when we ask who this is of whom they are spoken, there stands One before us "like a son of man," but One to whom the angels bend the knee, and He says, "I am the root and the offspring of David, and the bright and morning star." "These things saith He that is holy, He that is true, He that hath the key of David, He that openeth, and no man shutteth; and shutteth, and no man openeth!" We recognize Him. We sink with adoring reverence in the dust before Him, and exclaim with joyful voice, "Hosanna to the Son of David: Blessed is He that cometh in the name of the Lord; Hosanna in the highest!"